SO-AZM-249

SECULARISATION IN WESTERN EUROPE, 1848–1914

Secularisation in Western Europe, 1848–1914

HUGH McLEOD

CABRINI COLLEGE LIBRARY
610 KING OF PRUSSIA ROAD
RADNOR, PA 19087

#43791239

SECULARISATION IN WESTERN EUROPE, 1848–1914

Copyright © 2000 by Hugh McLeod

All rights reserved. No part of this book may be used or reproduced in any manner whatsoever without written permission except in the case of brief quotations embodied in critical articles or reviews. For information, address:

St. Martin's Press, Scholarly and Reference Division, 175 Fifth Avenue, New York, N.Y. 10010

First published in the United States of America in 2000

This book is printed on paper suitable for recycling and made from fully managed and sustained forest sources.

Printed in China

ISBN   0–312–23510–0 clothbound
ISBN   0–312–23511–9 paperback

Library of Congress Cataloging-in-Publication Data

McLeod, Hugh.
Secularisation in Western Europe, 1848–1914/Hugh McLeod.
p. cm. – (European studies series)
Includes bibliographical references and index.
ISBN 0–312–23510–0 (hardcover) – ISBN 0–312–23511–9 (pbk.)
1. Secularism—Europe, Western—History—19th century. 2. Europe, Western—Religion—19th century. 3. Secularism—Europe, Western—History—20th century. 4. Europe, Western—Religion—20th century. I. Title II. Series.

BL2765.E85 M35 2000
274'.08—dc21

00–035257

To my parents

Contents

List of Tables

Acknowledgements

I wish to thank the School of Historical Studies in the University of Birmingham for research grants, and the Humanities Research Board for financing a period of research leave, without which completion of this book would have been very much more difficult. Various parts of the book have been tried out at conferences or seminars. I would like to thank for their helpful comments all those who participated in the conference 'The Decline of Christendom in Western Europe', held in Paris in April 1997, and in the relevant meetings of the History of Religion Seminars at Queen's University, Belfast, and the University of Birmingham, the Theology Seminar at the University of Bristol, and the joint History Seminar of the Universities of Strathclyde and Glasgow. I owe a special debt to John Breuilly, Mary Heimann, Sarah Williams and my father, T. S. McLeod, for reading and commenting on draft typescripts. Many other people have generously helped by discussing aspects of the book or sending me copies of their own unpublished work, and I would like to make particular mention of my debts to Callum Brown, Steve Bruce, Gérard Cholvy, Jeff Cox, Sheridan Gilley, Martin Greschat, Roísín Healy, Yves-Marie Hilaire, David Hempton, Lucian Hölscher, Hartmut Lehmann, Peter Marsh, David Martin, Stuart Mews, Sue Morgan, Geoff Robson, Michael Snape, Werner Ustorf, Till van Rahden and Peter van Rooden. I would like to thank Sue Wright for advice on translations from French and Harry Buglass for drawing the maps. As always, I am grateful to all members of my family for their varied forms of encouragement, and most especially to Jackie.

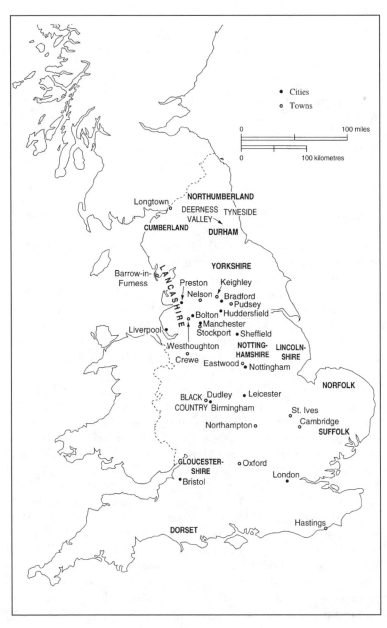

Map 1   England

Map 2   France, 1870

xii

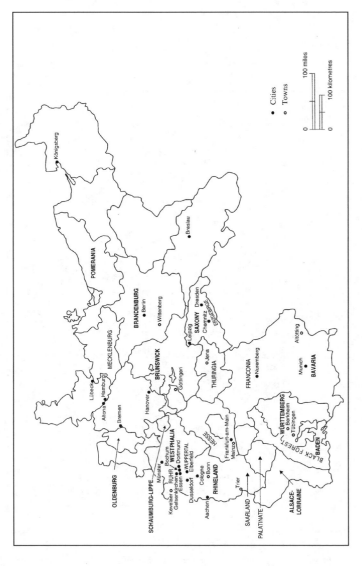

Map 3 The German Empire, 1871

Introduction

Until about the middle of the nineteenth century 'secularisation' referred to the process by which church lands were transferred to lay ownership (as happened, for instance, during the Reformation or the French Revolution), or whereby priests, monks or nuns abandoned their orders. But then the term began to be used in a wider sense. The first to do so seems to have been the historian W. E. H. Lecky who, in 1865, referred to a 'general secularisation of the European intellect' and specifically to a 'secularisation of politics'.[1] By this he meant that there had been a long-term tendency for reason of state to replace religious considerations in relations between states and decisions to go to war. Soon other authors were claiming to detect secularisation in such areas as economics or art. But the *idea* of secularisation seems to have been already current before it was given a name. The French pioneer of sociology Auguste Comte argued in his highly influential *Cours de philosophie positive* (1830–42) that knowledge passed through three phases, the theological, the metaphysical and the positive or scientific. Now, with the dawning of the scientific age, religion in its traditional forms was doomed, and Comte devised a Religion of Humanity, which would perform for the modern world those necessary functions of providing meaning, ritual and a basis for morality, which had once been the province of the churches.[2]

The search for a Religion of Humanity, which had already begun during the French Revolution, has remained a central theme of nineteenth- and twentieth-century history – though the search is still no nearer to its goal than it was in Comte's day.[3] Meanwhile, Comte's framework of long-term historical change, according to which religion begins as an all-powerful force and then gradually

1

dwindles to insignificance, has continued to exercise an enormous hold over the Western imagination. While the idea of science gradually taking the place of religion has had a great influence over the general public – and over natural scientists – historians and social scientists have tended to accept the basic concept of secularisation, while seeing its causes in social 'change' (a neutral term), rather than in intellectual 'advance'. The three most influential figures in the history of sociology – Marx, Weber and Durkheim – all accepted some version of the theory of a universal long-term trend towards secularisation. Most explicitly, Emile Durkheim, a follower of Comte, writing in France at the end of the nineteenth century, proposed that the whole of history revealed a process by which religion, which had once embraced all areas of life, was pushed back into fewer and fewer domains through a process of 'differentiation', whereby specialised agencies and personnel displaced the clergy. Marx did not neglect intellectual factors in secularisation – he claimed that demolition of religion at a purely theoretical level had begun with the philosophers of the eighteenth century and had been completed by writers such as Feuerbach in his own day. But in accordance with his belief in the fundamental role of the class struggle, he argued that the practical destruction of religion must await the proletarian revolution and the construction of a society in which illusions would no longer be needed. Weber's version of secularisation was less explicitly spelt out, less optimistic, but maybe equally triumphalist, albeit in a much more subtle way – since it also assumed a designation of religion as 'backward' and as inevitably doomed in its struggle with the modern world, represented by science, rationality and bureaucracy.[4]

During the twentieth century, the idea that the modern world is essentially irreligious has become widely accepted – both by those who welcome this situation and by those who deplore it. Perhaps the most famous example is the letter written from a Nazi prison in 1944 by the German Protestant theologian Dietrich Bonhoeffer: 'We are proceeding towards a time of no religion at all: men as they are now simply cannot be religious any more.'[5] But it is only since the 1960s that these ideas have been systematically developed and widely debated. A number of highly influential sociological expositions were published around this time by such authors as Bryan Wilson, Peter Berger and Thomas Luckmann,[6] as well as a more popular work, *The Secular City* (1965) by the American theologian, Harvey Cox, who did more than anyone else to bring some of these ideas to a wider audience. In spite of differences of emphasis and perspective, these authors shared a commitment to the 'secularisation thesis'. This thesis holds that the dwindling social significance of religion is an inevitable consequence of the processes of social development in modern societies. Differentiation leads to a narrowing of the social spheres in which religion has an influence, as professional specialists take over more and more of the roles previously performed by the clergy. Science replaces theology as the principal source of authoritative knowledge. Growing pluralism leads to a sophisticated relativism, in terms of which the moral absolutes prescribed by the various religions lose their binding force. In so far as religion survives, it does so as a private concern, important perhaps to some individuals, but with little influence on public institutions or on the world of work.

Although in the 1960s and 1970s the secularisation thesis seemed to have the status of sociological orthodoxy, there were some sceptical voices even then. In the 1980s the number of doubters rapidly increased. The chief reason for this was the rising public profile of religion from the later 1970s onwards, as a result of the political mobilisation of evangelicals in the United States, the advance of militant Islam, and the role of the churches in many of the revolutions in the Eastern Bloc countries. These developments called in question the assumption that religion would inevitably be privatised and marginalised in modern societies. In the United States, some sociologists of religion rejected the concept of secularisation altogether.[7] In Europe the tendency has been to suggest that it is not so much wrong as oversimplified, and that it tends to underestimate both the complexity of religious change and the variety of possible paths of religious development in the modern world.[8] At the same time there have been other sociologists, most notably Steve Bruce, who have reaffirmed and refined the theory, essentially in the form advanced by such authors as Bryan Wilson in the 1960s.[9]

Secularisation and the Historians

Historians of nineteenth-century religion have been influenced by these debates among sociologists, and they have obviously felt the impact of the same changes in the general intellectual, cultural and political climate. But whereas sociologists have often concentrated on identifying and explaining long-term trends, historians have usually wanted to trace in much greater detail the 'how', as well as the 'what' and the 'why', of historical change. This concern has been reinforced by modern developments in the writing of history. A major theme in historical scholarship since the 1960s has been the ambition to write a 'history from below'. One aspect of this has been the discovery of 'popular' religion, and the resulting attempt to write a religious history of the 'ordinary person', making no assumptions about the relevance to this history of the writings of theologians or scientists, the pronouncements of archbishops or the decrees of monarchs and parliaments.[10]

There are many possible ways of 'telling the story' of religion in Western Europe during the nineteenth and twentieth cenuries. All are to some degree arbitrary. Each involves a vast process of simplification, in order to allow some kind of overall sense to be made of events of baffling complexity. Clearly the dominant version of the story at present is that which sees the central theme as secularisation.[11] Crucially important here has been the fact that since the 1960s the churches in most parts of Western Europe have suffered a severe decline.[12] Anyone writing in Western Europe during the last thirty years or so on modern religious history has inevitably been keenly aware of this fact, and the temptation has been strong to study the nineteenth century mainly in order to trace the origins of this decline.

While many historians have agreed in identifying secularisation as the central theme of Western Europe's modern religious history, they have disagreed radically about the extent, causes and timing of this secularisation.

To begin with timing: most historians have identified a crucial period in which the trend towards secularisation became unquestionably dominant, even if they accept that other periods may also have played a part. In Germany and France, though much less frequently in England, many historians have argued that the turning point was the eighteenth-century Enlightenment, and that in spite of some temporary interruptions in the intervening period, there has been a process of secularisation continually at work from the eighteenth century to the present day. A second approach, more favoured by British historians, has been to focus on the Industrial Revolution and on the massive shift of population from villages to towns and cities from about 1800 onwards. A third approach, favoured especially by historians of ideas and of literature, has been to highlight various developments in science, philosophy and the study of religion around the middle of the nineteeenth century, with Darwin usually being identified as the central figure and the publication in 1859 of *On the Origin of Species* as the central event. A fourth approach has been to focus on the period since about 1960, when the decline in religious practice has been much more rapid.

These contrasting chronologies reflect different views of how and why secularisation has come about. I will group the main approaches to answering these questions under the headings of (1) 'The march of science', (2) 'Modernisation', (3) 'Postmodernity', and (4) 'Selling God'.

The account of secularisation in terms of 'the march of science' often starts with the assumption that the crucial battles were fought out within the human mind.[13] The basic theme here is the rise of science as the dominant way of understanding the world. The ground was prepared by Copernicus and Galileo, by Newton, and by philosophers, such as Descartes, Locke and Hume. But the turning-point came in the middle years of the nineteenth century. Of the many revolutionary developments at this time, three were of paramount importance. Darwin laid the basis for a radically new way of looking at humanity, according to which men and women, rather than being made in the image of God, were to be seen simply as a part of nature, subject to the same laws as the rest of nature. As a result, age-old concepts such as 'the soul' or 'free will' were to be dismissed as meaningless, and the conscience, if it existed at all, was a product of evolution. The Tübingen School of biblical scholars subjected the Scriptures to scientific investigation, and writers like Strauß and Renan reinterpreted the life of Christ, divesting it of all supernatural elements. Meanwhile, Comte and Spencer pioneered the scientific study of society, and in doing so provided explanations for religion as a product of a particular stage of human development. Of course, all this leaves unresolved the question of how, and to what extent, these ideas were transmitted to the masses of the people. But studies of Imperial Germany have shown that materialist science was fairly widely popularised, and was adopted by many working-class Social Democrats – mainly because they saw the churches as allies of the state, and they therefore welcomed anything that might discredit their theology.[14] In the French Third Republic, where many teachers, as well as leading politicians and prominent figures in the education system, were believers in the liberating potential of an anti-religious science, it might plausibly be suggested that such views were propagated through the state school system.[15] Another line of argument has been to suggest that however little most people knew about recent scientific developments, scientists were successful during the later nineteenth century in establishing their authority as the principal carriers of mysterious knowledge, largely supplanting priests and theologians, who seemed less 'modern'.[16]

The interpretation of secularisation in terms of 'modernisation' highlights social rather than intellectual changes. The central focus has usually been on the transition from a mainly rural, agrarian, and very hierarchical society, to one that is predominantly urban, industrial, relatively democratic and relatively affluent. Those historians who have simply seen a direct link between the spread of industry and the decline of religion have had to face the awkward fact that England in the first half of the nineteenth century saw a massive growth in the Nonconformist churches and a growth in evangelical influence in most sections of society. A more subtle version of the relationship between industrialisation and secularisation has, however, been proposed by Alan Gilbert.[17] He argues that in the short run industrialisation actually increased the importance of religion in English society. Religion offered a form of security in the face of bewildering social change. More especially, joining a Nonconformist chapel was a mark of independence for craftsmen and small businessmen, newly emancipated from the rural social order and subjection to squire and parson. The industrial village, in particular, became the favoured site for more intense, emotional and personal types of religion, such as Methodism. This phase reached its peak about 1840. But in the longer term industrialisation undermined the position of religion in English society. By the second half of the nineteenth century the majority of the population were enjoying significant improvements in their standard of living; medical advances reduced the frequency of epidemics; and the growth of towns was leading to more anonymous and individualistic forms of community in which such organisations as the churches found it harder to establish a base. As a result of these changes the range of situations in which purely human solutions to human problems were available had been greatly extended, and the crises in which people had 'turned to' religion became correspondingly less frequent. Religion had not necessarily become less true, but it had become less salient to most lives, and increasing numbers of people were becoming convinced that major improvements in the human situation were possible. Other historians have questioned the details of Gilbert's argument while still assuming that the most important sources of secularisation lay in the development of the industrial economy.[18] For instance, Stephen Yeo, in an influential study of the biscuit-manufacturing town of Reading, was one of several British historians who have argued that religion and the churches were central to the life of British industrial towns in the period from about the 1850s to the 1880s, but that major changes took place between about 1890 and 1914. These included the decline of paternalism, leading to increasingly impersonal relations between employers and workers, and frequently to more severe class conflict; the increasing role of the state and a corresponding decline in the significance of decisions made at the local level; and a decline in the importance of voluntary organisations. At the same time, the development of the entertainment industry took up an increasing proportion of people's free time, often supplanting older leisure facilities provided by the church, and sport became a matter of passionate concern, especially to young men, and often the emotional centre of their lives.[19]

Both of these versions agree that the nineteenth century was a crucial phase of secularisation, even if they disagree as to why. The account in terms of 'Postmodernity' view, however, suggests that the major theme of the nineteenth century and the first half of the twentieth is the continuing centrality of religion and the churches, and that 'real' secularisation has happened only since about 1960.[20] This has been proposed in respect of Britain by Callum Brown, but many of his points could be applied to other West European countries. According to this argument there had indeed been a considerable decline in church attendance in the nineteenth and early twentieth centuries, but the great majority of the population attended Sunday School or went to catechism classes as children, and as adults claimed membership of one of the Christian churches; most couples continued to marry in church and to have their children baptised there; and above all the moral influence of the churches remained great. They had a crucial influence on the definition of moral behaviour, and even if many people did not practise these standards very strictly, few were prepared to challenge them in principle. Especially important here was the role of women: although there was considerable tension between most forms of religion and working-class definitions of masculinity, religion remained an important component of femininity, and women continued both to uphold religiously-based moral rules, and to pass on religious beliefs and practices to the next generation. According to this version, the social position of the churches only began to crumble from the later 1950s onwards, with the development of a rebellious and hedonistic youth culture, strongly influenced by popular music, and with a revolution in women's self-understanding, as a result of which older models of femininity rapidly retreated in the face of new ideals of individual self-fulfilment. Somewhat similar arguments have been advanced by Peter van Rooden who, in a survey of long-term religious change in The Netherlands, concludes that only from the 1960s can one speak of a general trend towards secularisation. Up to that time, any sign of apparent secularisation in one area – for instance, the growth in the numbers of those without religious affiliation – had to be counterbalanced by contrary signs in other areas – for instance, the continued domination of Dutch politics by confessional parties and the tendency towards more tightly knit confessional subcultures. During the period between the later eighteenth century and the middle of the twentieth, there were several major changes in patterns of individual religious belief and practice, in the public role of the churches, and in their teachings, but none of these can usefully be defined or explained in terms of a trend towards secularisation.[21]

While proponents of these three theories differ radically as to when, how and why it happened, they are all agreed that at some point in the last 250 years Western Europe has been secularised. It is no accident that the more sceptical voices have come mainly from the United States, where religious trends since the 1960s have been more confusing and ambiguous than in Europe.[22] During the 1960s it did seem that the United States were undergoing a rapid secularisation, very similar to that which hit Western Europe at the same time. Even then, however, there were some counter-trends. While most of the 'mainstream' churches were losing members and there was a significant growth in the number of declared atheists and those with no religion, some of the more conservative or 'fundamentalist' evangelical churches were growing, and there was also a wave of religious experimentation, reflected especially in growing interest in various forms of Buddhism and Hinduism. These trends became more clearly defined in the later 1970s, when conservative Protestants disturbed by what they regarded as rampant liberalism, closely connected with various symptoms of moral decline, began to organise politically. By the mid-1980s evidence of secularisation in the United States was not lacking, but the picture seemed much more complicated than it had done fifteen years before. While most of the 'mainstream' denominations were continuing to lose members and the number of those without any religion had substantially increased, other churches were growing, a wide range of new forms of religiosity had emerged, and religion had a high public profile, mainly because of the activities of conservative Protestants. According to public opinion polls, about 90 per cent of the population claimed to believe in God and about 40 per cent claimed to have taken part in religious worship during the previous week – figures that in both cases were considerably above those reported in most west European countries.[23] American historians have therefore been less willing than their European counterparts to see secularisation as an inevitable concomitant of 'modernity', or as the overriding theme of modern religious history.[24]

The fourth account of secularisation, which I have called the 'Selling God'[25] interpretation, highlights the many-sidedness of modern religious history. Its most skilful exponent is Jeffrey Cox. This version, which accepts that secularisation has happened but denies its inevitability, has been favoured mainly by American historians. In refuting the assumption that religious decline is an inevitable concomitant of modernity (or postmodernity), they have often drawn comparisons between declining churches in Europe and thriving churches in the United States. According to these historians the central fact of the modern religious situation is competition: competition between churches, competition between religious and secular ideologies, and indeed competition between the claims of religious or political idealism and those of, for instance, sport or entertainment. In this environment religious belief-systems and organisations will only survive if they actively and intelligently sell themselves. This requires, for instance, an energetic recruitment policy and efforts to identify the church with the aspirations of large sections of the people. Historians in this school argue that the relative success of churches in the United States arises from the fact that they have done these things much more effectively than churches in Europe, which have frequently been hobbled by complacency-inducing traditions of State-establishment, or by over-close links with unpopular elites.[26]

So historians of many different kinds are agreed that secularisation is the central 'story' of Western Europe's modern religious history, but they offer quite different, and sometimes incompatible, versions of how it actually happened. It would, indeed, be possible to draw elements out of each of these stories to make a new synthesis. The result might even be more convincing than any of those versions which place overriding emphasis on one master-factor, be it science, industrialisation, or whatever. Nonetheless, it should be recognised that the result would be a fifth 'story', which would be unacceptable to many of the tellers of other versions. This is partly because there are many scholars for whom it is an article of faith that one kind of explanatory factor, be it social, intellectual, political, religious, or whatever, is fundamental, and any narrative which attached equal importance to factors of another kind would therefore be unacceptable.[27] It is partly because questions of chronology are central to many of these arguments and any dilution of this chronology would lead to a completely different kind of interpretation.

However, in history, as much as in sociology, sceptical voices have been heard more widely in the 1980s and 1990s. The grounds for this scepticism vary greatly. But the overall effect has been an increasing wariness among historians of modern religion about the use of the term 'secularisation' and its status as the supposed key to modern religious history.

In the first place, there have been many recent studies which, without directly challenging the concept of secularisation, have questioned the standard accounts of how it is supposed to have happened. For instance, the general trend of recent research has been to emphasise the continuing importance of religious belief and of the churches in nineteenth-century Europe, and even in the first half of the twentieth century. The assumption that indifference or unbelief spread rapidly as a result of 'modernisation' and the rise of science, or that the churches were forced back into a narrow 'religious subculture', seems much less persuasive than it did twenty or thirty years ago.[28] Recent research has tended to emphasise the importance of religiously-based political and social movements, and to question the extent of religious alienation – even in the great cities and in the urban working class (usually regarded as the most secularised areas of nineteenth-century society).[29] The growing interest in the history of women has also played a part in this re-evaluation: histories of secularisation have often been very largely histories of the secularisation of men, and the question of whether it happened differently for women has been put on one side, or simply ignored.[30]

Another approach does not so much deny the fact of secularisation as suggest that it is not the most interesting or significant aspect of the situation. So, for instance, Anthony Steinhoff in his study of Protestantism in Strasbourg argues that the most important theme of modern religious history is not the decline of Christianity, but its resilience in the face of drastic social, political and intellectual change.[31] Cynics might comment that specialists in the history of Christianity have a vested interest in emphasising its importance. However, it is worth noting that rather similar conclusions were reached in a study of German child welfare policies from the Bismarck era to the age of Adenauer. One of the major themes of the book was 'the sheer stamina of the Christian churches and Christian culture', reflecting the adaptability and the 'continuing relevance (the "modernity") of Christianity'.[32] In the light of such points, some scholars have suggested that pluralism, rather than secularisation, is the central theme of modern religious history. Thus Kselman in a study of religion in Paris during the Third Republic stresses both the continuing importance of Catholicism, the emergence of new religious movements, such as Spiritism, and the ways in which the Freethought and Socialist movements, rather than being merely irreligious, offered alternative beliefs and rituals, which had more in common with those of the Catholics than either side would wish to admit.[33]

Sarah Williams and Gérard Cholvy have challenged conventional conceptions of secularisation by redefining religion. Cholvy, focusing on changes in the intellectual climate, traces the decline and renewal of 'religious feeling'. This is understood in much broader terms than the doctrines and practices of the churches. Thus, writing in 1991, at a time when attendance at mass and other conventional indices of religious fervour were in decline, he insisted that the period since 1975 had been a time of religious revival. This was because of the many new religious currents which were emerging, often outside the churches, after the religious drought of the 'neopositivist' 1960s. He argued that the same had happened during the Romantic era. Sarah Williams criticises historians of secularisation for their preoccupation with those forms of religion which can be readily quantified, and for their consequent neglect of popular religion.[34] Indeed Williams and Cholvy, like Lucian Hölscher, have raised more fundamental objections to the concept of secularisation. Cholvy rejects the attempt by historians of religion to identify a linear trend. Instead, he argues for a cyclical pattern marked by successive periods of decline and renewal: the nature of religion has changed, but one cannot speak of any long-term decline. Williams's approach depends on enabling historical actors to tell their own story, in language which makes sense to them and which reflects their own concerns, without the imposition by the historian of alien categories. She sees 'secularisation' as an example of such an alien category. In somewhat similar terms, Hölscher highlights the ways in which understandings of 'religion' and the 'religious' have changed. Because of this, he argues, there can be no objective basis for measuring religious decline.[35]

One of the most cogent criticisms of the literature on secularisation is that made by David D. Hall in a paper on religious change in North America from the seventeenth century to the nineteenth. He argues that:

> American culture is characterized by the co-existence of the secular and the religious. It is the dialectical relationship between these forces on which we should focus, tracing out how each involves the other and how the boundary between the secular and the religious is continually negotiated.... this process of negotiation has been as much a part of our past as of our present, occurring, for example, even in Puritan New England, a time and place when, according to conventional wisdom, religion was all-important.[36]

Assumptions and Methods of the Present Book

First, it must be stressed that my subject is the secularisation of European *society* – not *The Secularization of the European Mind*, as in the title of Owen Chadwick's famous book. There is already a very extensive literature on changes in religious thought in the nineteenth century, and on the religious implications of developments in science or philosophy, and I have no desire to add to it. I am concerned with such developments only in so far as they affected the beliefs and practices of the mass of the people, or the relationship between religion and public institutions. Second, I see secularisation as a question to be put to the evidence, rather than as a preconceived conclusion. I think there is a strong *prima facie* case for thinking that West European societies underwent a significant degree of secularisation in the nineteenth century; but, as the summary given above of recent historical scholarship would suggest, the extent, chronology and causes of this secularisation remain unclear.

It seems probable that there have been major differences in the chronology and causes of secularisation in different countries and different social milieux. It is also too readily assumed that secularisation is a coherent 'process', moving in one direction, and impelled by the same force. But there is no necessary reason why this should be so, and it is equally possible that it affected different areas of life for different reasons and to a greatly varying extent.

Since some of the confusion surrounding this subject arises from different understandings both of religion and of secularisation, some explanation of how I will be using these terms is needed. By 'religion' I mean belief in an all-powerful and benevolent Creator, worship of whom, and obedience to whose commandments offers the only path to individual and collective well-being, together with the practices and the institutions founded on such belief. No doubt other definitions might be more appropriate to other societies at other points in time. But so far as Western Europe in the nineteenth century is concerned, this seems to me to summarise the distinctiveness of the Christian and Jewish faiths *vis-à-vis* the various other views of the world current at the time. I shall be using 'secularisation' in three different senses. It is essential to my argument that these senses are different, and that in asking how far and why secularisation happened during this period, one needs to look at each of these areas separately. The answers may prove to be quite different. The first two senses are fairly obvious, and most writers have concentrated on one or the other. Firstly there is individual religious belief and practice. To what extent has there been a decline in the proportion of the population having a religious view of the world, belonging to religious organisations or engaging in religious rites? Secondly there is the role of religion in public institutions. To what extent has there been a separation between church and state, or between church and school? The third area is less clearly defined, and perhaps for that reason it has been relatively neglected. It is the question of how far religion provided a common language, shared to some extent by the great majority of the people, through which a wide range of ideas, demands and needs could be expressed.

In the 1840s Pierre Proudhon argued that those like himself who wanted to rebuild French society on a completely new basis were obliged to retain a religious language because 'our monuments, our traditions, our laws, our ideas, our languages and our sciences, all are infected by this indelible superstition outside of which we can neither speak nor act, and without which we do not even think'.[37] This reluctant testimony to the ubiquitous social presence of theistic religion, whether Catholic, Protestant or Jewish, in Western Europe at the middle of the nineteenth century provides an indication of what I have in mind. From this point of view, a secular society might be seen as one in which religious language or practices or institutions, rather than being part of the taken-for-granted daily reality, which everyone is obliged to accept and come to terms with, whatever their personal belief or non-belief, become one option among several, a result of conscious individual choice. Philippe Boutry argues that just such a change in the social position of the Catholic faith took place in the department of the Ain in eastern France between 1815 and 1880:

> At the dawn of the Restoration it was an aspect of *mentality*, deeply stamped upon the social life and cultural traditions of the rural parish; by 1880 it has become a collection of *religious opinions*, that is to say individually motivated beliefs, ideas and practices, which for this reason are subject to general or particular challenge within the now disunited parish.[38]

It is likely that changes of this kind will come about in some areas of life, but not in others, or will progress more quickly in certain areas than in others. It is therefore necessary to examine the question at several different levels. One of the most important dimensions was hinted at by Proudhon: the question of how far religion offers a common point of reference, used by those in authority to justify their power, and by the oppressed to legitimate their protest. Another area for investigation is the relationship between religion and identity. To what extent was religion a fundamental social category shaping the self-image and behaviour of the majority of the population, or was it only important for the identity of those who were highly devout? Finally, a good test of the degree to which religious ideas, assumptions and symbols were a familiar feature of everyday life, rather than being limited to a pious subculture, is the place of religion in popular culture – the most elusive of all the areas I have mentioned, but one that is of major importance for any assessment of secularisation in my third sense.

If secularisation is defined in these broad terms, approached in a similarly open-minded way, and used flexibly, most of the objections mentioned above lose their force. Investigating the extent, nature and causes of secularisation does not preclude the recognition that other themes in modern religious history are equally central, or even more so, that the Christian churches continued to have a major role in West European societies throughout this period, that popular religion is as significant as more institutionalised forms, and that understandings of the 'religious' and the secular are continually evolving. Nor does it involve any kind of determinism.

There is one way of understanding secularisation which I shall *not* be using. An allegedly 'traditional' form of Christianity or Judaism has sometimes been presented as 'the real thing', and any change therefrom as a form of secularisation[39] – in complete disregard of the fact that these religions have been in continuous evolution, and that there has been constant interaction between Christianity or Judaism and their social and intellectual environment. One of the major themes in the religious history of Western Europe in the nineteenth century is the response of believing Christians and Jews to the threat of secularisation: a wide variety of strategies, radical, liberal and conservative, were devised to counter this danger. All of these deserve to be taken seriously. The attempt by some historians to dismiss the liberal and radical strategies as 'a form of secularisation' is as unjust and unenlightening as the attempt by other scholars to dismiss the conservative strategies as merely 'reactionary'.

The period chosen for this study, the years 1848–1914, saw many developments that are very significant for our theme. Non-religious belief-systems became generally accessible to the mass of the population, rather than being the preserve of relatively small circles of intellectuals or political radicals. Questions of the relationship of church and state, and especially of the place of religion in the system of mass education, became central political issues throughout Europe. The advent of mass politics, growing industrial conflict, and the rise of nationalism all had important implications for religion and the churches. In many parts of Europe, though by no means all, this period saw a substantial drop in attendance at church services or participation in communion. Other periods are also of great interest for historians concerned with secularisation in Europe, including, for instance, the 1790s and the 1960s. But I think there are good reasons for seeing the period between the revolutions of 1848 and the outbreak of the First World War as being of special importance.

Most studies of secularisation have either focused on a single country or region or have adopted a much more global approach, identifying trends common to Europe, the West or the whole world, without emphasising local differences. In selecting three closely related countries, I hope to be able to show both what is common to all three, and what is distinctive to each. I shall also pay considerable attention to regional and confessional differences, or class and gender differences, within countries. Potentially this seems to me one of the most productive ways of approaching the question of whether any general trend towards secularisation can be identified in nineteenth-century Europe and, if so, what its causes were.

The selection of France as a unit for study raises no special problems, though two boundary changes need to be noted: the annexation of Savoy and Nice in 1860, following the successful war against Austria, and the loss of Alsace and parts of Lorraine in 1871 following defeat by Prussia. However, Germany and England pose bigger problems, and no solution is going to be entirely satisfactory. In the case of Germany, one could make a case for including the whole of the German Confederation as it existed in 1848, thus including Austria, or at the other extreme, one could limit oneself to a single state, such as Prussia. I have taken a middle path, defining 'Germany' as those states which came together to form the German Empire from 1871 until 1919, and consequently became subject to homogenising influences, including a common consciousness of belonging to a state dominated by Protestants. It needs to be remembered, however, that church policy remained a matter for the individual states, and in spite of basic similarities between the religious constitutions of the various states, there were considerable differences in the details.[40] Rather than isolating England, one could make a case for taking the whole of the United Kingdom on the grounds that it was the state of which England was only a part, though the religious situation in nineteenth-century Ireland was so completely different from that in Britain that this would not be a very practicable approach.[41] One could make a case for taking the whole of Britain, though a difficulty here would be the fact that England and Wales on the one hand, and Scotland on the other, were completely separate in ecclesiastical matters, and the differences between them were much greater than the differences between the German states.[42] A case could be made for taking England and Wales as a unit, since throughout this period they had a common Established Church as well as numerous other common institutions.[43] There were, however, major cultural differences between England and Wales, most notably the much greater strength of Protestant Dissent in the latter country, and above all the

difference of language. This leads on to two decisive practical arguments for restricting myself to England. Firstly, I cannot read
Welsh, so that much of the relevant literature is inaccessible to me.
Secondly, it is a sufficiently formidable task to become fully familiar
with the literature on the social history of religion in England. This
is by now very extensive – comparable in size to the literature on
France, and much greater than the literature on Germany, where
many of the issues discussed here are only beginning to be
explored.

The Situation in the 1840s

In all three countries, church and state were closely linked and the
churches had a central role in education and social welfare. England
and France had gone through periods of revolutionary upheaval in
the seventeenth and late eighteenth centuries respectively, during
which the established church was overthrown. In both cases a compromise was eventually agreed in which the power of the established church was partly restored, but the position of religious
minorities was guaranteed. In England the Church of England
had been restored with the monarchy in 1660. Major modifications
of its powers were imposed as a result of the Revolution of 1688–89,
which produced the Toleration Act, providing freedom of worship
for Protestant Dissenters. In the later eighteenth century there was
a progressive relaxation of the laws prohibiting Roman Catholic
worship. Finally, the position of the church was fundamentally
changed by the constitutional revolution of 1828–32, and by the
Whig reforms of the 1830s. The former brought about the political
emancipation of Dissenters and Roman Catholics, though in the
1830s and 1840s a series of measures for the emancipation of
Jews, passed by the lower house of Parliament, were rejected by
the upper house. The latter included the Registration Act of 1836,
which greatly extended the very limited possibilities of marrying in
non-established places of worship, and also permitted a purely civil
ceremony. The highly controversial Poor Law Amendment Act of
1834 removed the care of the poor from the parish, where the
clergyman had a central role, placing it under newly formed Poor
Law Unions, under elected Guardians.

Anglican bishops were nominated by the monarch (on the recom-
mendation of the Prime Minister), and Anglican bishops sat in the

House of Lords. The monarch was supreme governor of the
Church of England, which was under the ultimate control of Parliament. The clergy were recruited mainly from the gentry and the
established middle class (in spite of a significant and growing clerical
proletariat, especially in the north, where clerical incomes tended
to be lower).[44] They had a powerful social presence, arising partly
from their incomes and closeness to other holders of power,
partly from their uniquely wide contacts with all sections of the
population. In particular, the Church of England had a leading
position in elementary education, as a result of the activities of the
National Society, founded in 1811 to establish schools for the poor.
By the 1840s, with the assistance of government grants, it was by far
the largest provider of elementary education. Meanwhile, many
clergymen were elected as Guardians to the new Poor Law authorities, just as many were appointed magistrates. Although, therefore, the ex officio powers of the clergy were being cut back, at least
for a time they remained formidably influential figures within the
newly emerging pluralistic, rationally organised, and relatively
democratic society.[45]

In France, the Roman Catholic Church had fallen very swiftly
from a position of immense wealth and privilege under the *ancien
régime* to suffer brutal persecution under the Revolution. However
the latent strength of French Catholicism was demonstrated by the
religious revival of the later 1790s, which persuaded Napoleon to
reach an accommodation with the church. The result was the Concordat with Pope Pius VII which came into operation in 1802, and
which Napoleon unilaterally modfied by the so-called 'Organic
Articles'. This was a deal tilted in favour of the state, but one
which enabled the church to reorganise after the devastation of
the 1790s. The state recognised the Catholic Church as 'the religion
of the great majority of Frenchmen'. The state was to pay the
salaries of the clergy, but no new parishes could be established
without the state's authorisation. Bishops were to be nominated by
the state, subject to the Pope's consent. The state subsequently
recognised the Lutheran, Calvinist and Jewish religions, and introduced similar provisions for the state payment of pastors and rabbis,
for the centralisation of religious authority, and for state control
over those exercising this authority. In some respects the position of
the French Catholic Church was more favourable than that of the
Church of England. In particular, the strength of all kinds of religious dissent in England contrasted with the overwhelmingly

Catholic composition of the French population. Clearly Protestants (about 2 per cent of the French population) and Jews (less than 1 per cent) had an importance out of proportion to their small numbers. Clearly also, the concentration of Protestants in certain areas (notably in and around the cities of Nîmes and Strasbourg, and in Paris), and of Jews in Paris and Alsace gave them a high local profile. But most parts of the country were homogeneously Catholic. The overwhelming majority of the population had been baptised, catechised and married by the Catholic Church and would be buried there, and in many parts of the country the great majority of the female population and a large proportion of the male population attended mass Sunday by Sunday. Elementary education was closely linked with the church, the schoolmaster often being the church organist. Nuns were growing in number rapidly and were taking a leading part both in the education of girls and in the care of the sick. On the other hand, the French Catholic Church suffered from the extent of its dependence on the state and from the legacy of the revolutionary years. The state could and did use its power of withholding salaries in order to put pressure on troublesome clergy. Bishops (whose dioceses generally corresponded with a department, the main unit of local administration), were closely watched by the prefect, the supreme civil administrator of the department. Their activities were the subject of regular reports to the Ministry of Religious Affairs, and they would come under pressure from the prefect or the minister if they stepped too far out of line. An annual *Budget des Cultes* was the chief determinant of the resources available to the church, and even governments otherwise sympathetic were naturally reluctant to authorise the formation of new parishes or other measures likely to result in increased spending. Naturally too, the church sought to supplement the state's reluctant grants through other sources of funding.[46]

In Germany the religious situation was inevitably much more complicated, since the unification of a multitude of smaller states into the German Empire was completed only in 1871, and in the 1840s there were still some thirty German states, each with their own arrangements for relations with the churches.[47] Apart from Austria, they included the large state of Prussia (crossing a large part of north Germany from Königsberg to the Rhineland), the medium-sized states of Bavaria, Baden, Württemberg, Hanover, Saxony and Hesse-Darmstadt, the city-states of Hamburg, Bremen, Lübeck and Frankfurt am Main, and numerous smaller states. All were explicitly

Christian. All recognised in principle 'parity' between the three major Christian confessions (Lutheran, Reformed and Roman Catholic), though in practice most states favoured one of these confessions (usually some form of Protestantism, but in the case of Bavaria, the Catholics). In a number of states the Protestants had formed a United church – most notably in Prussia, where Friedrich Wilhelm III had marked the tercentenary of the Reformation in 1817 by forcibly uniting the Lutheran and Reformed confessions – in the face of fierce opposition from many Lutherans. Some refused to join the new church, and became the first large body of Protestant dissenters in Germany, where at least until the 1840s the formation of free churches was fraught with legal difficulties. The great majority of Protestants in fact remained within the various *Landeskirchen* (territorial churches); the ruler of the territory was supreme bishop of the Protestant church and regulated its affairs through a ministry responsible for religion and education. The close relationship between these two spheres was reflected in the fact that although schools were under state control, they had a confessional character, and were subject to inspection by the pastor or priest (depending on the denomination of the school).

The occupation of various parts of Germany by French armies from the 1790s onwards had especially dramatic effects in traditionally Catholic areas. In 1803 Napoleon had imposed the Secularisation, by which all ecclesiastical states were dissolved and all church property confiscated. In Protestant Germany the later eighteenth century had been a period of rationalism in which traditional forms of piety were under fire. The church's hymn-books were being rewritten in the light of the contemporary bias towards the ethical and the socially useful aspects of religion, with its corresponding bias against the dogmatic and the miraculous.

In most parts of Europe, the period after 1815 saw a return towards more conservative forms of Christianity.[48] These were favoured by governments, which tended to see liberal religion and religious scepticism as major factors in the revolutionary upheavals of the previous generation. In the intellectual and cultural spheres, this trend was favoured by the rediscovery of tradition, of the Middle Ages, of the mysterious and the non-rational. The many aristocrats who were returning to their ancestral faith in the early years of the nineteenth century also threw their powerful weight behind this association of religion with conservatism. In France the alliance of throne, altar and chateau reached a high point under

Charles X (1824–30), whose reign was brought to an abrupt halt by the July Revolution of the latter year, provoked partly by opposition to his association with ultra-conservative Catholics. In Germany the alliance had a longer innings, notably in Prussia, where Friedrich Wilhelm IV (1840–61) aimed to bring about a 'Christian State'.

In all three countries, the period 1815–48 had seen important signs of religious revival and reconstruction. In France the Revolution had struck a devastating blow at the church's parochial machinery. Many priests either were killed or abandoned the priesthood during the 'dechristianisation' of 1793–4, and for several years the recruitment of new clergy came to a halt. Most religious houses were suppressed. The closure of churches and the lack of priests meant that the long-established practices of attendance at mass, confession, communion, participation in processions, and so on, were interrupted, and many children were not baptised, nor were couples married in church.[49] The process of reconstruction began very slowly with the relaxation of religious persecution in the later 1790s and somewhat more rapidly after the Concordat in 1802. However, the Napoleonic years were still a troubled time for the church, marked by increasing conflict between Napoleon and the Pope, with many episcopal sees remaining vacant, restrictions on the state's religious budget, and of course almost continuous war. Reconstruction of the church could be pursued much more vigorously after the final defeat of Napoleon in 1815 and the restoration of the Bourbons. In spite of the initially anti-clerical character of the July Monarchy, the renewal continued under Louis Philippe in the 1830s and 1840s. After 1815 there was a massive recruitment of new clergy, and the beginnings of a revival of the religious orders, which continued until the 1870s. In the short run the most visible aspect of this revival was the re-emergence of the Jesuits, expelled from France in 1764, as well as of other preaching orders. In the longer run the most significant development was the growth of orders for women, and the increasingly central part played by nuns in French Catholic life.[50]

The Catholic revival in France was strongly supported by the aristocracy, whose patronage was important not only in many rural areas but in cities with a strong aristocratic presence, such as Toulouse.[51] In some parts of France very high levels of Catholic practice had once again been attained by the 1840s. Yves-Marie Hilaire entitles his history of religious life in the diocese of Arras 'A Christendom in the 19th century?' And in spite of the question

mark, the main emphasis of his study is on the great strength of the
Catholic Church in this northern diocese, at least until the economic
and social upheavals associated with the development of coal-
mining in the second half of the century and the political revolution
resulting from the establishment of the Third Republic.[52] However,
the revival was uneven, both socially and regionally. In some
regions of France, in fact, the church seems never fully to have
recovered from the events of the Revolution.[53] Problems were
especially acute in areas where most of the population had supported the Constitutional Church, which broke with the Pope in
1791, and threw in its lot with the Revolution. Although Napoleon
had hoped to bring together constitutional and non-juring Catholics in a reunited church where former divisions would be forgotten, the bitter feuds of those years were not so easily forgotten. In
any case, the Pope was determined that former constitutionals
should be marginalised under the new order. A start was made
with this under the Napoleonic regime. The work was finished
after 1815, when new bishops were always former non-jurors, who
did their best to make life as hard as possible for those among their
clergy who had been constitutionals.[54]

In areas where the Constitutional Church had been dominant,
unhappiness with the new regime was reflected in low rates of
Catholic practice, and resistance to the numerous missions staged
by Jesuits, Redemptorists and other orders under the Restoration.
In particular, religious practice remained low in most of the Paris
and Bordeaux regions during the Restoration and the July Monarchy, and there was little of the growth seen in many other parts of
the country. A good example of the situation in the Paris region
would be the diocese of Orléans. A survey in 1850 showed that there
was no canton where more than 5 per cent of the men or more than
20 per cent of the women received communion at Easter. There
were ten parishes where not a single man received communion, and
two where not a single woman did so.[55] More generally, the bourgeoisie, and especially bourgeois men, remained relatively detached
from the church in this period. Intellectually they were still rooted
in the eighteenth-century Enlightenment and in the writings of
such figures as Voltaire and Rousseau – indeed 'Voltairian' was the
word typically used to describe the religious outlook of men of this
class during this period. Politically their attitudes varied, many
identifying with the July Monarchy, some harking back to Napoleon, and others looking forward to a future republic. But they were

generally agreed in opposing the Legitimism supported by many of the Catholic clergy, and in being suspicious of the reactionary political influence exercised by the church.[56]

In England, as in most other predominantly Protestant countries, the years around the end of the eighteenth and the beginning of the nineteenth century saw a powerful growth of evangelical religion, often in the form of 'revivals' involving mass conversions.[57] Most sections of the population were to some degree affected, though the precise forms taken by the evangelical movement varied between different social environments. Among the aristocracy and the upper middle class the movement was largely contained within the Church of England, and was often associated with strongly conservative political and social attitudes. In the middle class it was more often associated with the Independent and Baptist churches and with the emergence of political liberalism. In the working class in town and countryside it most commonly took the form of Methodism, and could equally often be associated either with forms of radical protest or with an apolitical attitude. Two other religious currents in this period were important because of their influence on the clergy and on the educated public, namely the High Church Tractarian movement within the Church of England and the liberals, who in the 1850s came to be known as the 'Broad Church'. Thus, the forms of Christianity existing in mid-nineteenth-century England were very varied – much more so than in France or Germany – and there were few members of the upper and middle classes who were entirely outside the churches.[58] Among the small number of avowed religious sceptics in the middle class, the most important group were the so-called 'philosophic radicals', guided by Utilitarian principles, who had a considerable influence on the Whig reforms of the 1830s. The main resistance to the all-pervasive influence of Christianity in England during the first half of the nineteenth century came, however, from lower down the social scale among sections of the working class and lower middle class, especially in London and in the industrial districts of east Lancashire and west Yorkshire. Here the biggest influences were Robert Owen, the pioneer of co-operation and socialism in Britain, and Tom Paine, whose *Rights of Man* (1791), the Bible of popular radicalism, was followed by *The Age of Reason* (1794), the first widely read attack on Christianity to be published in Britain. Paine's works were a principal target of the prosecutions of blasphemous publications which were at their peak in the 1810s and 1820s. However, deists and atheists were relatively small in numbers in comparison with the huge numbers of those who flooded into the Dissenting chapels in these years. It was the Dissenters, far more than the Secularists, who posed the main threat to the Church of England. In 1851, worshippers in the Established Church made up 51 per cent of all those attending church in England, while Protestant Dissenters made up 44 per cent. The threat came from two directions. In terms of religious and social influence the Church of England had by the mid-nineteenth century become a minority church in the large parts of northern England where Methodism was dominant. In political terms, the Municipal Reform Act of 1835 opened the way to new local elites, many of whom were newly rich, and most of whom were Liberal in politics and Dissenting in religion.[59]

In Germany too the early nineteenth century was a time of religious 'Awakenings' (the *Erweckungsbewegung*), but their scope was more localised than in England. Their major influence was on the aristocracy (especially in Prussia's eastern provinces), on the rural population (most notably in Westphalia), on small town artisans (especially in Württemberg) and on some industrial districts (such as the Wuppertal). Many regions of Germany were little affected and in particular the middle and working classes in the towns were seldom involved. As in France, the bourgeoisie, and especially bourgeois men, were more strongly influenced either by religious liberalism or by scepticism. The liberal currents were represented by the Friends of Light and the *Deutschkatholiken* (German Catholics), two movements of the 1840s, the former initiated by Protestants and the latter by Catholics, and both combining demands for a more open and democratic society with a liberal and rationalistic form of theology. The episode which more than any other exposed the religious tensions within German society at this time was the display by the cathedral authorities at Trier in 1844 of their most prized relic, the seamless robe of Christ. This attracted huge numbers of pilgrims, and also provoked protests, most notably from a priest in Breslau, Johannes Ronge, whose objection to this piece of Ultramontane 'superstition' led him to separate from the Roman Church and to found the *Deutschkatholiken*. At the same time another influential group within Germany's educated middle class was taking this rejection of religious tradition a step further. At Tübingen University, a group of scholars was submitting the text of the New Testament to scientific investigation, the most famous result of these researches being the *Life of Jesus* by D. F. Strauß.

Others were subjecting Christianity to philosophical criticism, most notably Ludwig Feuerbach in his *Essence of Christianity* (1841). Already in the 1830s and 1840s ideas of this kind were having a considerable influence not only on the intellectual avant-garde and on political radicals, but on wider sections of the educated middle class, especially in north German Protestant cities such as Berlin and Hamburg, where religious participation was already low.[60]

While the poor tended to be infrequent church-goers, religion remained an important part of the language of social protest, answering the equally frequent use of religious language by those in authority. In Eileen Yeo's memorable phrase, Christianity was 'contested territory'[61] – quite literally so in the summer of 1839 when, first in Stockport, and then in some thirty other towns, the Chartists marched in a body to the parish church on Sunday morning, occupied most of the seats, and asked the clergyman to preach on a text which they presented to him. At Stockport the Chartists gave the vicar a choice of four texts, but he ignored them all, preaching instead on 'What must I do to be saved?', and urging his hearers 'not to struggle for temporal things, but for eternal salvation'.[62] This was largely the story of the following weeks, as the Chartists, drawing especially on the Old Testament prophets, the gospels and the epistle of James drew messages of equality, social justice and condemnation of the rich, while most of the clergy, drawing from the epistles of Paul and Peter, appealed for submission to God-given authority. The Chartists gradually abandoned the attempt to reclaim the parish churches for the people, and turned instead to holding their own services, often conducted by those among them who had been Nonconformist preachers.[63] But speakers at political meetings and writers in their newspapers claimed the support of Christianity for their demands, and Chartist banners made frequent use of biblical texts.[64] Christianity and especially the Bible still provided a common language, accessible to all social classes and those at most points in the political spectrum, and for this reason it was potentially more effective than any more sectional discourse. The same seems to have been true in France, where Edward Berenson has analysed some of the songs sung by worker-poets to working-class and peasant audiences in the 1840s. Typically these songs presented a kind of Christian socialism, based on the principles of co-operation and social equality, together with a moral critique of the regime of cut-throat competition and the remorseless pursuit of wealth.[65]

The role of Christian symbols and language in the maintenance both of community amd of systems of authority also remained enormous. For instance, in France and in Catholic regions of Germany annual festivities in honour of the patron saint of the parish brought together the whole population in rituals which derived their special quality from the mixing of sacred and profane.[66] Protestant communities were more sparing in the use of symbolism. But here as much as in a Catholic environment the parish church evoked strong emotions, as an object of local pride, as a place associated with important events in individual and family history, as a link with past generations, as well as being the place where God was most likely to be found.[67] One of the most important functions of the parish church was the provision of an appropriate setting and ritual for celebration of the great turning-points of life and for mourning the dead. In France, the Revolution had decreed that the only legally recognised marriage ceremony was that which took place at the town hall, but by the 1840s the overwhelming majority of couples followed the legal ceremony with a ceremony in church.[68] In England a purely civil ceremony was available from 1837, but the proportion of couples taking this option was initially small.[69] In none of the German states was this option yet available. Many forms of religious observance, belief and morality, together with other requirements of social and civic virtue, were enforced by powerful community pressures, providing the necessary underpinnings to the authority of the clergy.

The first half of the nineteenth century had seen major changes both within the Jewish communities of France, Germany and England and in the social position of these communities. The latter changes went furthest in France, where Napoleon made Judaism one of the four officially recognised religions, and where from 1831 Jewish rabbis shared the privilege already accorded to Catholic priests and Protestant pastors of being paid by the state. Emancipation came step by step in England and Germany, but here too there were important advances. In Germany, the entry of Jews into many of the *Vereine*, which were central institutions of middle-class life seemed to indicate that Jews could become like other Germans in everything but their religion.[70] At mid-century, about 1 per cent of the German population was Jewish, as against 0.3 per cent in France and 0.2 per cent in England. In some cities, as well as in certain smaller towns in Prussia's eastern provinces, the proportion was far higher. In Frankfurt it was 8 per cent, in Hamburg/Altona and in

Breslau it was 7 per cent, though in Berlin, where the great expansion of the Jewish community came later in the century, it was still only 2 per cent.[71] So the Jewish presence was from every point of view much greater in the German states than in France or England, and developments within German Jewry were closely watched by Jews in other countries.

The effect of wider opportunities in German society, greater openness to outside influences, and the weakening of internal authority structures from the later eighteenth century onwards was to provoke deep divisions within German Jewish communities. Prussian legislation from 1750 eroded the powers exercised by rabbis, and the same happened in, for instance, Bavaria in 1806 and Baden in 1809. The result was that Jews were free to decide which parts of the Jewish law they would observe and which they would ignore. In Berlin, by the early nineteenth century, there were many Jews who seldom went to synagogue and who partly or wholly ignored the Sabbath and the dietary laws.[72] Partly in response to this decline in observance, a powerful movement for religious reform emerged in the early nineteenth century. The reformers aimed to revitalise the synagogue by providing services that were more modern, dignified and German, and rabbis who were more like Protestant pastors, preaching inspiring sermons and providing pastoral care for the congregation. The first congregation to implement these ideas was the Hamburg Temple, established in 1818, which issued a prayer book making extensive use of German and including a declaration that German Jews regarded Germany as their homeland and did not desire another.

In the following decades many Jewish communities saw confrontations between traditionalists and reformers. In Breslau, for instance, between 1838 and 1842 the two parties polarised around the rival figures of senior rabbi Titkin and the second rabbi Abraham Geiger, one of the outstanding leaders of the reform movement, who had the support of the majority of the communal board. After traditionalists heckled a funeral address by Geiger in 1842, Titkin was suspended. Finally in 1856 a compromise was agreed which was typical of the situation in many German cities: Geiger was appointed joint rabbi with Titkin's son. Each effectively catered for a different part of the community, while the communal board continued to be responsible for welfare matters. By this time, as Meyer writes, 'there had arisen at the edge of German Jewry a generation so fully Germanised and Europeanised that its non-

Jewish identity all but crowded out ancestral loyalties'. They often felt some attachment to the Jewish community, while having little or no interest in the Jewish religion.[73]

Similar battles were being fought on a much smaller scale within the English and French communities – with the difference that the Consistory system introduced by Napoleon in France and the office of Chief Rabbi in England led to a considerable degree of central control, whereas in Germany there were major differences between the Jewish communities in different states and different cities.[74] Thus in England too a reform movement developed, leading to the formation of the West London Synagogue in 1842, but the Chief Rabbi (powerfully assisted by the president of the Board of Deputies) was able to ensure the continuing dominance of orthodoxy.[75] In France, it was the other current of religious change that was most conspicuous, namely the emergence of a large group of prosperous, highly acculturated, and largely non-observant Jews.[76] In England, the Jewish community had always been overwhelmingly urbanised and heavily concentrated in London. In France and Germany there were also significant numbers of rural and small-town Jews, but there were strong trends towards urbanisation and embourgeoisement. By the second half of the nineteenth century the Jewish communities in all three countries were highly urbanised and, at least until the influx of Russian and Polish immigrants after about 1880, they were predominantly middle class.[77]

Summary of the Book

I agree with Kselman and Cox[78] that pluralism is the key to the religious situation in later nineteenth-century Europe, and that trends towards secularisation have to be seen in the context of intense religious competition, whether between rival branches of Christianity or between religious and secular views of the world. Nineteenth-century pluralism did not necessarily lead to the sceptical relativism[79] that some writers have suggested: in fact there can have been few periods of history in which fervent ideological commitments of varying kinds were so widely held. Rather than seeing secularisation as an impersonal 'process' (the term most commonly used in the sociological and historical literature), it would be better to see it as a 'contest', in which adherents of rival world-views battled it out. Certainly the role of more impersonal forces in undermining religion and the churches needs to be considered, but insufficient account has been taken of the role of human agency. Secularisation happened at least in part because there were large numbers of people who were trying their hardest to bring it about. In some parts of Western Europe these efforts were very successful. The fact that in other areas secularisation was much more limited was at least partly due to the efforts of those who devised strategies for resisting the trend.

Chapter 1 will begin the story in the 'crazy year' or the 'holy and terrible year', as it was variously named, of 1848 – a year that cast shadows across the rest of the nineteenth century, powerfully influencing the history of religion, as of so much else. In France and Germany, though much less in England, the events of this year strengthened the connections between the churches and political conservatism and furthered the tendencies towards secularity on the Left. This leads on in Chapter 2 to a consideration of the role of religion in public institutions. This offers a contrast between the systematic secularisation pursued by French governments from the later 1870s onwards, the tendency towrds a very gradual and unsystematic institutional secularisation in England, and the privileged and powerful public role which the churches continued to exercise in Germany. The different balance of political forces in the three countries brought about very different relationships between church and state. This leads to a recogniton that in the nineteenth century there were huge divergences between the patterns of religious development in different sections of society. Chapter 3 considers which social groups were most supportive of secularising policies, and why. Chapters 4 and 5 move away from public institutions to focus on the trends in individual belief and practice. With the pressures towards religious conformity weakening and with the availability of an increasingly wide range of alternative belief-systems, the trend was clearly towards a greater religious individualism, with belief and practice becoming much more a matter of personal choice and commitment and both taking a considerable variety of forms. However, Chapter 5 also emphasises that the chronology and circumstances of these changes varied greatly as between different parts of Europe, and to some extent between members of different religious confessions. In Chapters 6 and 7, which look at religion as a source of identity and at the relationship between religion and popular culture, the emphasis is more on continuity. Chapter 8 brings the story to an end in the even crazier, more terrible and completely unholy year of 1914, and reconsiders these various dimensions of religious change in the light of the ways that the English, French and Germans responded to the outbreak of war.

One final comment on my approach: historians of secularisation have often exaggerated the extent and rapidity of the changes described by emphasising the most religious aspects of the period covered in the earlier part of their narratives, and highlighting all the most secular aspects of later periods. My assumption is, however, that in most societies there has been a tension between the professed beliefs of the people and their actual practice, there have been major variations in individual belief, and some areas of life have been more influenced by religion than others. Certainly I shall stress the extent of such tensions, ambiguities and variations in the years 1848–1914.

1 1848

The revolutions of 1848–9 mark a turning-point in the religious history of modern Europe. The Pope, the Catholic bishops in France and Germany, leaders of the German Protestant churches, were all forced to take sides. The choices made during these fateful years would continue to shape relations between church and state and between church and society over several generations.

In the short term the revolutions ended in failure. In France, where the Second Republic was established in February 1848, with all adult males having the right to vote, Louis Napoleon was elected president in December of that year. This proved to be the infant democracy's suicide, since the president went on to limit the right to vote in 1850, to stage a *coup d'etat* in 1851, and to declare himself emperor with the title of Napoleon III in 1852. The Second Empire continued until 1870 when defeat in the war with Prussia forced Napoleon into abdication and exile.

The revolution in France was followed in March 1848 by mass meetings, demonstrations and sometimes street-fighting in the cities of the German states. Frightened rulers, fearing that they might soon be following France's Louis Philippe into exile, responded quickly by appointing 'March ministries', with liberal ministers and promises of constitutions. Elections were held all across Germany for a national parliament, which met in May in the St Paul's church in Frankfurt, and began the task of preparing a constitution. During the summer, however, the conservative forces were reorganising, encouraged by the growing divisions between moderate liberals and radical democrats. In November the Prussian king felt strong enough to stage a *coup d'état*. He followed this by promulgating a constitution, which granted some of the liberal demands, but strictly as an act of royal grace. In the king's eyes, it was entirely a matter for himself, as the ruler appointed by God, to decide what he would give his people. In March 1849 the Frankfurt parliament produced a national constitution, but it was promptly rejected by Prussia and Austria. The Parliament soon began to disintegrate, as deputies drifted home. In May there were armed uprisings and the establishment of revolutionary governments in Saxony, the Palatinate and Baden. But each of these was suppressed by Prussian troops. In July 1849 the revolutions finally came to an end with the mass execution of revolutionaries in Baden, followed by the emigration of many of the survivors to the United States. All over Germany, conservatives were in control.

The revolutions in Italy and Hungary met a similar fate, but they are beyond the scope of the present book. One of the Italian revolutions, however, was of wider significance. Pope Pius IX, who ruled not only Rome but most of central Italy, fled in November 1848, and in January 1849 the Roman Republic was established. One of its leaders was Giuseppe Mazzini, the hero of Italian radicals, nationalists and anti-clericals. French troops overthrew the Republic after only six months, and for the time being the whole of central Italy was again under papal rule. Pius IX had begun his reign with a reputation for liberalism. But after his return from exile, and for the remainder of his long reign, he was an uncompromising foe of liberalism and of democracy, inside or outside the church.

Churches in Revolution

In their early stages the revolutions were accepted or even welcomed by the clergy of the dominant churches. Except in Vienna and in Lyon, there was little evidence of the militant anti-clericalism which had been part of the 1830 Revolution in France.[1] In Berlin two events came to symbolise the religious atmosphere of the first days of revolution. On 19 March, after a night of fighting in which over two hundred people died, the bodies of some of the barricade-fighters were brought to the royal palace, where the king was called to the balcony and told to take off his hat as a mark of respect to the dead, while the crowd sang the funeral hymn '*Jesus, meine Zuversicht*'. Three days later, most of the city's Protestant clergy, as well as a Catholic priest and a Jewish rabbi, participated in the funeral of 183 fallen insurgents. The liberal Protestant pastor Adolf Sydow delivered a graveside address which was enthusiastically received because of its praise for the heroic sacrifice made by the fallen and his celebration of the revolution as 'a turning-point in the history of our Prussian German fatherland'.[2] Meanwhile, the rhetoric used by a number of the leading radicals was notable for its Christian language.[3] At this stage a common religious idiom, expressed through biblical references, familiar phrases, hymns and rituals provided common ground between the monarch and the common people of Berlin, and between those at different points in the political spectrum.

In the spring of 1848 the links between church and revolution and the religious flavour of much revolutionary rhetoric were even more conspicuous in France. Although by 1848 the anti-clericalism of the Orleanist monarchy had largely dissipated, there was little enthusiasm for Louis Philippe among the clergy. Some welcomed the Republic, especially those who identified themselves with their poorer parishioners and wanted social legislation as well as democracy. Many others looked forward to a return of the Bourbons, the 'legitimate' rulers of France. And there were also those whose concerns were more exclusively ecclesiastical, and who expected that the new regime would allow the church more freedom especially in the field of education. All three groups hoped that the revolution might be the first step on their chosen path. This support was symbolised in the blessing by priests of 'Liberty Trees' which was a characteristic event in the early weeks of the revolution. Among the leaders of the new regime there were fervent Christians such as Buchez, but even those who were less personally devout believed that the support of the clergy was important for the success of the revolution.[4]

Among the most enthusiastic supporters of the revolutions were members of religious minorities, including French Protestants, French and German Jews, Protestants in the Bavarian-ruled Palatinate, Roman Catholics in other German states, and German Dissenters.[5] Here we need to distinguish between two kinds of support for the revolutions. In the German states, where church and state were closely bound together, and all religious activity was closely watched by police and bureaucracy, nearly all religious minorities expected that the revolutions would improve their own position by broadenening the range of religious freedom.[5] (A rare exception were the Calvinist dissenters in the Wuppertal, who were loyal monarchists, totally opposed to the revolution.[6]) On the other hand, there were also certain religious minorities whose demand for religious liberty fed into a more general enthusiasm for freedom and democracy, and became some of the most active supporters of the revolutions. In France, where the overwhelming majority of the population were Catholics, the role of minorities in 1848 was much more peripheral. In many parts of Germany, however, it was central. The best example of opportunistic support for the revolution would be the Roman Catholic Church in Prussia, Württemberg, and other Protestant states. The best example of the mingling of religion with revolutionary idealism would be the German Dissenters.

To begin with the latter: the 1840s had seen intense conflict between liberals and conservatives within the German churches, leading to the secession of many of the liberals to join the Free Parishes and *Deutschkatholiken*. The latter movement attracted not only Catholics, but also many Protestants and even some Jews, who saw in it the beginnings of a new national church which would overcome the old confessional differences by providing a 'rational' faith and 'modern' forms of worship which all Germans could agree upon. It was particularly attractive to confessionally-mixed couples, who saw the new church as a way of reconciling the difference.[7] Admittedly there was considerable disagreement as to what form the movement's theology should take. While its founders were looking for a more tolerant, undogmatic form of Christianity, they were soon joined by those who wanted to move beyond Christianity and into a 'religion of humanity'.[8] In spite of the rapid growth of *Deutschkatholiken* and Free Parishes, their members were no more than about 0.5 per cent of the German population in 1848. However, they played a part in the revolutions out of all proportion to their numbers.[9] The most famous example was Robert Blum, founder of the congregation of *Deutschkatholiken* in Leipzig and leader of the moderate democrats in the Frankfurt Parliament, whose execution by the Austrian military made him the most revered martyr of the German revolutions. But there were numerous other examples both at local and at national levels. The Dissenters' critique of religious orthodoxy provided a stimulus to critical rethinking in many other areas of German society, and their own religious ideas provided an alternative vision of the future. A good example of their creative potential is their pioneering role in the history of women's emancipation. In 1850, when the Free Parishes and *Deutschkatholiken* united, they gave women the right to vote in congregational elections and to hold office, a step which the Protestant churches took only in 1920 and the Catholic Church in 1924.[10]

The Roman Catholic Church had a much more ambivalent attitude towards the German revolutions. The clergy saw the events of March 1848 as a God-given opportunity to liberate the church by ending the numerous controls and restrictions on its activities which the states imposed.[11] Accordingly, Catholic priests stood as candidates for the Frankfurt Parliament and for many state parliaments, and a large number of Catholic associations were formed, named *Piusvereine*, in honour of the Pope. Their chief purpose was to defend Catholic interests, by campaigning against state interference and for the maintenance of confessional schools.[12] But they had a more general role in organising the Catholic community in other directions – for instance by setting up charities or establishing newspapers – and in maintaining Catholic consciousness at the highest possible level.[13] Clearly very few Catholic clergy in Prussia or other Protestant states wished to return to the *Vormärz* (the time before the March revolution). But neither did they have much sympathy with the more radical democrats. There was certainly a minority of radical priests: a secret government report on the political views of the clergy in the Trier district after the suppression of the uprisings in 1849 suggested that 16 per cent of Catholic priests were democrats.[14] Most Catholic priests in Prussia, however, seem to have been moderate liberals, preferring a constitutional monarchy, but mainly preoccupied with the rights and needs of the church.[15]

Even in the euphoric spring days there were some out-and-out enemies of the revolution, especially on the Pietist and orthodox Lutheran wings of the German Protestant churches. In Berlin, Ernst Wilhelm Hengstenberg, editor of the influential organ of conservative Protestantism, the *Evangelische Kirchen-Zeitung*, was from the first scornful of the revolution in Paris, and bitterly hostile to the revolutions in Germany, which he saw as acts of sinful rebellion against rulers appointed by God.[16] Hengstenberg had founded his paper in 1827, at a time when liberals and rationalists were a powerful force within the Protestant churches, and Friedrich Schleiermacher was still a central figure in Berlin. Hengstenberg's primary concern was the defence of Protestant orthodoxy through unremitting attacks on its enemies both inside and outside the church. But in his mind it was difficult to separate the religious from the political. Christians had a duty to submit themselves to the

Obrigkeit – a key concept in the thinking of conservative German Protestants, which might be translated as 'legitimate authority', though it really has no English equivalent. But the alliance of 'throne and altar' also had practical advantages – the Prussian kings Friedrich Wilhelm III and IV were strongly supportive of conservative Protestantism, whereas political liberals and democrats were generally sympathetic towards liberal theology and a wide-ranging religious toleration.

In the course of 1848, the majority of the Protestant clergy in Germany and the Catholic clergy in France moved more clearly to the Right. In France the most important turning-point was the working-class uprising in Paris in June – 'the June Days'. After four days of fighting the rising was suppressed with much bloodshed, but it had provoked widespread panic within the middle and upper classes, and also among the clergy. Even those clergy who had been concerned with the 'social question', now insisted that armed uprisings were not a legitimate way for workers to claim their rights. The revolution in Rome in November 1848 and the Pope's exile also horrified the French clergy. They rallied strongly to Louis Napoleon as the most conservative of the candidates in the presidential election the following month. By the time of the parliamentary elections in May 1849 the position of the great majority of the clergy was clear. While they might differ as to the precise form of conservative politics that they favoured, they were united in voting for the 'Party of Order', an alliance of 'white' legitimists and 'blue' republican moderates against the radical republican 'reds'. Many of the bourgeois supporters of the 'Party of Order' were very recent converts to the Catholic cause, but they claimed to be standing for 'religion, the family, work and property', and they alleged that a victory for the 'reds' would mean a return to the terror of 1793.[17] The minority of 'red' priests, who had been to the fore in the spring of 1848, were now isolated. Napoleon's coup of 2 December 1851 provoked uprisings in many strongholds of the Left, most notably the south-east, but received the approval of most of the Catholic hierarchy.[18]

The response of German Protestant clergy to the revolutions was much more complex, varying as it did both between states and to a considerable extent within them. Many clergy simply swam with the tide, accepting or even welcoming the revolutions in their early months, and later accepting the triumph of reaction. There were also many Protestant clergy who played an active or even prominent

part in the revolutions. Most of these belonged to the liberal wing of
their churches, and hopes for democratisation and liberalisation of
the state generally went hand in hand with hopes for similar
reforms within the church. The two principal demands of these
church reformers were elected synods, whereby the laity could
take an active part in church government, and freedom for the
clergy to follow the dictates of their conscience, rather than being
required formally to subscribe to the Confessions of Faith drawn up
during the Reformation. These objectives were indeed achieved in a
number of states during 1848–9, though as with every other reform
enacted in the revolutionary year, they were heavily diluted, or
destroyed entirely, after the triumph of reaction.[19] One of the few
clergymen to become a local leader of the revolution was the Bremen pastor, Rudolf Dulon.[20] But there were many who supported
the revolutions in a less prominent way, through sermons, newspaper articles or standing for elective office. In Breslau it was
claimed that the majority of the clergy supported the revolution.[21]
In Baden there were twenty-three clergymen whose support for the
revolutionary government was sufficiently active to warrant pro-
secution after the government fell, and a study of Württemberg
identifies eighteen Protestant clergy who were active democrats
during 1848–9.[22] In the Palatinate a number of factors combined,
including an objection to Bavarian rule in general and the Bavarian
church leadership in particular, to ensure that the radical element
among the clergy was unusually large: a government report after
the suppression of the revolutionary government in 1849 indicated
that out of a sample of Protestant clergy 73 per cent were Leftist
sympathisers.[23]

However, in most parts of Germany, the decisive role was played
by those among the Protestant clergy who either (like Hengstenberg) rejected the revolution from the start, or else came to reject it.
Theological factors played a major part here. The prominence in
the revolution of liberal Protestants, Dissenters and Jews, and the
emergence of political Catholicism, were all alarming to orthodox
Protestants. Anti-revolutionary leanings were particularly strong in
Prussia, where they were reinforced by deep loyalty to the Prussian
crown, and lack of enthusiasm for a united Germany, in which
Prussianism might be diluted by liberal and Catholic influences.[24]
But in other German states too, conservative theology and anti-
revolutionary politics were closely linked – and this at a time when
the conservative forces within Protestantism had for some years

been in the ascendant.[25] As one rather striking example of the
trends, in the Palatinate, where 82 per cent of clergymen aged 35
and over were reckoned in 1849 to be Leftists, only 37 per cent of
their younger colleagues shared these sympathies.[26] The major
reason for this seemes to have been the growing influence of
Lutheran orthodoxy with its accompanying political conservatism
or quietism, inculcated in this case through the Theology Faculty of
the University of Erlangen.[27] In Prussia, Protestant pastors contributed to the development of conservative politics by preaching sermons, writing newspaper articles and joining (or even founding)
conservative associations. The first national Protestant congress, the
Wittenberg *Kirchentag* in November 1848, was dominated by
theological and political conservatives, and the speeches included
anti-revolutionary diatribes, as well as the more constructive contribution of Johann Wichern, founder of the Inner Mission, who
outlined his proposals for a paternalist programme of social reform.
Conservative politicians, for their part, emphasised their closeness
to the clergy, and defence of the 'Christian State' was a major plank
of conservative propaganda.[28] In Bavaria, the only German state
where both the ruling house and the majority of the population
were Catholics, the church leadership took a similar line to that of
their Protestant counterparts in Prussia. The Catholic bishops
remained strongly wedded to the alliance of throne and altar, and
they preached obedience to the monarch as a Christian duty.[29]

With the triumph of reaction, church and state frequently worked
hand in hand. Church leaders provided legitimation for authoritarian governments. Parish clergy preached loyalty and obedience.
Governments offered favours to the church, both in gratitude for
their support, and because they believed that lack of religion, or at
least lack of religion of the approved orthodox and conservative
kinds, had prepared the ground for revolution. In German Protestantism, an important first step was a purge of those clergy who had
actively supported the revolutions. Some were imprisoned. More
often they were dismissed from their posts, which was easily done,
in view of the very close links between church and state and the
existence of effective disciplinary machinery in the German Protestant churches. Dulon, the Bremen revolutionary pastor, was among
those who emigrated to the United States after losing his post.
Others stayed in Germany, and struggled to make a living in
jobs where they no longer had any public influence.[30] The clergy
of the 1850s were thus a more conservative body than the clergy of

the 1840s had been. This was also true of French Catholicism, where the number of outspokenly radical clergy was in any case smaller, and where bishops were generally quite ready to transfer or suspend those who stepped too far out of line; if the bishop showed any hesitation he would certainly be prompted by the prefect, who kept a close eye on the politics of the clergy.[31]

German governments of the 1850s also took a close interest in the various religious minorities. Since *Deutschkatholiken* and Free Parishes had taken such an active part in the revolutions, they were inevitably a major target. Numerous Dissenting preachers were imprisoned or exiled.[32] Several states, including Bavaria, Saxony and Hamburg, banned Dissenting congregations.[33] In Prussia, where a law of 1850 prohibited women and children from attending political meetings, Dissenting services were frequently stopped on the grounds that they were political meetings and that the presence of women was thus contrary to the law.[34] Under the weight of repression and the loss of so many of their leading members, the Dissenting movement went into a decline in the 1850s from which it never fully recovered. Many former *Deutschkatholiken* returned to Roman Catholicism – in spite of the requirement that they do a public penance.[35] With the liberalisation of the 1860s, radical Dissent enjoyed something of a revival. It continued to have an influence out of proportion to its numbers, as many of its members were active in Left Liberal or Social Democratic politics, or in campaigns for women's rights. But it was never again a mass movement as it had been in the 1840s.[36]

Working on the general assumption that the most dangerous forms of religion were the more liberal, some German governments intervened in the affairs of the Jewish community to support the Orthodox against their Liberal or Reform opponents. Thus, for instance, in Frankfurt in 1849 the city authorities authorised the Orthodox to secede from the existing Jewish parish and to appoint their own rabbi; Friedrich Wilhelm IV of Prussia in 1854 gave an Orthodox rabbi the status of 'Royal Rabbi'; and at the same time the Grand Duke of Mecklenburg-Schwerin placed the Orthodox in control of the divided Jewish community.[37]

Friedrich Wilhelm IV also tried to foster better relations with the Catholic hierarchy, which he saw as a potential support for political conservatism, and whose theology was at least preferable to the liberalism of so many Protestants. The constitution of 1850 marked a breakthrough for the Catholic Church in Prussia, since the guarantees of religious freedom lifted many of the restrictions on Catholic activity and, in particular, allowed the previously banned religious orders to establish themselves, and to hold the big missions which were a typical feature of the 1850s.[38] The 1850s and 1860s were a period of expansion for the Catholics in Prussia, marked by increasing numbers of vocations and many new organisations. When in the 1870s the state turned again to the attack, the Catholics were well prepared to meet the challenge.[39]

In France too, the 1850s were a period of great Catholic prosperity, during which Louis Napoleon rewarded the church for its support. The most important piece of legislation was the Falloux Law of 1850 (named after the Minister of Education), which lifted restrictions on the opening of private secondary schools. It was followed by a great increase in the number both of primary and secondary schools run by religious orders. State spending on the church increased (albeit modestly), and a generally authoritarian government allowed the church a degree of freedom that was granted to nobody else. The numbers of priests and nuns increased and many new churches were built.[40] The civil and military authorities gave their moral support to the church – sometimes in ways that were more revealing than they perhaps intended: the Mayor of Rouen, laying the foundation-stone of a new church in 1857, compared it to a new prison recently built nearby, both being institutions 'for the moralisation of the people'.[41] With similar considerations in mind, the business elite were much more generous than ever before in giving money to the church.[42] The support given by the Emperor to the Pope in these years was also much appreciated by Catholics. Admittedly, relations cooled between 1859 and 1863 as Napoleon threw his weight behind the establishment of the Kingdom of Italy. But they improved again in the later years of the Second Empire.[43]

The alliance between the church and the Second Empire was widely regarded as a marriage of convenience.[44] A large proportion of the clergy remained Legitimists, and saw Napoleon as simply the best available option pending the return of the Bourbons. Napoleon's view of the church seems to have been entirely pragmatic. But in Germany, where a similar conservative alliance operated in most states during these years, the cause of the 'Christian State' was upheld by a number of highly devout rulers and statesmen.[45] In particular, Friedrich Wilhelm IV of Prussia was a convinced Pietist, as were a number of his ministers and advisers. Many of them were drawn from the aristocracy of Prussia's eastern provinces, where the

Protestant Awakenings had led to the formation of numerous aristocratic Bible-reading and prayer circles. These Christian conservatives placed overwhelming stress on human sinfulness, the need for submission to God-given authority, and the belief that the movement towards democracy generally, and the revolutions of 1848–49 in particular, were products of human pride and rebellion against the divine order.[46] The 'Christian State' should combine firm government (in Prussia the number of executions shot up during the 1850s)[47] with an increased emphasis on religion in schools, and other measures to re-affirm the Christian basis of society.[48] An important symbol here was 'Sunday rest', which liberals saw as a matter for free personal choice, whereas conservatives saw its legal enforcement as a sign of a collective submission to God's laws.[49] Some German rulers offered special favours to the more conservative wings of their churches, which they saw as less tainted than their liberal counterparts by involvement in revolutionary activity, and more likely to recognise the secular ruler as divinely ordained. The triumph of the Lutheran confessionalists in Bavaria and Hanover and of the Pietists in Württemberg over their rationalist or moderate adversaries owed a lot to the patronage of the state.[50]

The Emergence of a Secular Left

Meanwhile, the Left was becoming gradually more secular. A local study of the Tarn department in south-west France has shown the importance of the years 1848–51 in the evolution of the 'clerical/anti-clerical' polarisation which dominated French politics and much of daily life in the years 1870–1914. During 1848 and the early months of 1849 there was still no trace of anti-clericalism in the oratory of republican politicians or in the local republican press. They hoped to win the support of the priests by praising the work of the lower clergy, by promising to remedy some of their grievances, and by giving approving publicity to the views of those clergy who were already committed to the republican cause. The elections of May 1849 were a turning-point. While right-wing orators and journalists were increasingly making appeals to religion, and the majority of clergy supported the Right, from late 1849 the republican paper L'electeur du Tarn attacked the clergy with increasing frequency, and in 1850 it began to identify 'the clerical party' as a

powerful and dangerous political force.[51] By 1851 the official position of the paper was still that there was a bad clergy who unfortunately had too much influence, but that there was also a good clergy,
who represented true Catholicism, and who were sympathetic to
republicanism, or at least politically neutral. But in practice most of
the paper's space was devoted to attacking the bad clergy, sometimes employing a rather wild rhetoric of a kind likely to alienate
most Catholic readers. Thus in 1851, championing the moderate
Archbishop of Paris in a dispute with the more aggressively cleric-
alist Bishop of Chartres, the paper commented: 'the Archbishop
of Paris will have against him all the Jesuits, all of the clerical
party, which places the altar on the throne, which traffics in amulets,
manufactures miracles and would like to bring back the Inquisition,
he will have on his side the true priest of Jesus Christ, he will have
on his side the people, he will have on his side the gospel...'.[52] As
Faury sums up:

> full of concern and of a certain hope vis-a-vis the clergy and
> Catholicism in general in 1848–9, the republicans have come,
> especially after the hard electoral battle of May 1849, to a resolute
> anti-clericalism. This anti-clericalism is essentially political; but we
> observe that once they have entered along this path, the repub-
> licans begin to criticise certain abuses, certain dangers of religion
> itself. ...these attacks will develop much further in the years to
> come: attacks against the actual content of religious practice and
> against the anti-scientific character of religion....[53]

Napoleon's *coup d'état* of 2 December 1851 marked a final break.
Opposition politicians were arrested or went into exile. After the
suppression of the uprising in the south, thousands of insurgents
were transported. Many Catholic bishops declared their explicit
support for the coup, and the Archbishop of Paris held a *Te Deum*
in Notre Dame. Some clergy were suspected of having betrayed
participants in the rising to the police.[54] In his study of the diocese
of Montpellier, one of the strongholds of the insurrection, Cholvy
concludes that:

> the events of December 1851 open a profound breach – the first
> since the Revolution of 1789 – between the Church and the
> common people of a large part of the diocese. The Church rallied
> the party of order. In turn it can expect that some of the

bourgeoisie will rally to the Church. But it risks losing all hope of winning back the souls of those peasants and artisans of [the parts of the diocese close to the Mediterranean coast] ... The anti-clericalism which will win more and more supporters in France during the years 1860–80 must find in these regions a natural stronghold.[55]

One priest of the diocese was in fact among those arrested after the uprising, and another went to Paris to plead (successfully) for the lives of eleven local men condemned to death. However, the more general souring of relations between the clergy and the militant republicans was reflected in the situation in another village, where the priest's offer of help to the families of men who had been transported, though initially favourably received by some, sub-sequently met with a concerted rejection.[56]

The fact that an open rejection of the Catholic faith was spreading among convinced republicans in the 1850s was indicated by the fact that 'civic' (i.e. purely secular) funerals first became common among French political exiles in Brussels during the 1850s.[57] In the repressive climate of France in the 1850s and early 1860s, direct attacks on the Catholic church or faith were relatively rare, though attacks of a more subtle kind were much more numerous. However, the political opening of the last years of the Second Empire, between 1867 and 1870, was accompanied by a large outpouring of anti-clerical sentiment, which made it clear how far the break with Catholicism had gone among those on the political Left.[58] Anti-clericalism was not necessarily irreligious. The critics of the church included a small but influential group of Protestants and a larger number of what were termed 'spiritualists' – mostly ex-Catholics who rejected the institution and many of its doctrines, but retained a belief in God, often an attachment to some kind of undogmatic Christianity, and a rejection of materialism. However, there was by now a large element of atheists, agnostics and sceptics on the Left, and the public language of the Left was very largely secular.[59]

Under the Third Republic, religion would constitute the most fundamental line of division between Left and Right, not only because of the very different religious policies favoured by the two sides, but also because of a difference of language. While the Left justified its policies in purely secular terms (admittedly often enlivened by anti-clerical rhetoric), the Right readily used religious language, and justified its policies by reference to the teachings of the church. This latter tendency was at a high point in the era of the 'Moral Order' in the mid-1870s, when devoutly Catholic aristocrats were in the forefront of politics, the restoration of the Bourbons still seemed to be a possibility, and French defeat in the war against Prussia was widely seen as a divine punishment for national sins.[60] But appeals to religion remained a staple of right-wing rhetoric, often because of the personal beliefs of right-wing politicians, but more generally because religious authorities were those which carried most weight with the majority of right-wing voters, and because religious symbols had a force which no others could equal. A striking example of this was the nationalist and monarchist *Action Française*, founded in 1898 by the poet, Charles Maurras. He was not himself a believer, but he found in Catholicism the only possible basis for national identity and unity, and he successfully sought Catholic support. 'France is "by heart Catholic" and also by tradition, habit, morals and spirit', Maurras wrote in 1903. With its principles of authority, tradition, and the subordnation of individual ideas and desires to the needs of the whole community, the Catholic Church provided the model for the kind of society which France ought to be.[61]

In Germany there were similar secularising tendencies after 1848 on the part of those liberals and radicals who had supported the revolutions. Rüdiger Hachtmann, author of the most recent study of the revolution in Berlin, argues that the year 1848 marks a turning-point in the development of popular anti-clericalism and irreligion in the Prussian capital. While he finds evidence of a growing gulf between Protestant clergy and large sections of their parishioners in the 1840s, he suggests that the opposition of many clergy to the revolution led to more numerous and intense manifestations of hostility than any seen before. Several conservative pastors were subjected to *Katzenmusik* – noisy and scurrilous demonstrations outside their homes. Religious services in the Berlin workhouse were disrupted. And while the moderate liberals of the Frankfurt Parliament were calling for inter-denominational schools, some working-class radicals in Berlin were demanding that religious teaching in schools be stopped altogether.[62] The scientific materialism which was in vogue in the 1850s and 1860s was often propagated by political radicals who hoped that by undermining belief in orthodox religion, they could undermine the forces of political reaction.[63] German Liberalism in the period from the 1860s to the First World War included both Protestant and secular strands, with

Protestant Liberalism being especially to the fore in south-west Germany, while secular forms predominated in North Germany. The secular forms of Liberalism often directed their attacks primarily at Roman Catholicism, while being more tolerant of Protestantism, at least in its liberal forms. But even where not explicitly anti-religious, the German Liberalism of this period was predominantly expressed in non-religious terms, and often combined with a critique of those forms of religion which were deemed dogmatic, authoritarian or unscientific. For many German Liberals the crucial authorities, cited with as much reverence as others quoted the Bible, were the heroes of German literature, above all Goethe and Schiller.[64]

In Germany, as in most other parts of Europe, socialism was strongly influenced by liberalism, and socialist attitudes to religion were partly shaped by the previous history of relations between Liberals and the churches. A typical case was that of August Bebel, who was to become the most popular leader of the German Social Democrats in the later nineteenth century. Having earlier belonged to both Protestant and Catholic workers' associations, he lost his faith after attending classes at the Leipzig Workers' Educational Association, where he fell under the influence of materialist writers, such as Büchner and Wundt, who were 'scientific, modern, and actively concerned about the "social question"'.[65]

Bebel was fiercely anti-Christian, especially in the aftermath of his imprisonment between 1872 and 1875 – later he was more inclined to see parallels between socialism and early Christianity, while remaining resolutely opposed to the churches. Throughout the period from the 1860s to the First World War the ethos of German Social Democracy remained heavily secular. The main division was between those, like Johann Most in the 1870s or Karl Liebknecht in the 1900s, who regarded attacks on religion and the churches as a high priority and who supported movements of mass resignation from the churches and from the Jewish community, and those who insisted that religion was 'a private matter', and that the party should maintain a complete neutrality on the question of the truth or falsity of religion, while continuing where appropriate to attack the privileges of the churches and the power of the clergy.[66] Seldom in these years did socialist propaganda use religious arguments, or claim the support of religious authorities or association with religious symbols.

In the years 1890–95 a considerable number of Protestant pastors, theologians and theology students joined the Evangelical

Social Congress, set up to discuss social problems and propose Protestant solutions. The strong language with which some members of the Congress criticised landowners and industrialists caused alarm on the part of the Emperor, Conservative politicians and the church authorities. After a particularly strongly worded report on the condition of the rural poor in Prussia's eastern provinces was published in 1894, the church authorities in many parts of Germany imposed a clampdown on political activity by the clergy. A few members of the Congress went so far as to join the Social Democratic Party and were promptly subjected to disciplinary hearings, leading to their dismissal or resignation. In spite of the suspicion which these pastors encountered on the part of some of their new comrades, they seem on the whole to have been warmly welcomed. The Württemberg pastor Blumhardt was elected as a Social Democratic deputy to the state parliament very soon after joining the Party. The Prussian socialist pastor Paul Göhre was sought as a Reichstag candidate by three constituencies, and Party presses printed half a million copies of his pamphlet 'How a Pastor became a Social Democrat'. The major reason for printing the pamphlet was no doubt the hope that it would persuade church-going workers to vote Social Democrat. However, the fact that so many socialists apparently wanted to be represented by Göhre suggests that there may have been a considerable number who retained a lingering Protestant loyalty and found the mixing of socialism and religion congenial. A more ambiguous example of the closeness of many Social Democrats to Protestant culture was the adaptation for socialist purposes of Protestant hymns, including most frequently the most famous and popular of them all, Luther's 'Ein' feste Burg'. This implied not so much a simple rejection of the Protestant faith, in which the great majority of the socialists of this time had been brought up, as an appropriation and reinterpretation of Protestant ideals and emotions, together with a claim that all that was best within them had found ultimate fulfilment in socialism.[67]

In spite of the strong secularising tendency in German socialism, and to a lesser extent in liberalism, religious arguments and language continued to play a major part in German public debate, both because of the strength of political Catholicism, and because of the fact that the various branches of Conservatism were all highly Protestant. Ursula Krey, in analysing the world-view and rhetoric of Conservatives in east Westphalia at the turn of the century, notes that the slogan 'With God for King and Fatherland' runs 'like a red thread' through party literature.' In it was articulated both the mentalities of wide sections of the population, and the monopoly of the Conservatives who claimed their value-system as their own. While she stresses the pragmatism of the Conservatives in dealing with most questions of policy, she also provides a revealing comparison between the ways in which local papers in Bielefeld looked back on the nineteenth century from the vantage-point of January 1900. The Conservative paper agreed with both the Liberals and the Social Democrats in celebrating scientific and technological progress and the emergence of Germany as a great power. But only the Conservative Party added a lengthy discussion of moral and religious developments – generally evaluated in a very negative way.[68]

Why England was Different

In England the political and religious history of 1848 and the years immediately following was quite different. The 1830s and 1840s had been one of the periods of most severe social and political conflict in British history. At national level the Whig governments of 1830–34 and 1835–41 had reformed Parliament, the Church of England, town government and the poor law in the face of bitter opposition from a large part of the aristocracy and gentry, the urban oligarchies, the Anglican clergy and, in the latter instance, the working class. In the towns the reform of municipal corporations in 1835 enabled *nouveau riche* industrialists to supplant old established wealth, while militant Nonconformists were powerfully challenging the entrenched power of the Church of England. Then from 1838, Whig and Tory, urban and rural elites, new and old wealth, all faced the challenge of Chartism, a mass movement with its strongholds in the working-class communities of the industrial north. While Tories could rely on the support of High Church and Evangelical Anglicans, and the Whigs were supported by most liberal Anglicans and the great majority of Dissenters, relatively few clergy of any denomination were willing to declare their support for the Chartists.[69] In the years of greatest political excitement in the later 1830s and early 1840s the church loyalties of many of the working class were placed under severe strain. Some Chartists retained their links with their churches (most commonly some branch of Methodism) in spite of the lack of official support; some rejected the churches, while remaining Christian; some adopted the secular philosophy of Owenite socialism. There were also some who resolved an apparently insoluble dilemma by setting up Chartist Churches. The first of these came in 1839, when two Primitive Methodist chapels in West Yorkshire turned themselves into Chartist Churches. Arthur O'Neill, who founded a similar church in Birmingham in 1840, was regarded as the leader of this branch of the movement.[70]

In England the later 1840s and early 1850s saw nothing comparable to France or Germany's 1848, but also nothing comparable to the triumph of reaction in those countries. These years brought the collapse of Chartism, but also with the slackening of social tensions and rising material prosperity, the beginnings of a period of modest liberalisation. The period from the 1850s to the 1880s was one of exceptional prosperity in the history of the English churches, in which every social class and political faction was to some degree reached by one of the many religious denominations and levels of involvement were high. The dominant political force of this era, the Liberal Party, took shape in the 1850s as a coalition of Whigs, Peelite Free Traders who had seceded from the Tories, and Radicals. Among the latter were many former Chartists. Some of them joined the Secularist movement, established in 1851, under the leadership of the former Owenite lecturer, George Jacob Holyoake, who had served a term in prison for blasphemy. Many more remained with or returned to one of the numerous branches of Nonconformity. A striking feature of the 1850s and 1860s was the frequency with which Dissenting radicals who had left their chapels in the 1830s and 1840s returned to their former religious home.[71] Among the most famous examples is that of Thomas Cooper, the Chartist poet and leader of the movement in Leicester. He had been a Wesleyan preacher, but in 1840 he lost his faith, because he thought it irrelevant to the political and social action on behalf of the poor which was now his overriding concern. Later he was influenced by reading the *Life of Jesus* by D. F. Strauß. In 1858, however, he returned to his former beliefs and decided to devote the rest of his life to lecturing on the evidences of Christianity. Arthur O'Neill, the pastor of Birmingham's Christian Chartist church, reconstituted his church in 1847 as a Baptist church, naming it 'The People's Chapel'.[72] As in Germany and France, therefore, the political situation had considerable influence on perceptions of the religious options.

In England, as in France and Germany, religion remained an essential part of conservative ideology and rhetoric throughout this period, while liberalism, radicalism and socialism could develop in more purely secular directions. The difference between England on the one hand and France and Germany on the other lies in the frequency with which not only moderate liberalism, but also the various branches of radicalism and socialism, continued to take religious forms. While the Conservative Party in England was closely associated with the Established Church, the Liberal Party, and later the Labour Party, were religiously pluralistic, linked most closely with Nonconformity, but also containing significant Anglican, Catholic, Jewish and Secularist elements.[73]

So far as the Liberals were concerned, religious language and religiously-motivated concerns came more to the fore in the 1860s and 1870s, as increasing numbers of Nonconformists entered parliament, and as the fervently High Anglican William Gladstone took the place of Whig aristocrats, such as Lord Palmerston, whose interest in religion was often very limited and who at most had favoured a very low profile piety. Gladstone established a particularly close rapport with the Nonconformists. They made up the core of his electoral support, delighting in his ability to present political issues in terms of clear-cut moral choices. He found it easiest to do this when dealing with events outside Britain, and a high point was reached during the Bulgarian atrocities of 1876–77, when his bitter criticism of Disraeli's alliance with Turkey won warm support in Britain. The potentialities of a biblically based rhetoric were shown even more clearly in the rural labourers' movement of the early and mid-1870s, which often began meetings with a hymn, which drew heavily on support from the Bible (especially the Prophets), and which included among its leaders many Methodist preachers.[74]

With the rise of socialism in the 1880s the Social Democratic Federation emerged as Britain's first self-consciously secularist political party. However, it was soon overshadowed by the Independent Labour Party, with its 'ethical' socialism and its openness to various forms of religion. A survey of the religion of Labour MPs undertaken around 1930 throws a good deal of light on the pre-war situation, as the great majority of those who answered the questionnaire were already active in the labour movement at that time, many of them prominently so. An example is George Lansbury, one of the most widely admired figures in the Party, and its leader between 1932 and 1935. Elected MP in 1910 for Bow and Bromley in east London, he also had a distinguished career in local government, including a spell in prison in the 1920s when Poplar council refused to pay contributions to the London County Council. Lansbury told the author of this survey:

> Religion is not a matter for Sunday and Monday but for the whole life. Education cannot be carried on apart from religion. Anything in industry or politics that conflicts with our Lord's teaching must be removed, and men and women must be given opportunity so to live that they express in their daily life the law of love. We Labour believe that it is a denial of our Lord's teaching that we should fight each other for our daily bread. In fact, we believe that it is that personal struggle to get above each other which causes most of the evil in the world and consequently we are always working to substitute in place of that struggle co-operation.

Nor was the Christian rationale for Lansbury's socialism a purely private conviction. When in 1922 the Poplar Labour Party published a defence of the imprisoned councillors, they began with a quotation from the Epistle of James, and Lansbury himself wrote in 1924 a pamphlet on *Jesus and Labour*. Meanwhile Stanley Baldwin, as leader of the Conservative Party, was offering an equally explicit Christian justification for his politics of patriotism and class-reconciliation.[75]

Conclusion

So in England Christianity was still in the 1920s 'contested territory'. But in France and Germany the political use of the Bible had for long been a conservative monopoly. In these two countries, the two or three decades following 1848 marked an important stage in the process by which religion ceased to provide a common language. In public debate, religious concepts, rhetoric and symbols had become rallying-cries for those at one end of the political spectrum, but had lost most of their meaning for those at the other end. Religion had not become thereby less politically significant, but in terms of one of the criteria suggested in the Introduction, French and German society had become substantially more secular.

The events of 1848–49 in France and Germany, and the triumph of reaction in the 1850s, helped to crystallise tendencies which up to then had been latent and which might not have developed in such a clear-cut way but for the polarisation brought about by revolution and counter-revolution. In France before 1848 anti-clericalism was certainly widespread in the bourgeoisie, but various forms of Christian radicalism were also widespread. The religious standpoint of the workers and peasants was very varied, but in many areas attachment to the church was still strong. Legitimism was very popular among the clergy, especially in the south and west, but the 1840s were a period of experimentation when a wide range of new possibilities were also emerging. In Germany both the atheism of the Social Democrats and many Left Liberals and the Christian Conservatism and Ultramontanism that triumphed after 1848 within the churches had their intellectual roots in the 1830s and 1840s. But there was no necessary path from the atheism of Marx and Feuerbach and the ultra-conservatism of Hengstenberg and the Gerlach brothers to the radical separation between the world of the church and the world of the progressive bourgeoisie and socialist worker that was so common in the years around the end of the century. As the example of England shows, it was also possible for a more fluid relationship between religion and politics to develop in the nineteenth century.

2   Institutions

Under the *ancien régime*, one of the foundations of west European states was religious unity. Even in countries where religious minorities had the right to worship in public, they suffered civil disabilities, which were often very extensive. The parish was the basic unit of education and poor relief, and the registration of births, marriages and deaths was also in the hands of the clergy. Blasphemy laws, systems of censorship and restrictions on unauthorised preaching offered further protection to established religion. But, in the century after 1789, the confessional state was largely dismantled, first in France, and then more gradually in other parts of western Europe.

In France the crucial changes took place during the Revolution or under Napoleon. These included the granting of political rights to all citizens, regardless of their religion; civil registration, with the civil marriage ceremony being from 1792 the only one which was legally valid; assumption of responsibility by the state for education and poor relief; and the system introduced, following Napoleon's Concordat with the Pope in 1801, whereby the state recognised four religions – Catholic, Reformed, Lutheran and Jewish – granting rights to each, while also imposing considerable state control over their organisation and activity. (Until 1859, other religious groups, such as Baptists, continued to be harassed by the police.)

In England, the most important changes came between 1828 and 1841, including the granting of full political rights to Dissenters and Roman Catholics (though the Jews only achieved full emancipation in 1858), civil registration (though here couples had the right to choose between a religious and a civil marriage ceremony), the placing of poor relief under the control of Poor Law Unions rather than the parish, and the beginnings of state involvement in education.

In the German states, changes came more gradually, and the pace of change naturally varied in the different states. Generally speaking, the German states were far ahead of England in the development of state bureaucracies, and the state tended to take on a major role in such areas as education and poor relief at an earlier stage. For instance, the Prussian state assumed responsibility for education in 1794, and in 1788 the city of Hamburg introduced a system of poor relief largely independent of the church, which was seen as a model in many other parts of Germany. Some German states also had a long history of granting freedom of worship to various specified minorities. However, the rights granted to recognised minority communities went hand in hand with considerable limitations on individual religious freedom, which often continued until after the unification of Germany in 1871. Until then, for instance, it was in many German states a requirement that one belonged to a religious denomination of some kind. Jewish emancipation was also a long drawn-out process, only completed in some states in 1871. Civil registration came first in Baden in 1869, in Prussia in 1874, and finally throughout Germany in 1875.

After the Confessional State

England, France, Germany, and other west European countries did not move directly from a confessional state to one that was religiously neutral or militantly secular. In the middle years of the nineteenth century, considerable religious freedom was generally allowed, and the state was encroaching on territory previously dominated by the established church; but the state was still regarded by those in positions of authority as Christian, one of the Christian confessions usually still enjoyed a privileged position, and the church or churches still had a major role in education and social welfare.

The close links between church and state in both France and Germany in the 1850s have already been described. England might seem to be out of step with its continental neighbours, since the 1850s were years of cautious liberalisation,[1] including, for instance, the admission of non-Anglicans to study at Oxford and Cambridge Universities (1854–6), the appointment of officially commissioned Catholic army chaplains (1858),[2] admission of Jews to the House of Commons (1858) and a Matrimonial Causes Act (1857), which ended the jurisdiction of church courts and made divorces somewhat easier to obtain. These were steps in the direction of a more tolerant society, in which the existence of a considerable degree of religious pluralism was recognised by the state, and the many religious minorities were gradually accorded the rights that previously were reserved for Anglicans. While many of these changes were bitterly opposed by High Church Anglicans, and sometimes by most of the episcopate,[3] it seems to me wrong to equate them with secularisation.[4] The reform that provoked most Anglican opposition was the (very modest) liberalisation of the divorce law. But this was as much an argument within the church, as an argument between ecclesiastical and secular authority. While High Churchmen like Gladstone condemned the bill as a denial of the Christian basis of the country's laws, ten out of fifteen bishops voted for the bill in the House of Lords, and the Bishop of London said that it did not go far enough. Much of the debate in Parliament focused on rival interpretations of the relevant scriptural texts.[5] The Act, which remained in force until 1937, was much more limited in scope than the corresponding legislation in the German states or, after 1884, in France, since it only allowed for divorce on the grounds of adultery. In any case, it would be a very one-sided view of church-state relations in this period that emphasised these adjustments, while neglecting the strongly Christian (and, of course, Protestant) character of the British state, and the close association between the Church of England and the holders of power in many different areas of society.

At the top, the piety of Queen Victoria and Prince Albert [6] helped to confirm the status of regular church-going as 'one of the recognised proprieties of life', as Horace Mann put it in his famous commentary on the national Religious Census of 1851.[7] It might even be argued that the growing tendency of prime minsters to consider possible bishops in the light of their theological tendencies and their quality as pastors, rather than simply in terms of how they would vote in the House of Lords, represented a form of desecularisation. Certainly there is ample evidence that prime ministers took ecclesiastical appointments seriously, and for a few it was a matter of consuming interest.[8]

A clearer example of desecularisation in this period is the attempt in the aftermath of the Crimean War to create a 'Christian Army'.[9]

In the first half of the nineteenth century religion seems to have played a limited role in the British Army. After the Crimean War, the government decided to maintain a permanent corps of military chaplains, including Roman Catholics and Presbyterians, as well as Anglicans (with Wesleyans later being added). The chaplains were to be officers and after 1860 they wore uniforms. The big military encampments built in this period all included a large interdenominational chapel, and from 1864 the religious affiliation of new recruits was recorded so that they could be issued with Bibles or other religious literature of the appropriate kind, and required to attend the church parades of their denomination. Whether the result was a 'Christian Army' is more doubtful. Olive Anderson argues that the main strongholds of military religion in the mid-Victorian period were the Artillery and the Engineers, where officers came from a more middle-class background than in other sections of the Army, and where large numbers of civilians were employed. And Bob Bushaway suggests that regular soldiers in the pre-First World War period were generally distinguished by a fatalistic mentality and a lack of interest in religion.[10] In this it would seem that not much had changed since the time of the Napoleonic Wars. What is lacking, however, is any evidence of institutional secularisation.

Patterns of Change after 1870

The major divergences between the three countries took place with the onset of mass politics. In England this can be dated from the Second Reform Act in 1867, which for the first time established a relatively broad electorate, and in France from the end of the Second Empire in 1870. At about the same time Germany entered a transitional stage. With manhood suffrage in elections to the North German Reichstag in 1867 and to the new imperial Reichstag in 1871, Germany was in this respect ahead of England. On the other hand, the extensive powers retained by the emperor and other German rulers, together with the operation of the discriminatory 'three-class' voting system in state and local elections meant that the extent of democratisation was really more limited than in England or France, and that national institutions continued to be shaped largely from above. In all three countries, democratisation was associated with anti-clericalism, attacks on the power of established churches and demands for greater religious freedom. However, the subsequent course of events in the three countries was entirely different.

France offers a model for the systematic secularisation of the state. In England, where Gladstone's government of 1868–74 launched a major attack on the privileges of the Church of England, the aim of liberal reformers was not secularisation, but religious equality. However, it can be argued that the trend in England during the later nineteenth and early twentieth centuries was towards a creeping, and largely unplanned, institutional secularisation. In Germany, the secularisation of much of everyday life during this period contrasted with the close ties between church and state, which continued until the fall of the monarchy in 1918. The formal separation of church and state came together with democracy in 1919. But the position of the 'big' churches (the Roman Catholic Church and the Protestant *Landeskirchen*) under the Weimar Republic remained relatively favourable, and only with the Nazi, and later Communist, dictatorships can one speak of a systematic secularisation. So the third stage in the development of church–state relations in modern western Europe could take many different forms. At the opposite extreme to France would be the situation in The Netherlands, especially after 1917, or in the Irish Free State after 1921, where church and state were legally separated as much as they were in France, but where a mainly church-going electorate was able to vote into power parties strongly sympathetic to church interests. In The Netherlands this meant the system of 'pillarisation', whereby education and a variety of social and cultural services were mainly provided by the churches or by other groups with a distinct ideological basis, each of which received state funding for its work. In Ireland the state funded a church-dominated education sysem, and was very sensitive to Catholic opinion on a number of other issues. Germany and England lay somewhere between these extremes.[11]

In England where, as in Wales and Scotland, the main division was that between the Established Church and Protestant Dissenters, and where secularism was relatively weak, Liberalism was almost as strongly influenced by religion as Conservatism, but intense interdenominational competition placed a serious strain on the resources of all denominations. The picture from 1870 is that of a gradual and continuing encroachment by the state onto areas previously dominated by the churches, resulting in some degree of *de facto* secularisation.[12] The chief driving force behind this expansion of state power was the inability of the churches, organised on a voluntaryist basis in a situation of very considerable pluralism, to provide comprehensively for society's needs. Many of the strongest advocates of the expanding state were in fact those within the churches, especially the Nonconformist churches, who believed that the state could do the job better. The first major landmark was the Education Act of 1870. In the years following, and especially after about 1890, local authorities became increasingly active in areas of social welfare previously dominated by the churches, including the provision of evening classes, free meals for poor children, Infant Welfare Centres and the employment of health visitors. Gradually from the 1870s onwards, but on a very large scale from the 1920s, local authorities also took over responsibility for building cheap housing. The churches were not entirely ousted from their long-standing welfare role. In fact, as one sphere of church activity was displaced by the expanding national or (more often) local state, the churches tended to discover new areas of unmet need.In the early decades of the twentieth century the big growth area was the running of youth clubs. Jeffrey Cox's study of the borough of Lambeth in south London shows that in 1938 there were no less than 257 youth clubs in the northern (strongly working-class) half of the borough, and that the great majority of these were based in a church or chapel.[13]

However, Cox is no doubt right to argue that the role of the churches in welfare, which had been central in the mid-Victorian years, had become much more marginal by the early twentieth century, mainly because of the greatly increased role of central and local government.[14] He also shows that Nonconformists played a large part in bringing this change about. Those who had supported the National Education League in the years around 1870 were at least partly motivated by sectarianism: the extension of the role of the state would be good, because it would displace the Church of England, the power of which was a threat to religious freedom.[15] In the period of late Victorian and Edwardian Progressivism, the Nonconformists, who were among the most enthusiastic advocates of a high-profile local government, were inspired by the vision of a benevolent authority, acting on behalf of the whole community against selfish vested interests and in the cause of health, moral welfare and social improvement. Nonconformist chapels – the churches of the people – might have a vanguard role in this process, but only the local council had the authority to act on behalf of the whole people and the resources to do the job effectively.[16]

In Germany the main religious cleavage was that between Protestant and Catholic, and the Jews also had an important presence. The well-established system of state-funded confessional schools provided a precedent for regarding the population as primarily divided into these three confessional communities. Under the *ancien régime* the Jews had been expected to provide for their own poor through taxation of their community, and at least in law the obligation of all Jews to belong to the *Gemeinde* and to contribute to its costs continued until 1876. With the introduction of the 'church tax' in many parts of Germany around this time a similar model was applied to Protestants and Catholics. Money to support the work of the church was collected together with income tax by the state, and then passed on to the religious community to which the tax payer belonged. Those who were too poor to pay income tax were exempt; on the other hand, those with high incomes made a correspondingly large contribution to the costs of their church. The system was first introduced in Oldenburg in 1852, and most other states followed during the later nineteenth or early twentieth century.[17] It was now possible for anyone to leave her or his religious community and become *konfessionslos* – though anyone doing so lost the right to be married, buried or have their children baptised by a minister of religion.

However, very few people did choose to leave their religious community. The regularity and size of the income derived from church taxes, in addition to the income already derived from state subsidies and from church-owned property, gave the various communities the opportunity not only to build many more places of worship, but also to expand their involvement in social welfare, by building hospitals, orphanages, old people's homes, and so on. As in England, city councils were expanding their operations in these areas around 1900. But there were strong pragmatic arguments for co-operating with the many church-based charities.[18] The city authorities were often willing to offer the churches substantial subsidies rather than bear the whole cost themselves. This continued after the separation of church and state in 1919. Indeed Borg argues that the formal separation was little more than symbolic, since the states went on paying subsidies to the churches, the church tax system continued, and confessional schools remained the norm in most parts of Germany until they were destroyed by Hitler.[19] The collaboration between public authorities and the mainly church-based private charities also continued. For instance the law of 1922 on the welfare of youth provided for local Youth Bureaux, in which two-fifths of the seats would be reserved for representatives of private charities. The prominent role of the German churches in welfare provision continued after the Second World War, and right up to the present day, in the East as well as the West. In the early 1990s it was estimated that private charities were responsible for 65 per cent of welfare provision in Germany, and the largest of these was the Roman Catholic *Caritas*.[20]

The German model therefore tended to produce powerful religious institutions, though with relatively high levels of anti-clericalism, and low levels of religious participation. The English model produced weak institutions, with low levels of anti-clericalism, and medium levels of participation. The French model produced a polarisation between extreme anti-clericalism and very low levels of participation in some parts of society, together with a powerful Catholic subculture, which sustained a wide range of alternative institutions, and was enormously influential in certain regions and in some social milieux.

Systematic Secularisation in France

When in 1879 the French republicans, who already controlled the the Chamber of Deputies, won a majority in the Senate, the relationship between the Catholic Church and the state moved to the top of the political agenda. After the many years in which conservative governments had worked hand in hand with the Catholic clergy, republicans were eager for revenge. And even politicians of a more moderate and conciliatory disposition recognised that the enormous social influence wielded by the Catholic Church posed a threat to the Republic's survival. In particular, the thousands of monks and nuns teaching in public schools were suspected of training the young in political conservatism. Many republicans thought that it was difficult, or even impossible, for a practising Catholic to be a loyal servant of the Republic: any Catholic who occupied a public position was therefore potentially suspect. There were also questions of religious freedom and civil rights at stake. The ties between the church and public authority both at national and at local level, the presence of Catholic symbols in public places, and the Catholic basis for many of the country's laws might all be justified on the grounds that Catholicism was, as the Concordat had stated, 'the religion of the great majority of Frenchmen'. But they could also be seen as infringing the rights of non-Catholics. For more moderate republicans the watchword was 'neutrality': the state should do nothing which might seem to favour Catholics by comparison with adherents of other faiths, or believers by comparison with unbelievers. More militant republicans argued that the state had a responsibility towards its citizens to free them from harmful influences: that included a duty to do everything in its power to undermine the Catholic Church, or even to undermine the influence of religion more generally. Republicans of every colour also knew that anti-clericalism was an invaluable rallying cry and political cement, and moderate republicans were especially conscious of its value as a substitute for more socially radical policies. By the same token, Socialists were often divided between their hatred of the church and their suspicion of those 'priest-eaters' who seemed to be using attacks on the clergy as a divertionary tactic.

In the period between 1879 and the outbreak of war in 1914 a wide-ranging programme of secularisation was carried out both by republican governments and by numerous local authorities. The conflict between church and state was at a high point in the early 1880s. There was a lull in the early 1890s, when moderates on both sides looked for an accommodation. But the Dreyfus Affair ended such hopes, and in the early 1900s the struggle reached its climax.[21] Major items of legislation at the national level included in 1880 repeal of the laws requiring 'Sunday rest', restrictions on the 'free' (Catholic) universities (which, among other things, could no longer call themselves 'universities'), and the exclusion of ministers of religion from national and departmental education comittees; in 1881 abolition of the confessional character of cemeteries; in 1882, abolition of religious teaching in state schools; in 1884 legalisation of divorce, and a ban on the saying of prayers during the meetings of public bodies; in 1886 exclusion of priests and nuns from teaching in state schools; in 1899 the exemption of seminarists from military service was stopped; in 1901–4 various measures were passed restricting the activity of religious orders, including a ban on teaching even in private schools; in 1903 the use of religious symbols, such as crucifixes, in schools was prohibited; and in 1904 the ban was extended to courts of law.[22]

During all this period, the Concordat of 1801 remained in operation. Separation of church and state was already being demanded
by one of the most prominent republicans in 1867, and in 1882 a
League for the Separation of Church and State was formed with the
support of eighty-six Deputies. However, many republican politicians, including the arch-anti-clerical Émile Combes, Prime Minister from 1902 to 1905, were convinced that the Concordat and
Organic Articles offered the best means of keeping the church
under firm state control.[23] Bishops were nominated by the French
government. Once appointed, they could not go anywhere outside
their own diocese without permission from the Ministry of Public
Worship, nor could new parishes be established without such permission. Bishops were also prohibited from publishing Papal ency-
clicals in France without state approval – though the development of
the press meant that this was largely meaningless. And the fact that
the state paid the salaries of the bishops and parish clergy meant
that there was an excellent means of whipping trouble-makers into
line. Combes himself made free use of this threat, suspending the
salaries of a record-breaking 632 clergy, including an archbishop
and eleven bishops.[24] Combes met his equal in intransigence in
Pius X, who became pope in 1903, and by 1905 relations both
between France and the Vatican and between church and state
within France had reached a very low level.

The separation of church and state had come to have great symbolic significance for many French Radicals and Socialists, for whom
it symbolised the liberation of the French state. The Dreyfus Affair
had a radicalising effect, as many anti-clericals believed that the
Catholic Church had connived at an act of gross injustice. The
pace was forced by the Socialists, and in 1905 a law of Separation
was passed. The main practical consequences of the law were that
municipalities assumed ownership of most churches and presbyteries, and that the state abandoned responsibility for paying the
salaries of clergy, so that the churches were accordingly forced to
undertake a massive fund-raising drive. The law envisaged that
Catholic, Protestant and Jewish believers would form 'Worship
Associations', and that the local authorities would allow them rent-
free use of the churches and other religious buildings. The Protestants and Jews did this, and a conference of Catholic bishops
voted (with some qualifications) to do the same. However, they
were overruled by Pope Pius X, who insisted on a policy of non-
co-operation, both as matter of 'honour', and because he felt that

the role of laymen on the proposed committees would undermine Catholic hierarchical principles. As Pope he was also obliged to take a global view, and he believed that an uncompromising response to the French government would send the right signals to anti-clericals in Spain, Portugal and the Latin American countries, who threatened to follow the French lead. In response to the church's refusal to co-operate, the French government did climb part of the way down, since it allowed Catholic parishes continued free use of churches, under direction of the clergy. But bishops' palaces and large numbers of presbyteries were expropriated, some being sold, while others were rented back to the clergy, so that the financial cost of non-co-operation was very considerable. The other, unintended, consequence of Separation was to push the French church further to the Right. The French government in abrogating the Concordat had renounced its right to nominate French bishops. The new men appointed by Pius x to the many sees left vacant in the latter days of the war between church and state were all drawn from the more conservative wing of the church. Moderates were distinctly out of favour, and anyone suspected of Modernism faced persecution.[25]

But the Separation was also an event of immense symbolic potency for devout Catholics. The moment which more than any other defined their rulers as desecrators of the holy was the drawing up of inventories of church property in early 1906. As state officials, guarded by gendarmes, appeared at the church doors, they often found the way barred by crowds of angry parishioners, determined that no unbeliever should lay hands on the sacred vessels or on their saints. Sometimes only a token resistance was offered. Sometimes it took violent forms. And sometimes more ingenious forms of defence were devised. In Pyrenean parishes bears were chained to the church porch, and in one western parish the demonstrators armed themselves with chamber pots which they emptied over the gendarmes.[26] These confrontations had little practical effect – beyond hardening the Pope's resolve to be as unconciliatory as possible. But they dramatically confirmed the French Catholics' self-image as an embattled minority, fighting a desperate rearguard action against the forces of evil, and their sense of being, in Michel Lagreé's words, exiles in their own country.[27]

For enemies of the church, including many Protestants, as well as anti-clerical Catholics and Freethinkers, the passing of the law of Separation was an act of cleansing, from which France emerged as a freer and a nobler nation. The political battle caught the popular imagination, to the extent that it became a subject for street-singers. A song current in Lyon compared the clergy to snakes and to crows, complained of their fine living and their constant demands for money, and concluded that if the state stopped paying the clergy, the multitude of 'grey sisters, monks and parish priests', 'posing as victims', would rapidly disappear.[28]

At the local level, zealous mayors often took the secularising crusade further than the law required. The most hotly debated issue here was the religious neutrality of public space. Until 1879 Catholic symbols were everywhere. The Catholic faith was interwoven with every aspect of daily life and of public institutions.[29] Crosses stood in innumerable town squares and beside countless country roads. Small statues of saints stood at street corners. Religious processions had an important place in the calendar of most communities. Celebrations in honour of the patron saint of the parish would involve most of the population, including those who seldom went to church at other times. Streets were named after saints. Crucifixes hung on the walls of schools, hospitals and courts of law. Most of this, probably, was generally taken for granted. In the republican era, much that had previously been taken for granted began to appear offensive, and attacks on these symbols of the Catholic past became an effective means by which local authorities could demonstrate their zeal.

For instance, in the years 1879 to 1881 the Paris city council was carrying through a programme of secularisation of schools and hospitals in advance of national legislation. In 1893 when conservative proposals to resacralise the hospitals were a major issue in the Paris municipal elections, horror stories abounded in papers both of Left and Right about the atrocities committed by nurses of 'the wrong kind'.[30] Carcassonne in 1881 was among the first councils to order the removal of all crosses and statues of saints from public places. Many local councils stopped some or all religious processions through the streets. When republican councils tried to avoid antagonising their Catholic voters, they were kept up to the mark by anticlerical newspapers, which publicised cases of laxity. Processions could thus take on the character of political symbols. In Nantes they were banned in 1881, allowed again by a more Catholic council in 1888, and banned again (this time by the prefect of the department) in 1903. On the latter occasion Catholics responded by staging a 'spontaneous' march through the streets, during which the two thousand participants were involved in fights with hostile onlookers.[31] The need to preserve public order by averting conflicts of this kind provided a means of combining anti-Catholic effect with an ostensible religious neutrality. Some municipalities took a more frankly anti-Catholic stance. Streets named after saints were renamed after such anti-clerical heroes as Voltaire. In Paris, where the erection of the Sacré Coeur basilica during the 1870s on the top of the Butte of Montmartre was a striking example of the church's continuing ability to stamp its presence on the modern cityscape, the municipal council voted money in 1904 for the erection of a statue of the Chevalier de La Barre opposite the entrance to the basilica. La Barre had been executed for sacrilege in 1766 and so stood beside Étienne Dolet, executed for atheism and heresy in 1546, as a martyr of freethought, frequently celebrated by republican councils.[32]

Since many Catholics were known to be hostile to the Republic, practising Catholics could also face various forms of direct or indirect discrimination by the state. Indirect discrimination included the law of 1913 which excluded those who had not been educated for at least three years at a state school from entry to the civil service or the officer corps of the army. Since devoutly Catholic families tended to send their children to private schools in order to escape the 'irreligious' teaching in state schools, the effect was to make it even harder for practising Catholics to enter state employment. Various forms of direct discrimination were already in operation. The army had from 1900 kept reports on the religious activities of officers, with the result that practising Catholics were held back, while Freemasons had good prospects of promotion. Government ministries varied in the degree to which they excluded Catholics, but some particularly important positions, notably that of prefect, were effectively closed to practising Catholics from the 1880s until the 1940s. (In fact, Larkin found one example of a practising Catholic who was a prefect for several months in 1930.)[33]

While the Third Republic's programme of secularisation was many-sided, its centre-piece was the secularisation of the state school system. In 1876–77, 30 per cent of the teachers in state primary schools were members of religious orders; by 1906–7 the proportion had dropped to less than 1 per cent. [34] Meanwhile the number of lay teachers had more than doubled, and a large proportion of them were convinced republicans, often very hostile to the Catholic Church. From the later 1870s, teacher training

colleges multiplied, many of them noted for their strongly republican and anti-clerical ethos. And even where teachers began their
career as Catholics or as religiously neutral, the logic of their situation pushed them in an anti-clerical direction. Often bitterly
opposed by the parish priest and by his more devout parishioners,
they found their keenest supporters among militant republicans.
Where there was a Catholic 'private' (republican terminology) or
'free' (Catholic terminology) school, the lay teacher was in direct
rivalry with the priest. Certainly in the 1880s and still, though to a
diminishing extent, in subsequent decades, there were teachers
who were pious Catholics, and there were also those who wished
to avoid any kind of confrontation. But by the first decade of the
twentieth century the younger generation of teachers was very
largely made up of men and women on the new model – to the
Left in politics and more or less distanced from the Catholic
Church. Clearly a wide spectrum of religious attitudes was represented among these teachers. While some were militantly anti-
religious, there were also many who claimed to have a religious
view of the world, while refusing affiliation to any church. But
common to both groups was a negative view of Catholicism. This
clearly affected the ways in which subjects such as history were
taught. The teacher might be officially neutral in relation to pre-
sent-day events, but study of such episodes as the Inquisition, the
Wars of Religion or the Revocation of the Edict of Nantes provided
plenty of opportunities for criticising the church's past record.[35]

The most significant aspect of the secularisation of the curriculum
was the abolition of religious teaching, and its replacement by
teaching on morality and civics. A range of manuals were written
to help teachers cover these subjects, and some of these manuals
became centres of controversy, as Catholics accused them of bias.
The elimination of Christianity from the curriculum was a more
gradual process. In the 1880s and 1890s, for instance, it was still
common for teachers to emphasise that morality derived ultimately
from God, while after the turn of the century, claims of this kind
were becoming rare.[36] The teaching of morality had a foundation in
a strong commitment to the Republic and to what were seen as
republican values, such as democracy and equality. While teachers
often tried their best to avoid any explicit taking of sides on religious
questions, there were some occasions when controversy was un-
avoidable. One example was the 'Quarrel over the Manuals' which
split many communities in 1882–83, when the church condemned a

number of the manuals approved for use in state schools. Some local authorities and some teachers regarded it as matter of principle to ignore such condemnations, and Catholic parents sometimes responded by withdrawing their children from schools where the manuals were used. In 1882 fierce controversy was caused by a manual, adopted for use in the schools of the Tarn department, which defended civil marriage, and attacked the Catholic view that only a marriage performed by a Catholic priest was a real marriage. Some of the other manuals approved for use in schools were more directly anti-Catholic, including, for instance, attacks on the Catholic belief in miracles.[37] However, Jean Baubérot's study of what was actually taught in the schools, as revealed in some two hundred surviving exercise-books, suggests that direct attacks on Catholicism were the exception: the secularising effect of education in the *école laïque* lay more in the inculcation of a moral code which was independent of Catholicism, or even of belief in God, and which was in tension with certain aspects of Catholicism, even if there was no outright contradiction. The key concepts of this code included human dignity, the supremacy of the individual conscience, work, solidarity and progress – the supreme example of the latter being French history, culminating in the glories of the Third Republic.[38]

There was a minimal and a maximal version of the religious implications of the secular school. Jules Ferry who, as Minister of Education from 1879 to 1884, pushed through the crucial legislation, favoured the minimal version. He claimed that the school must be religiously 'neutral' – 'We have neither dogma nor symbols' – and he poured scorn on the idea of the teachers becoming 'a new sacerdotal caste'. The aim must be to give the children the freedom to choose between different views of the world.[39] He saw it as essential to the future of the secular school and indeed of the Republic, that they win the support of the majority of Catholics, and he was therefore prepared to move slowly on non-essential issues. For instance, he was in no hurry to remove crucifixes from school walls in places where most parents wanted them, and at the turn of the century there were still teachers who took their class in a group to church for catechism.[40] Ferry's close collaborator, Ferdinand Buisson, who was Director of Primary Education, and later a prominent Radical deputy, was typical of those who took a maximal view. In his book *La Foi laïque* (1912) he declared: 'Yes, there is a religion which the school teaches and propagates. What is this relgion? To live in equality.' And an enquiry into the ideas of teachers of the 1905 generation found many of them claiming that the secular school stood for a 'universal morality' which transcended the particularisms of the various religions.[41]

The Catholic Counter-Culture

France thus came closer than any other country in pre-1914 Europe to achieving a system of primary education that was (to quote the republican watchwords) 'free, compulsory and secular' and under the firm control of the state. There was, however, one weak link in the chain. The compulsion to attend school did not preclude the choice of a 'private' or 'free' school – generally of a strongly Catholic character. In 1878–79, 15 per cent of primary school children were attending private schools; by 1912–13 the proportion had risen to 19 per cent.[42] Thus the problem of 'les deux France' or 'les deux jeunesses', frequently lamented by republican orators. The secularisation of the state system had certainly placed the majority of children in an environment that was emphatically republican and generally non-Catholic. But it had further emphasised the fervently Catholic and anti-republican character of the environment in which a substantial minority of children were educated – the majority in many parts of Brittany and the Vendée, the principal strongholds of the Catholic school. In Breton villages the school was often run by the Brothers of Christian Instruction. When in the 1880s schools were secularised, parents refused to send their children to 'the school without God'. The village priest, sometimes with assistance from local aristocratic families, organised the building of a private school, and the dispossessed Brother of Christian Instruction resumed teaching, with most of his former pupils still in front of him.[43]

Equally worrying from a republican point of view was the strength of the church in secondary education, which actually increased during the 1880s and 1890s. By 1899, 43 per cent of secondary school pupils were attending church-run schools.[44] Middle-class parents had for long preferred a Catholic schooling for their daughters,[45] but many of them were now sending their sons too. The prestige of some of the Catholic boys' schools, especially those run by Jesuits, appealed to many parents, including some who were uninterested in the religion. The famous Sainte-Geneviève school in the rue des Postes in Paris had been said in 1867 to include among its pupils the children of 'Voltaireans, very well known as such', and one father was reported as 'caring no more about the religious and political question, where the Jesuit fathers are concerned, than he would have thought about the orthodoxy of his dentist in the case of toothache'.[46] But whatever the motives were that led middle-and upper-class parents to send their children to a Catholic school, the religious atmosphere was frequently catching. In the upper reaches of French society during the second half of the nineteenth century, a familiar figure was the devoutly Catholic son of a sceptical father.[47] Under the Third Republic these schools trained a rival elite with its strongholds in the army and navy. The armed forces recruited huge numbers of graduates of the elite Catholic schools in the 1880s and 1890s, and continued to do so even after the Dreyfus Affair led to acute republican anxiety about right-wing influence in the armed forces.[48]

As more and more positions of official authority passed to militant republicans, Catholics hit back by building an extensive network of distinctively Catholic institutions. In every sphere where the republicans had an important presence, the Catholics had a counter-organisation. 'Bad newspapers' had unquestionably played a major part in the development of anti-clerical propaganda from the 1860s and 1870s. Parisian papers like *Le Matin* and *Le Journal* had a national influence. But even more widely read were regional papers, like *La Dépêche de Toulouse*, and the multitude of local papers. Catholics responded to the threat by establishing their own popular papers. 'The time is past,' declared the Archbishop of Rennes in 1908, 'for building churches and decorating altars; the urgent matter now is to cover the country with newspapers which will teach it the truth once again.'[49] This was the era of the priest-journalist, of whom the prototype had been Fr. Vincent de Paul Bailly, editor of the sensationalist and ultra-Rightist *La Croix*. His more sober counterparts included the 'democratic priests' who wrote for *L'Ouest-Eclair*, which became the leading paper in the west of France.[50]

Especially from the 1890s, there was an enormous growth of Catholic youth clubs, which came to play a big part in the growth of organised sport in the years following. In 1898 a Catholic sporting federation was formed, the *Fédération gymnastique et sportive des patronages de France* (FGSPF), in opposition to the well-established *Union des sociétés françaises de sport athlétique* (USFSA), the ethos of which was seen as republican. Republican sport was mainly organised in connection with the secular school. Associations of former pupils, known as '*Les Petites Amicales*', were formed,[51] and in many places there was the familiar phenomenon of two rival organisations, more or less indistinguishable in what they actually did, but one catering for Catholics and the other for those detached from the church. The rapid growth of Catholic sports clubs in this period caused some anxiety to government officials, who saw them as a major source of support for the church,[52] even in some areas where it was otherwise weak, such as the rural regions surrounding Paris.[53] Sporting success enabled Catholics to win symbolic victories even at the moment of republican political triumph. In 1905, while the law of Separation was in preparation, the Catholic soccer champions of France, Étoile sportive des Deux-Lacs, met Gallia Club, champions of the secular league. 'The match was played in a climate of passion' and when the Catholics won 2–1, the victory was greeted by the Catholic papers as an event of both political and spiritual significance.[54] At the same time the choice of sport could have a religious significance: in 1905–6 the Catholic association's decision to give priority to soccer over rugby was partly influenced by the fact that the spread of rugby in the south-west had been especially promoted by anti-clericals and Protestants – though the main argument used was the brutality of rugby.[55] Relations between Catholics and anti-clericals in the years between the Separation and the war were so bad that teams from the rival leagues stopped playing one another.[56] In an age when practising Catholics had become a minority of the French people, organisation, militancy, shows of strength were all important for Catholic morale. For activists, giant congresses played this role – 35,000 took part in the eucharistic congress at Lyon in 1914[57] and the numerous diocesan congresses held in the years following the Separation often attracted several thousand.[58] For Catholics of all kinds, pilgrimages were the most important form of collective activity. Lourdes, especially, attracted not only the sick in search of miracles, but also those who loved the feeling of being part of a huge crowd of people sharing the same beliefs.[59]

The Slowness of Institutional Secularisation in Germany and England

At first sight the attack on the Catholic Church pursued by Bismarck between 1871 and 1878, the so-called *Kulturkampf*, has much in common with the attack on the Catholic Church by the French republicans.[60] In both cases the religious orders were a particular target. For instance, the Jesuit Law of 1872 (which applied to the whole German Empire) expelled all foreign Jesuits, and placed such extensive restrictions on German Jesuits as to make most of the Society's work impossible. In Prussia, the schools were an important battleground, with Catholic and Protestant schools being forced to merge and clerical school inspectors being replaced by professional educators. Money was used as a weapon too, with many Catholic clergy being denied their salaries. The intro-duction of civil registration, with only the civil marriage ceremony being legally valid, placed Germany in line with the long-standing French practice. In some respects Bismarck's methods were more brutal than those of his French counterparts. For instance, there was the notorious case of the apparitions of the Virgin Mary at the Saarland village of Marpingen. Within a very short time large crowds of pilgrims were arriving at the village. This so worried the Prussian government that troops were sent to occupy Marpingen, and some twenty villagers, including the priest, were put on trial.[61] More generally, five bishops, as well as large numbers of priests and lay Catholics were imprisoned, the Catholic press was constantly harassed and Catholics who were state officials fre-quently suffered dismissal.[62] Attacks on the Catholic Church, in Germany as much in France, had the effect of pushing Catholics into organising, developing a stronger *esprit de corps*, and often a ghetto mentality.

When, however, one looks at the objectives of Bismarck's policy, as opposed to the methods he used, it becomes clear that they were much more limited than those of the French republicans in the years following. Bismarck's policies had much more of an *ad hoc* character, and they were driven largely by political concerns, rather than the much more wide-ranging recasting of society that was proposed by French anti-clericals. (Certainly some of the Liberal supporters of the *Kulturkampf* had ideas much closer to those of the French anti-clericals, but they never had a determining influence on policy.)[63] For instance, in the crucial matter of the role of religion in education, there was never any suggestion that the Catholic faith would cease to be taught in the schools; and even the policy of setting up inter-confessional schools proved to be very short-lived.[64] Nor was there any campaign to secularise hospitals, or pull down crucifixes. And with the halting of the government attack in 1878, and its abandonment in 1887, the Catholic Church was free to rebuild its institutional strength.

The biggest battleground between the secularisers and the champions of the Christian State in the nineteenth century was generally education. The solutions adopted in England and in the German states resembled those seen in France in so far as the state was in Germany, and increasingly became in England, the dominant voice. But they differed from France in so far as religion remained an essential ingredient of the English and German systems of publicly funded education, and the role of the various religious denominations also remained important.

In England the major turning-point in the evolution of elementary education was the Education Act of 1870, which instituted the 'Dual System' that has characterised the English school system ever since.[65] This consists of the co-existence of religiously neutral schools, supported largely or entirely from public funds, and denominational schools, supported partly from public funds. The Dual System was a compromise, which at first was bitterly opposed from a variety of conflicting standpoints by important sections of public opinion. Many Anglicans argued that education needed to have a consistent religious basis and that it should socialise children into membership of a specific religious community, since religion could not be practised in isolation. They therefore wanted a continuation of the older system whereby most elementary schooling was provided by churches or church-based educational societies, assisted by government grants. Their solution to the problem that there were far too few such schools to educate all the nation's children was simply to increase the size of the grants. In the 1850s and early 1860s most Nonconformists had been 'Voluntaryists', who opposed any form of state intervention (which, in their view, usually favoured the Anglicans), and argued that the provision of schools should be left entirely to voluntary efforts. However, by the later 1860s large numbers of Nonconformists had come to realise the impracticability of this method. By now there were many Nonconformists supporting the National Education League, which campaigned for a comprehensive system of free and non-sectarian publicly funded schools. Nonconformists were, however, divided between those who thought that such schools should provide religious teaching of an undenominational character, and those who wanted these schools to be entirely secular, leaving religious teaching to the churches. The latter position was naturally also favoured by the Secularists, as well as by a section of the liberal intelligentsia and by the Trades Union Congress.

The Education Act is a good example of a compromise which at first upset almost everyone, but, since it offered something to almost everyone, came in the end to be generally accepted. It upset the Anglicans by establishing School Boards, authorised to set up non-sectarian schools supported from local taxation. It upset Noncon-formists and Secularists by stating that these Board Schools would supplement, rather than replace, the denominational schools, and that denominational schools would continue to receive state grants. It upset Secularists and some Nonconformists by permitting the new schools to provide religious teaching, provided they did not teach the formularies of any specific denomination. At the same time it defused criticism slightly by introducing a 'Conscience Clause' permitting parents to withdraw their children from reli-gious instruction. In the 1870s a few School Boards, such as that in Birmingham, the principal stronghold of the National Educa-tional League, did decide that the teaching would be purely secular. But this decision was overturned in 1879 and was never reinstated. Before long the overwhelming majority of School Boards were providing religious teaching, though it varied considerably in scale and content. Two of the largest Boards, those of Birmingham and Manchester, stood at opposite extremes. Birmingham, from 1879 to 1900, provided only Bible-reading, with no comments or explana-tions by the teacher being allowed. Manchester provided fifty min-utes a day of religious teaching, with a syllabus claimed by one Anglican observer to be more elaborate than the one operating in church schools.[66] The compromise position, adopted in London and Leeds, was to base the lessons round the reading of the Bible, supplemented by 'such explanations and such instruction there-from in the principles of morality and religion as are suited to the capacity of the children'.[67]

Some historians have seen the Education Act as a major step towards secularisation. For instance, Jeffrey Cox sees it as the first stage in the direction of a Welfare State, in which the churches would be marginalised by the all-embracing role of central and local government as providers of knowledge and health care and relievers of poverty.[68] For K. D. Wald, the old system of National and British Schools had played a key role in socialising children into a society where denominational identity was fundamental, and nearly everyone belonged to the church camp or the chapel camp, which in turn provided an essential part of the basis for the conflict between Conservative and Liberal. Children growing up in Board Schools, according to Wald, had no such strongly defined denominational identity, and so were ripe for integration into a political system where class rather than denomination was the principal influence on voting. At the same time, the fact that even on the eve of the First World War a substantial minority of children were attending Anglican schools helped the Tories to hold on to a significant number of working-class voters in the 1920s, when the Liberal working-class vote was collapsing.[69]

My own view would be that the secularising effects of the Act have been exaggerated. The non-sectarian religious teaching provided by the overwhelming majority of Board Schools is an example of the continuing attempt by those at the top of English society to use religion as an integrating force, though in the changed context of greatly increased pluralism, and the undermining of the Anglican Church's central position. Jeffrey Cox, in fact, credits the Board Schools with considerable success in teaching basic information about the Bible and Christian doctrine – they weakened the churches while, at least in the short run, increasing the extent of 'diffusive Christianity'.[70] Others are more sceptical. For instance, J. S. Hurt stresses the significance of such factors as large classes and lack of support from parents in limiting the effectiveness of all aspects of Board School teaching. And a recent oral history-based study suggests that the religious beliefs of elderly residents of the Black Country have been shaped much more strongly by Sunday School than day school.[71] The evidence seems to be inconclusive. However, Wald surely overstates the importance of day schools as shapers of religious identity. Other factors played an equally large role, including Sunday Schools and discriminatory employment practices, as well as family tradition. If Wald's argument were correct, the Anglican dominance of elementary school provision in the period up to the Second Reform Act would have been reflected in a Tory electoral hegemony from 1868 onwards. Similarly the decline in the percentage of elementary school children being taught in British or Wesleyan schools from 24 per cent in 1872 to 8 per cent in 1900 would have been reflected in a declining Liberal vote long before 1918.[72]

The continuing prominence of religion in English education is even clearer when one looks at the public schools, attended by the sons of the upper middle and upper classes, including many of the nation's future rulers. John Honey, the leading historian of the

Victorian public school, has produced a ranking list of schools in terms of their status in the later nineteenth century. Of the top fifty, forty-eight were Anglican – which meant that they had a school chapel where daily Anglican services were held, they provided Anglican religious instruction, and boys were prepared for confirmation in the Church of England (though in a few cases separate provision was made for Jewish pupils).[73] There were also some Nonconformist and Roman Catholic public schools, but in the nineteenth century none of them was in the top rank.

Up to about 1870 the majority of teachers in the leading public schools were clergymen. There was then a rapid laicisation, with the proportion dropping to 29 per cent in 1889 and 13 per cent in 1906. This was probably due to a combination of factors, including both an increase in the number of those staff who were religious sceptics and, more crucially, increasing professionalisation both in the teaching and in the clerical profession.[74] The tendency in the later Victorian period was for schools to prefer the career teacher, and for parochial work to be seen as the clergyman's *real* business. This was the period later termed by Archbishop Lang the 'golden age of parochial work in the Church of England', when the most admired clergymen were those who, like Lang himself, or like Arthur Winnington-Ingram, who became Bishop of London in 1901, had made their name in large city parishes.[75] So far as the ethos of the public schools is concerned, the decline in the proportion of clergymen-teachers was less significant than the fact that in all of the top public schools in this period the headmaster was a clergyman. Thomas Arnold, the famous liberal Anglican and headmaster of Rugby seems to have set the pattern when in 1841 he united the offices of headmaster and chaplain. In 1903 Marlborough became the first major school to appoint a lay head, and a number of others followed in the years immediately before the war. But the most famous school of all, Eton, waited until 1933 before doing so. Sermons in chapel and confirmation classes were the most important means by which the official ethos of the school was inculcated. And, according to Honey, 'The sermons of Vaughan at Harrow, of Farrar and Cotton at Marlborough, of Benson at Wellington, created an indelible impression on generations of their pupils, who discussed them in letters home, in their diaries, and later in their memoirs'. [76] Admittedly this intertwining of the role of pastor and ruler repelled some of those who were subjected to it. The writer Roald Dahl claimed to have turned against Christianity as a result of witnessing the beatings administered with gusto by Geoffrey Fisher, headmaster of Repton, and later Archbishop of Canterbury.[77] But for better or for worse, the upbringing imposed on the future rulers of the British Empire, and on most of those who would take leading positions in commerce, industry and the professions, was of an emphatically religious character.

The only sector of English education that might seem to have been clearly secularised during the Victorian period is the university, but even here it would be more accurate to describe the changes as a move towards pluralism and religious freedom. At the middle of the nineteenth century the only non-sectarian institution of higher education in England was University College, London, founded in 1828 under strong Utilitarian influence, and favoured by Dissenters and Jews. King's College, London, the Anglican answer to the 'godless' University College, together with Durham, Oxford and Cambridge were exclusively Anglican, and the majority of fellows of Oxford and Cabridge colleges were clergymen. Students at the two ancient universities were required to attend chapel and to take an examination in theology. Most of this changed with the legislation of 1854, 1856 and 1871, which abolished all religious tests at Oxford, Cambridge and Durham, except in Faculties of Divinity, though at King's, London, this happened only in 1902. The new colleges, established mainly from the 1870s onwards in the major provincial cities, such as Manchester, Liverpool and Birmingham, were all non-sectarian. Especially in Oxford, with its strong High Church traditions, a polarisation between clerical and anti-clerical parties had developed by the 1860s, and in the 1870s it was claimed that a large proportion of college fellows were 'argumentative agnostics'.[78] A strong agnostic element emerged in Cambridge at a slightly later date. A change in atmosphere among the student body at the ancient universities may also be indicated by the decreasing frequency with which graduates entered the Anglican ministry. A rather striking example of this is the drastic decline in the proportion of outstanding students going on to be ordained. In the years 1841–43, 65 per cent of those graduating from Cambridge with first-class degrees had been ordained, while in the years 1881–83 only 18 per cent had done so – still perhaps quite a considerable number, so long as one overlooks the extent of the decline.[79]

However, by comparison with, let us say, the French universities under the Third Republic, the English universities were far from being secular institutions. Most had chapels and chaplains, and in some Oxford colleges compulsory attendance at chapel only ended in the 1950s.[80] Oxford and Cambridge established Theology Faculties in the 1870s, and the Cambridge Faculty earned a distinguished and, by German standards, rather conservative reputation in biblical criticism. Many of the new universities had strong Nonconformist associations, and Manchester established a non-sectarian Faculty of Theology which attracted some outstanding Nonconformist scholars.[81] The appearance of a strong agnostic element among the academics at Oxford in the 1860s and 1870s, and later at other universities, reflected changes in the intellectual atmosphere, and to some extent the special circumstances of Oxford, where the militant Anglicanism of some college fellows provoked an equally strong reaction. But the growing religious pluralism within the universities was equally reflected in the emergence of a large body of evangelical students, especially at Cambridge, where the Inter-Collegiate Christian Union was formed in 1876.[82] In fact from the later nineteenth century right up to the present day English universities have been marked, by comparison with English society in general, by unusually high proportions both of committed believers and of committed agnostics or atheists.[83]

Germany differed from England, in that the religious emphasis was stronger in the schools attended by the masses than in those of the elite. As a prominent Left Liberal politician said, it was 'practical Christianity for the masses, cultured humanism for the cultured classes'.[84] In the *Gymnasium*, Latin, Greek, Mathematics and German dominated the curriculum, and Religion was limited to two hours a week. Most schools were inter-confessional, though in practice one confession usually was overwhelmingly dominant. However, the relatively small quantity of religious teaching was possibly counterbalanced by superior quality, since it was given by specialists, who had taken a theology degree.[85]

As for the *Volksschulen*, which were attended by over 90 per cent of German school children in the later nineteenth century, religion ranked alongside reading as the principal subject. In Prussia, a comprehensive system of state-controlled primary schools and compulsory attendance had existed since the later eighteenth century – though the attendance requirement was only strictly enforced from 1860. A decree of 1822 laid down that the system should be organised on a confessional basis. While ultimate control lay with the state, each school would teach the doctrines of a specific faith, whether Protestant or Catholic, would be staffed by teachers and attended by children of that denomination, and would be inspected by the local pastor or priest. From the 1820s in Württemberg and from 1847 in Prussia, Jewish state schools were also available. In spite of a temporary change of direction in the 1870s, this remained the basis of the Prussian elementary school system until after the revolution of 1918–19.[86]

There were indeed frequent objections, whether from the teachers themselves, or from Liberal and Social Democratic politicians. Already in the 1840s there were many criticisms of the subordination of teachers to the local clergy, arising from the role of the latter as inspectors and from the fact that teachers sometimes had to do jobs in the church – for instance, play the organ. In 1848 the Frankfurt Parliament voted for inter-confessional schools (*Simultanschulen*) and an end to clerical inspection. Of course, all of this was forgotten in the 1850s. One of the high points of the conservative reaction of these years was the curriculum, drawn up in 1854, for Protestant schools in Prussia, which included prayers at the start of the day, and six hours a week of religious instruction. In spite of some later reductions in the time devoted to religious teaching, the links between church and school, both in Prussia and in most other German states, remained close right up to the revolution of 1918. Pupils learnt an extensive repertoire of hymns and biblical verses and stories, as well as the catechism. It was also common for them to attend services at the beginning and end of the school year and on other special occasions, including the king's or grand duke's birthday.[87]

In 1861, 99 per cent of Protestant children were attending Protestant schools, and 97 per cent of Catholic children attended Catholic schools, though most Jewish children went to a Protestant school, while having separate religious teaching.[88] But with the dawning of the New Era it seemed that the future would lie with the Liberals, and that with them would come the *Simultanschule*. The model here was Baden, where inter-confessional schools were introduced in the 1860s, provoking the first of the German *Kulturkämpfe*, pitting state against Catholic Church. With the appointment of Adalbert Falk as Minister of Education and Religion in 1872, it seemed that Prussia might be going in the same direction. As part of the package of measures which was setting the Prussian state and the Catholic Church on a collision course, he started a programme of introducing inter-confessional schools and of replacing clerical

inspectors by professional inspectors with a background in education. Predictably, he won the enthusiastic support of Liberal city
councils and provoked fierce Catholic opposition, including mass
rallies organised by the Centre Party. By 1876, however, he was also
facing considerable opposition from Protestants, and that was to
prove a decisive factor in the failure of Falk's programme.[89] Conservative Protestants were worried by the dilution of confessional
consciousness in mixed schools, especially in areas where most of
the teachers and pupils were Catholics. From 1879 until the fall of
the monarchy the Prussian Ministry of Education and Religion was
generally held by Conservatives of strongly Protestant background.
They were all wedded to the principle that elementary schooling should have a confessional basis, and while they always put
Protestant interests first, they were generally more conciliatory
towards the Catholics than Falk had been. They insisted on the
inter-confessional school only in Polish-speaking areas, where it
was used as an instrument of Germanisation. In the west, many
schools were reconfessionalised, and there was a considerable
increase in the proportion of Catholic schools which were inspected
by Catholic priests. In 1906, 95 per cent of Protestant children and
91 per cent of Catholic children, though only 27 per cent of Jewish
children, were being taught in schools of their own confession.[90]

The teaching profession became increasingly highly-organised
and vocal after the formation in 1871 of a national teachers' union
(*Deutscher Lehrerverein*), which tended to be Left Liberal in politics,
though by the early twentieth century it also included a significant
element of socialists. The Liberals also thought the clergy had too
much influence on the running of the schools and wanted the state
to take full control of inspection. But their chief bugbear was con-
fessionalism, which they saw as divisive. In practice, their main
objection was to *Catholic* confessional schools, though they tended
to argue for inter-confessionality as a matter of general principle.
Their solution was the *Simultanschule*, in which the children would
separate only for religious instruction – though by the early twentieth century some were arguing for non-sectarian teaching on
similar lines to that provided in English Board Schools. By this
time there also tended to be growing differences between Left
Liberals, who were prone to argue on lines of abstract principle,
and the more pragmatic National Liberals, for whom defence
against the dangers of Catholicism and/or socialism tended to override mere principle.[91] The Social Democrats wanted a purely

secular system – but of course until after 1918 they had no possibility of putting any of their ideas into practice, and the main effect of
the growing socialist strength was to push the other parties into
closing ranks against them. Meanwhile, Conservatives (most of
whom were Protestant) and members of the Catholic Centre Party
remained firmly wedded to the confessional principle. Both
believed that religion must be at the core of the system of popular
education. Personal religious conviction certainly played a part in
this. Conservative politicians and higher state officials included in
their ranks considerable numbers of Pietists, who believed that
education must contribute to the salvation of the soul as much as
to the welfare of the state, and that the two kinds of consideration
were quite compatible. Similar convictions influenced many members of the Centre Party, not least those who were priests, though
equally important in influencing Catholics was suspicion of the state
and a strong sense of confessional identity. Conservatives, for their
part, regardless of personal religious convictions, believed that religion provided the best foundation for the inculcation of patriotism,
industry and respect for authority. The Emperor Wilhelm II spoke
for many when, in 1889, he declared:

> The prime object of the schools will be to lay the foundations for a
> sound comprehension of both civic and social relations by
> cherishing reverence for God and love for the fatherland.... The
> school must endeavour to create in the young the conviction that
> the teachings of social democracy contradict not only the divine
> commands and Christian morals, but are, moreover, impractical
> and, in their consequences, destructive alike to the individual and
> the community.[92]

On the eve of the First World War, the confessional school still
dominated German elementary education. Only in Baden and
Hesse-Darmstadt was the inter-confessional school widespread.[93]
Admittedly the criticisms of Liberals, Social Democrats and the
teachers themselves highlighted the enormous gap between the
views of those who governed Germany and a considerable proportion of those whom they ruled. In the Weimar Republic the tables
would be at least partly turned. But until then, power in the
German states remained in the hands of those who regarded conservative forms of religion as an essential basis for the maintenance
of the existing social order.

While it would be hard to claim that the English and German school systems were overtly secularised in the second half of the nineteenth century, some historians have argued that there was a secularisation of the content of education. Mangan, in a study of English public schools, highlights the tension between the Christian values to which these schools professedly subscribed and the qualities of toughness and harsh competition fostered by the games cult which played such a large part in the daily life of the public schoolboy. He suggests that beneath the Christian rhetoric the dominant ethos was that of Social Darwinism.[94] Blessing and Humphries, dealing respectively with Bavarian and with English elementary education in the years around 1900, argue that the central theme was the promotion of patriotism. For instance, Humphries notes that a portrait of Queen Victoria hung on the walls of every Bristol Board School, and that the history textbooks 'described a heroic national stereotype, compared to ignorant and inferior races', and were full of passages 'glorifying the monarchy and celebrating Britain's commercial wealth and progress'.[95] Blessing, whose main emphasis is on the mentality of the teachers themselves, stresses their 'National Liberal *Weltanschauung*', which included fervent German nationalism, mixed with devotion to Goethe and Schiller. Humphries argues that religion was relegated to a secondary role, and Blessing speaks explicitly of 'secularisation'.[96]

While the evidence concerning the centrality both of the games cult in English public schools and of patriotism and imperialism in English and in German elementary schools is clear, I would be more cautious about some of the ways in which these have been interpreted. First, there are within any institution tensions between rhetoric and reality, and often between different aspects both of theory and of practice. Certainly it is one of the tasks of historians to expose these contradictions. But it would be naive to suppose that there was once a time when no such tensions existed: all one can say is that the areas of tension tend to change over time. Secondly, it needs to be recognised that in both England and Germany around 1900 nationalism and religion were often so intermingled that the two cannot always be easily separated. I shall return to this theme in a later chapter. But two examples will illustrate the problem.

Blessing, in describing the generation of Franconian Protestant pastors who had lived through the wars of the years 1864–71, notes that the 'cosmopolitan humanism and pragmatic patriotism'

tending towards 'cultural unity' of the late Enlightenment generation
had given way to a more emphatic German nationalist orientation
and a tendency to glorify military success. The results were vividly
displayed within the households of the pastors themselves:

> On the study wall there now hung, beside the cross and the
> portrait of Luther, a picture of Bismarck and, beside Leonardo's
> 'Last Supper' and Dürer's 'Apostles', Werner's 'Proclamation of
> the Kaiser at Versailles'. In the bookcase, next to theological
> literature and the canon of German and European poetry recog-
> nised by the educated bourgeoisie, there stood memoirs from the
> war against France. The pastor's daughter played on the piano
> not only chorales, pieces from operas and romantic *Lieder*, but
> also Hoffmann von Fallersleben's '*Deutschland über alles*', the
> hymn to the Kaiser '*Heil Dir im Siegerkranz*' and Becker's
> '*Rheinlied*'. The sons received for Christmas not only stories
> from the life of Luther, but popular war books and card games
> with portraits of the generals of 1870–1.[97]

To understand the context of this blending of the religious and
the patriotic, one has to take account of several things. Firstly, to
place Luther beside Bismarck would have seemed to most German
Protestants of the time completely logical. As they saw it, Luther's
Bible had played a central role in the development of the German
language, and his rejection of the Papacy was a daring blow for
German independence; his stand for the rights and obligations of
the individual conscience was the basis of German national character and of the greatness of the German people; Bismarck, in establishing the *Reich*, was building on the foundations laid by Luther. An
essential part of the cult of Luther which was a central feature of
German Protestantism, and which had been heavily reinforced by
the confessionalist movement (so powerful in Bavaria), was a strong
sense of his Germanness – he was often referred to as 'the German
man'.[98] Secondly, most Protestant pastors of the time, and especially
those on the Lutheran confessionalist and Pietist wings of the
church, believed that Prussian military triumphs and the establishment of the Reich were no accidents of history, but a part of God's
plan and a sign of God's favour.[99] Thirdly, they believed that it was
of the essence of the German Empire that it was a Protestant state,
and owed all that was greatest in it to its Protestantism.[100] This
meant among other things that Catholicism and Judaism were

alien presences, however sincerely patriotic individual Catholics and Jews might be.[101] And fourthly, of course, Protestant pastors shared a considerable part of the values and ways of thinking of the educated bourgeois milieu from which they came, and equally they naturally chose to preach Christianity to their contemporaries in a language which they understood and in terms of concepts to which they could relate. For all these reasons, religion and nationalism were not always clearly distinguishable in the Germany of the later nineteenth century. For instance Kuhlemann notes that a handbook for teachers used in east Westphalia around 1900 'spoke of Christianity and the Germans (*Deutschtum*) in the same breath', and claimed that the Christian duty to love one's neighbour referred above all to one's duty to love those speaking the same language and belonging to the same race. From the 1880s it was common to hang life-size portraits of national heroes on the school walls, and the figures chosen typically included the emperor, Bismarck, Blücher, Moltke and Luther.[102]

The other example, which I shall consider more briefly, is a quotation, cited by Humphries, from an interview with Florence Mullen, a Bristol factory worker and housewife, born in 1899:

> The best thing about school in them days was that they taught you right from wrong. They taught us we were the best nation in the world and must live up to it. We mustn't cause any trouble or bring disgrace on the country, because if we did anything wrong we should disgrace not just ourselves but the nation.[103]

To interpret this statement with any confidence, one would need to put it in the context of the rest of the interview, and one might also want to know more both about the school and about the interviewee herself. But what is immediately striking is that patriotism is apparently being used as a support for morality – rather as the fear of God was often used. One might suggest that this represents a secularisation of morality – but it might equally be seen as a more religious conception of patriotism – the greatness of the nation lying not in the extent of its conquests but in the moral quality of its citizens. And what are the origins of the concepts of 'right' and 'wrong' which Florence Mullen regards as the essence of education? It is unlikely that they were derived from consideration of the empire – more probable that they arose out of some form of religion or humanism. In this case it would seem that the rhetoric is patriotic, but that the primary concern is moral or religious. In fact these concerns were often so tightly intermeshed at this time that it is difficult, and possibly misleading, to separate them.

Whereas in France, the secularisation of the state ran ahead of the secularisation of everyday life, in England, and even more in Germany, the reverse was true. The tendency for law to lag far behind practice in matters of religion and morality, except where radical politicians are able to force the pace, is well illustrated by the history of sabbatarian legislation.[104] In nineteenth-century England the greatest symbol of national piety was the 'English Sunday'. Up to about the 1850s the law was struggling to keep pace with the rising tide of sabbatarian opinion. But by 1860, when public support for such legislation was at its highest point, there was an extensive body of laws and by-laws on Sunday trading and entertainment and on the Sunday opening of pubs, emphasising the set-apartness of 'the Lord's Day', and offering a standing provocation to less devout members of the English nation and to visitors from France and Germany. Probably no aspect of nineteenth-century English life was a cause of so much adverse comment by foreign observers, and there was at least a substantial minority of the English who openly resented the sabbath. Men waiting outside pubs for the doors to open at 1 o'clock were said to jeer at the worshippers leaving church, and *Punch*, the favourite humorous journal of the middle class, was one of several papers that subjected sabbatarians to constant ridicule. There were many gradations of sabbath observance. But throughout the Victorian period Sunday was recognised as a day set apart by the majority of the population, including not only the middle and upper classes, but many of the working class, and including not only fervent evangelicals, but church-goers of other kinds, and indeed many non-church-goers.[105] By about 1880, there were signs of some relaxation. In London society, Sunday dinner parties – previously taboo – were coming back into fashion, and wealthy families were beginning to play croquet and tennis on Sunday afternoon. Soon golf clubs were starting to allow play on Sunday, and with the cycling craze of the 1890s, large crowds of cyclists could be seen leaving London or Manchester on a Sunday morning in search of country lanes. In France or Germany all of this would have been totally taken for granted. In England it marked a minor social revolution, and one which most evangelicals regarded with distaste and anxiety.

It needs to be emphasised, though, that public opinion was a long way ahead of the law. Private golf courses opened on Sundays long before public golf courses. Municipal parks usually banned Sunday sport at least until the 1920s, and in the Nonconformist stronghold of Northampton, the council voted overwhelmingly in 1932 to reaffirm the ban.[106] It was only in 1932 that Sunday cinema shows were legalised – though in some areas, such as seaside resorts, they had been allowed by local councils since before the war; throughout the inter-war period, the BBC had a distinctive pattern of radio broadcasts on Sundays with religious services in the morning and evening and serious music and talks in the afternoon;[107] and of course restrictions on Sunday trading and Sunday opening of pubs were only substantially removed in the 1990s.

The English Sunday was one of the most potent symbols of the Victorian religious era and its decline has been a very long drawn-out process. It was perhaps the longest-lasting example of a form of collective religious observance recognised by most of the population. The belatedness of the legal recognition of its decline was partly a matter of inertia; partly of the fact that at any given time most legislators came from the older generation and often retained religious attitudes and habits which they had learnt thirty or forty years earlier; partly of the fact that many people liked at least the idea of the 'quiet Sunday', whatever they might choose to do on that day themselves. But also very relevant was the fact that the period from the 1880s to the 1920s, when sabbatarianism was declining but laws concerning sabbath observance changed little, was one when Nonconformist political power was at its height. The growing presence of Nonconformists in Parliament, culminating in the election of some 200 in 1906, is well known. But even more important from this point of view, since Sunday observance was predominantly subject to local regulation, was the very large number of Nonconformist local councillors.[108]

Conclusion

One of the weaknesses of those accounts of secularisation which present it as an aspect of modernisation is the tendency to see societies in the grip of inexorable and impersonal forces, operating largely independently of anyone's volition. Certainly religious developments in the nineteenth century have to be related to a changing economic and social context. But there was generally more than one possible way of responding to these changes, and the choices that people made stemmed at least partly from religious and political ideology, as well, of course, as economic interests. Secularisation did not just happen: it was welcomed or actively promoted by some social groups, and resented, or even resisted, by others. In explaining the different nature, extent and pace of secularisation in different countries one needs to consider the balance of power between different social classes, political parties, or religious communities. For instance, in Germany the separation of church and state, which had been proposed by the Frankfurt Parliament as long ago as 1849, became a political impossibility in the subsequent era of reaction, and remained out of the question until the fall of the monarchy. In spite of a flurry of radically secularist decrees during the revolution of 1918–19, the balance of power in the Weimar Republic ensured that the separation of church and state enacted in 1919 took a much gentler form than in France. In England the fact that the main opposition to the established church came from devout Nonconformists, rather than from Secularists, ensured that public bodies and national institutions continued to be strongly influenced by religion, even if it often took a non-sectarian form. In the longer term, the Liberal preference for non-sectarian municipal and state institutions weakened the public role of the churches, but the introduction of such institutions was warmly promoted by many Nonconformists, and was seldom accompanied by the Secularist ideology that was so prominent in France. The next chapter will look at the religious attitudes of various sections of the population, with a special emphasis on those groups which were most precocious in the rejection of religious belief and practice, and in supporting steps towards secularisation.

3   The Pace-Setters

In all three countries some social groups were precocious in their alienation from religious institutions, in their adoption of irreligious ideas or their promotion of secularising tendencies in society. Aristocrats were generally close to their church, and whatever their personal convictions might have been, seldom supported secularising measures.[1] The urban working class were generally the group most alienated from the church, though they varied in their openness to irreligious ideas and their attitude to secularising policies. The position of other groups, such as the professional and business classes, the lower middle class, the peasantry or the rural working class was more varied, both between countries and often within countries. The rest of this chapter will look at those groups which played a significant part in advancing secularisation in one or more of these countries.

The Socially Marginal

In January 1838 Edward Derrington, a missionary attached to Carr's Lane Independent Church, was going door to door in a poor district of central Birmingham, preaching the Calvinist gospel to anyone who would listen, and trying to persuade people to attend a mission. He recorded in his journal the conversations that ensued. Some did listen with interest to his message. There were also a few who were already active members of another church, and friendly discussions sometimes ensued. For instance, he had a long and amicable talk with a Roman Catholic, 'the most liberal of that denomination I had ever met with'. Some of the Catholics, and rather more of those who were against all religion, got into arguments with him, abused him or threatened violence. However, two other kinds of response were more common. Some people welcomed his visit, but primarily because they felt he could be of use to them in a practical way, by providing food tickets or helping them find work. And there were also many whose energies were entirely taken up with the struggle for survival. As Derrington wrote: 'The anxieties of the present life so incessantly occupy and fill the mind that [preaching the gospel] is like putting more in that which is already full'. Another missionary in 1842 recorded a conversation with 'an elderly female whom I found at her washtub in the court where I was visiting today'. When the missionary had spoken to her about Christ and salvation, 'she very readily replied that she knew all these things and did them all, said her prayers every night regular... Grieved by her self-confidence and delusion, I endeavoured... to impress eternal things on her unawakened mind when, with the utmost indifference, she intimated she had enough to attend to without troubling about these things and no-one had ever been to the next world and returned to tell us how things stood there'.[2]

There was also a further dimension to this indifference born of poverty. Some of those who had been church-goers in more prosperous times had subsequently dropped out. Derrington met one family with four children, a father who was unemployed and a mother who was seriously ill. The father had a sitting in a Wesleyan chapel for fifteen years and had been a teacher there for seven years, 'but was so reduced that he cannot attend'. In a neighbouring house, the wife was a Wesleyan who used to attend class, but had been excluded when she could not keep up her subscription, and the husband had belonged to a Baptist Adult School, but left when he had to pawn his clothes.[3] In a similar case, a man who had been a regular church-goer, gave it up because 'he did not want his old acquaintances talking of his poverty'.[4] So there was also an element of pride in the absence of the poor from church. They did not want to go if they could not dress in suitably respectable clothes and be treated as equals by other members of the congregation. The free seats which most English churches provided for those who could not afford a pew-rent were often spurned by those who would rather not go at all than be visible recipients of charity.[5] The stigma of charity, and maybe the contamination of close association with those who were constantly dependent on such help, may also have discouraged many people from attending mission chapels.[6]

Those least involved in organised religion were generally those most socially marginal, including the poorest sections of the urban population and sometimes those living in isolated rural areas, as well as such groups as migrant labourers and sometimes recent immigrants from other countries. The religious census of London showed that there was a high correlation between the standard of living and the level of church-going in the various districts of London, with the poorest districts recording the lowest levels. A study of church attendance levels in eighty-one relatively homogeneous areas of the city, which were then divided into seven groups according to social character and income levels, showed that the lowest level 5.8 per cent, was found in the working-class district of Stepney, and that the 'poor' category had the lowest median level of attendance, 11.7 per cent.[7] A similar correlation between standard of living and regularity of church attendance could be seen in other English cities, including, for instance, Birmingham, Bristol and Sheffield. The one major exception was Liverpool where church attendance by Catholics in poor districts was high.[8] In France and Germany, though the correlation between church-going and standard of living was seldom as direct as in England, the poorest districts still had some of the lowest figures. In Berlin in 1900, Wedding was the poorest district in the city and also had the lowest ratio of Protestant communions to population (3.4 per cent).[9] In Paris between 1909 and 1914 the most strongly working-class *arrondissement*, the 20th, had the second lowest rate of attendance at mass (5.8 per cent).[10] Similarly, enquiries in Marseilles in the 1860s and 1870s suggested that detachment from the church was greatest in the poorest districts, especially those where large numbers of Italian immigrants lived.[11]

The non-involvement or limited involvement of the poorest or most marginal sections of the population in the church was nothing new. Lucian Hölscher notes that although the laws of many German states in the seventeenth and eighteenth centuries required pastors to ensure that everyone attended church regularly, this was only enforced in the case of those parishioners who had their own seats in church – which excluded servants and many journeymen and labourers.[12] The idea that *everyone* should be attending church regularly seems only to have become widely accepted in the early nineteenth century – partly under the influence of the evangelical movements of the time, and partly because of fears that the irreligious were potential rioters or radicals.[13] Similarly in eighteenth-century England, the fact that many of the poor seldom went to church was a commonplace, deplored by some of the clergy, but by many accepted as a fact of life. A typical comment was that by the vicar of the small Lancashire town of Westhoughton in a report to his bishop in 1778. In reply to a question about the extent of irreligion in his parish, he said that few professed irreligion, but that 'many absent themselves from all public worship: owing as they tell me to their Poverty, and want of decent cloaths to come in'.[14] There was both an Anglican church and a Presbyterian meeting-house, but many people went to neither.

In the more impoverished rural districts there might be no easily accessible place of worship at all. An example would be the village of Futeau on the borders of Lorraine and Champagne. It was situated in a forest area settled in the sixteeenth century by glass-workers, who turned to wood-cutting and seasonal migration after the collapse of the local glass industry in the early nineteenth century. The village had no church or school until 1848. In spite of the efforts of a vigorous priest, fewer than 5 per cent of adult males were communicants in 1880. By then, republican propaganda, spearheaded by the teacher, was reinforcing local habits. But these were primarily a product of economic factors of long standing: the poverty which made it difficult for the community to sustain a church and a priest, and often required Sunday labour; and the economy of seasonal migration – and, indeed, long periods of living in the woods when they were 'at home'. The latter meant that the roots of the men in this or any other place were shallow, and it excluded them from the daily and weekly rhythms of Catholic worship, and the ties with a priest, a church building and a congregation, which were available to those living a more settled existence. Bonnet concludes: 'Working-class irreligion is not a spontaneous generation, but a tradition. The weak social and religious integration of the *day-labourer* preceded the religiously marginal position of the *worker*.'[15]

From about the 1830s onwards the task of integrating the city poor and isolated rural communities into the church was being taken up by religious agencies of many kinds. The first of the many city missions was established in Glasgow in 1826. Typically they combined door-to-door evangelism and material assistance with preaching and Bible classes in unpretentious back-street chapels.[16] Church-building programmes brought not only buildings, but clergy, other church-workers and a range of parochial institutions to neglected proletarian suburbs on the edge of the city and to isolated communities in forest, mountain or marsh.[17] Some clergy had a vocation to live among the poor – like the Anglo-Catholic 'slum priests', who came to special prominence in the East End of London during the cholera epidemic of 1866.[18] One new religious denomination, the Salvation Army, which grew out of the East London Mission, founded in 1865, had its whole *raison d'être* in evangelising the poor through open-air preaching and music, and a variety of social schemes, including providing work for the unemployed and beds for the homeless, and setting up hostels for those wanting to get out of prostitution.[19]

For reasons already mentioned, the conditions of life experienced by a large proportion of the working class made any regular involvement in organised religion, or organised anything else, very difficult.[20] Radical political groups faced many of the same problems when they tried to recruit from the very poor. In the early twentieth century, for instance, London socialism had its strongholds in artisan districts. It took much longer to establish itself in the very poor East End boroughs of Bethnal Green and Stepney where, according to Paul Thompson, 'the most serious difficulty was probably the chronic poverty typical of the inner working class districts, breeding a political apathy which made a labour or socialist movement peculiarly hard to establish'.[21] Established churches, and those with a large middle-or upper-class membership, were also likely to experience additional difficulties in attracting the loyalty of the poor. In Berlin, for instance, where, in the later nineteenth and early twentieth centuries, working-class attendances at services of the Evangelical *Landeskirche* were very low, devout working-class Protestants preferred to attend what were called Bible Hours, or else the services of the various Free Churches, where they would be among people of similar social standing to themselves. A London man, who had been in the Anglican church choir when living in a dockland area, gave up going to church when he moved to a parish with a larger middle-class presence: 'the church boys at the parish there, St Dunstan's, were quite lofty, they were somebody. They were the sons of local businessmen'.[22] Working-class church-goers were likely to complain that they were shunned by better-dressed fellow-worshippers or even that the mere presence of better-dressed people made them feel uncomfortable, that the clergy mixed more readily with their middle-class parishioners, or that the sermon was over their heads. And even those working-class people whose political awareness was low were likely to resent the way that religion was often mixed up with the exercise of authority, and that religiously-based charity was combined with heavy-handed conversionist messages.[23]

Church leaders were aware of these areas of tension, and many of them made energetic attempts to respond to working-class grievances. Nonetheless the direction of social change during the nineteenth century was to exacerbate these problems. Even more important than the rapid growth of urban populations around the middle of the nineteenth century were changes in social relations within the cities. In the eyes of many contemporaries this period was marked by the decline of urban community. In England these changes had started earlier, but in France and Germany they were in full swing in the 1840s and 1850s. They included a growth in the size of industrial units, more impersonal relationships between employers and workers, greater residential segregation, and an increasing sense of working-class identity, partly overriding distinctions between artisan, factory operative and labourer. This process has been traced with unusual precision in a massive study of christening ceremonies in Leipzig. Here patriarchal relations in the dominant printing industry were still quite common in the 1820s and 1830s, and were reflected in printers' choice of their masters as godparents for their children. In the middle years of the century, as production became increasingly concentrated in large factories, workers abandoned the hope of becoming masters, and relations with employers became more impersonal, godparents came more and more exclusively to be chosen from those in working-class occupations, including growing numbers of those from other occupations or at different levels of skill.[24] This clearer sense of working-class identity developed partly in reaction to the emerging middle-class ideology, which included liberal economics, and the concept of 'character'. The latter could be used to condemn both the inherited wealth of the aristocrat or rentier and the poverty of the worker.[25] At this stage the sense of betrayal and humiliation was strong among many working-class people. In the next generation, as successful businessmen moved out into exclusive suburbs and cultivated a more ostentatiously luxurious lifestyle, relations between classes may have been less emotionally charged, but the sense of separation was deeper. So the feeling of marginalisation, rather than being the experience of certain minority groups, became common to most of the working class.

An anonymous poem published in a local paper in the German textile town of Elberfeld in 1855 captures this feeling rather poignantly:

Ihr tituliert den armen Mann
Als Bruder noch im Gotteshaus:
Doch schließt ihr mit der Bildung Bann
Gleich vor der Tür ihn wieder aus
Von euren Geistgenossen, euren Gästen,
Von euren Tischen und euren Festen.[26]

[In the house of God you still give the poor man the title of brother: but right in front of the door, with the spell of education, you shut him out again from your spiritual community, your guests, your tables and your celebrations.]

The increasingly distant and often tense relations between workers and bourgeoisie made it difficult for them to worship together in the same church. Since members of the bourgeoisie often held most of the positions of lay leadership,[27] it was generally the workers who left – sometimes to join a different church, but more often to give up church-going altogether. In Bradford, for instance, up to the 1820s, many Nonconformist chapels had a socially mixed membership. The mixing was placed under strain by the weavers' strike of 1825, and in the 1830s and 1840s it broke down as newly rich businessmen came to dominate many of the Baptist and Independent chapels, making them strongholds of the ethos of self-help.[28] In Bradford there were strongly working-class denominations, such as the Primitive Methodists, which could to some extent provide a haven for those who felt excluded by more prosperous churches. The breach was often more sharply defined in France, where there were few alternatives to the Roman Catholic Church.

Marseilles offers an example of the connections between economic, demographic and political changes and the decline of popular Catholicism.[29] In the first half of the nineteenth century the great port city was a stronghold of Catholicism and Legitimism, but in the second half of the century the working class became increasingly alienated from local religious and political traditions, cutting many of its ties with the church and moving to the Left. The strength of Catholicism and of Legitimism had been interconnected and both depended on relationships crossing class lines: popular

Catholicism declined as Legitimism disappeared, and as class antagonism became an essential fact of economic and political life. The workers seem to have remained strongly Catholic at least until the 1840s. The hold of the church and of Catholic faith were reflected in the enthusiastic support for the missions held during the Restoration and subsequent defence of the mission crosses, which became a prime target for anti-clericals after the revolution of 1830; the response to the cholera epidemic of 1834–5; the popularity of Catholic processions; and the links between the church and such trade organisations as the fishermen's corporation. In the 1840s and 1850s all this began to change. In those two decades the population more than doubled as a result of massive immigration, and rates of Catholic practice began to drop rapidly. In these middle years of the century there seems to have been a tripartite division of the city's working class. Local traditions seem to have survived best in the older districts, among workers born in Marseilles, speaking Provençal and belonging to certain exclusive trades where employment was often hereditary, including dockers and fishermen belonging to their own corporations and a variety of port-based artisans. The working-class radicalism, which first became a significant factor between 1848 and 1851, had its basis among artisans, especially building workers, born outside the city. Meanwhile, the many unskilled immigrants, drawn especially from Italy, remained remote both from the church and from radicalism. Isolated by language, by long hours of labour often including Sunday, by frequent moves in search of work, and often by severe poverty, they remained in the first generation a group apart. The decline of Catholic practice in these years affected all areas of the city, but it was in the poorest districts that the drop was sharpest. In the long run, the old-established local working class was affected too. So all sections of the working class in Marseilles found their relationship with the Catholic Church placed under strain in the middle and later years of the nineteenth century. For some, though by no means all, this was associated with growing political radicalism. I shall return to this radicalism in a later part of this chapter.

To what extent this lack of involvement in the church was associated with atheism or agnosticism is harder to say. There is certainly plenty of evidence that poverty and deprivation could lead to resentment towards God, and a cynical attitude towards idealists and activists of all kinds, whether religious, political or simply humanitarian.[30] On the other hand, church charities could play an important part in the survival strategy of many poor households, so that the cultivation of good relations with clergy, nuns, district visitors, or other representatives of the church might be a necessity, and in some cases could lead to warm personal ties.[31] Moreover those who had no wish to be part of a religous congregation might still pray, hang pictures of saints on the wall, or go on pilgrimages.[32]

The bitterness that the poorest often felt towards God, the church and those in comfortable circumstances was less often translated into action. The cynicism was applied as much to militant secularists as to militant believers. So the very poor seldom played a prominent part in secularising movements. The leaders of such movements were indeed often found at the opposite end of the social spectrum, among the members of new elites, for whom established churches were part of the old order that they wished to sweep away.

New Elites

In 1872 the French republican leader Léon Gambetta welcomed the arrival on the political stage of 'a new social stratum', which would provide the basis for the new order.[33] They were a middle bourgeoisie, consisting of such groups as lawyers, doctors and middle-ranking businessmen. They were obviously sharply set apart from the workers and peasants, who had not yet become a major political force, but whose votes would be useful. More important for the time being was the fact that they were also clearly distinct from the 'notables' drawn from the aristocracy and the upper bourgeoisie, who had dominated French society during the Second Empire.[34] The members of this new elite were liberals and republicans, but more than anything else they were anti-clericals, and during the 1870s and 1880s men drawn from this background would lay the foundations of the modern French secular state.

Many of the 'notables' who supported the conservative and pro-Catholic 'Moral Order' in the mid-1870s were the sons and grandsons of the 'Voltairian' bourgeois of the Restoration and the July Monarchy, when the Catholic Church was associated with Legitimism and the dominance of the aristocracy.[35] In the 1820s and 1830s bourgeois men had been the section of society most alienated from the church, and many of them had kept the spirit of the eighteenth-century Enlightenment alive. But the years 1848–51 had seen a major religious split within the bourgeoisie. Among one section, including many of the wealthiest members of this class, there was the beginnings of a 'return to the church'. Another section broke more decisively with the Catholic Church. In their eyes the church in throwing in its lot with Louis Napoleon had betrayed the democratic ideals of 1848 and given its support to arbitrary government. While Napoleon enjoyed a considerable degree of support, not only from the very rich, but from devout Catholics, and from large sections of the rural population, there were also those who resented the loss of freedoms under his rule. They included many members of this middle bourgeoisie. The lawyers among them saw themselves as the main defence of the citizen against the over-powerful state embodied in the Emperor. The academics resented interference with the University, and the journalists objected to press censorship. The middle-ranking businessmen felt that commercial policy was determined by the interests of the giant mining, metal-working and textile combines.[36] And all of them thought that the Catholic Church had too much power, especially within the education system.

Protestants and Jews were relatively numerous in this middle bourgeoisie, and many of them were convinced republicans. Both of these religious minorities had a prominence in the Third Republic that was out of all proportion to their small numbers – in 1880, after the loss of Alsace-Lorraine, about 2 per cent of the French population were Protestant and about 0.2 per cent Jewish.[37] But most republican politicians had been brought up as Catholics, and most had subsequently rejected their church. Many had become Freemasons. Under the Second Empire, Masonic Lodges had been strongholds of the anti-clerical middle class. Until 1876 the lodges declared their belief in 'The Great Architect of the Universe' (after that date this belief became optional), but their universalist faith repudiated what they saw as the particularism – as well as the superstitions and the authoritarianism – of the Catholic Church. Freemasonry also provided meeting-places for those who shared a common political and religious outlook and often similar social background, and it offered a network that could be used for defence in the hostile climate of the Second Empire and the Moral Order, for attack in the favourable climate of 1879 and the decades following. In these years, the lodges moved from being a refuge for rebels to being hives of careerism, as Masons were in a position to offer one another jobs on a huge scale, and to prevent jobs going to Catholics.[38]

Middle-class republicans, whether Protestants, Jews, anti-clerical Catholics, or Freethinkers, shared a number of common objections to the contemporary Catholic Church.[39] It was very hierarchical, whereas republicans were, at least in principle, committed to democracy and equality. The clergy, bishops and Pope were, at every level from the global to the most parochial, accused of having 'a spirit of domination'. This was the essence of Gambetta's famous speech of 1877, concluding: 'Clericalism? That is the enemy!':

> Gentlemen, if we do not act quickly to resist this spirit of invasion, which touches everything and neglects nothing – because it is for this reason that in families, in workshops, in the fields, every-where in fact, the opinion, the certainty has spread that ultra-montanism, clericalism, is all-powerful to protect the material interests of their clientele – if, I say, we do not act quickly to resist this spirit of invasion and of corruption, it will achieve its double goal of conquering the state and directing the masses.[40]

So, as Gambetta clearly indicated, questions of power were crucially involved. The most important objection to the church was that its links with reactionary old elites and influence over the people posed a double threat to the liberal republic. And even those republicans who had some sympathy with Catholicism in its liberal or gallican forms were repelled by the dominant ultramontanism of the second half of the nineteenth century, both because of the Syllabus of Errors and the dogma of Papal Infallibility, and because of the 'insult to the progress of science' contained in the claims that miracles had taken place at La Salette and Lourdes.[41]

Though liberal republicans were fairly much agreed as to what was wrong with the contemporary Catholic Church, they had widely varying views as to what forms of religion or world-view ought to take its place. The Freemasons, for instance, included among their ranks, as well as Protestants and Jews, the two main currents of middle-class Freethought, the 'materialist' and the 'spiritualist'. The materialists rejected all forms of supernaturalism. They hoped to subject all areas of the world and of human life to scientific analysis. In the 1860s materialist scientists, with their stronghold in the Paris Medical Faculty, had found themselves in conflict on various occa-sions with the university authorities or the imperial government. In a *cause célèbre* of 1868 a thesis submitted to the Faculty entitled 'A Medical-Physiological Study of Human Free-will' (which concluded that there was no such thing) was rejected by order of the government.[42] With the advent of the Third Republic many of these former rebels moved into prominent academic positions.

The spiritualists, by contrast, believed in God and the immortality of the soul. Their religion was both universal and progressive – they rejected the specificities and the alleged finality of revealed religion. At the same time, in spite of their great respect for science, they saw moral regeneration, rather than advancing scientific knowledge, as the indispensable key to human progress. And rather than rejecting, as the materialists did, all the prophets of previous faiths, they tended to claim them all as their own. If the materialists had Zola, the spiritualists were able to call on the support of an even bigger name – that of Victor Hugo. Spiritualism merged into the most liberal end of Protestantism where, around the end of the nineteenth century, the passionate commitment to free enquiry and liberty of conscience had led to a drastic pruning of traditional dogma. By the 1880s, however, atheism was advancing within the organised Freethought movement, where spiritualism was often regarded as a survival from an earlier era. How far such views retained a hold on the rank and file of anti-clerical republicans is harder to say.

One small pointer to the continuing vitality of both the materialist and the spiritualist traditions within French secularism is provided by an enquiry conducted by Jacques and Mona Ozouf in the 1960s. They sent questionnaires to thousands of retired primary school teachers, who had started teaching before 1914 – the secular profession par excellence in the heyday of anti-clericalism. When they were asked which authors had influenced them, by far the most frequent mentions were of Anatole France (19 per cent), Hugo (18 per cent) or Zola (15 per cent) – all writers noted for their anti-clericalism, but of three very different kinds, Zola being an atheist, Hugo a deist, and France being noted mainly for his ironic scepticism. The authors of the study note that the respondents frequently reported that having been believers in their childhood and sceptics in their young adulthood, they had more recently returned to a kind of belief, though without dogmas or formal practice. They often approved of 'religious feeling', while being suspicious of the church. Their views seemed close to those of the ultra-liberal Protestants of the late nineteenth century, with their stress on the conscience, the infinite, and the mystery at the heart of life.[43]

In Germany the liberal bourgeoisie exercised a wide-ranging social and cultural influence through the press, through their position in the universities, and through their role in adult education. Their political influence was much more limited. They were an important force at the local level, especially in city government, which they dominated from the 1860s to the First World War. At the level of the states, and later of the Reich, they were at their peak in the 1860s and 1870s. Among their greatest political monuments were the *Kulturkämpfe*, directed against the Catholic Church in Bavaria, Baden and then in Prussia, together with various measures enacted around the same time, designed to provide greater equality between religious bodies and wider freedom of religious choice for the individual.

Those German bourgeois who were actively involved in the churches tended to be theologically liberal.[44] In the 1830s and 1840s Protestant liberals wanted to free the church from its over-close ties with the state. They wanted elected parish councils, elected pastors, elected synods and maximum freedom for theologians to write, pastors to preach, and individual church-members to believe as their consciences led them, with a minimum of direction from above.[45] In 1848–9 ideas of this kind were put into practice in some states, but in the 1850s ties between church and state were again close, and in most cases conservatives were in control. In 1863 the Protestant Association (*Protestantenverein*) was founded, which became the chief organisation of Protestant liberals, campaigning for the maximum of doctrinal freedom within the church and autonomy for each parish. Unfortunately for them, greater democracy did not always work to their advantage.[46] Conservative Protestants took a closer interest in church affairs, turned up with greater regularity to vote, and on the whole were more successful in church elections. In Berlin, which was a stronghold of the Protestant Association, church elections showed a clear class pattern. The conservatives were strongest in working-class and lower-middle-class areas to the north and east of the city, and in areas like Dorotheenstadt and the Tiergarten, with large numbers of aristocrats, bureaucrats and army officers, while the liberals won in bourgeois Charlottenburg.[47] In the later nineteenth and early twentieth centuries, a lot of liberal energies went into defending freedom of conscience within the church, as the dominant conservatives tried to exclude pastors suspected of heterodoxy. This phase culminated in 1911 and 1912 with the Prussian church dismissing two very popular liberal pastors, Karl Jatho and Gottfried Traub.[48] In most areas the liberals were fighting an uphill battle in these years, and though they were influential in the universities, they had the support of a large part of the press, and they had local strongholds in Berlin, Bremen, Baden, Oldenburg and the Thuringian states,[49] there must have been a strong temptation to give up the fight, and accept that the church was conservative territory.

Of course liberals had an even harder time in the Catholic Church. The secession of many liberals to join the *Deutschkatholiken* in the 1840s naturally had the effect of strengthening the hand of the ultramontanes who had the support of Rome, a growing number of clergy, and some important members of the hierarchy. The dogma of Papal Infallibility, defined by the Vatican Council in 1870, led to the secession of the Old Catholics, who were drawn mainly from business and the professions, and especially from those who were National Liberals. Even among those middle-class Catholics who remained loyal to Rome (the great majority), there were many who were deeply unhappy with what they saw as the ultramontane dominance of their church.[50] But with the onset of the *Kulturkampf* Catholic solidarity became the overriding priority, and for many years liberal Catholicism was a private phenomenon that seldom found public expression.

In this situation, religious scepticism was widespread. There was also a phenomenon typical especially of men, but also of many women in the prosperous middle class, which does not quite fall into any other category – what was called *Unkirchlichkeit*. This is variously translated into English as 'irreligiousness', which is not quite precise, or as 'unchurchliness', which is not really an English word. Like its opposite, *Kirchlichkeit*, it does not denote any particular degree of dogmatic belief or religious fervour; rather, it reflects degrees of closeness to, or distance from, the church as an institution. By contrast with England where, in the first half of the nineteenth century, regular church-going had come to be seen as a requirement of respectability, frequent church-going came to be seen in wide sections of the Protestant bourgeoisie in north Germany as evidence of exceptional religious fervour, and most often linked with highly dogmatic beliefs. In Hanover in the early-twentieth century frequent church-going was criticised as being 'Catholic'.[51] In such cities as Berlin and Hamburg, as well as in many smaller towns, there was a large section of the educated middle class which was emphatically Protestant, reasonably well versed in the Bible and in Protestant doctrine and history, strongly committed to Christian ethics, as they understood them, but devoted to the rights of the individual conscience, and suspicious of anything overtly 'pious'.

This emerges clearly from Gunilla-Friederike Budde's study of middle-class childhoods in England and Germany in the years 1840–1914, based on autobiographies, diaries or interviews. All of the 211 Germans were brought up as members of a religious denomination – 77 per cent as Protestants, 13 per cent as Catholics and 10 per cent as Jews. But while the overwhelming majority of the English memoirists remembered their family going to church regularly in their childhood, this was much less common among the Germans. There was in fact a major confessional difference in Germany: 62 per cent of the Catholics had been brought up in church-going families, but Catholics were very much of a minority within the heavily Protestant German middle class. Among the Protestant majority, only 23 per cent had been brought up in church-going families.[52] The great majority of Protestants had been confirmed, and many of them had also been taught prayers or heard the Bible read at home. However, there was a widespread feeling that religion was a necessary part of childhood that, at least for men, did not extend into adulthood.

In families where the children *did* go to church – perhaps with their mother, grandmother, older sister or a servant – father would often be in his study working.[53] In accounts of the mentality of the *unkirchlich* German bourgeois around the end of the nineteenth century, one gets the sense that religion was seen as a suitable concern for women, children, aristocrats, and members of the lower classes, who either had time on their hands or whose work was of an intellectually undemanding kind, whereas the work of the businessman, professional man or academic left no time for more frivolous concerns, and could indeed be seen as a higher form of religion. Note, for instance, the stress on work in Nietzsche's comments on middle-class religious indifference in 1886. He stated that religious indifference was typical

> of the great majority of German Protestants in the middle classes, especially in the great industrious centres of trade and commerce, and of the great majority of industrious scholars and the whole university population, except for the theologians, whose existence and possibility there provides ever fresh puzzles for the

psychologists to solve.... They are no enemies of religious customs; if these are required, for instance by the state, they do what
is needed, as one does so many things – with a patient and modest
earnestness and without much curiosity or unease.[54]

Max Weber, in his famous lecture on 'Science as a Vocation' presented arguments on somewhat similar lines. To be a scientist was a
high and testing vocation, and one that by implication had a quasi-
religious quality. How else is one to interpret the almost poetic
language used by the normally sober Weber to describe the nature
of the scientist's calling? Yet the way in which he defined the calling
was one which excluded any kind of loyalty to a church.[55] In 1902
Paul Drews, one of the academic theologians whose existence
Nietzsche deplored, came to rather similar conclusions in his invaluable study of Protestantism in Saxony. Writing on the big cities,
Drews stated that: 'First of all the population divides itself into two
great camps: the women as a whole are devout (*fromm*) and *kirchlich*,
but the world of men, busy with a thousand questions of life, is
either completely indifferent to religious questions, or allows itself
to be as religious as custom seems to require'.[56]

To be *fromm*, however, was not necessarily to be *kirchlich*. *Kirchlichkeit* was bound up with all sorts of questions concerning one's view
of the church as an institution, of the clergy in general and, specifically, of the kind of people who made up the local congregation – and
indeed one's attitude to the state. For many state officials going to
church was seen as part of the job, and for many aristocrats it was
seen as a matter of duty; in some peasant communities there were
social pressures to attend church. But for the urban professional
and business classes in Germany (unlike England) it was largely a
matter of individual choice. Apart from the many middle-class men
who were religiously sceptical or indifferent, there were quite a lot
of educated middle-class women who were highly religious, but
seldom or never went to church.

One of the most powerful instruments for spreading the
opinions of the liberal bourgeoisie was the press. With the general
processes of liberalisation in the 1860s there was a great flowering of
the press in Germany, and especially of papers that combined a
liberal approach to politics and religion. As well as numerous local
papers, a number sprang up in these years, such as the *Berliner
Tageblatt*, *Kölnische Zeitung*, or *Frankfurter Zeitung*, which had a much
wider readership and assumed a powerful role in the shaping of

public opinion. Typically the editors of these papers were men who had been involved in the revolutions of 1848–9, often suffering subsequent persecution, and who were fierce critics of the conservative elements in German society.[57]

One of the most widely read of all the new journals to appear at this time was the Leipzig-based *Die Gartenlaube*, a weekly magazine, founded in 1853. At the height of its popularity in the 1870s, it sold 375,000 copies, and reached a huge readership with a combination of fiction, educational articles, numerous illustrations, and more discreetly presented political and religious comment. Its stance was typical of many of the papers of the time, and of the large element of middle-class opinion whose views it reflected and helped to shape. Its founder, Ernst Keil (1816–78), who came from a Saxon middle-class family, was a fervent liberal and an admirer of Heinrich Heine. After spending nine months in prison for his satirical journalism, he conceived the idea of a paper which would avoid direct political or religious comment, but would spread liberal and nationalist ideas indirectly. The targets included not only the aristocracy and the military, but also conservative forms of religion. Keil wrote that the *Gartenlaube* would 'enlighten the German bourgeoisie in such a way, that it would instil in it an aversion to every kind of church orthodoxy or superstition and, by educating people, fight against all forms of conservatism and romanticism'. So the fight against reaction had a religious and cultural, as well as a political and social, dimension. At least until the 1870s the paper was notable for its positive depiction of Jews – Jewish emancipation was representative of the extension of freedom, the self-made businessman (often Jewish) was the ideal citizen of tomorrow, and Jewish family and home life was frequently presented as a model. On the other hand, the undogmatic humanitarianism which they saw as the essence of true religion excluded theology, and made religious institutions and hierarchies suspect. As Wasserman comments, the symbol of Christianity became the Christmas tree rather than the cross.[58]

E. A. Roßmäßler, who wrote on science for the *Gartenlaube*, was also a leading member of the workers' evening class movement (*Arbeiterbildungsvereine*) set up by members of the liberal bourgeoisie in 1850s and 1860s. He had been a deputy at the Frankfurt Parliament in 1848, and he believed that the revolution had failed because of superstition and the lack of scientific knowledge. By educating the people, they would lay the foundations of the liberal and democratic society of the future. Instead of the hymns, catechisms and stories from the Old Testament learnt in the public elementary schools, they would teach the people Gerrman history, economics and modern science. This sense of being at the cutting-edge of 'modernity' was central to the self-image of the leaders of the movement. Very often this 'modernity' was identified with a specific intepretation of science as materialist, as incompatible with any kind of belief in the supernatural, and as providing the tools for the understanding of every aspect of the universe and of human life. While some of the leaders of the workers' educational movement and many of the popular writers on science explicitly condemned religion, or even claimed that they were offering a new and better religion, there were also many who avoided any direct attacks, and even suggested that their ideas were quite compatible with more liberal forms of religion. However, they were openly hostile to con-servative forms of Christianity, and especially to ultramontane Cath-olicism.[59] The attack on the Roman Catholic Church in Prussia in the 1870s brought together those like Bismarck, whose motives were overwhelmingly political, and many middle-class Liberals who had a much more deep-seated ideological objection to Catholicism.

Anti-Catholicism, which in England was often closely linked with evangelical Protestantism, was in Germany most fervently preached by liberal Protestants and religious sceptics – and used by them as a weapon in their battle against the conservative wing of the Protes-tant churches. The most famous of all the German anti-Catholics, Rudolf Virchow, who dubbed the fight against the Catholic Church the *Kulturkampf* (struggle for culture), was a militant unbeliever. Virchow, a prominent medical scientist at the University of Berlin, had beliefs very similar to many of his counterparts in France, including a deep confidence in science and its potential to improve the human condition, and bitter hostility to anything 'mystical' or non-rational.[60]

Within the Protestant churches, the main stronghold of anti-Catholicism, the Protestant League (*Evangelischer Bund*) founded in 1886 to continue a struggle in which the state had lost interest, depended on the support of liberal and moderate Protestants. Liberal Protestants and religious sceptics shared three major points in their critique of Catholicism (and by implication, conservative forms of Protestantism). Firstly they attached fundamental importance to the principles of freedom and the supremacy of the individual conscience. Luther's 'Here I stand, I can do no other' was quoted *ad nauseam*, and asserted as the fundamental basis of true

Protestantism. This meant that church hierarchies and official confessions were condemned. Secondly *Wissenschaft* (science) and *Bildung* (education) were the basis for all social progress – and indeed they carried an aura of the sacred. So Catholic claims concerning visions of Mary and miraculous healings were not only delusions – they were an affront to all that was most sacred. And by implication Protestant appeals for a change of heart and preaching of salvation by faith alone were also suspect – liberals were more inclined to believe in salvation by education alone. Thirdly, liberals could not accept the idea of creeds or confessions valid for all time: just as the world was in a process of continuous evolution, and knowledge in a process of constant advance, so must religion progress. The attack on ultramontane Catholicism was highly visible, while that on conservative Protestantism was less often openly avowed, but the historian and *Kulturkämpfer* Heinrich von Sybel was at least partly right when he declared that the battle was not one between confessions, but 'the struggle within both confesions between the spiritual compulsion imposed by the hierarchy and the spiritual freedom represented by the state'.[61]

In the 1860s and 1870s middle-class liberals were confident that history was on their side. They already had a dominant position in the worlds of industry, commerce and education, and now it seemed that political power was also coming to them. With typical self-confidence the journal of the Society for the Extension of Popular Education, headed by such Liberal luminaries as Virchow and the heads of the Borsig and Siemens engineering firms, condemned alike 'those who live in the past' ('feudal Conservatives', 'Romish Jesuits' and particularists opposed to the new German state) and 'those who live in the future' (Social Democrats and other ultra-radicals). As masters of the present, the Liberals could afford a certain amount of lofty disdain for those who opposed them. Where French anti-clericals liked comparing the clergy to reptiles or insects, the German *Kulturkämpfer* preferred light/dark imagery. The Catholic milieu was conceived in terms of *Finsternis* (darkness), and ultramontanes were *Finsterlinge* (creatures of darkness) or *Dunkelmänner* (dark men).[62]

This identification of Catholicism with darkness was further emphasised by a conception of German culture and German nationhood which saw both as specifically Protestant achievements. Daniel Schenkel, a founder of the Protestant Association, declared in 1862: 'We say with the deepest conviction: the entire cultural progress of peoples in our century is based on the foundation of religious, moral and intellectual freedom, and for that reason upon Protestantism'.[63] Similarly, while German literature was generally regarded as one of the foundations of German identity and a cornerstone of German claims to be regarded as a *Kulturvolk* (people of culture), Luther's Bible was regarded as the beginning of German literature and Catholic authors were frequently excluded from the canon or marginalised within it. Some of the most influential historians of the *Kulturkampf* era, such as von Treitschke and von Sybel, presented the struggle against Rome as a central theme of German history, linking otherwise disparate epochs.[64]

In England liberal members of the middle class were as important as they were in France in the fight to reduce the influence of the Established Church and to bring about a religiously neutral state. The big difference is that few of them were religious sceptics. Though the British Liberal Party represented a coalition of diverse religious forces, by far the most important of these was Protestant Dissent. Congregationalists, Baptists, Methodists, Unitarians and Quakers – many of them very devout – were at the heart of the attack on religious privilege and the union of church and state.

A microcosm of the interaction between socio-economic and poltical-religious change is offered by Bradford, the centre of the worsted industry, and said to be the world's fastest-growing city in the first half of the nineteenth century. In the period from about 1800 to 1830 the ruling oligarchy was Tory and Anglican, drawn from a combination of local gentry, professionals and rentiers descended from the successful merchants and manufacturers of earlier generations. But the 1830s and 1840s saw the emergence of a new elite of self-made businessmen, who had come from relatively modest lower-middle-class families, and most of whom had been born outside Bradford. They were Liberals, most of them were Nonconformists, and many of them had received a rather strict religious upbringing. They despised what they saw as an effete and parasitic old elite and they espoused the virtues of self-help. The most important institution associated with this new elite was Horton Lane Congregational Chapel, identified by Koditschek as 'a cathedral of Nonconformity', and attended by four of the town's first five mayors as well as the editor of the *Bradford Observer*. The links between their religion and their economic lives were a strong sense of calling and the concept of 'character'. While most had received little education, they were passionate self-educators, and later they tried to promote adult education more generally through Mechanics' Institutes. They also supported the temperance movement.[65]

The Municipal Reform Act of 1835 enabled similar groups of Nonconformist business and professional men to take over the government of numerous provincial towns, and from the 1830s to the 1880s there were intimate links between Liberal urban elites and the Nonconformist chapels. Simon Gunn, in his study of the middle-class elite in Manchester, notes the erection around the middle of the nineteenth century of a number of very imposing Anglican churches and Nonconformist chapels, and suggests that 'the size, cost and grandeur of religious buildings announced the wealth and power of the urban middle class a decade or more before the construction of the great town halls'. He goes on to argue that Nonconformist ministers were the 'organic intellectuals of the urban middle class' and that their prestige was at its peak in the 1860s and 1870s, when their sermons were 'a fulcrum for the complex of discourses linking class and culture, capitalism, politics and religion'.[66]

Birmingham in some respects offers a striking example – though its magnificent classical Town Hall was actually built in the 1830s. In the later 1860s the Midland city was the centre of the National Education League, and in the 1870s it was the site not only for a brief experiment in purely secular Board School education, but also for an ambitious programme of 'Municipal Socialism'. The political leader of Birmingham Radicalism was Joseph Chamberlain, a Unitarian screw manufacturer, and the most prominent politician to embrace the cause of disestablishment of the Church of England. But just behind him were a group of outstanding Nonconformist preachers, whose sermons provided legitimation and some of the theoretical underpinning for Chamberlain's 'Civic Gospel'. They included the Congregationalist R. W. Dale, of Carr's Lane, and George Dawson of the undenominational Church of the Saviour. Their chapels were attended by Liberal councillors, prominent businessmen and journalists, and their support at election times was eagerly sought by Chamberlain.[67] Typically the leader of the movement for the disestablishment of the Church of England was a Nonconformist minister, the Revd Edward Miall, whose Anti-State Church Association, founded in 1844, later became the Society for the Liberation of Religion from State Patronage and Control. As this latter title indicated, religious arguments bulked as large as Liberal political principles in the association's propaganda. Its constitution declared: 'the application by law of the resources of the state to the maintenance of any form or forms of religious worship is contrary to reason, hostile to human liberty, and directly opposed to the Word of God'.[68]

In England, at least until the 1880s, the predominant element in the liberal bourgeoisie was Protestant Dissent, though there also were liberal Anglicans and Freethinkers. The huge range of Non-conconformist denominations provided for many different kinds of theology and cultural orientation. The Unitarians were the most liberal in theology and the most open to literature and the arts, with the Baptists and in particular the Wesleyan Methodists tending to theological conservatism and cultural puritanism, the Congregationalists somewhere in between these extremes, and the other denomination with an important element of the prosperous middle class, the Quakers, standing outside most conventional categories.

The 1880s mark a turning-point in two respects. In 1886 the Liberal party split over the issue of Irish Home Rule. Many of the Nonconformist business elite were among those who left to join the Liberal Unionists – the beginning of a political journey which, at least in the next generation, usually ended in the Conservative camp. This move away from political Liberalism was often associated with a move away from religious Nonconformity, whether in the direction of the Church of England or of religious neutrality. Meanwhile the same period saw a substantial growth in agnosticism among the middle and upper classes. The last Liberal government of 1905–15, generally regarded as one of the greatest reforming administrations in British history, still depended on Nonconformist voters and local activists. But at the top it was to a considerable extent led by agnostic politicians and advised by agnostic experts and civil servants. This agnosticism was informed by specific intellectual developments, such as Darwinism and the critical approach to the Bible, but most important perhaps was a positivist mentality, in terms of which the way forward lay through the accumulation of facts and figures, and the reconstruction of society along more ordered and rational lines. Religion thus tended to be seen as irrelevant, though seldom regarded with the hostility that was common in secular liberal circles in France. And, in keeping with the less polarised religious atmosphere in England, there was in any case a considerable degree of religious pluralism in the

Edwardian world of liberal reform. If a discreet and low-key agnosticism was the prevailing tone, one of the rising stars of the Liberal Party, C. F. G. Masterman, was an Anglo-Catholic who had been strongly interested in ordination.

At the local level, Nonconformists, often drawn from lower down the social scale than their mid-Victorian predecessors, still played a crucial role in Liberal politics, and in furthering the expanding role of local councils. Nonconformist ministers were still among the most influential supporters of the Liberal cause. In the south London borough of Lambeth, for instance, around the turn of the century, the leaders of the Progressives, a coalition of Liberals, Radicals and Labour, included several shopkeepers, a builder, an undertaker, a Nonconformist minister, and some who were teachers or local government employees. Many of them were Congregationalists or Wesleyans. 'These local politicians', writes Cox, 'looked upon Lambeth's chapels as bases from which they struggled to promote social and political reform, to co-ordinate voluntary and government activity for the improvement of the condition of God's suffering poor, and to create a more just and Godly society in England.'[69]

The Expert

The religious radicalism of new elites frequently faded as they achieved the social status and a share of the privilege and power that they sought, and gradually merged with older-established elites. Some emerging professions, however, found themselves in a longer-lasting rivalry with the clergy, either because their fields of competence overlapped, or because of the pretensions of the clergy to regulate their activities.

In the eyes of many liberal reformers of the late nineteenth and early twentieth centuries, the place of the preacher, appealing for a change of heart, was to be taken by the expert – the scientist, the medical practitioner, the teacher, the social worker – with specialised knowledge and professional skills. In 1874 the English scientist Francis Galton had called for 'a sort of scientific priesthood', which would come to supersede the clergy.[70] Now such ideas seemed to be coming to fruition.

The clearest example of a 'new priesthood' in direct conflict with the old is that of the teaching profession in France. There had been a long-standing tension between the teachers' self-perception as an independent profession and the view held by many clergy who saw the teacher as an adjunct of the priest and responsible to him. But the tensions became much more acute from 1879 onwards, as republican governments made the secular school the key instrument in the inculcation of republican values and loyalties. Already in the 1860s, when attendance at chapel was compulsory, it was said that students at the *École Normale Supérieure* in Paris 'showed a studied disrespect for religion, shambling into chapel in slippers with a copy of Voltaire under arm'.[71] In the teacher training institutions (*Écoles Normales*) a strongly anti-clerical ethos seems to have developed, promoted by professors who were necessarily committed republicans, and who were often strongly opposed to the Catholic Church, whether from a Freethinking or from a Protestant point of view. Many future teachers seem to have lost their Catholic faith while at the training college, whether under the influence of fellow-students, who considered it 'good form' to stand hat on head and scarlet flower in button-hole while religious processions passed, or of teachers, who preached the 'scientific' ideal and encouraged the reading of Renan, Haeckel and Taine.[72] They often went out into the countryside as missionaries for the republican faith. In one Norman village in 1909 the newly arrived 20-year-old teacher found herself boycotted for a year by sixty-one of the sixty-three children in the village after she refused to withdraw a history textbook condemned by the bishops. She was very proud of the fact that she 'held up high the secular and republican flag' throughout the year, thus becoming a heroine of the secularists of the department, and eventually most of the children returned to school.[73] This teacher held a trump card, since hers was the only school in the village, but where there was also a rival Catholic school the conflict was likely to last much longer. Even where the teachers went to their schools hoping to keep the religious peace, the local situation often made neutrality, let alone any kind of practising Catholicism, difficult.

In the 1960s questionnaires were sent to thousands of retired primary school teachers who had begun teaching before 1914. Only 11 per cent of those replying to the questionnaire stated that they had been practising Catholics before 1914 – which was considerably below the proportion in the general population. Protestants (4 per cent) were slightly over-represented and Freethinkers (32 per cent) vastly so. The great majority were to the Left politically, with a significant element among them being committed

Socialists.[74] The generation of teachers represented in this survey may form an extreme case, since most of them would have started in the years around the Separation of Church and State in 1905, when tensions between republicans and the church were at their most acute. But the distinctive ethos which came to characterise a large part of the French teaching profession had deeper roots in the rivalry that had developed between priest and teacher, each with a mission to shape the mentality and morality of the common people.[75]

In England education was notoriously a major field of sectarian rivalry, but the secular ethos so powerful among the profession in France never seems to have made much headway. There are indeed some parallels with the French situation. Board Schools were regarded with great hostility by some of the Anglican clergy, especially those of High Church views. Supporters of Board Schools, including Joseph Chamberlain and some of his associates in the National Education League, sometimes ascribed a messianic role to the new schools in the spreading of enlightenment, uncontaminated by clerical interference and dogma, to the masses. Yet the reality of the Board Schools fell some way short of these dreams. In the first place, clergy of all denominations proved very successful in getting themselves elected to the School Boards, so that religious concerns and denominational interests played a bigger part in their running than those like Chamberlain had expected.[76] And partly for this reason, most School Boards provided for non-sectarian religious teaching in their schools. Contemporaries and subsequent historians have differed as to the merits and effectiveness of this teaching. But it could not be argued that English Board Schools were guided by a secularist ethos. Nor were teachers as a profession a notably irreligious group. Quite the reverse, in fact: one of the considerations leading Anglican clergy gradually to modify their hostility to Board Schools was the recognition that elementary school teachers were among the more devout professions and that they included many practising Anglicans among them.[77] A paean of praise to the Board School, and its healthy influence in a poor district of London, referred to 'not the teaching alone, but the influence of direct personal magnetism of right-minded, God-fearing men and women'.[78] One reason for the presence of many Anglicans on the staff of Board Schools was the fact that teachers trained in church colleges were lured away from church schools by the promise of better salaries[79] – which is an interesting example of the relative fluidity of ideological boundaries in England. There was indeed bitter controversy in London in 1894 following a circular by Athelstan Riley, a High Anglican and a leading member of the Moderate (Conservative) majority on the Board, insisting that religious instruction include explicit teaching of the doctrine of the Trinity. This was strongly opposed by the teachers' union (as well as by the Progressive minority on the Board), but their argument is revealing: they claimed that most teachers were happy to teach this doctrine, but that the circular violated the religious freedom of the minority who could not conscientiously do so.[80] Still less could charges of secularism be levelled against the grammar schools, attended by the middle class, or the public schools, attended by the upper middle and upper classes. Throughout this period these schools were generally pervaded by an Anglican ethos, and whatever the views of individual teachers might have been, the open expression of secularist views would have been out of the question.

In Germany the situation was somewhere between that in France and England. Here there were long-running tensions between the clergy and the teachers in the elementary schools (*Volksschulen*) over the issue of clerical inspection. There was also the issue of the so-called *Küsterschule* (only finally abolished by Hitler) in which the teacher was also expected to carry out what he regarded as menial duties in the church – a source of humiliation, but also of extra income. Consequently teachers had a reputation for anticlericalism. They were prominent on the democratic side during the revolutions of 1848–9[81] – so much so that Friedrich Wilhelm IV of Prussia actually blamed the revolutions on the bad influence of radical teachers. In the later nineteenth century, tensions between teachers and clergy seem to have been greatest in Bavaria, where the Catholic clergy were particularly assertive in pressing the view that the school was primarily a religious institution, and in condemning the Liberal and German nationalist politics of most of the teachers. An added problem was the fact that many of the clergy (and of the rural population) thought that the best teachers were nuns.[82] The national teachers' union was associated with the Left Liberals in politics and abolition of the direct links with the church was among its standard demands. Apart from wanting fellow teachers, rather than clergymen, as school inspectors, they also favoured inter-confessional *Simultanschulen*. However, there is little evidence of French-style militant irreligion. From about 1905 onwards, there were frequent calls for reform of religious teaching, but only in the radical strongholds of Hamburg and Bremen was there much demand for a purely secular school. More representative were the Saxon teachers, who, in a manifesto of 1908, adopted a liberal Protestant position, which included a central focus on 'the thinking of Jesus', teaching that would be 'in harmony with the well-established results of scientific investigation and the advanced ethical experiences of our time', and 'biographical sketches of proponents of our religious and moral culture in relation to our people in modern times'.[83] Whatever their reservations about clerical interference, most of the teachers seem to have been loyal members of their own denomination, and often active church-goers. For instance, teachers tended to be one of the largest occupational groups on Protestant parish councils, and were particularly prominent on the liberal side.[84] The fact that applicants for entry to teacher training colleges had to pass an examination in religious knowledge and that the colleges themselves imposed an extensive regime of religious observances may have filtered out many of the religiously indifferent.[85]

Tensions between clergy and the medical profession could be even more acute. Again, these were most visible in France, where there was probably no profession more commonly associated with anti-clerical or anti-Catholic views than that of medical doctor, and medical students were proverbially to the fore in anti-clerical demonstrations, masquerades and charivaris.[86] From the 1870s onwards a number of the most prominent figures in the medical profession were outspoken Freethinkers. For instance, in the early 1900s the Dean of the Paris Medical Faculty, Henri Roget, was also president of the Rationalist Union.[87] Two of the most fervently anti-clerical politicians of the Third Republic, Georges Clemenceau and Émile Combes, were medical doctors, as was Alfred Naquet, who introduced the bill to legalise divorce. Combes's choice of career was the more pointed in that he had turned to medicine after being rejected as a candidate for the priesthood. Nor were these celebrities isolated examples: no less than seventy-two Deputies in 1898 were doctors.[88] Doctors as a profession were generally associated with political Liberalism in later nineteenth-century Germany and had a reputation for *Unkirchlichkeit*.[89] But in this they seem to have been typical of the educated bourgeoisie, rather than standing out in the way that they seemed to in France. In England too, by the later part of the century, most doctors seem to have been typical members of the upper middle class – which meant that most were likely to be regular church-goers.[90]

But even where open conflict was lacking, major sources of tension between the clergy and the medical profession existed. Religious explanations of illness and prescriptions for cure could conflict with the medical version, and medical proposals for prophylaxis were sometimes subject to religious objections or counter-proposals. Medical men found themselves in direct competition with healers whose credentials were religious rather than academic. There could also be tensions between ultimate objectives: those doctors who believed that the relief of pain must always override all other concerns were in potential conflict with priests who believed that the pursuit of other-worldly salvation superseded all merely this-worldly concerns. And for some people the conflict was even more fundamental. For them, science was the faith of the new age, and the doctors were its miracle-working saints. At the same time, the polarisation was never complete. Approaches to questions of sickness and healing varied considerably within the various churches, and even in France, where the tensions were greatest, by no means all doctors were anti-Catholic.

One example is offered by the terrible cholera epidemics which hit western Europe at frequent intervals between 1831 and 1892. In the eyes of many clergymen these were to be seen as divine judgements, and the wrath of God was to be assuaged by public displays of piety and by turning away from the sins which had brought about the visitation. Catholic writers thought it significant that the first French city to be attacked by cholera in 1832 was Paris, which they regarded as a citadel of irreligion. Since the doctors could offer no convincing reason for the epidemic, these Catholic writers suggested that a supernatural explanation was the most credible.[91] Anti-clerical national and local officials in France rejected all demands for official days of prayer, and government and church saw themselves in competition with one another in the distribution of charity. In Britain, however, a national day of Fasting and Humiliation *was* decreed.

By the time of the next major epidemic in 1848–49 opinion was changing, and not only among medical men. In Paris, Catholic writers and preachers much less frequently interpreted the epidemic as a judgement, and more often insisted that prayers should be combined with medical precautions.[92] Meanwhile in Britain, the Bishop of London, in a sermon on the cholera, put the main stress on the need for improved sanitary measures. At the time of the next major epidemic in 1854, the Home Secretary, Lord Palmerston, rejected calls for a national day of prayer, arguing that prayers were only appropriate after all necessary medical and sanitary precautions had been taken.[93] He had the support of an important section of church opinion, among which the most outspoken was the Christian Socialist and novelist Charles Kingsley. Kingsley belonged to the liberal 'Broad Church' wing of Anglicanism, which was strongly opposed to all attempts to divide the world into sacred and secular spheres, which saw the pursuit of truth in all its different forms as a God-given task, and therefore saw the scientist, teacher or social reformer, if motivated by love of humanity, as doing what was essentially religious work. But there were still many clergymen who intepreted such disasters as the bad harvests in 1860 and 1861 and the cattle plague in 1866 in theological, rather than natural, terms. And while the clergy did show an increasing tendency to accept natural explanations for such disasters, they continued to believe in the possibility of divine intervention in response to prayer. Particularly fierce controversy flared in 1871. On Sunday 10 December prayers were ordered to be said in Anglican churches for the Prince of Wales, then seriously ill. When, the following Thursday, his condition began to improve, leading to eventual recovery, this was widely seen as an answer to prayer – except by the medical profession, which saw it as a triumph of modern medicine.[94]

In France, medical jealousy was also caused by Catholic priests – or, more often, pious laypeople acting independently of the clergy – who claimed healing powers, and who provided a service which was either free, or at least a lot cheaper than that provided by the qualified practitioners, who sometimes called the law to their defence.[95] Since the time of Napoleon, practising medicine without the necessary certificates had been an offence punishable by imprisonment, and throughout the century a regular trickle of clergy, as well as larger numbers of wise men or (more often) wise women found themselves behind bars. The importance in Catholic life of shrines such as Lourdes and of the miraculous cures claimed by pilgrims added an extra dimension to the tensions between religion and medicine.

Medical men also came into conflict at least with sections of religious opinion over measures prescribed for containing disease. Prostitution was one potential source of conflict. Medical opinion tended towards the view that prostitution was a necessary evil, and that its harmful consequences, such as the spread of venereal diseases, could best be contained by having tolerated brothels with compulsory medical inspections. In England, thinking of this kind lay behind the Contagious Diseases Acts of 1864–69 which regulated prostitution in towns with major military and naval bases, and which were fiercely opposed by Nonconformists and feminists.[96] The grounds for opposition included liberal, feminist and religious arguments, but probably the most widely accepted of these was opposition to any kind of state recognition of prostitution. In France the introduction of anaesthetics caused dispute, because of Catholic fears that a patient who died while under the anaesthetic would not have had the opportunity to prepare for death by confession and receiving extreme unction.[97]

In France, the hospitals were also contested territory in similar fashion to the schools during the early years of the Third Republic. Catholics preferred to be nursed by nuns, in hospitals under saintly patronage, with crucifixes and religious pictures hanging on the walls and official chaplains readily available to minister to their spiritual needs. By the same token, anti-clerical municipalities such as Paris, dedicated to the principle that public space must be religiously neutral, pursued a vigorous policy of secularising the hospitals, only allowing that patients could be visited by a priest from outside the hospital (not an official chaplain), if they explicitly requested it. Advocates of secularisation claimed that nurses belonging to religious orders not only violated freedom of conscience by forcing religion on those who did not want it, but also lacked professional training, had poor standards of hygiene, and were insufficiently deferential to the doctors. It was therefore essential to replace the nuns with a corps of well-trained secular nurses. Four training institutions were established in Paris between 1878 and 1895 under the direction of Dr Bourneville, who was also a Paris municipal councillor and a member of the executive of the National Association of Free-thinkers. Under his leadership the ethos of these colleges was as strongly republican and secular as that of the teacher training colleges.[98]

In the later years of the nineteenth century there were many people who regarded the doctor as a symbolic figure. Not only was he a standard-bearer of modern science: he also embodied the determination to apply this knowledge for the betterment of the lives of ordiary people. While priests offered illusory miracles now or the distant hope of rewards in a life to come, the doctor offered a better life here and now. The idealised figure of the doctor as modern saint takes particularly clear shape in the novels of Émile Zola. The hero of the 'Three Cities' trilogy, Pierre Froment, was a priest who lost his faith partly under the influence of Dr Chassaigne. The latter was 'a medical man of real merit, who, with the one ambition of curing disease, modestly confined himself to the role of practitioner'. In spite of the Catholic rural background from which he came, he 'had not set his foot inside a church during the forty years that he had been living in Paris'. The doctor was a friend of Pierre's father, a scientist, who had been killed in a laboratory explosion. Through him, Pierre rediscovered his father, seeing him as 'clear and gay, a worker consumed by a longing for truth, who had never desired anything but the love and happiness of all'. Thus 'little by little, despite himself, the light of science dawned upon him, an ensemble of proven phenomena, which demolished dogmas and left within him none of the things which as a priest he should have believed'. At the seminary he had been forced to keep 'the spirit of inquiry, his thirst for knowledge in check'. But now 'Truth was bubbling up and overflowing in such an irresistible stream that he realised that he would never succeed in lodging error in his brain again'. The association of science with images of light and of springs of pure water, and with ideas of health, joy and freedom, was characteristic of the scientific faith, and of course very closely paralleled much of the imagery associated with various forms of religious faith. But even more significant was the attempt to trump the religious believers' ace – the lives of the saints – by showing that secular saints were possible.[99] And in this endeavour the freethinking doctor was a key exhibit, since he was seen as combining commitment to science with compassion for human suffering and the practical skills that could make an effective difference. A real-life counterpart to Zola's heroic doctors was Dr Alphonse Vincent (1880–1935), 'the doctor of the poor', who was Socialist deputy and a director of secular charities in the Creuse, a department noted alike for its anti-clericalism and its devotion to its saints, and who was described as a 'secular saint'.[100]

Religious believers did not remain passive in the face of such attacks. In later nineteenth century France the claim that secular nurses had a better professional training was implicitly accepted and countered by an improvement in the training given to nuns. And in spite of the exclusions operated by secularist local authorities, such as Paris or Reims, the number of nuns practising as nurses continued to increase until the 1920s, although proportionately they suffered some decline. Catholic doctors countered the strength of secularism in the profession by forming organisations like the *Société Médicale St Luc*, which combined attempts to define the Catholic view of various medical issues with pilgrimages, and a job-finding network for Catholics within a profession where many influential figures were Freemasons. After a slow start, the society had over 2000 members in the 1930s, by which time the traditional medical anti-clericalism had considerably abated. This society, aided particularly by the Medical Faculty of the Catholic University of Lille, played a big part in formulating a Catholic counter-ideology to the appropriation of medicine for the cause of secularism by propagandists such as Zola. According to this Catholic view, the non-religious doctor was likely to be a mere 'technician', whereas the Catholic doctor was motivated by Christian charity to feel for the patient as a person, with spiritual, emotional and material, as well as medical needs.[101]

The greater tensions between clergy and medical profession in France than in Germany or England may be partly due to differences in the social background of the clergy. In Germany the Protestant clergy were unmistakably part of the educated bourgeoisie, and the great majority of them had a university education. Though their status was in some ways declining in the later nineteenth century, their social background was similar to that of doctors, and in many respects their way of life was not very different.[102] In England the social range of the Anglican clergy may have been somewhat greater, moving up into the gentry, and down into the lower middle class, but most were unquestionably 'gentlemen'.[103] The French Catholic clergy drew from lower down the social scale. Typically in the second half of the nineteenth century they came from peasant and artisan backgrounds.[104] They had been educated at seminary, rather than university. Where a rural Anglican clergyman or German Protestant pastor might naturally include the local doctor in his social circle, this was much less likely in the case of the French rural priest. The strengths and weaknesses of the French Catholic clergy were very different from those of their Anglican or German Protestant counterparts.

Radicals

Du passé faisons table rase
Foule esclave, debout! debout!
Le monde va changer de base,
Nous ne sommes rien, soyons tout . . .
Il n'est pas de sauveurs suprêmes,
Ni Dieu, ni César, ni tribun,
Producteurs, sauvons-nous nous-mêmes:
Decrétons le salut commun!

[Let us make a clean break with the past. Rise up, you crowd of
slaves! The world is going to change its basis. We have been
nothing, let us be everything.... There is no supreme saviour,
neither God, nor Caesar, nor any tribune of the people. Produ-
cers, let us be our own saviours, let us legislate for our common
salvation.]   (Eugène Pottier, *L'Internationale*, 1887)

The *Internationale* owed its unique popularity as the anthem of
international socialism more to its rousing tune than to its often
laboured text. But it expressed clearly enough the desire of many
radicals for a clean break from religion of every kind. Marx in the
1840s had claimed that the criticism of religion was the starting-
point for the criticism of society.[105] Since the most powerful
ideological underpinnings for existing social arrangements were
so often religious, it is not surprising that political radicals were
the most outspoken critics not only of the church, but also of
religious doctrine and ritual. In the 1840s, as we have seen, criticism
of the existing social order was more often than not expressed in a
religious idiom. From the 1850s and 1860s, religiously based radicalism was in sharp decline in France and Germany, though it
remained influential for longer in England.

The 1860s saw a major growth of anti-clericalism and anti-
religion in France, culminating in the events of 1871. The Paris
Commune seized priests as hostages, and shot twenty-four of
them, including the Archbishop of Paris, Mgr. Darboy, ensuring
that most Catholics hated the Commune and everything it stood
for. Pope Pius IX referred to the Communards as 'demons escaped
from hell'.[106] The bloody repression of the Commune which
followed ensured that the Left had a far larger number of martyrs.
The mass executions at the Mur des Fédérés in Père Lachaise

Cemetery provided the French Left with its most sacred site, while the building of Sacré Coeur on the heights of Montmartre, in reparation for the crimes of the Commune, was a highly visible provocation for those Parisians who cared more for those buried by the wall than for the murdered priests.[107]

In the decades following, French radical culture, whether in its working-class, its petit bourgeois, or its intellectual and bohemian forms, was saturated with anti-clericalism, often extending to a total rejection of all religious faith.[108] These tendencies developed very rapidly from about 1880 among supporters of the republican government. The church was seen as the principal pillar of political and social conservatism, and it was therefore mandatory for Radicals and Socialists to seek its destruction, even though Socialists claimed that religious issues should take second place behind social and economic issues. However, other considerations played a part beside the purely political. In particular the Radicals and Socialists of this time were heirs to long traditions of songs and jokes focusing on the wealth of the clergy, their love of good food and drink and, in particular, their abuse of the confessional in order to tyrannise and, where possible, seduce women.[109] In the case of the Socialists, rejection of older religious traditions was partly based on the conviction that Socialism contained within it all that was necessary for human salvation, and that anyone who retained older loyalties was trying to serve two masters, and must therefore be less than wholly loyal to the Socialist cause. From the 1880s French Freethinkers, including many Socialists, were devising new rituals, designed to cut their members off from the old Catholic world.

This tendency went even further in Germany where, especially after 1890, an elaborate network of Social Democratic institutions and accompanying celebrations and rites developed, designed to embrace every area of the comrade's life. Becoming a Social Democrat was not only a matter of voting, attending meetings, reading party newspapers and joining a trade union. It might also include marching through the streets on May Day, singing in a workers' choir, pedalling with a workers' cycling club, drinking in a socialist pub[110] – and formally resigning from the church. The latter step required two time-consuming visits to the municipal offices, and so was not undertaken lightly. The first movement of mass resignations from the churches (*Kirchenaustrittsbewegung*), organised by some Social Democrats in 1878, was a failure; but a second movement, in the years 1906–14, produced several tens of thousands of resignations in Berlin, as well as smaller numbers in Hamburg, Frankfurt and many other towns. The ratio of resignations to population was in fact highest in Bremen.[111]

In some of the early strongholds of Social Democracy, such as Berlin and Hamburg, the level of involvement in the Protestant church was already low. But in others, such as 'red' Saxony and the Thuringian states, the growth of socialism in the 1860s and 1870s was matched by a substantial decline in Protestant practice.[112] For Social Democratic activists a distinctive world-view became normative: a synthesis of Marx and Darwin provided a total explanation of the natural and social world, and all supernatural religion had been exposed as 'unscientific' – and, perhaps more importantly, as a tool of reaction. These objections to religion were reinforced by the popularity of anti-religious writers and orators, and by those of the German classics, such as Goethe, Schiller and Heine, who were seen as critical of religion. To be fully integrated into the powerful socialist sub-culture which was developing in later nineteenth-century Germany it was necessary to lose all religious beliefs and loyalties, and for many Social Democrats of this time it would seem that the loss of faith was thus a relief. This tended to be most difficult for Catholics, for whom the church, the clergy, religious symbols and pious observances of all kinds, were often a ubiquitous part of the environment in which they had grown up. It was easier for Protestants and Jews, whose ties with church or synagogue were often fairly loose before they became involved in socialist politics. From the point of view of most Social Democratic activists, the Protestant Church was condemned by its close links with the state, with Conservative politics, and sometimes with big business; the Catholic Church was condemned by its association with the Centre Party, one of the Socialists' major electoral rivals, as well as by the fact that papal teaching explicitly rejected socialism; and, more generally, religious 'prejudices' were seen as a major obstacle in the way of acceptance of the socialist world-view.[113]

In 1920 a German Social Democratic factory worker recalled the great turning-point of his life, some thirty years earlier, the time of his conversion to socialism. In the mainly Catholic district where he lived, the socialists were a small and isolated group. 'All "right-thinking" people turned their back on them, and the more pious people were, the crazier their ideas about the activities of the "reds"'. However, the socialists were always on the look out for new members, and the author was picked out as a likely candidate because he was known to have a sceptical attitude to 'the dear clergy' – though he still believed in God and an after-life, and saw in religion the source of his highest moral ideals. He was soon converted to the political and economic goals of socialism, but 'My greatest difficulty in the development which now began was the real inner conquest of all the religious ideas which lay within me and which influenced me through my environment'. For a long time he saw socialism as the practical application of the commandment to love one's neighbour, and of the religious duty to fight against injustice. Only gradually did he come to understand the materialist view of history and of nature – the latter through such books as Dodel's *Moses or Darwin?* and Haeckel's *The Riddle of the Universe*, which had a big influence on many socialists of that generation who were moving away from Christianity.[114]

Several points here are characteristic of the secularism of many political radicals during this period. In the first place, rejection of Christian belief was often a consequence rather than a cause of entry into radical politics. Secondly, becoming a socialist meant entering a sub-community that was self-consciously different and in conflict with the 'right-thinking' elements in society, for whom the acknowledged opinion-leaders were the clergy. And thirdly, to be fully integrated into this counter-culture, it was necessary to adopt a distinctive world-view, which was explicitly at odds with the orthodoxies of state, church and school. Scientific materialist and anti-religious writers, together with certain of the German classics, assumed an important role in the process of integration, since, although they had nothing directly to do with socialism, they provided a rationale for the rejection of Christianity or Judaism.

Nonetheless the overall picture was not so simple. In the first place, women were much less politically active than men – in fact they were not able to vote until 1919, and in Prussia they could not join a political party until 1908 – and they were much more likely to retain ties with the church. This was one reason why, for instance, the great majority of children continued to be baptised and later confirmed, in spite of the decline in church-going and participation in communion.[115] In the second place, there were Social Democratic activists – admittedly rather few in the pre-1914 period – who continued to belong to one of the churches, and to insist on the compatibility between their religion and their politics. This was perhaps easier in areas where the churches had a strong working-class following, and Social Democracy accordingly felt it wise to avoid antagonising potential voters by anti-religious rhetoric. In the Catholic stronghold of Munich, for instance, where the local party leaders were determined to avoid religious controversy, some prominent Social Democrats were church-going Catholics. In eastern Westphalia, one of the most strongly Protestant regions of Germany, propagandists for the socialist Free Trade Unions were said in the 1890s to go 'Bible in hand', and Carl Severing, one of the few socialist leaders of this period to remain a believing Protestant, came from this area. There was also a large group of those who voted Social Democrat, without becoming strongly integrated into the socialist subculture, who remained members of the Protestant church, though seldom attending its services, and who saw no tension between these two loyalties.[116] On the whole, the boundaries between the world of the church and the world of Social Democracy were sharpest in the cities, with their social segregation, and their concentrated working-class districts where the Social Democratic Party often had a dominant influence and, in the eyes of its critics, operated a form of 'terrorism'. The overlap between the world of the church and the world of the party was greater in areas of large villages and small towns, where industry and agriculture lived side by side, and many factory workers had a small plot of land.[117] In such districts observers were struck by the apparent discordance of the symbols decorating the walls of the people's homes. Thus Thuringian workers placed scriptural texts and framed confirmation certificates beside the portraits of leading Social Democrats. In another such area, the Erzgebirge, where Luther would hang beside the Virgin Mary, Bebel next to King Albrecht of Saxony, a pastor commented: 'In the soul of the people, it is the same as it is on the wall; they bring together harmlessly the things that are most opposed'.[118]

There was an important secular element in English radicalism too, though it never achieved the kind of dominance that it enjoyed in France or Germany. From the 1850s to the 1880s the Secularist movement was an important aspect of working-class and lower-middle-class radicalism. Its leaders, George Jacob Holyoake and Charles Bradlaugh, were widely popular, and Secularists were prominent in such important popular institutions as the Co-operative Societies and the trade unions, as well as in campaigns for democracy, republicanism and land reform. In a few industrial areas, including central and east London, south Lancashire, west Yorkshire and the north-eastern coalfield, Secular Societies had quite a

high profile. Even so, there were many radicals in the period from
the 1850s to the 1880s who were also chapel-goers, and in certain
branches of trade unionism, notably agriculture and mining, Nonconformists had a central role. Similarly, both Secularists and
Nonconformists were prominent among the growing number of
converts to socialism from the 1880s onwards. Ironically the socialist
movement weakened both Secularism and Nonconformity: recruits
to the Social Democratic Federation or Independent Labour Party
often retained their former religious or anti-religious beliefs, but
concentrated their energies on political activities, with the result that
their former affiliation lapsed or became largely dormant.[119]

For many, perhaps most, radicals of this era, rejection of the
established church was a matter of course. But relations with Dissent
were more complex.[120] There were indeed some very moderate
Secularists who had links with very liberal Nonconformist chapels,
but there were also many secular radicals who had either rejected
a Nonconformist upbringing, or who had become Secularists
after a period as a chapel-goer.[121] The secularist socialist view of
the world in the early twentieth century is presented with unique
vividness in Robert Tressell's caustic novel of Edwardian working-
class life, *The Ragged Trousered Philanthropists*. The continuing
resonance of these views (and also, probably, the continuing tension
between secular and religious versions of socialism) is suggested by
the fact that when in 1994 Labour MPs were asked which author
had influenced them most, Tressell was the winner – narrowly
ahead of R. H. Tawney.[122] It is significant that Tressell's attacks on
organised religion are directed at Nonconformity – the Church of
England is simply ignored. Many of the employers of Tressell's town
of Mugsborough belong to the Shining Light chapel, as does the
tyrannical foreman, Hunter. The fact that the employers bear such
names as Didlum and Sweater, while the pastor of the chapel is the
balloon-like Revd John Belcher, indicates that Tressell's satire is
sometimes heavy-handed, though more subtle irony is directed at
the charismatic assistant minister, Revd John Starr. But the most
savage invective is directed at working-class members of the chapel,
who are described as 'tame, broken-spirited, poor wretches',
'attendants at various P.S.A.s and "Church Mission Halls" who
went every Sunday afternoon to be lectured on their duty to their
betters'. 'They had to sit there like a lot of children while
they were lectured and preached at and patronised'. So for
Tressell the rejection of religion was above all a declaration of

independence – a decision by the worker to think for himself, and to reject every form of deference, and every kind of emotional tie to the exploiters and their minions.[123]

For large numbers of working-class people, all over Europe, these years around the end of the nineteenth century and the beginning of the twentieth marked the dawn of a new era of radical change. For many, traditional religion and the churches seemed at best an irrelevance, and at worst a major obstacle to the realisation of their hopes.[124] In France, rejection of the Catholic Church was more or less mandatory for Socialists in the pre-1914 period. There were French Socialists – including the most famous of them all, Jean Jaurès,[125] as well as many Protestants – who believed in God: the problem lay not in belief, but in institutional loyalty, and especially in submission to the hated *calotte*.[126] In Germany, by contrast, there was a significant, albeit small, minority, of those who managed to be both a loyal member of church or synagogue and of the Party. However, the pressure on party members to adopt the whole socialist world-view, including atheism, was greater than in France. In England, the situation was typically confused: every tendency that could be found in French or German socialism could be observed somewhere in England too, but there was no prevailing orthodoxy.

Men

'Women are different beings' (*'les femmes sont autres'*), the dying Dr Barois tells his son, the hero of Roger Martin du Gard's novel, *Jean Barois*.[127] In successive generations, the men of the Barois family have been engaged in spiritual warfare with their wives, mothers and daughters, and it is the women who seem to be winning. Dr Barois, a lifelong freethinker, has finally relented: on his death-bed he has said his confession, and he is about to invite the family to join him in receiving communion. The same drama was to be repeated in the next generation. Jean has been brought up by his devout grandmother, and in his youth he is himself a practising Catholic and marries a Catholic girl. As a science teacher in Paris he loses his faith. His marriage breaks down, since neither he nor his wife is willing to compromise. After being dismissed from his job in a Catholic school, Barois becomes the editor of a freethinking journal, and a leading Dreyfusard. Meanwhile his daughter is being brought up as a Catholic in a small country town. When she is eighteen, she comes to stay with her father in Paris. Jean, who has not seen her since she was a baby, falls under her spell. It emerges that she wants to be a nun, and that the time spent with her notorious father is a way of testing her vocation. It eventually appears that it is not *her* faith but *his* that is being undermined. A combination of factors including, not least, an increasingly obsessive awareness of his own mortality, is pulling the veteran freethinker back towards the Catholic Church (and towards his wife), and the dual influences of his devout and undoubting daughter and of a sympathetic and doubting priest provide the decisive push. In his last months, Jean too becomes a Catholic again. After his death his wife and the priest discover the testament, written some years before, in which Barois had declared that any death-bed conversion was to be seen as an aberration and disregarded – and the novel ends with the paper going up in flames.

The situation described by Martin du Gard would have been familiar to any of his French readers, and to many of those in England and Germany too. There was general agreement that where religion was advancing in the nineteenth century it was women who led the way, and where it was declining the way was led by men. Women played a crucial part in the reopening of churches after the French revolutionary persecutions in the 1790s, and in initiating family conversions during the American Second Great Awakening in the 1820s and 1830s.[128] In France the impressive growth in the number of male religious vocations up to 1880 was overshadowed by the even more impressive growth in the number of female vocations.[129] Analysis of the membership of English Nonconformist churches, which also were growing at least until the 1880s, shows that women chapel-goers were more likely than their male colleagues to apply for formal membership. This entitled them to participate in the Lord's Supper, and tended to reflect a higher level of commitment and probably a more confident faith. Clive Field, who has analysed records of Baptist and Congregational churches from the mid-seventeenth century to the mid-twentieth, has shown that throughout this period women were a clear majority, but that the proportion of women increased in the nineteenth century, reaching a peak in the early twentieth.[130]

However, our concern here is with trends towards secularisation, where roles were reversed. Where in nineteenth century Europe church attendance was declining it generally seems to be the case that men were leaving at a faster rate than women, and as a result a startlingly wide gender gap often, opened up. This was most spectacularly so in some regions of France. Already in the middle of the nineteenth century there were many rural parishes where not a single man received communion, and the number of such parishes increased considerably during the later years of the century, reaching its highest point during the first decade of the twentieth century.[131] This phenomenon developed first in the rural areas surrounding Paris, though later it would spread to other areas, most notably the Creuse. Already in a pastoral letter for Lent 1842, the Bishop of Chartres was telling the women of his diocese: 'You are almost, at least in the places where we live, the Church's only consolation'.[132] In fact, the proportion of women going to mass or receiving communion in these areas was not high either – but they completely outnumbered the men. In 1898, the first year when separate figures for adults of each sex are available, 2 per cent of men and 15 per cent of women in the Chartres diocese received communion at Easter.[133] In more devout dioceses women were always more practising than men, but the disproportion was smaller.[134]

In Germany and England the imbalance between male and female practice was much less. In 1891–95 the median proportion of women among the communicants in the various Protestant *Landeskirchen* was 55 per cent. However, the proportion was highest in the cities of Berlin (62 per cent), Hamburg (63 per cent) and Frankfurt (71 per cent).[135] In view of the fact that Protestant religious practice in Germany was much higher in rural than in urban areas, this would be consistent with the pattern seen in France. In 1902–3, 61 per cent of worshippers at places of worship of all denominations in the County of London were women, though women were only 53 per cent of the population aged fifteen and over. The gap was widest among Anglicans (66 per cent women) and Roman Catholics (64 per cent), but narrower in the various Nonconformist denominations. For instance, 60 per cent of Baptist worshippers were women, 57 per cent of Congregationalists and Wesleyans and only 52 per cent of Quakers or Primitive Methodists. Conversely, the German *Kirchenaustrittsbewegung* recruited more men than women – though the differential was not spectacular. Thus, 62 per cent of those leaving the church in Berlin in 1913 were men; a study in one Protestant parish showed that while most of those leaving were married couples resigning together, those who resigned individually were nearly all men.[136] Similarly, men were heavily predominant in Freethought and Secularist movements. In the late nineeenth century about 80 per cent of the members of the Secular Societies in Leicester and Huddersfield were men. Lalouette reports an average of 92 per cent male membership in French Freethought societies during the Third Republic.[137]

There was also a distinctively Jewish form of the divide between increasingly secular men and more faithful women. Judaism distinguished, in a way that Christianity did not, between those religious duties which were the responsibility of men and those which fell to women. The synagogue was men's sphere, while the home was women's. Simlarly, religious study and scholarship were male matters, while there were forms of religious observance prescribed for women, such as ritual bathing after menstruation. In the later nineteenth and early twentieth centuries, men continued to attend synagogue in far geater numbers than women. For instance the religious census of London in 1903 showed that 78 per cent of the adults attending synagogue on the first day of Passover were men. However, there is also a good deal of evidence to suggest that synagogue attendance was declining, while domestic religious observances declined much less. So the balance was shifting from forms of religious practice which were the responsibility of men to those which were mainly the responsibility of women. The sabbath eve meal with lighted candles, the kosher kitchen, and celebration in the home of the various Jewish festivals continued to be widespread, even while sabbath observance weakened, congregations dwindled, and Talmudic scholarship declined.[138]

Whether in Jewish or in Christian homes, the religious disengagement of many men was clearly a possible source of tension. This disengagement could take passive forms, as with the men who stayed working in their study or in the garden, or who drank and played cards in the pub while their wives and children went to church. In many households there seems to have been an accepted division of labour whereby religious matters were simply part of women's sphere of responsibility. However, where husbands were more actively opposed to their wives' piety, relations could become more strained. Some husbands discouraged their wives' church-going by sneers, or even by violence. Baptisms or funerals could occasion big battles, since women who had given up going to church on Sundays still often insisted that the great turning-points in life be marked with due solemnity and with religious rites. The fiercest conflicts often arose where the husband was a political radical, convinced that the church was not only wrong, but a powerful and dangerous enemy. In cities like Hamburg and Berlin around the end of the nineteenth century there are stories of babies brought secretly to baptism by their mother or grand-mother. In France around the same time, where the 'civic' funeral had become the most important symbol of rejection of the church, bereaved families quarrelled not only over the will but also over the manner of burial.

Conflicts of these kinds were common in France, but relatively rare in England, with Germany falling somewhere between the two extremes. Mary Hartman's study of middle-class women accused of murder in nineteenth-century Britain and France offers some vivid examples both of the ways in which religion might contribute to marital disharmony and of the differences between the two coun-tries. In most of the cases studied the alleged victim was the hus-band or lover of the accused. None of the British husbands or lovers adopted an explicitly anti-religious attitude, and most were church-goers. None of the French husbands or lovers is known to have been a church-goer and some did their best to oppose their wives' religious practices. For instance, Henri Lacoste, a retired shop-keeper, whose sudden death in 1844 led to his wife being charged with poisoning him, was said to have upset her by constant attacks on the church and clergy and to have strongly discouraged her from going to church. Marin Fenayrou, a Parisian pharmacist, con-victed together with his wife in 1882 of murdering her lover, was sufficiently voluble in his anti-clericalism to be labelled by the press a second Homais. His wife's piety, though not sufficient to prevent her taking part in the murder, led her to go to church beforehand to pray that her lover would not arrive at the fatal rendezvous.[139]

There were many reasons why it was men who took the lead in giving up church-going or other forms of religious practice, or in becoming avowed unbelievers. It should first be recognised that long before the nineteenth century Christian women tended to be more devout than Christian men, and that even in societies where declared unbelief was very rare, male anti-clericalism was often widespread.[140] It is not surprising, therefore, that when the nineteenth century offered an unprecedented degree of religious freedom, it was men who most often used this freedom to leave the church or drop all religious belief. However, there were other factors more specific to the nineteenth century which also contributed to this trend. Of these the most important was the fact that men tended to be far more politically active than women, at a time when religion and politics were deeply bound together. Sometimes religious and political loyalties could be mutually supportive, as with the Lib-Lab-voting Methodist miner in county Durham and the Centre-voting Catholic miner in the Ruhr, but at other times they might be in severe tension, as they were, for instance, for a Socialist-voting Catholic miner in the Pas-de-Calais. In the tension between religious and political loyalties in the second half of the nineteenth century, it was very often the religious loyalty which lost out.

As already mentioned, certain professions, for instance French doctors and teachers, found themselves collectively at loggerheads with the church. More generally, liberal political attitudes, implying at least some degree of distance from the church, were very wide-spread during the Restoration and the July Monarchy. And in spite of the 'return to the church' of the upper bourgeoisie after 1848, most professional men and many owners of small and medium-sized businesses remained republican and anti-clerical during the Second Empire and the early years of the Third Republic. They discussed politics with other men at work, in cafés, and at the Masonic Lodges, which were the spiritual home of the French anti-clerical middle class. They were less likely to discuss politics at home, where questions to do with the church were potentially explosive. There are numerous examples of prominent republican politicians whose wives and/or daughters were pious Catholics. Already in the 1840s, the historian of the French Revolution, Jules Michelet, had described in graphic terms the lack of spiritual comradeship in many middle-class homes: 'We can speak to our mothers, to our wives, to our daughters, on subjects about which we might speak to strangers...but not about those things which touch the heart of the moral life, eternal things, religion, the soul, God'.[141] In the later years of the century such republican luminaries as Jean Jaurès had pious wives, and the fictional Jean Barois had a real-life counterpart in the Positivist leader, Émile Littré, who seems to have undergone a death-bed conversion, partly under his wife's influence. (This episode was, in fact, bitterly disputed, with Free-thinkers alleging fraud, and Catholics celebrating this apparent proof of the insufficiency of Positivism in the face of death.)[142]

In Germany, too, liberal politics were often associated with a sceptical or luke-warm religious attitude, and middle-class marriages saw frequent differences in religious attitude between husband and wife. Nonetheless, because the confessional divide tended in Germany to be deeper than the divide between believer and unbeliever, the situation was different. Protestant Liberals who lacked religious faith tended to concentrate their fire on the Catholics, and to retain a sense of Protestant identity, however little they believed in God or Jesus Christ. Bismarck's *Kulturkampf* did wonders for the cause of Catholic solidarity. And most non-religious Jews remained nonetheless Jews. In the case of Protestants and Jews in Germany, piety was less closely bound up with public religious observances than it was with Catholics. There were many devout Protestant and Jewish women who practised their religion in the home, while seldom crossing the threshold of church or synagogue. One rather striking example of a middle-class woman whose religion was entirely private, but nonethelss central to her whole understanding of the world, was Caroline Valentin (1855–1923), who belonged to the educated bourgeoisie of Frankfurt, and who left behind her a diary from the 1880s, when she was a young mother, unhappily married to a husband who was a disciple of Schopenhauer. Crushed by her husband's coldness, and full of guilt because of an affair with one of his colleagues, she confided in God all her cares and concerns, and also her thankfulness for her two children. They were her chief joy, and she saw them as divine gifts.[143] There were also many middle-class women who had little to do with the church, but prayed, read the Bible and sang hymns at home. The household in which the future Protestant theologian and martyr, Dietrich Bonhoeffer, grew up in the early twentieth century would be an example. His father, Professor of Psychiatry in Berlin, was a political Liberal and a religious sceptic. His mother was a devout Lutheran, and Dietrich learnt his faith from her. But as a theology student in the 1920s he remarked that until then he had very little to do with the church.[144]

Such situations may have been even more common in Jewish families. When the father had completely given up religious observance, and the passing on of religious tradition had become the sole responsibility of mother or grandmother, it tended to be domestic observances that they passed on. Marian Kaplan quotes numerous examples.[145] The son of a wealthy Berlin family, born in 1876, recalled that he received no religious education and his family took no notice of the dietary laws or of the Sabbath, but his mother taught him to pray every night, while his grandmother herself prayed every morning in a singsong Hebrew, rocking backwards and forwards, and bowing – all of which he found rather comical.[146] The son, born in the same year, of a couple who ran a small business in a Saxon town, recalls that his parents never went to synagogue and observed Christian rather than Jewish festivals (because that fitted the needs of their business better). But every Friday evening his mother read from the prayer book, standing at the prescribed moments.[147]

Conflicts between employer and worker contributed to the development of a strong sense of class-consciousness on the part of many male workers, which often found expression in hostility to churches and clergy. Class-consciousness flourished in the hierarchical and strictly disciplined atmosphere of factory and mine, where workers had immediate experience of the tyranny of employers and the arrogance of officials, and also of community with workmates and the need for organisation. Women, on the other hand, might have more first-hand experience of the tyranny of their husbands than of employers, and their community of neighbours and kin was not necessarily limited to members of their own class – especially in areas where the working class was not concentrated, and where many workers came from a peasant or lower middle-class background, it would probably be women who retained their links with members of other classes for longest. Furthermore, the characteristic division of labour between spouses could be a source of serious tensions. Women, faced with the task of feeding and clothing a family, could resent the diversion of scarce resources into political or trade union funds, the purchase of books and newspapers.[148] Certainly there were women who were strongly committed radicals and socialists; women who took an active part in the revolutions of 1848 or the Paris Commune; and of course women who campaigned for the right to vote and for other rights. But the fact that women continued throughout this period to be barred from voting in national elections, and that even where female membership was permitted few parties did much to encourage female membership, all contributed to relatively low levels of political interest among women.

Some historians have argued more generally that the churches remained strongest in pre-industrial sections of society, whereas involvement in modern industry led to a rational and mechanistic outlook, hard to reconcile with supernaturalist religion. In the most eloquent version of this argument, Bonnie Smith has suggested that the bourgeois women of Lille remained devoutly Catholic, because they lived in a world dominated by the tasks of giving birth to and bringing up children, both largely subject to factors beyond human control. Their husbands, however, whose life was dominated by the highly mechanised textile industry, were mostly religiously indifferent.[149] Similarly, sociologists and historians have noted that the social classes closest to the church in nineteenth-century Germany – the aristocracy, the peasantry, and the lower middle class of craftsmen and small shopkeepers – were those least involved in the modern industrial economy. Their 'pre-industrial' way of life has been suggested as the explanation for their religiosity.[150]

These kinds of argument stress too one-sidedly the influence of people's work on their beliefs. Beliefs could also shape people's understanding of their work. Furthermore, the relationship between work and belief is not a constant, but is shaped by the social, political and religious context. The religious proclivities of particular occupational groups owe much more to this situation than to anything inherent in their profession. Thus industrialists, who in the mid-nineteenth century were often religiously indifferent in France or Germany, were in England very likely to be prominently involved in church or chapel. Artisans and shopkeepers, who in Germany were often regarded as the most devout section of the urban population in the second half of the nineteenth century, were in France regarded as the group most prone to militant anti-clericalism.[151] This point has been demonstrated particularly clearly in a history of English and Scottish fishing communities from the later nineteenth century to the present day. This showed both that the religious situation in different fishing ports varied very widely – some, for instance, being strongly influenced by Methodism, some by Calvinism, and some showing little interest in religion of any kind – and that religion could have a major impact on the local economy and culture, as well as vice versa.[152] If, in the second part of the nineteenth century, a large part of the male population was alienated from the church, this was due much less to the nature of the work they did than to the social conflicts arising out of their work situation, and the political loyalties that often arose out of these.

Other factors contributed to the detachment from religion or the church of specific sections of the male population. Access to higher education was a male monopoly for much of the nineteenth century, and with it came access to a vast range of new ideas on religion, often of a highly critical kind. In this, Germany, where Strauß and Feuerbach were major influences in the 1830s and 1840s, was a little ahead of France, where Comte and Renan had a big following in the 1850s and 1860s, and both were ahead of England. The significance of higher education should not be exaggerated, since most of these authors were soon widely popularised. But it remains true that middle-class men often had access to a wider range of new ideas than did their wives.

As Magraw suggests, there was also an important element of machismo in male anti-clericalism.[153] In both Protestant and Catholic environments men who went to church could be accused of being under the thumb of their wives, and thus being traitors to their sex. So in the Wuppertal in the 1880s, the Protestant Workers' Association was referred to as the *Schluffenverein*, (*Schluffen* being a dialect word for 'slippers', and a man who 'wore slippers' being one who took orders from his wife).[154] In the Tarn in 1899 a Socialist deplored 'the lamentable spectacle' of seeing men at church because they 'have been unable to resist their wives'. Priests could be looked down upon as not being 'real men' – a Tarn republican paper in 1870 ridiculed them for 'dressing like women'[155] – and yet at the same time regarded with suspicion and jealousy because of their influence over, and alleged skills in seducing women. In his book of 1845 entitled *On Priests, Women and the Family*, Michelet had vehemently attacked the clergy for subverting the authority of the male head of the family: 'Your mother sadly shakes her head, your wife contradicts you, your daughter silently disapproves. They are on one side of the table, and you on the other side, alone.' And 'sitting opposite you in the middle of the women' is 'the invisible man', the priest.[156] Many other men of all social classes echoed these thoughts. They especially objected to the confessional, both because the requirement to confess was seen as a blow to male pride, and because it was seen as a key weapon in the priests' bid to control women. Indeed the objection to confession was so strong that in some otherwise devout dioceses there were many men who went regularly to mass but could not receive communion, as they would not go to confession.[157]

The Tarn Socialist mentioned above referred to 'our wives, fascinated by these men of lies'.[158] This sexual jealousy was mainly directed against Catholic priests. The ability of Protestant preachers to attract a large female following was a frequent theme for humorous comment – but the humour was more often directed at the

women than at the preachers.[159] Nevertheless there were Protestant forms of anti-clericalism too, and in the nineteenth century they
were a predominantly male phenomenon. Critics of the Protestant
clergy who really wanted to draw blood focused on two opposed
stereotypes. One version which was prevalent in the early and
middle years of the nineteenth century presented the clergy as
men of power and often wealth, well-dressed and well-fed, hand
in glove with members of other elite groups – and by implication
totally removed in spirit from anything one might find in the
gospels.[160] A rival view, which became more frequent as the century
progressed, reflected the decline in the status and influence of
the clergy: now they were presented as well-meaning but ineffectual
observers of the world, the humour or pathos arising from the
discordance between the pretensions of the church and its real
power. A striking example of the genre was a sardonic depiction
of an execution in the German satirical magazine *Simplicissimus*
in 1899, which showed the chaplain praying, with an expression
of pious anguish, while everyone else (except, of course, the victim)
appeared to be thoroughly enjoying themselves.[161] Either way, anti-
clericalism in the nineteenth century was a predominantly male
phenomenon. It was mainly men who saw clerical power as an
affront to their own rights. And when clergymen were accused
of 'feebleness' or 'effeminacy' the attacks also came mostly from
other men.

In all three countries, religion was a normal part of childhood, for
boys as well as girls. They were taught prayers by their mothers,
they received religious teaching at school, they went to Sunday
School or to catechism classes. Only towards the end of the nineteenth century, with the emergence of a self-consciously secularist
minority, some children being brought up in an entirely non-
religious way, and this remained very much the exception. With the
onset of adolescence, however, the paths followed by the two sexes
began to diverge – very sharply in many parts of France, though the
gap was narrower in England and Germany, or in more strongly
Catholic regions of France. The differences were already visible
around the age of thirteen or fourteen. This may partly reflect
differences in the way that boys and girls were brought up. In
France, for instance, far more girls than boys were sent to schools
staffed by religious orders. But even where girls and boys were
educated in the same way, they responded differently. German
Protestant pastors found that the girls' confirmation classes were

much more attentive and better behaved than those for boys. In England, where the great majority of working class children went to Sunday School, both boys and girls – but especially boys – often gave up going to church when they started work.[162] In the later teenage years, the difference between the religious behaviour of the two sexes became quite marked. In many parts of France it was expected that girls and young women would continue to go to mass until they married, whereas there was no such expectation for young men. In fact male youth were allowed a certain amount of space for rowdy behaviour that was denied their female counterparts. A striking example from a slightly earlier period was the response to the efforts of the curé d'Ars, Jean-Marie-Baptiste Vianney. By the time of his death in 1859 he was regarded as a saint, and he attracted pilgrims from all over France to his remote rural parish. But when he came in 1818 he had faced an uphill task in a parish where religious practice had declined since the Revolution. His earliest successes were among the teenage girls, many of whom joined his Confraternity of the Rosary, which met on Sundays at the same time as the dances which Vianney condemned. The last group to fall under his sway were the young men who, up to 1830, continued to protest loudly against all attempts to interfere with their leisure activities.[163]

Rowdy and sometimes irreverent teenage boys did not necessarily grow into irreligious men. But by the later nineteenth century there were many parts of western Europe where piety was seen as a normal and desirable part of womanhood, and irreligion as an equally normal part of manhood. Young women who sought respect and acceptance within their community were likely to emulate the religion of their mothers; and young men were most likely to gain such acceptance if they followed their fathers by rejecting the religion of their childhood. So in France, especially, and to a lesser extent elsewhere, the religious differences between men and women often went back to adolescence, and to two contrasting patterns of religious bevaviour learnt at home, and reinforced within the peer group. Those French bourgeois men who came from religiously divided homes, and who carried over their Catholicism from childhood into adulthood, seem often to have been strongly influenced by their mothers and to have had a bad relationship or none at all with their fathers.[164]

In conclusion, two points need to be stressed: firstly, that the growing gap between more religious women and more secular men is to be observed in all three countries, in all social classes, and within each of the major confessions; secondly, that the extent of this gap varied greatly as between these different environments – for instance, it was very wide indeed in some parts of France, whereas in England it was generally much narrower. The general phenomenon of women's greater religious involvement in nineteenth-century (and twentieth-century) Europe has to be explained in terms of a very wide range of contributory factors, some of which have been discussed in this section. The more specific phenomenon of the almost complete alienation of men from formal religious practice in some parts of France and Germany was primarily a result of liberal, radical or socialist politics. Where such alienation existed, other considerations, such as the husband and father's fear of losing control over the female members of his household, might arise to reinforce a rejection of church and clergy that was mainly politically motivated.

Catholics, Protestants and Jews

It is often remarked that a Catholic atheist is something very different from, let us say, a Methodist atheist. And while one cannot say that any one of the major religious confessions in western Europe was more vulnerable than the others, it is possible to point to typically Catholic, Protestant or Jewish patterns of secularisation.

In the later eighteenth and nineteenth centuries it was Catholic France that led the way in the development of popular irreligion and in the passage of anti-clerical legislation; yet in Germany and England between about 1890 and 1960, Catholics were much more resistant than their Protestant neighbours to the secularising trends.[165] Though clearly the differences are partly explained by differences in the situation of Catholics in the three countries, the defeats suffered by the church in many parts of France and the successes achieved in Germany, England and, indeed, other parts of France, could also be seen as two sides of the same coin. In fighting the dangers of secularisation in the nineteenth century the Catholic Church employed a high-risk strategy. It involved a central role for priests and nuns,[166] the building of a network of strongly Catholic institutions and organisations, and a heavy emphasis on the maintenance of dogmatic orthodoxy and moral conformity, often reinforced by explicit threats of hell, as well as by exclusion from the sacraments, and by naming and shaming from the pulpit. Where the clergy succeeded in keeping the respect and trust of the majority of the people, this high-profile style of leadership could be very effective in maintaining a tightly-knit, cohesive and disciplined Catholic community. But when this respect and trust were weakened, Catholic loyalty could collapse very rapidly. Anti-clericalism was central to the Catholic form of secularisation in a way that it seldom was in a Protestant or Jewish environment.

Many aspects of the priest's role were double-edged. Celibacy was an important part of the mystique that surrounded the highly-regarded priest, and it had consequences that were potentially positive for the priest's popular image. While the family life of the Protestant pastor, and such things as the clothes worn by his wife or the schools attended by his children, helped to place an indelible stamp of class upon him, the social status of the Catholic priest was more ambiguous and flexible.[167] Similarly, while the Protestant pastor often felt a tension between the demands of his family and his parish, the Catholic priest was more likely to be available whenever his parishioners decided that they needed him. On the other hand, the priest's celibacy, together with his ambiguous form of dress, led to the definition of the clergy as the 'third sex', and thus as beings outside the normal dispensation of nature. This could be a subject of derision, but also of unease, mixed with a degree of respect – in the folklore of Catholic cultures, the priest has often been seen as a figure with mysterious powers, not always used for benevolent purposes. These feelings were not entirely absent in Protestant cultures – for instance George Eliot refers to 'the clerical sex', and tales or 'superstitions' concerning the clergy have their place in Protestant, as well as Catholic folklore.[168] But this bundle of conflicting feelings towards the clergy was much more typical of Catholics. Similarly with the confessional: the resentments and jealousies which it provoked have already been described. Yet, it was in the confessional that Jean-Marie-Baptiste Vianney, the curé of Ars, won his reputation as a saint, and in his later years, penitents would come from all over France to confess to him. Another example is that of the Irish-born Fr. Murnane, regarded as a saint in his London dockland parish: he was 'in tremendous demand as a confessor – and at most inconvenient times', 'a peacemaker with a wonderful way with him of solving troubles, especially family troubles'.[169]

More generally, in exalting the role of the priest and the part played by him in the salvation of his people, the church raised expectations extremely high. When a priest lived up to these expectations the gratitude and devotion of his parishioners could be very great, but when he failed, their disappointment was correspondingly bitter. The need for each village to have its own priest was partly a matter of local pride: in Zola's novel *The Earth*, the far from pious municipal council finally decided that its long-standing refusal to pay for repairs to the church and presbytery, and the consequent lack of a priest, had given their commune a reputation for meanness and thus damaged its prestige. But the people also needed the sacraments. Even in Zola's Rognes (based on a village near Chartres), the municipal councillors were influenced by the knowledge that some of the women preferred to be married and buried by a priest.[170] In the more pious diocese of Belley, the absence of a priest was felt most keenly when the dying were unable to receive extreme unction. In 1839 one such priest, who had accepted an invitation to dinner, rather than going to visit a dying parishioner, was the subject of a petition to the Ministry of Public Worship asking for his removal.[171]

The sources of potential conflict between a Catholic priest and his parishioners were numerous. An analysis of the causes of disputes between priests and parishioners in this diocese[172] showed that the most common causes of trouble were local politics, faction fights, personality clashes, and so on – potential minefields for any minister of religion. But there were a number of other recurrent problem areas: notably disputes concerning the sacraments, arising either, as mentioned above, from the priest's absence at the vital moment, or more commonly his determination to impose unpopular conditions for the reception of the sacraments; disputes over money; the morality and life-style of the priest, with sex and to a lesser extent drink, being the main causes of complaint; and national politics – which in this diocese came to the fore from 1859 onwards, when many clergy, putting the interests of the papacy first, condemned Napoleon III's support for Italian unity. In the 1840s, 1850s and 1860s such disputes frequently led to the majority of parishioners boycotting the church, at least temporarily.[173] In a period of militant anti-clericalism, such as the 1880s, they were likely to become a part of wider political struggles. The extraordinary variety of abusive epithets devised by French anti-clericals to designate the clergy offer one indication of the depth of feeling involved and the obsessive quality that this hatred frequently acquired. Priests were most commonly referred to as 'crows' (because they wore black), but rats, spiders, snakes and pigs were among the numerous other zoological similes. Many new words were coined to designate the clergy, and the republican politician and later Minister of Education, Paul Bert, speaking at a banquet in the wine-growing department of the Yonne in 1879, even compared the clergy to phylloxera.[174]

In France both Protestants and Jews were attracted to secular liberalism. For Jews it seemed to offer the hope of a society in which they would be treated as equals, in which merit rather than confessional origin would be the key to advancement. In the case of the Protestants there were considerable continuities between secular liberalism and some of the more modernist forms of Protestantism, and the one shaded easily into the other. This step-by-step conversion to some kind of humanism as, in effect, the highest form of Protestantism, was one of the characteristically Protestant forms of secularisation. It was seen very clearly in the evolution of the German Free Parishes in the 1850s and 1860s. There are hints of this in the British Labour Churches, formed from 1891 onwards, mainly in northern England, by socialists and trade unionists, many of whom had been Nonconformists, but had left their chapels in protest at the support of most of their ministers for the Liberal Party. Members of the Labour Churches came from a variety of religious backgrounds, ranging from evangelical Protestant, via Unitarian, to Marxist. And here was one of the major practical problems that these new churches faced. The only way to preserve some kind of unity was to suppress all potentially contentious theological issues and to focus on socialism as the goal of all their efforts and the labour movement as the instrument by which it would come about.[175] As one Scottish socialist later recalled, they were guided by 'Religion the binder without Theology the Separator'.[176] Some of those who continued to value the theology returned to the older churches. But an equally common tendency was for the religious basis for socialism to fall into the background as practical political activity took precedence, and for the politics rather than the religion to be passed on to the next generation. Similar tendencies can be seen within French liberal Protestantism.

In the early years of the Third Republic, Protestants, mostly on the liberal wing of their churches, played a big part in republican politics, especially in the field of education policy.[177] In many cases, their passionate identification with the cause of the Republic and equally passionate hostility to the Catholic Church and to all forms of 'dogma' and religious hierarchy (including those embodied in the evangelical wing of their own church) led them in a direction of a humanist faith in which all specifically Christian elements were gradually eroded. The most notable example was the former pastor, Ferdinand Buisson, appointed Director of Primary Education in 1879, and a principal author of the Republic's programme of secular moral education. While the dogmatism and clericalism of the Catholic Church often provoked a bitter reaction, ending in a total rejection of the Christian faith and church, liberal Protestantism potentially endangered Christianity and the church in the opposite way. By its radical rejection of 'dogma' it opened the way to a questioning of all orthodoxies, which sometimes, though not necessarily, led to agnosticism or atheism, and more often led to a purely personal theology, which had little relation to any previously existing orthodoxy. By its equally radical relativisation of the church, it opened up the possibility that God might be working primarily through political and social movements,[178] and that any involvement in the church might be a diversion from more urgent tasks. Among those from a liberal Protestant background, a continuing emotional attachment to Christianity was often combined with considerable distance from most Christian institutions and traditions.

There was another characteristically Protestant form of secularisation. The reaction against Catholic dogmatism had its counterpart in the revolt against Protestant puritanism. In the period between about 1880 and 1914 this revolt was hitting English Nonconformity with special severity. The chapels which had been so much in tune with the spirit of the times in the early and middle years of the century were now coming to be seen by many of the younger Nonconformist generation as 'ugly', 'dull, dull, unfathomably and inexpressibly dull'[179] and filled with 'cant and rant'. Evangelical Anglicanism was subjected to many of the same charges. One solution to these discontents was conversion to Roman or Anglican Catholicism, and the great expansion of Anglo-Catholicism in the late Victorian years was partly fuelled by the influx of disillusioned evangelicals. One early twentieth-century Methodist who became an Anglican monk was said to have seen this conversion as 'a door of escape from meanness of culture and narrowness of life into all the grandeur, beauty, dignity and wisdom of Christian civilization'.[180] But the anti-puritan reaction could also lead to agnosticism, to socialism, or to the religion of art and literature, which was so familiar in Germany at this time, but which found converts in England too.[181]

Jews mainly lived in three contrasting kinds of environment in England, France and Germany during this period, and there were major differences between them so far as the religious situation was concerned. In Alsace and in various parts of southern and central Germany there had for centuries been rural Jewish communities, sometimes placed in entirely Jewish villages, sometimes in religiously-mixed villages or in small towns. Many of them were quite poor, though their inhabitants might include moderately prosperous merchants and artisans. Then there were increasing numbers of middle-class Jews, above all in Berlin, London and Paris. In all three countries there were a few extremely wealthy Jewish bankers, as well as large numbers of merchants, manufacturers, shopkeepers and (in Germany) professional men. And, especially from the 1880s onwards, there were growing numbers of Yiddish-speaking Russian and Polish Jews, in flight from persecution and discrimination, many of whom settled in the working-class districts of London, Manchester, Berlin, and other cities, where a large proportion found work as tailors, capmakers or shoemakers.

There were distinctively Jewish forms of secularisation, which varied according to these contrasting environments. Traditional forms of Jewish life and religious observance continued with relatively little difficulty in the rural and small-town environment of many parts of Alsace, Baden or Württemberg. In villages where everyone was a Jew it was taken for granted that, for instance, businesses would close on the sabbath. Rabbis were highly regarded, and the force of public opinion ensured high rates of religious practice. Such institutions as the ritual bath survived and continued to have a regular clientele. In the mid-1920s, when 51 per cent of Jewish couples marrying in Berlin had a religious ceremony, 96 per cent of those marrying in Württemberg still did so.[182] Here, as elsewhere, the Christian environment had an influence on patterns of Jewish religious observance. In areas of the Rhineland and Westphalia where most of the population were practising Catholics, levels of Jewish religious observance tended to be high too. In the Weimar period, when the majority of Jews in Berlin stayed away from the synagogue even on the high holidays, those in Westphalia and the Rhineland generally observed the rites of passage, the sabbath and the dietary laws, and went to synagogue on the high holidays – and a considerable proportion went on the sabbath too. And while Jews in most other parts of Germany voted Liberal, those in the Rhineland often joined their Catholic neighbours in voting for the Centre.[183]

Not that life in a small town provided in itself any protection against secularising tendencies: where the number of Jews in a place was low, it became difficult to find a *minyan* (quorum) for the sabbath services, and there was a strong possibility that many families would drift away from the Jewish community, or even convert to Christianity. This happened in many parts of southern France in the nineteenth century, where Jewish communities were often too small to be viable, and it happened in the first generation of German-Jewish settlement in various English towns in the nineteenth century. When the first synagogue was established in Bradford in 1873, there were two or three hundred Jews in the town, some of whom had been living there for years, and in many cases they had given up all practice of their religion. The first generation of German-Jewish migrants to Manchester often became Unitarians. Most of those who arrived after 1830, by which time there was a well-established Jewish middle class and many Jewish institutions, stayed within the community.[184]

In London, Paris or Berlin, there was no lack of synagogues, but living as a Jew was difficult in other ways. Observance of the sabbath was a major problem, since many Jews worked for gentile employers, and even Jews who owned their own business often felt that they had to follow the same hours of work as their competitors. There were also many urban Jews who felt that if they were going to win acceptance, they would have to adapt to local custom. So the men cut their hair, shaved off their beards and removed their skull caps. Married women took off their wigs.[185] Throughout the nineteenth century, as village Jews moved into the cities, adjustments of this kind took place. In the years around 1900, when huge new Jewish quarters were formed by migrants from Poland and Russia in areas like the East End of London, there were severe tensions between those who remained strictly orthodox, and those who were willing to compromise with the new environment. The former joined the numerous backstreet synagogues (*chevrot*) which brought together immigrants from the same east European town for worship, sociability, and various forms of mutual support.[186] The latter declared England 'a *"freie Medina"* – a country where the restrictions of orthodoxy cease to apply', and some of them revelled in the unrivalled freedoms that the great city offered.[187] Others broke with tradition more reluctantly. As one Manchester tailor said: 'I just put up with it, but . . . I hated it . . . I remember the first day, it's a *shabbos* . . . I was broken-hearted . . . Yes they used to work *shabbos* them days, tailors.' However, they generally remained emphatically Jewish, speaking Yiddish and living in mainly Jewish neighbourhoods; and their children, even though they spoke English, were likely to marry a Jew, and continue living among Jews, even if further out in the suburbs. Rather than rejecting Judaism entirely, they more often reached a compromise, where some forms of religious observance were dropped, but others remained, including most often the lighting of candles and the family meal on the sabbath eve, keeping a kosher kitchen, and attendance at synagogue on the high holidays. This kind of compromise was still apparent in 1980 when, in one east London suburb 10 per cent of Jewish adults attended synagogue regularly, while 70 per cent of households lit candles on the sabbath eve. So a strong sense of Jewish identity might remain, while knowledge of Jewish religious beliefs and practices declined.[188]

Something similar had happened at various points in the nineteenth century in the German cities to which migrants from rural Jewish communities in Baden, Hesse or Prussia's eastern provinces were moving. The difference here was that the abandonment of many aspects of Jewish tradition was often much less reluctant. These socially mobile Jewish families had a strong wish for acceptance by their Protestant and Catholic middle-class neighbours. Their aim, as Sorkin says, was to be like other Germans in everything but religion. This objective was to be achieved especially through education and culture – ideals common to middle-class Germans of all religious confessions, but ones to which Jews were the most fervently committed.[189] In the second half of the nineteenth century, the proportion of Jewish students in Prussian institutions of higher education was far above the proportion of Jews in the population; Jews were the keenest theatre-goers, and (at least until his anti-Semitic views became known) the most fervent Wagnerians; and of course there was a deep divide between the Yiddish-speaking rural or immigrant Jew, and the educated middle-class Jew, for whom High German was mandatory.[190] Many who had entered on this path were influenced by the values and perspectives of an educated middle class which was mainly either religiously sceptical or liberal Protestant. Their faith placed overriding stress on the individual's relationship with God and on 'practical' religion, and it was hostile to ritual and dogma. In the light of such assumptions, traditional synagogue worship seemed crude and undignified, and much of daily Jewish religious practice seemed narrowly legalistic.[191] Ideas of this kind had a big influence on the Jewish reform movement in the early nineteenth century, and in the later part of the nineteenth century the great majority of German city synagogues were liberal.[192] But there were also many Jews whose contacts with the synagogue were very limited and who, like their Protestant counterparts, practised their religion in the home or adhered to a purely individual form of faith.

In England, where middle-class church-going was much higher than in Germany and where conservative forms of religion were more socially acceptable, attendance at synagogue was also higher, and the synagogues remained predominantly orthodox. Involvement in the synagogue was especially high within the Jewish elite in west London which, according to Endelman, was strongly influenced by contemporary conventions of upper middle-class piety. Though not orthodox by east European standards they were 'far more observant than wealthy Jews elsewhere in the West': 'They observed the major Jewish holidays, kept the Sabbath, and adhered to the dietary laws, although their manner of doing so did not always agree with Jewish tradition and was considerably influenced by contemporary Christian practice'.[193] This was partly because of a strong sense of loyalty to and responsibility for the Jewish community, and some who held prominent communal positions were privately agnostic or disliked many aspects of Jewish worship. (This was very similar to the position of those Anglican squires or Nonconformist businessmen whose church-going was a matter of social obligation rather than personal faith.) Middle-class Jews were, however, less involved in the synagogue than the elite, and towards the end of the century, as members of the elite increasingly went to public schools and to Oxford and Cambridge, intimate contacts with members of the Anglican ruling class sometimes had a corrosive effect on their faith and communal loyalty.[194]

Both in England and in Germany there were those who felt that their life was narrow and enclosed and who, either by choice, or just through the logic of events, found themselves breaking away from the Jewish community. There were parallels here with the situation in later nineteenth-century British Nonconformity, where the chapel sometimes seemed claustrophobic, and conversion to Anglicanism, Roman Catholicism, or the religion of literature seemed to promise the vision of a wider life. The many writers who decried their Nonconformist origins had their Jewish counterpart in Julia Frankau. Her novels of the 1880s and 1890s remorselessly satirised the materialism and philistinism of the prosperous Jews in Maida Vale and Bayswater.[195] In Germany at various points in the nineteenth and early twentieth centuries there were considerable numbers of Jewish conversions to Christianity. In England this was much less common, but there were still Jews who broke away entirely from their community.[196] In some cases this was linked with a hatred of all things Jewish. From the later eighteenth century, especially in Germany, there were some Jews who wished for total assimilation, who saw their own Jewishness as a burden and who accepted all the criticisms levelled by anti-Semites against Jewish culture, values and personal traits. For instance, in nineteenth-century Germany there was a derogatory verb, *mauscheln*, which denoted a Jewish way of speaking. It was used not only by anti-Semites, but very often by Jews.[197] Such people identified themselves completely with German cultural achievements, and saw everything specifically Jewish as infinitely inferior. Classic examples were Karl Marx (whose father had converted to Protestantism) and Walther Rathenau, the industrialist, who became Foreign Minister under Weimar, and was assassinated by ultra-nationalists.[198] In England, from the later nineteenth century onwards, there were wealthy Jews who aspired to join London society or to become country gentlemen, and who tried to obscure everything connected with their Jewish origins in order to facilitate their acceptance.[199]

The various forms of secular faith which emerged during these years also had a special attraction. While converts to Protestantism or Catholicism continued to be seen as 'baptised Jews', the religions of socialism, science or art seemed to promise a universalism in terms of which all traditional faiths were equally condemned, and all converts entered as equals. In the 'ghettos' of London's Whitechapel, Manchester's Red Bank and Strangeways, Berlin's Scheunenviertel, at the turn of the century, socialism – and indeed other radical creeds, such as anarchism – had a powerful attraction for the working class immigrant.[200] While the radicals may have been influenced by traditional Jewish concepts of social justice, these were often now presented in purely secular form. Thus in the

East End of London, where a Yiddish radical press emerged in 1884, these papers presented everything specifically Jewish as backward, and they blamed the weaknesses of trade unions on the failings of Jewish culture and religion, rather than on economic factors. The way forward was through education, science, the English language and secularism.[201] Similarly in the German universities, Jewish scholars were coming to the fore around the turn of the century in many fields, especially those which were more innovative or unconventional, such as psychoanalysis or sexology.[202] These scholars had often dropped most of their connections with the Jewish community and religion, and it could be argued that they were transferring Jewish traditions of study and scholarship into a sacralisation of secular intellectual activity.[203]

4 Belief

In 1846 the radical journalist Friedrich Saß described Berlin as a model example of the consequences of religious freedom: every kind of belief and unbelief was flourishing, from Pietism to atheism. The second half of the nineteenth century was a time of growing religious pluralism – especially in the cities, with their newspapers, lectures, cafés and pubs, and many sub-cultures.[1] But the same was happening more gradually in small towns and rural areas too. Christianity and Judaism were challenged by the spread of agnosticism or atheism and by the development of rival belief systems.

In the late twentieth century, public opinion polls have provided a mass of information about the percentage of the population claiming to believe in God, or in life after death, to pray or to read the Bible. Clearly no such figures are available for the nineteenth and early twentieth centuries, but other pointers may throw light on the trends in belief.

One pointer would be the appearance of religious doubt as a central theme in novels and plays. Here the peak period would seem to be the 1880s and 1890s. The most famous example would be Dostoyevsky's *Brothers Karamazov* (1880). But one could also mention Zola's 'Three Cities' trilogy (1890s), Thomas Hardy's *Tess of the d'Urbervilles* (1891) and *Jude the Obscure* (1895), Samuel Butler's *The Way of all Flesh* (published in 1903, but much of it written in the 1870s and 1880s), Mrs Humphry Ward's *Robert Elsmere* (1888), and Ibsen's *Ghosts* (1881), where freethought arrives at the furthest outposts of western Europe on the Norwegian fjords. Of course, throughout the nineteenth century there had been many novelists who repeatedly subjected clergymen or religious zealots to hostile caricature (for example, Charles Dickens), who professed

147

religious scepticism in strident terms (for example, Stendhal) or more subtle terms (for example, George Eliot), or who gave a prominent role in their novels to outspoken sceptics (for example, Flaubert's Homais – who, admittedly, is almost as much a caricature as Dickens's Stiggins or Chadband). The characteristic feature of many of the novels of the 1880s and 1890s was that religious doubt and/or the tensions between believers and sceptics, rather than being either a colourful sideshow or a subtly intruded subtext, is explicitly discussed and is central to the whole structure of the work.[2]

Robert Elsmere was a best-seller in both Britain and the United States, and was hotly debated in the periodical press, where critical reviewers included the former Prime Minister, W. E. Gladstone. It tells the story of an Anglican clergyman who loses his faith, and accordingly resigns his orders and devotes the rest of his life to social service in the East End of London. The novel included large amounts of autobiography, as Elsmere's crisis of faith closely corresponded to that which the author had herself undergone as the wife of an Oxford don in the 1870s. The crisis was largely a result of solitary study combined with discussions with sceptical acquaintances, and its main cause was doubt as to the reliability of the gospel accounts of Jesus' life. In the short run, these doubts caused immense anguish – greatly exacerbated in Robert Elsmere's case by the fact that his wife remained a devout evangelical – though one of the purposes of the novel was to show that in the longer run a new version of Christianity, in keeping with modern knowledge, was both possible and necessary. The immense interest which the book aroused showed that Mary Ward was touching on themes and experiences familiar to her contemporaries. And indeed there were many well-known mid- and late-Victorian intellectuals who experienced a crisis of faith of a somewhat similar kind.[3] A classic example would be Thomas Hardy who, as a young architect in London during the 1860s, began to doubt the Anglican faith, in which he had been brought up, and which up to then he had devoutly practised. The precise nature of the doubts are obscure, but he definitively abandoned his earlier hopes of becoming a clergyman, and for the rest of his life his religious position seems to have been one of complete scepticism, though he continued to be steeped in the Bible and the Prayer Book and to enjoy going to church.[4] In *Tess of the d'Urbervilles*, he referred to 'the chronic melancholy that is taking hold of the civilised races with the decline of belief in a beneficent power', and Hardy himself would certainly appear to illustrate this tendency.[5]

Yet it may be that agnosticism of this particular kind is a phenomenon typical of nineteenth-century Britain, but found much less commonly in France or Germany. The educated middle class, from which so many of the celebrated doubters came, was in England the most strongly devout section of the population – far more so than their counterparts in Germany and France and, unlike in France, the men of this class were almost as devout as the women. Moreover, the evangelicalism which was the prevailing form of religion in this class laid enormous emphasis on the importance of individual conversion and regular Bible-reading. It was often an intensely personal faith, the loss of which could be highly traumatic.[6] In the educated middle class of Germany and France, the impact of new intellectual developments in the later nineteenth century was less, because religious scepticism had for long been widespread, especially among men. In fact, by the time that agnosticism was hitting England in a major way in the 1880s and 1890s, the fashion among French intellectuals was for the rediscovery of Catholicism.[7] It is also likely that the model of loss of faith presented by Robert Elsmere assumes a degree both of intellectualisation and of consistency that was relatively rare.[8] In reality, questions of personal and communal loyalty, of custom, of sentiment, or of the need to make symbolic statements all affected religious belonging as much as more abstract intellectual considerations. Mergel quotes the example of Johannes Janssen, the leading German Catholic historian of the *Kulturkampf* era, admired by his co-religionists for his vigorous rebuttal of the prevailing Protestant version of the nation's history, and regarded as a 'saint of scholarship'. When in 1891 Janssen was dying, he told one of his closest friends that all the doubts he had expressed in former years still applied. He had no time for dogma of any kind, and Buddha, Abraham, Moses or Christ were all the same to him. But he wept with emotion at the news that a priest was saying mass for him daily.[9]

Paths to Salvation

While the 'Robert Elsmere' version of the spread of religious unbelief in the second half of the nineteenth century is certainly one part of the story, more typical is the situation where Christian faith and loyalty to the church was undermined by the attractions of rival forms of belief – offering not the cosmic bereavement endured by Thomas Hardy, but the 'new life' promised by so many secular prophets of that era. A characteristic figure of this time was the secular guru. The first such figure was certainly Voltaire. But the second half of the nineteenth century produced a whole series of scientists, writers and other pundits who owed a large part of their fame and popularity to the fact that they were seen as champions of secular ideas and values, and thus as offering both inspiration and legitimation to more obscure rebels against religious orthodoxy. Godwin Peak, the hero of George Gissing's novel *Born in Exile* (1892) noted a big demand for 'anti-dogmatic books written by men of mark'. There was 'a growing body of people who, for whatever reason, tend to agnosticism, but desire to be convinced that agnosticism is respectable'. 'They couldn't endure to be classed with Bradlaugh, but they rank themselves confidently with Darwin and Huxley'.[10]

In the second half of the nineteenth century non-religious views of the world became a possibility for the mass of the people, rather than only for small elite groups. Just as much as the older faiths, these newer world-views offered a path to salvation – a model of the good life, dignity and fulfilment for the individual, and a way forward for humanity. Five such paths to salvation were widely followed in the later nineteenth century. I shall call them the 'religious', the 'political', the 'scientific', the 'aesthetic' and the 'spiritualist'.

The most widely followed was still the 'religious'. But two more recently discovered paths to salvation were also being widely followed, one through radical politics, and the other through science. The doctrine of 'salvation by politics alone' had its origins in the French Revolution, and was eagerly preached by republicans, radicals, nationalists and, most importantly in our period, socialists. By the later nineteenth century the belief that science alone offered the way to truth, a solution to humanity's problems, and a basis for everyday living, was widely held, and advocated by influential politicians, writers and of course scientists. A fourth way to salvation was the 'aesthetic', according to which the deepest level of human experience and the only path to such truth as humanity is capable of reaching was through art, music and literature. What I have called the 'spiritualists' were those who were seeking a third way between orthodox religion and orthodox science, rejecting any

purely materialist interpretation of the world, insisting on humanity's spiritual nature, affirming the existence of supernatural forces,
but rejecting many of the doctrines of the churches. Proponents of
each of these five paths to salvation were often in conscious opposition to one another. But this was not necessarily so. There were
many people who, for instance, linked science and radical politics
or religion and radical politics as necessary allies in the shaping of
the future. There were also many people who were much more
eclectic.

Like Protestantism, Catholicism or Judaism, these rival faiths
could be the cause of passionate commitment, and sometimes intol-
erance. 'Honest doubters' of the Robert Elsmere kind seldom
became militant anti-Christians. But those who fervently believed
not only that the old faith was wrong but that they had found the
right answer often committed themselves to making life as difficult
as possible for those who insisted on remaining loyal to the old
gospel. This is one reason why political radicalisation was a major
factor in many aspects of secularisation. The doctrine of 'salvation
by politics alone' led many political radicals to give up religious
commitments which either seemed to conflict with their political
loyalties or diverted them from more important political tasks.
Only political loyalty could shape collective identities almost as
powerfully as religion did. And political passions generated much
of the energy which powered campaigns against the role of religion
in public institutions. This was a period in which collective identities
were vitally important, an age of organisations, of mass meetings, of
oratorical spell-binders, of flags and banners. Only political organisations rivalled the churches in these areas, sometimes working in
harness, sometimes in opposition.

Numerous examples could illustrate the 'religious' aspect of
much of the radical politics of this era. I will note three examples,
all of which show radicals claiming to define the criteria by which a
person's life might be judged. The first is that of one of the earliest
secular funerals in Paris, held in 1876, where the deceased, a man
named Despierres, was praised in the graveside oration for his
role in the revolution of 1830, for his life-long commitment to
the principles of 1789, and for his rejection of the 'lying words of
the priests'. The second is from the autobiography of a formerly
Catholic German factory worker, who had become a Social Democrat and, after a good deal of soul-searching, had adopted the
scientific-materialist world-view: 'I finally came to the conclusion

that it was impossible to know anything about the last things; but it was sufficient for me to know that if there is an after-life and a reward, I could stand before God with my socialism'.[11] The third example goes back to 1839, when an evangelical missionary visited a dying man in a poor area of Birmingham:

> After conversing with him in the most solemn manner on the subject of faith and repentance he said, without anything that would lead to such an observation, 'Do you think the present ministers will go out?' On my wishing to evade the subject he said he had been a Reformer and really did not think a Tory could be saved and evidently comforted himself with the hope that it would fare better with him in another world because he had always voted against the abuses of government and church rates.[12]

Radicals thus claimed that political activity was the highest test of virtue. At times of intense political enthusiasm that often meant a turning away from religious activity by those who believed that politics took precedence. Also typical of this period was the linking of radical politics with the cult of science. This was particularly common in Germany from about the 1880s onwards, where a synthesis of Marxism and Darwinism became characteristic of many Social Democrats, and was often seen as representing the mature socialist viewpoint towards which recruits to the movement should aim, and to which they would be gradually led.[13]

For an important section of the population in the later nineteenth and early twentieth century, including most typically male skilled workers in the cities and industrial centres, socialism became a way of life – and, indeed, in a word that was often used, a religion.[14] Quite frequently in England, much less often in Germany, and very rarely in France, 'Christian Socialists' sought a reconciliation of the new faith and the old. But there were all sorts of obstacles on the way. There were, for instance, close links between the churches and older political parties. Even in England, where many Nonconformist ministers were self-consciously 'progressive' and 'friends of labour', they often had a firm loyalty to the Liberal Party. A symbolic moment was the election of 1892 in Bradford, a strongly Nonconformist town, and also a centre of the emerging labour movement. At a meeting of the town's Nonconformist Association a resolution calling on members to vote Liberal was passed, but in the face of

bitter opposition from Labour supporters, led by the Congregationalist, and later Labour MP, Fred Jowett. Jowett declared: 'if the
reverend gentlemen [on the platform] would persist in opposing
the Labour movement there would be more reason than ever to
complain of the absence of working men from their chapels [loud
cheers], and the labourers would establish a Labour Church . . . and
they would cheer for Jesus the working man of Nazareth [cheers]'.
Two months later a Labour Church was set up, with Jowett as
chairman.[15] In many instances the attitude of the churches
towards socialism was openly hostile. So far as Catholics were concerned, Leo XIII's encyclical of 1891, *Rerum Novarum*, in which he
explicitly condemned socialism, was often regarded as the final
word. There were certainly some Catholic socialists in Britain who
evaded this condemnation by declaring that the British form of
socialism was not the kind that had been condemned by the Pope.
Again, Catholic socialists were rare in Germany, and even more so
in France. There were differences between the Protestant churches
and within them. The greatest hostility to socialism was found in the
German *Landeskirchen* where official condemnations of socialism
were numerous in the 1890s, and where it would have been very
difficult for a pastor to actually join the Social Democratic Party
before 1918.[16]

In England there were no such official condemnations. Clergy,
both Anglican and Nonconformist, could and did join the Independent Labour Party (ILP), and sometimes preached socialist
sermons. On the other hand, there were many more clergymen
who belonged to the Conservative or Liberal Party, and church
members who were known to be active socialists might well face
opposition from either the minister or lay leaders. Similarly, Nonconformist ministers, who depended for their livelihood on their
congregations, could come under strong financial pressure to
preach in ways acceptable to the wealthier members of their congregation.[17] Two examples from the early history of the ILP in the
1890s illustrate both the significant role of Nonconformity and
some of the resulting tensions. In the small industrial town of
Nelson, in north-east Lancashire, where the local branch of the
ILP grew out of the Young Men's Mutual Improvement Society at
Salem Independent Methodist church, most of the original group
of activists dropped out of the chapel, feeling that it was too much
identified with Liberalism. In Crewe one of the original leaders of
the ILP was the town's Unitarian minister, Rev Harry Bodell Smith.

This led to a period of conflict in the church, culminating in the resignation of its treasurer, a successful businessman, and leading local Liberal. This proved a pyrrhic victory for the socialists, since the departing treasurer had been the church's leading financial supporter. The church soon found itself unable to pay the minister's salary, and it eventually closed down.

Moreover, as already mentioned, socialism frequently came as part of an intellectual package which included Darwin, and a variety of anti-religious writers, as well as Marx. The socialism of these years, especially in Germany, but also in France, and to some extent in England too, tended to become a society within a society, a self-contained subculture, within which the comrade could spend all of his (or occasionally her) non-working and non-sleeping hours. Socialist leaders did their best to insulate their members from dangerous contacts with the unbelieving world. They were contemptuous of comrades who 'sang with the bourgeoisie'.[18] The thinking of the party loyalists of this era was well described by a Berliner brought up in a strongly socialist household in the early twentieth century. For people like his parents the way towards the socialist state of the future was not through fighting on the barricades:

> The way to get there was to strengthen the organisation: trade unions, party, co-operatives; the freethinkers against the reactionary churches, the workers' sports clubs against their bourgeois counterparts, the workers' choirs as part of an autonomous proletarian culture over against bourgeois culture, the party newspaper over against the reactionary and the boulevard newspapers. ... In the solidaristic identification of the individual with the whole, they built the powerful organisations and communities which, like great religions, placed people under their spell. They gave them a view of the world, a country and a home. Here people did not only take part in politics: they also sang and drank, celebrated and made friendships. What was impossible elsewhere was possible here: you could be a human being.[19]

The other major alternative to the religious view of the world was faith in science. Auguste Comte's positivism was the first widely influential attempt to devise a systematic alternative to supernaturalist forms of faith. By classifying theology as a primitive way of understanding the world, a necessary stage, but one now superseded by the advent of science, he provided a persuasive way of explaining, and indeed explaining away, religion. In emphasising the importance of altruism and of the identification of each individual with the whole of humanity, he reassured those who feared that the rejection of religion would mean a descent into moral anarchy. In the 1850s and 1860s his system was adopted by large sections of the intelligentsia both in France and, to a lesser extent, in England.[20] His ideas gained special significance from the influence which they had on many of the founders of the Third Republic. Gambetta claimed that Comte was the greatest thinker of the nineteenth century. Ferry, who made the study of Comte's works compulsory in state schools, owed to his master the vision of a humanity 'no longer a fallen race, doomed by original sin, dragging itself painfully in a valley of tears, but as a ceaseless cavalcade marching forward towards the light'. By seeing himself as 'an integral part of this great Being which cannot perish, of this humanity which is ceaselessly improving', Ferry 'had conquered his liberty completely because he was free from the fear of death'.[21] Comte also devised a Religion of Humanity, which admittedly was not to the taste of all his admirers. For many of his French disciples his deliberate adaptation of such Catholic observances as saints' days reminded them too much of the hated original.[22]

In Germany and England many of the most popular critics of religion were practising natural scientists. In Germany the 1850s and 1860s saw the publication of numerous works of popular science, written from a materialist point of view.[23] In the 1850s the major influences were Ludwig Büchner, Jakob Moleschott and Karl Vogt, all of whom were political radicals who saw the popularisation of materialist science as a means of undermining the reactionary forces which had defeated the revolutions of 1848–49. In the 1860s many of the disciples of Büchner eagerly adopted the ideas of Darwin and his German popularisers such as the Jena zoologist, Ernst Haeckel. Haeckel's *History of Creation* (1868), was the first German book to use Darwinism as the basis for a whole world-view, and his ideas were more fully developed in his *Riddle of the Universe* (1899), which became an international best-seller. Even more widely read in Germany was Wilhelm Bölsche, whose works of popular science combined Darwinism, sex, a love of nature and mysticism in a mixture that proved irresistible. When one young Berliner was asked in 1908 why he was leaving the church, he replied 'My Gods are Haeckel and Bölsche'.[24] In England 'The Conflict between Science and Religion', to quote the title of a book published in the United States in 1874, became a matter of wide-spread public interest and debate in the 1870s and 1880s. Charles Darwin was certainly the greatest symbol of this conflict and the greatest hero of those who championed an anti-religious science. But he himself was not interested in the role of guru. This was taken up by T. H. Huxley in the field of the natural sciences and by Herbert Spencer in the fields of philosophy and sociology.

As has been shown, there were many working-class radicals who believed that the alliance of socialism and science was the key to the future. There were even more middle-class Liberals who believed that science alone held all the answers. Arnold Dodel, whose *Moses or Darwin?* (1889) was so popular in Germany, spoke for many when he concluded: 'With the overwhelming power of an uncontrollable force, the conception of a *realisable and desirable happiness of ALL mankind during our LIFE-TIME, not beyond the grave,* has taken root, spread, and become an intrinsic part of the moral ideal of this age'.[25] These views found their most eloquent expression in the novels of Émile Zola, with his scorn for the mystical and the miraculous, his attempt to understand human behaviour in 'naturalist' terms as primarily determined by heredity, and his messianic faith in the power of science to transform human life for the better. Zola, indeed, saw criticism of science as a form of blasphemy. He was particularly incensed by the claim, attributed to the writer Ferdinand Brunetière, that science was 'bankrupt', and much space in his novels was devoted to rebutting this claim. In *Paris*, the scientist Bertheroy spoke for the author when he declared 'science alone is the world's revolutionary force, the only force which far above all paltry political incidents, the vain agitations of despots, priests, sectarians, and ambitious people of all kinds, works for the benefit of those who will come after us, and prepares the triumph of truth, justice, and peace. ...Ah, my dear child, if you wish to overturn the world by striving to set a little more happiness in it, you have only to remain in your laboratory here, for human happiness can only spring from the furnace of the scientist'.[26]

In 1874 Francis Galton closed his book *English Men of Science* by expressing the hope that scientific occupations in the universities, industry, sanitation and statistical enquiry would address themselves to the nation's practical problems, and in return would receive public financial support. And Turner comments that 'The spokesmen for the scientific professions desired the social prestige and recognition that had been and to a large degree still was accorded to the clergy'.[27] The new faith received its most decisive impetus from those professions which saw their own identity and interests as bound up with advancing the authority of science, and often with side-lining ecclesiastical authority. This applied most obviously to research scientists and doctors, but potentially academics and teachers in other areas could adopt similar perspectives, and the same happened with new professions such as social work, which found themselves entering territory previously dominated by the clergy. The other important underpinning of the scientific faith lay in certain sections of middle-class liberalism and radicalism, where it was hoped that major social improvements could be brought about by education and the application of science, without the drastic social re-organisation, let alone the revolutionary violence, which many socialists were demanding. Here a representative figure was Rudolf Virchow, both a Berlin medical scientist and a Left Liberal politician, who declared in 1860 that the sciences had taken the place of the church, and in 1865 that 'science has become a religion for us'.[28]

The scientific faith was spread more thinly and advanced more slowly than the faith in socialism, but it was spread more widely, and it was apparently able to show results. It spread partly through the writings of popular scientific writers; partly through the prestige of such scientific heroes as Darwin, Pasteur and Liebig, whose achievements seemed to promise an infinite progress in human understanding of and control of the world; partly through appreciation of advances in technology and medicine. Eugen Weber shows how in the 1880s and 1890s such ideas were spreading even to the remoter parts of the French countryside. In the swampy Sologne, where victims of malaria had for long made pilgrimages to the shrine of St Viâtre, the availability of quinine was beginning to provide more effective remedies, and artificial fertilisers were boosting crops without the need for supernatural help.[29]

The doctrine of salvation through art had its origins in Germany in the later eighteenth century, and its greatest prophet was Goethe. This doctrine could take many different forms. In part it arose from the rejection of over-narrow and too-explicit doctrinal formulae, and the need for a religion that would reflect the mystery, the beauty and the strangeness of life and of the divine. In part it was one aspect of the typically nineteenth-century search for a Religion of Humanity, which would unite all of humankind through generally acceptable ideals and goals, and would thus escape the particularism and the peculiarity of each of the existing religions. For some of those who had rejected Christianity or Judaism, but without finding any compensatory faith in science or radical politics, art was simply all that remained beyond the triviality of everyday life and the sordidness of individual ambition. On the other hand, for many in late Victorian and Edwardian England, art meant emancipation – it pointed to a life which would be lived to the full, free from the constraints imposed by antiquated creeds and restrictive moral codes.

Throughout the nineteenth century these ideas had a large following in Germany's educated middle class. In England, they only became widely current after about 1880, and in France they never seem to have gained the same degree of influence. In Germany the religion of art, literature and music appealed to the many members of the educated middle class who had distanced themselves from the church, but continued to see themslves as 'religious'. It was especially attractive to the women of this class, who were relatively resistant to the cult of science that appealed so much to their husbands and fathers.[30] In England, the growing interest in ideas of this kind at the end of the nineteenth century was part of the reaction against 'Victorianism' then underway, and the rejection of the powerful British tradition of puritanism.

When, in 1911, the popular but highly unorthodox Cologne pastor, Karl Jatho, was charged with heresy by the Prussian church authorities, he was alleged to have said that 'Music is the only really adequate experience of religion', that 'the "God experience" is fluid, one can never be sure of being constant to this or that means of expressing it', and that 'copulation … is the highest level of revelation of God's love'.[31] Clearly none of this was close to the Protestant Church's official teaching, and Jatho was dismissed; but it is not surprising that he was popular – these ideas were typical of an important current of German middle-class thinking at that time. Wagner, in his essay on Beethoven, claimed that the composer was 'holy', 'a tone-poet seer' who 'reveals to us the inexpressible', his 'suffering' being his 'penalty for the state of inspiration'. Traditional religion had become 'artificial', but music offered 'the essence of Religion free from all dogmatic fictions'. By 'teaching redemption-starved mankind a second speech in which the Infinite can voice itself', music would give modern civilisation a 'soul', 'a new religion'. As Obelkevich comments,[32] Wagner himself became the object of the greatest of musical cults, and visits to Bayreuth became 'pilgrimages'. As one example, in Fontane's *The Woman taken in Adultery* (1882), the heroine and her future lover recognise their affinity at their first meeting because of a common passion for Wagner – 'we belong to that small parish whose name and middle point I do not need to tell you'.[33] Similarly, Nipperdey notes two stages of distancing oneself from traditional forms of Christian observance while still recognising the sacred dimension of life, to which the Christian festivals were one pointer. The first step was to observe Good Friday by going to hear Bach's *St Matthew Passion*; the second was to go instead to Wagner's *Parsifal*.[34]

Music, apart from its own inherent power, also had the advantage of ambiguity. It could nourish forms of belief that were totally independent of any kind of traditional religion. Yet it could also be accepted as a reinterpretation of older religious themes. Literature often marked a more explicit and decisive break from religious tradition. In Germany there was a well-established tradition according to which the revelation to modern humanity came through poetry and drama. The writings of Goethe and Schiller, in particular, superseded all previous revelations, providing the basis for a religion of freedom, self-fulfilment, creativity and belief in humanity, which men and women of all nationalities and religious backgrounds could share. As Hölscher writes:

> Goethe's philosophy and poetry formed for his admirers an enclosed religious cosmos; his poems were learnt and recited like prayers, and received like binding religious interpretations of the world. Goethe calendars and breviaries accompanied (and still today accompany) their readers through the year with their maxims, in a similar way to the Christian watchwords; Goethe's birthday, August 28th, is and was celebrated by his devotees more or less as a secular counterpart to Christmas.[35]

In November 1859 admirers of Schiller marked the centenary of his birth by processing through the streets holding aloft statues of the poet, rather as Catholics might process with a statue of the Virgin Mary.[36] In Lutheran Hamburg these celebrations gained special piquancy from the fact that the actual date of Schiller's birth, 10 November, had been designated by the city authorities as the annual Day of Prayer and Repentance, and the Schiller festivities had to be postponed until the days following. This caused considerable resentment, and when the birthday celebrations took place, there were undertones of criticism of the secular and religious authorities. Not that Protestantism and the religion of art were altogether mutually exclusive: the 'Culture Protestantism' that came to the fore from the 1860s, called for 'a renewal of the Protestant church in the spirit of evangelical freedom and in harmony with the general cultural development of our time'. Pastors from this wing of the church sometimes preached on texts taken from Goethe and Schiller – though texts from Nietzsche, as used by some preachers in the radical stronghold of Bremen, were not generally appreciated.[37]

The German aesthetic faith was nothing if not reverent. Its English counterpart, coming as it did much later, as part of the late Victorian revolt against puritanism, was often fiercely irreverent. Its favourite target was 'cant', in which was included anything unduly serious or high-minded, or any resort to high-flown language. The mocking tone favoured by the enemies of 'cant' took its most strident form in Richard Aldington's novel, *Death of a Hero*, published in 1929, but set during the First World War and the years immediately preceding the war. The novel was an attack on 'the "Victorians" of all nations' and 'the regime of Cant before the War which made the Cant during the War so damnably possible and easy'.[38] The novel's purpose was mainly destructive. But in his autobiography, *Life for Life's Sake*, Aldington made a more positive statement of the aesthetic faith which was his alternative to the religion, the politics, and much else, that he rejected:

> In religion and even in politics I was more or less a Gallio, caring nothing. What I wanted was to enjoy *my* life in *my* way... I wanted to know and enjoy the best that had been thought and felt and known through the ages – architecture, painting, sculpture, poetry, literature, food and wine, France and Italy, women, old towns, beautiful country.[39]

This was only a particularly clear and frank expression of a view that had gradually being gathering strength from about 1890. In 1888, the conflict between older puritan traditions and the 'modern gospel of the divine right of self-development' had been vividly presented in *Robert Elsmere*. The two main female characters, Catherine Leyburn and her younger sister, Rose, are tightly bound in a relationship of love and mutual resentment. Catherine, an old-fashioned evangelical, suspicious of anything 'worldly', devotes her life to the well-being of the poor in the remote rural parish where they live. Rose, a talented violinist, longs to return to the artistic circle she had known in Manchester – or, even better, to escape to London or Berlin. In Manchester, at the home of her uncle, a businessman who patronised the arts:

> she found long-haired artists and fiery musicians about the place, who excited and encouraged her musical gift, who sketched her while she played, and talked to the pretty, clever, unformed creature of London and Paris and Italy, and set her pining for that golden *vie de Bohème* which she alone apparently of all artists was destined never to know. For she was an artist – she would be an artist – let Catherine say what she would! She came back from Manchester restless for she knew not what, thirsty for the joys and emotions of art, determined to be free, reckless, passionate; with Wagner and Brahms in her young blood... [40]

What I have called the 'spiritualist' path to salvation is the hardest of all to define, as well as the one most frequently dismissed, both by sceptical contemporaries and by historians, as representing some kind of lunatic fringe. Yet it is both a very widespread current in the western Europe of this time, especially from the 1870s onwards, and one which had resonance at many social levels. Its best known manifestation was the Spiritualist movement (or 'Spiritist' as it is known in France, where 'spiritualism' has a wider meaning), which was based on the belief that it is possible to make contact with the spirits of the dead. Originating in the United States this movement got established in western Europe in the 1850s, and initially won widest support in France,[41] where its leading figure, Allan Kardec, published the movement's classic text, *The Book of Spirits*, in 1856, and founded a *Spiritist Review* in 1858. Initially, the interest in Spiritism came mainly from those on the Left, the most notable example being Victor Hugo, and it reflected their search for forms of religion uncontaminated by the Catholic Church. But the interest spread much more widely – indeed in 1857 the emperor and his family had several sessions with a famous Scottish medium.

In England too, the Spiritualist pioneers in the 1850s were political radicals, including most notably Robert Owen, and throughout the Victorian and Edwardian periods Spiritualists were active in radical, socialist and trade union organisations, as

well as in temperance and adult education. The first strongholds
of the movement were among the working class in the woollen
towns of west Yorkshire.[42] Early recruits were often Secularists,
who had rejected the churches and clergy on political and social
grounds, but were open to new forms of supernatural belief –
especially if these emerged from individual exploration and
experiment. In the mid-Victorian years the doctrine of hell
probably caused more disquiet than any other aspect of Christian
orthodoxy: perhaps the most attractive aspect of Spiritualism was
that it purported to prove the fact of immortality, while rejecting
hell. Spiritualism also related to another important aspect of
popular culture. Spiritualist mediums were often keenly interested in unorthodox healing techniques, ranging from herbal
medicines to methods which drew on the resources of the spirit
world. Some were heirs to ancient rural traditions. For instance,
Joseph Ashman, a prominent Spiritualist in the 1870s and
1880s, had begun his working life as a Suffolk farm labourer,
and had used traditional methods of curing both humans and
horses and cattle. Some mediums were heirs to the 'wise men'
and 'wise women' who advised on personal problems and the
finding of lost objects, or foretold the future. A book on Berlin
spiritualism published in 1905 gave examples, such as that of the
'consultations' held every afternoon by a carpenter's wife with
a reputation as a medium at which she advised 'the servant-girls
of the neighbourhood, love-lorn shop-girls, mourning widows,
anxious mothers'.[43]

By the mid-1860s there was a growing interest in spiritualist
phenomena among academics and scientists. Leading figures in
this group were the scientific polymath and associate of Darwin,
Alfred Russel Wallace, and Henry Sidgwick, Fellow of Trinity
College, Cambridge, and later Professor of Moral Philosophy
in the university. The desire to submit these phenomena to
scientific investigation led to the formation in 1882 of the Society
for Psychic Research. Members of this group had broken away
from Christianity, but they rejected the claims of science to be
the new religion. They resented the dogmatism of such leading
exponents of scientific orthodoxy as Huxley and Galton; they
were often strongly concerned with moral questions, which they
felt science was unable to answer; and they accused materialist
scientists of simply ignoring, or dismissing as nonsense, those
aspects of human experience which were not consonant with their

theories. Many of them were particularly concerned to place belief in human immortality on a scientific basis.[44]

But this is only one aspect of wider tendencies in contemporary thinking, summed up, as I suggested earlier, by the search for a 'third way' between orthodox religion and orthodox science. This led on typically to the idea that there are powers inherent in human beings which, because of the influence of rigid dogmas and the increasing distance of modern humanity from nature, are seldom exploited – the ability to communicate with spirits might be one such power, but there could also be others, including the ability to see into the future and to heal. So closeness to nature, a sense of the unity of all nature including humanity, and belief in the possibility of experiencing God through nature were all typical parts of this current of thinking. Another was the rediscovery of ancient sources of wisdom, especially via Eastern religions. A characteristic figure was Annie Besant, one of the British pioneers of birth control and of socialism, and later an associate of Gandhi and president of the Indian National Congress. Brought up as an evangelical, she became in her teens an Anglo-Catholic, and then successively a liberal Anglican, a Comtian, and a leading Secularist, before converting in 1889 to Theosophy. As so often, the move away from Secularism began with an interest in psychic phenomena. As a result of attending seances and investigating examples of clairvoyance, she became convinced that 'there was some hidden thing, some hidden power, and resolved to seek until [she] found'. What she found was pantheism – 'He is in everything and everything is in Him' – and a belief in reincarnation and the law of karma.[45]

The 'third way' often involved a challenge to current sexual orthodoxies. Annie Besant in her later years advocated celibacy. A different kind of challenge came from Edward Carpenter, a former Anglican clergymen and Cambridge don, who resigned his orders and went to live in a village near Sheffield, working as an adult education lecturer. Best known as one of the pioneers of British socialism, he was the author of *Towards Democracy* (1885) and of the popular socialist hymn, 'England Arise'. He also wrote *Sex-Love, and its Place in a Free Society* (1894) and *Homogenic Love in a Free Society* (1895). Besides advocating sexual, and especially homosexual, liberation, Carpenter was a spiritualist with a keen interest in Hinduism and other Eastern religions, a vegetarian and teetotaller, a believer in closeness to nature, and a critic of contemporary science.[46] Nipperdey notes the ubiquity in German middle-class circles around 1900 of 'religion outside the church' or what he calls a 'vagrant religion'.[47] There were many people who had rejected first orthodox Christianity and then scientific rationalism, and were searching for a view of the world which would be 'spiritual' but without submission to any formal creed. As a typical example he notes Rudolf Steiner, a former disciple of Haeckel, whose Anthroposophy, formulated in 1913, drew both on Theosophy and on Christianity.

As the case of Edward Carpenter suggests, 'spiritualism' overlapped in one way or another with each of the other forms of contemporary faith. 'Spiritualists' shared with Christians and Jews the critique of materialism, they often – though not always – believed in God, and they were particularly sympathetic to the liberal reformers within the older religions. They often shared the social reforming zeal of socialists and other radicals. There were also many people who were fascinated by science, but critical of the 'rigidity' of more conventional scientists. And, given their flexible views on the sources and content of divine revelation, they had no difficulty at all with the idea that it might as readily come through art or music as, for instance, Bible-reading.

By the late nineteenth century the typical situation in western Europe was a religious pluralism in which a variety of relatively well-developed world-views were generally available. The Christian churches still reached a much wider and more socially varied section of the population than any of their rivals, but they faced powerful competition in many areas of life which they had previously dominated, including the interpretetion of the world, morality and the shaping of identity.

Organised Freethought

Some of those who were moving away from Christianity or Judaism joined secularist, freethought or humanist movements. Organised alternatives to Christianity and Judaism had their origins in France and England in the revolutionary years of the 1790s, and in England the 'infidel' tradition, with its strength among radical artisans and shopkeepers, continued under the leadership of such figures as Richard Carlile and George Jacob Holyoake in the 1820s, 1830s and 1840s. Since the keystone of English popular Christianity was the Bible, regarded as inspired in all its parts and as the final

authority on every question, English 'infidels' devoted a large part
of their energies to exposing inconsistencies and absurdities in the
sacred text. Their principal guide was Tom Paine's *Age of Reason*
(1794), an attack on Christianity written from a deist viewpoint. The
other, equally important dimension of the English secular movement was practical and political. From Paine, through Holyoake to
Charles Bradlaugh, the leading English Secularist of the later
nineteenth century, the movement was dominated by political radicals, whose attacks on religion focused as much on the wealth of the
clergy and the ties between church and state as on more abstract
theological issues.

It was in the later nineteenth and early twentieth century that
organised irreligion reached its greatest strength. In England the
most popular anti-religous organisation in this period was the
National Secular Society, founded in 1866, which developed out of
the London Secular Society, founded in 1851. By comparison with
its counterparts in France, the National Secular Society remained a
relatively small body, with 120 branches and several thousand members in the peak year of 1883, and with a membership drawn mainly
from the working class and lower middle class.[48] However, in the
period from about the 1850s to the 1880s it had a considerable
influence on the politically active and self-educating sections of the
working class. Even if the membership of Secular Societies was
small, Charles Bradlaugh, who was not only President of the
National Secular Society, but a leading campaigner on a variety of
other radical issues, could attract huge audiences to his lectures
both in his London headquarters, the Hall of Science, and in the
provinces. Just as Nonconformist chapels had 'hearers' who regularly attended services without becoming members, and who were
very often more numerous than the membership, Secularism
included a large penumbra of sympathisers, who probably shared
many of the movement's principles and goals. However, Royle
suggests that even the most generous estimate of the number of
Secularist adherents in the 1870s and 1880s would put it no higher
than 60,000 – which was tiny by comparison with, for instance, the
number of Methodists, who recruited within a similar upper
working class/lower middle class milieu.[49] From the 1890s there
were a number of relatively small bodies appealing to religious
sceptics in the educated middle class. These included the Ethical
Societies, which acted as a kind of church for rationalists, and the
Rationalist Press Association, which had a primarily educational and

propagandist role, publishing freethought classics and scientific works with an anti-religious slant.[50]

In France during the Third Republic organised freethought became a mass movement in a way that it never was in Germany or England. The first freethought societies were formed in Paris during 1848, but under the Second Empire and the Moral Order this was impossible. Freethinkers met either through bodies, such as the Masonic lodges, which were not formally committed to free-thought, or through one-off events such as Good Friday banquets. These were held in numerous places in 1869 and 1870, during the final more open phase of the Second Empire. Only with the coming to power of the republicans in the later 1870s were all restrictions lifted, and then the growth of organised freethought was very rapid. An almanac of 1894 listed 567 societies formed in the last fifteen years. A further 357 societies were formed in the period 1901–14.[51] Naturally the movement was well represented in Paris and other big cities. But the most striking evidence of the widespread diffusion of organised freethought was the formation of numerous branches in mainly rural regions. For instance, the years 1880–85 saw the for-mation of eighteen societies in the Yonne and sixteen in the Eure, neither of which contained any large town. At the national level the leaders of the movement tended to be lawyers, doctors and Radical or Socialist politicians. At the local level, the key figure was very often a teacher, though there were also numerous mayors who belonged to a freethought society. Among the rank and file, the largest occupational groups were farmers and wine-growers, with building and metal workers, innkeepers and small shopkeepers also well represented.[52]

In Germany an important role was played by the Free Parishes, originally established by Christian rationalists. After their brief hey-day in 1848–49, and the repression of the 1850s, they gradually evolved in the direction of a more thorough-going rationalism, minimising or dropping altogether all supernatural elements in the Christian creed and arriving in some cases at atheism. By 1859 when they re-organised under the title League of German Free-Religious Parishes (*Bund freireligiöser Gemeinden Deutschlands*), many parishes had removed the altar and stopped singing hymns; the preacher had become a 'speaker' and his sermon a 'lecture'.[53] In some areas, including Berlin and Saxony, many of the pioneers of socialism belonged to the Free Parishes,[54] and during the period of the Anti-Socialist Law in the 1880s meetings of the Parishes could provide a front for Social Democratic activity. In Germany organised irreligion reached a high point in the period between about 1880 and the First World War, when many new organisations were founded. Those who thought the Free-Religious were still *too* religious joined the German Freethinkers League, set up in 1881 by followers of Ludwig Büchner, one of the most uncompromising exponents of scientific materialism, and an international freethinking celebrity. By this time Büchner's popularity was rivalled by that of Ernst Haeckel, under whose direction the Monist League was formed in 1906. In 1908 Social Democrats, who felt that the existing groups were too much influenced by middle-class Liberals, formed a separate Proletarian Freethinkers' League.[55] There were also numerous small freethinking groups, and in 1909 an umbrella organisation called the Weimar Cartel was set up. Simon-Rits puts their combined membership on the eve of the First World War at 43,000, which would be more than the membership of equivalent groups in England, but much less than in France.[56]

Eclecticism

Freethinkers were often as doctrinaire as any religious believer. But there was another less well-defined though equally important tendency at this time – an aversion to 'dogma' of any kind, and an eclectic readiness to mix beliefs drawn from many different sources. In the early twentieth century, the Bishop of Birmingham, Charles Gore (a leading Anglo-Catholic), summarised this latter trend by saying that 'some thirty years ago' 'there was a sort of Protestant religion' 'which for good or evil could be more or less assumed', but that now 'religious opinions are in complete chaos'.[57] Kselman presents a similar picture in his account of religious pluralism in French cities in the later years of the nineteenth century. The 'unchurched' were not necessarily 'irreligious': many of them 'constructed religious systems from a combination of sources that included Catholicism, the occult, socialist ideology, and nationalism'. As one rather striking instance, he mentions the veteran republican journalist and politician, Claude-Anthime Corbon, who in a series of books in the 1860s and 1870s advocated a mixture of Christian socialism and belief in reincarnation. But he also cites various examples of spiritualist mediums who claimed to be loyal Catholics and of Catholics with a keen interest in the occult.[58]

The dogmatic rejection of 'dogma' was well illustrated in a correspondence which ran for several months in 1904 in London's *Daily Telegraph* focused on the quesion 'Do we believe?' Several thousand letters were sent to the paper – another illustration both of the keen interest in questions of faith and doubt at the time and of the very divided state of public opinion – and a selection was later published as a book. The editor of the paper, W. L. Courtney, detected a degree of confusion in many of the letters. He attributed this to the fact that science had made people sceptical of many orthodox religious teachings, but that many scientific findings were hard to accept, and the will to believe in God and in a purpose for human life remained undiminished. As a result people were 'keeping in separate pigeon-holes, as it were, what they want to satisfy their religious instincts, and what they want to satisfy their intelligence and their reason'. 'Dogmatic Christianity' had decayed, but 'the form of Christianity which is most common in our own day does not repose upon dogmas at all'. Indeed, 'A hard, definite, logical and systematic religious faith is almost an impossibility in the England we know'.[59]

The letters that followed included many written by dogmatic Christians or dogmatic atheists. But there was also a large group for whom 'dogma' or 'orthodoxy' of any kind was objectionable. Many professing Christians saw their religion either as essentially practical or as based on faith – in either case formal creeds tended to be dismissed either as secondary, or even as irrelevant. Some correspondents adopted a pluralist approach to religion, referring, for instance, to 'the basic and fundamental truths, whether taught by Buddha, Plato or Christ'.[60] And others were more self-consciously constructing a belief-system drawn from a variety of sources. Thus one writer called for:

> belief in a God who loves and saves Hindoos and Buddhists and Mohammedans, as well as Christians of a hundred sects, and prepares each, by the experience of one or more earthly lives, for the next school of training in the great evolutionary march of embryonic souls from chaos towards that perfected state which can gaze upon the face of God Himself.[61]

According to another correspondent:

> though Englishmen have lost faith either in the absolute truth of the Gospel, or in the orthodox creed of the Churches, a very large

and increasing number of them cling tenaciously to the following creed, namely – that there is a God and a future life, and that this world has in the life of Christ the nearest approach to a Divine example to follow ever sent down among sinful men. Whether Christ was able to work miracles or not does not concern them, though they are inclined to doubt it. What does concern them is their belief that a great, inscrutable, living force and intelligence is slowly evolving order out of chaos, and bringing about that state of human perfection which we call 'Heaven'.[62]

Most participants in the *Daily Telegraph* correspondence were middle class and many of them were highly educated. They came from a social background where, until quite recently, concern for Christian doctrinal orthodoxy had been widespread, and where there was also a significant minority of those whose faith in science included an uncompromising resistance to 'heresy'. In working-class communities, as Sarah Williams has shown, an eclectic approach to questions of belief was long-established and more widely accepted. Working-class Londoners in the early years of this century frequently combined belief in Christianity and practice of various Christian rites with a range of 'folk beliefs' of a kind often deemed pagan.[63] In the mid-nineteenth century, working-class Methodists often combined their evangelical doctrinal schema with belief in boggarts and ghosts and the practice of various luck-bringing rituals, while working-class Spiritualists often combined their novel and 'heretical' ideas with a liberal and undogmatic form of Christianity. At successive seances in the 1850s, the Christian Spiritualists of Keighley took eclecticism to the length of making communication with the spirits first of Tom Paine and then of Martin Luther.[64]

Conclusion

The mixing of Christianity with a variety of other supernatural beliefs has a very long history, and in spite of the objections of the clergy, most people usually saw this mixing as unproblematic. But in the nineteenth century Christianity and Judaism were in a direct competition with a variety of rival views of the world, whose exponents frequently aimed to replace the older faiths. Two of these, the 'scientific' and the 'political', were particularly important because of the evangelical zeal with which they were propagated and because of the influence which they acquired over wide sections of the educated middle class and the working class respectively. Those west Europeans who broke away from their ancestral faith or who joined secularising campaigns in these years did so predominantly under the influence of one or both of these new faiths. The emergence of a significant minority of avowed unbelievers also undermined the status of religion as a 'shared language', providing rites, symbols and concepts, available to the whole community at times of celebration or of mourning, drawn upon by those in power to legitimate their authority and by oppressed groups to vindicate their claims. But if one looks at how this growing pluralism affected the beliefs of the majority of people, the prevailing trend is not the rejection of older beliefs, but a degree of eclecticism, and of accommodation between old and new.

5 Going to Church

In the seventeenth and eighteenth centuries there were many parts of Europe where regular church-going or participation in communion was legally required – even if the enforcement of the law could never be totally effective. In England, the Elizabethan statute prescribing weekly attendance at the parish church was repealed only in 1846, though it became a dead letter after the Act of Toleration in 1689. By removing all penalties from Nonconformist worship the Act also opened the way to those who worshipped nowhere. In most of the German states, there were laws requiring attendance at church, though these were no longer enforced after about the middle of the eighteenth century. In France, church-going was not required by the state, but those failing to receive communion at Easter could be barred from marrying or acting as godparents. By the eighteenth century these penalties were seldom rigorously applied, but participation in Easter Communion continued to be very high, at least in rural areas, until the Revolution.[1]

It is meaningless to compare levels of participation before and after the lifting of such requirements. But as increasing degrees of religious freedom became available, patterns of observance began to diverge, and statistics of the various forms of religious practice became the means favoured, both by contemporaries and by historians, of measuring the levels of fervour or alienation in different regions or social classes.[2] There are certainly many pitfalls awaiting those who do this. Anyone who assumes that a full church means a parish of devout Christians might take note of Samuel Butler's typically sardonic account of the congregation at his father's Nottinghamshire church around 1840:

171

They were chiefly farmers – fat, very well-to-do folk, who had come some of them with their wives and children from isolated farms two and three miles away; haters of popery and of anything which any one might choose to say was popish; good, sensible fellows who detested theory of any kind, whose ideal was the maintenance of the status quo with perhaps a loving reminiscence of old war times, and a sense of wrong that the weather was not more completely under their control, who desired higher prices and cheaper wages, but otherwise were most contented when things were changing least; tolerators, if not lovers, of all that was familiar; haters of all that was unfamiliar; they would have been equally horrified at hearing the Christian religion doubted, and at seeing it practised.[3]

Conversely, sympathetic commentators on Victorian working-class life objected to the idea that low levels of church attendance could be taken as evidence of irreligion, and such historians as Sarah Williams have developed this point at length.[4] In France, both contemporary observers and historians have made a great deal of what was called 'respect humain', which meant an unquestioning acceptance of the locally prevailing norms of behaviour.[5] In some parts of nineteenth-century France this led to full churches and in others it led to empty churches. There were many people who kept their beliefs to themselves and followed the local custom.

There were also differences between different religious traditions, and between those of similar traditions in different countries, as to the relative importance attached to different rites. For instance, in the nineteenth century English Protestants attended Sunday church services in much greater numbers than German Protestants, while far more German Protestants participated in communion at least once in the year than did those in England.[6] And while regular attendance at Sunday services was generally regarded by nineteenth century Protestants as being both a religious and a social duty, this could not have quite the force of the Catholic teaching, according to which those who missed Sunday mass without good reason were in a state of mortal sin. In general, the failure by a Catholic to go to church on Sunday, to receive communion at Easter, to marry in church, or to have children baptised, was more likely than a corresponding failure by a Protestant to represent a deliberate defiance of the church or rejection of the faith. Catholic teaching was much more explicit and insistent than that of most Protestant churches in inculcating these duties and in warning of the divine punishment awaiting those who neglected them.[7]

The great appeal of religious statistics is, of course, that they allow a degree of precision that is otherwise impossible. The exact date when church-going began to increase or decline can be identified, and fluctuations in the size of congregations can be related to political or economic events, to the publication of particular books, or the preaching of a popular evangelist. Statistics of church attendance or participation in communion provide the best evidence of the extent and distribution of attachment to the various churches. They cannot, however, be used as evidence for religious belief or a lack of belief. In view of the differences between countries and between religious traditions in the significance of particular rites, it is also more revealing to use the statistics to trace developments within particular countries and traditions, rather than to make comparisons between them.

Patterns of Religious Observance c.1850

Patterns of religious observance in western Europe already varied enormously at the middle of the nineteenth century. Around 1850 the proportion of the adult population attending church on an English Sunday varied from around 70 per cent in the St Ives district of Huntingdonshire to about 13 per cent in Longtown, a remote district of Cumberland, running along the Scottish border. In France the proportion of Easter communicants in the population aged thirteen and over varied from 86 per cent in the diocese of Nantes to 7 per cent in the diocese of Versailles. If figures for smaller units were available, they would clearly show even more extreme variations. In Germany in 1862 the number of Protestant communions in relation to the total Protestant population in 1862 varied from 83 per cent in Hesse-Nassau and Schaumburg-Lippe to 17 per cent in Berlin. (To discover what proportion of adults were communicants, one would clearly need to deduct children from the population total and multiple communions from the communion total. A study of Hanover suggests that the number of the latter was small, though in some rural areas they may have been more frequent.)[8]

Unfortunately, statistics of Jewish attendance at synagogue, or other forms of Jewish religious practice, are scarce. Rare examples are the British religious census of 1851 and the religious census of

London in 1903, the former counting attendance on an average sabbath, and the latter on the first day of Passover. These figures confirm a number of points that are also suggested by other sources: that attendance at synagogue was mainly an activity of adult males – no less than 78 per cent of the adults counted at the London census in 1903 were men; that attendance on an average sabbath was relatively low – Endelman estimates that about 10 per cent of British Jews went to synagogue on the day of the census in 1851; and that attendance was much higher on certain festivals – an estimated 25 per cent of London Jews were counted at services in the census of 1903, and there were others attending smaller synagogues omitted by the census-takers.[9] Throughout the nineteenth century, and into the early twentieth century, complaints of declining attendance at synagogue were rife. We find them in, for instance, Hamburg, in the early nineteenth century, where they provided a major pretext for the reform movement, in Paris in the 1870s, and in London in the early twentieth century.[10] But since precise figures are so seldom available, it appears to be impossible to trace the changes over time. In the remainder of this chapter, therefore, I shall concentrate on the various branches of Christianity, and I shall not attempt to enlarge on the impressionistic discussion of trends in Jewish religious practice which I provided in chapter 3.

Trends in Religious Practice

If we look at trends across the period from 1848 to 1914, we can divide the regions of western Europe into several groups:

(1)   Those where there had already been a large drop in the level of religious practice during the period 1750–1850 (e.g., Paris and the Paris region, most north German towns).

(2)   Those where there was a substantial drop during the period from the mid-nineteenth century to the First World War (e.g., England, most towns and industrial regions in France, most predominantly Protestant regions of southern and central Germany).

(3)   Those where the level of religious practice remained high throughout this period (e.g., much of Brittany and the Massif Central, most predominantly Catholic regions of Germany).

(4)   Those where religious practice increased during this period (e.g., those parts of Alsace-Lorraine that were annexed by Germany in 1871).

There were also some places where religious practice has always been low – or at least had been low since long before 1850. This was the case in some forest, marsh, heath or coastal settlements, where no church had ever been built, and the people seldom had much contact either with the clergy or with other figures of authority. For instance, the 'wild men of the marshes' at Guînes near Calais were said to live 'isolated, without religion, speaking who knows what language'. Here, as in many such areas, the first churches came in the second half of the nineteenth century, and as Hilaire comments, Catholicism and 'civilisation' tended to advance together.[11] In the Harz mountains in the early twentieth century it was claimed that the scattered communities of miners and iron-workers had never been well provided for religiously, and that Christianity and the church were regarded as 'foreign imports'.[12] The religious census of 1851 showed that the lowest level of attendance in England was found in a belt of remote rural districts in Cumberland and North-umberland, close to the border with Scotland. As in many parts of northern England, large parishes with a scattered population meant that contacts with the church had for long been much less frequent than in other parts of the country; and while many such areas had been successfully evangelised by the Methodists in the later eight-eenth and early nineteenth century, the border area had remained relatively detached from both church and chapel.[13]

Moving on to those areas where the biggest drop came in the period 1750–1850: in many German towns the decline of Protestant religious practice began about 1750, and there was a dramatic drop during the second half of the eighteenth century. In the early eight-eenth century it was common both in town and country for Protest-ants to receive communion three times in the year. By the early nineteenth century there were clearly many Protestants who did not participate in this central rite of the church at all. Between 1750 and 1800 the ratio of communions to Protestant population dropped most spectacularly in Hanover, where it fell from 150 per cent to 20 per cent; but it also fell from 100 per cent to 45 per cent in Ham-burg, and from over 100 per cent to 40 per cent in Berlin. In Dresden and Nuremberg, where most of the population were still communicants in 1800, the decline had also already begun in the later eighteenth century.[14] Figures for church attendance are less often available. But it is clear that by the 1840s, and probably at an early date, the proportion of Protestants attending church on an average Sunday was already fairly low. For Berlin there were estimates of about 10 per cent, and for Hamburg in the 1820s and Frankfurt in the 1840s there are comments on the sparseness of congregations, but without any precise figures.[15]

Clearly, the decline of Protestant religious practice in Germany began long before the onset of industrialisation, and in some cases, such as that of Hanover, before the period of rapid urban growth. Hölscher explains the decline partly in terms of social and economic changes, which applied mainly to larger cities such as Berlin and Hamburg, and partly to intellectual and cultural changes which applied more widely. Among the former he notes the rapid growth and increasing mobility of the urban population, and the development of extensive entertainment facilities, such as theatres, concert-halls and beer-gardens which competed strongly with the churches.[16] It might be added that in Berlin, where no new Protestant church was built between 1739 and 1835, the shortage of churches which became notorious in the later nineteenth century when Berlin was dubbed 'the most irreligious city in the world', was already apparent in the later eighteenth century.[17]

Among the intellectual and cultural developments, the influence of the Enlightenment both on the educated middle class generally and also on a large part of the Protestant clergy is clearly important. According to Hölscher it did not often lead to an outright rejection of Christianity; but it favoured a highly individualistic approach to religion in which dogma and external observances were both seen as being of minor importance, while individual faith was all-important. One of the major practical consequences of this new religious approach was a relaxation of church discipline. Pastors no longer thought it appropriate to regulate the behaviour of their parishioners by naming sinners from the pulpit or excluding them from acting as godparents.[18] A particularly important development during this period was the formation of numerous voluntary associations (*Vereine*), which took on wide-ranging intellectual, recreational and sometimes charitable functions, and for some of their members came to operate almost as alternative churches. Originally the province of bourgeois men, the *Vereine* expanded enormously during the nineteenth century, often drawing in women or members of other social classes, and becoming a central feature first of urban life and then of rural life too in the German-speaking world. While these developments went furthest in predominantly Protestant cities, Schlögl's research on Aachen, Münster and Cologne suggests that there may have been similar trends in Catholic cities too.[19]

In Paris and the surrounding rural areas, as well as in some other parts of France, including much of the Bordeaux region, the turning-point seems to have been the period from 1789 to 1801. These years saw the Catholic Church split in two, then the persecution of the non-juring church, followed by the terror and forced dechristianisation, and then, even after the churches began to reopen, a severe shortage of priests, and continuing disputes bewteen constitutionals and non-jurors. There were many ways in which the events of these years might precipitate an exodus from the churches. In the first place, the Revolution offered an unprecedented degree of freedom. This was particularly welcomed in the area round La Rochelle, which had been a Protestant stronghold in the seventeenth century, and where large numbers of people were forcibly converted to Catholicism.[20] Their descendants were among the first to give up practising what had generally been a very lukewarm Catholic faith. Secondly, the opposition to the Revolution of many of the clergy and of the strongly Catholic peasantry of the west helped to unleash a violent anti-clericalism, which left a permanent mark in Paris and other strongholds of revolutionary militancy. Thirdly, the church faced special problems in the first half of the nineteenth century in regions, like the Île de France, where most of the clergy had taken the oath of loyalty to the constitution in 1790. During the dechristianisation of 1793–94, the majority of the non-juring clergy were already in exile, while the constitutional clergy were still in their parishes. Many thousands of them succumbed to the severe pressures that were put upon them and abdicated their priesthood, often marrying as well. Even after the Concordat of 1801 and the gradual reconstruction of the church, these areas suffered from a shortage of clergy. In 1816, 15 per cent of the parishes in France were vacant, but in parts of the Paris region, the centre and the south-west the proportion was over 30 per cent.[21] In some of these areas there was a generation brought up during the revolutionary era who had not been catechised, had not received their First Communion, had not been married in church, and had never learnt habits of church-going. Even when priests were available, problems often arose from the fact that they were out of sympathy with local religious traditions. After the implementation of the Concordat in 1802, and even more after the restoration of the Bourbons in 1814–15, former non-jurors held most of the key positions in the church, and there was often a deliberate policy of marginalising or completely excluding those who had belonged to the constitutional church. Many of these priests retained a popular following and became a focus for dissatisfaction with the restored church and opposition to the priests who had supplanted them.[22]

Throughout the period from the restoration of the Bourbons in 1815 to the establishment of the Second Republic in 1848, indifference or positive hostility to the church, often justified by reference to Voltaire and other heroes of the Enlightenment, was very widespread among bourgeois men in all parts of France, including those regions where the mass of the people and most bourgeois women were fervently Catholic.[23] In Paris and the surrounding countryside, however, peasants and workers tended to be as anticlerical as the bourgeoisie, and the proportion of women going to mass – though still much higher than the proportion of men doing so – was relatively low. Sometimes the timing of the decline in church-going can be documented quite precisely: in Bayeux, according to Hufton, the majority of the population stopped going to mass some time between Christmas 1791 and Easter 1792.[24] More often the precise timing is not so clear, but by the middle of the nineteenth century there was a broad belt of low religious practice running across central France from Paris to Bordeaux. There is a wealth of impressionistic evidence, especially in the form of clerical complaints, though accurate statistics are not often available.[25]

The Importance of the Years 1848 to 1914

However, there were still at the middle of the nineteenth century large areas of western Europe where going to church on Sunday or going to communion at Easter were things taken for granted by the majority of the population, and not signifying any special degree of piety or religious commitment. By 1914 such areas were the exception rather than the rule. By then there were some areas where those who went to church on Sunday exposed themselves to ridicule;[26] there were many more where church-goers were regarded as 'religious people', whose piety, whether respected, admired, or merely tolerated, was the result of a personal choice.[27]

All three countries saw an overall decline in church-going during this period, in spite of numerous local variations (see tables 1–3). The period between the revolutions of 1848 and the outbreak of the First World War marks a very important stage in the decline of church-going in England, France and Germany. Two types of general explanation have most commonly been advanced to explain this fact: the impact of Darwinism and of other new intellectual developments, such as biblical criticism; and the impact of industrialisation and urbanisation, and associated processes of 'modernisation'. A variant on the second explanation is the idea that increasing prosperity in the later nineteenth century encouraged the idea that religion was no longer needed, and thus led to indifference.

However, the more closely one looks at the evidence, the harder it becomes to fit it into any such overall scheme. In the first place, it needs to be noted that the patterns of change in the three countries were very different. In England the decline in church-going came relatively late – mostly after about 1890 (see table 3). But when it came, it affected all regions and social classes, though Catholics less than Protestants. However, with Catholics comprising only about 5 per cent of the population in this period, they were a much less important minority than in Germany. In Germany, as already mentioned, there had been a substantial decline in Protestant religious practice in the later eighteenth and early nineteenth centuries. There was a further decline, in most parts of Protestant Germany in the 1860s and 1870s. Then between about 1880 and 1895 the level of practice stabilised, before going into another period of less rapid decline between 1895 and 1913[28] (see table 1). In Germany, however, the confessional divide was fundamental: while Protestant religious practice declined in all social classes and in all regions during the second half of the century, Catholic practice remained high, and followed its own quite different patterns of development. In France, Gibson interprets the figures as showing a gradual increase in the first half of the century, reaching a high point around 1860, a stabilisation in the 1860s and early 1870s, and then a steady decline in the period 1879–1905, followed by a slight recovery in the period up to the First World War I.[29] However, regional variations are so great that generalisation is difficult (see table 2). The polarisation between the most strongly Catholic and the most

Table 1　Trends in Protestant religious practice in Germany

Communions per 100 members of the Protestant *Landeskirchen*			
	1862	*1880*	*1895*	*1913*
Old Prussia	52	42	39	30
Hanover (Lutheran)	63	59	48	47
Hesse-Nassau	83		42	48
Bavaria	78	65	68	62
Palatinate	73	61	58	43
Saxony (Kingdom)	72	49	44	35
Württemberg	70	54	51	40
Baden	69	52	54	44
Hesse-Darmstadt	69	54	57	47
Mecklenburg-Schwerin	39		34	30
Mecklenburg-Strelitz	29	23	23	19
Brunswick	42	28	27	24
Saxony-Weimar (Thuringia)	63	44	40	31
Oldenburg	35	24	21	15
Saxony-Meiningen (Thuringia)	60	36	38	28
Hamburg		8	9	8
Lübeck	34	19	18	14
Bremen		14	14	7
Berlin	17	13	16	14

Source: Lucian Hölscher, *Weltgericht oder Revolution* (Stuttgart, 1989), p. 143.

strongly anti-clerical regions had taken such extreme forms by the second half of the nineteenth century that national developments were received within highly specific regional environments, many of which remained immune to the tendency to declining religious practice until after the First World War I, or even until the 1960s.[30]

When one looks at the various general explanations that have been offered, difficulties soon become evident. The explanation in terms of the impact of Darwinism and biblical criticism works best for England, where the decline in church-going began in the later nineteenth century, and where it was initially most rapid among members of the upper middle and upper classes, who might be expected to be those most familiar with new intellectual developments.[31] However, it should be remembered that even after this decline was underway, church-going by the upper middle and upper classes was higher than that for other social groups, and that right up to the present day in

England the highly educated are more likely to be church-goers than those with little education.[32]

Table 2 Trends in Catholic religious practice in France

Easter communions as percentage of population aged 13 and over in various dioceses

Châlons	**1870**: 20	**1892**: 15	**1911**: 12
Chartres	**1868**: 22	**1909**: 8	
Clermont-Ferrand	**1807–13**: 97	**1903–5**: 60	
Le Mans	**1830–47**: 54	**1908**: 31	
Luçon	**1876–8**: 66	**1894–6**: 65	
Moulins	**1805–16**: 94	**1877–8**: 64	**1904**: 43
Nantes	**1839–45**: 86	**1863–9**: 83	**1899–1902**:89
Orléans	**1852–6**: 19	**1865–9**: 27	**1883**: 21
Périgueux	**1841**: 49	**1874**: 57	**1901–6**: 54
Rennes	**1883–4**: 94	**1899**: 95	
Troyes	**1865**: 17	**1878–80**: 14	**1908–10**: 7
Versailles	**1834**: 7	**1859–61**: 15	**1893–1901**: 11
City of Paris	**1854**: 17	**1889**: 15	**1903–8**: 18

Source: Ralph Gibson, *A Social History of French Catholicism, 1789–1914* (London, 1989), pp. 174–6.

Table 3 Trends in religious practice in England

Attendances at places of worship of all denominations on Sunday of census as a percentage of total population

London (County)	**1851**: 29	**1886–7**: 29	**1902–3**: 22
Liverpool	**1851**: 40	**1881**: 33	**1912**: 27
Birmingham	**1851**: 28	**1892**: 24	
28 large towns*	**1851**: 37	**1881**: 35	
8 large towns**	**1851**: 43	**1902–4**: 27	

* These were spread across most regions of England and ranged in size from about 20,000 up to 500,000.
** These were all in the north or north midlands, and included few very large towns.

Source: Robin Gill, *The Myth of the Empty Church* (London, 1993), pp. 302, 305, 313, 319, 322.

The explanation in terms of intellectual developments does not work at all for France, where the alienation from the Catholic Church of a large proportion of middle-class men dated back to the time of the Revolution and was strongly influenced by political factors, where the years 1848–51 had seen the beginnings of a 'return to the church' by a significant section of the upper middle class, and where the period after about 1890 saw a religious revival specifically among intellectuals. In France the major theme of the period 1848–1914 is the religious alienation of a large section of 'the people'. In this period we have the origins of the situation that became highly visible as a result of statistical enquiries in the 1950s and 1960s whereby in many French cities very low levels of Catholic practice on the part of the working class and lower middle class contrasted with very high levels in the upper middle class.[33]

In Germany it is true that the educated middle class was noted for low levels of church-going in the second half of the nineteenth century, and that Darwinism and scientific materialism had consider-able influence on members of this class. However, as already men-tioned, non-church-going by upper middle class Protestants seems very often to have been a continuation of habits already established over several generations, rather than the result of new ideas. Equally Darwinism had a big influence on the thinking of working-class Social Democrats in the late nineteenth century, but it seems more likely that their enthusiasm for Darwin was a consequence rather than a cause of their alienation from the church. In any case, the impact of Darwinism does not provide a convincing explanation for the decline of church-going among the mass of impoverished and poorly educated German Protestants during this period.

At first sight the impact of industrialisation and urbanisation does provide a much more convincing explanation. There are many instances where the decline of church-going was associated with either the establishment of factories and mines in areas previously dominated by agriculture, the mechanisation of previously home-based industries, or the onset of rapid urban growth. It does not follow, however, that these devlopments provide in themselves a sufficient explanation of the decline in church-going. In some parts of western Europe the same things happened, but with only a slight decline in church-going, or none at all.

Two examples will illustrate this. Geoffrey Robson undertook an intensive analysis of church-going in 1851 in the Black Country, the zone of mining and metal-working towns and villages to the north-west of Birmingham, with a combined population of around 350,000. Within this relatively small area adult church attendance on the day of the census varied, for reasons that are often far from clear, between about 30 per cent and 60 per cent. Some towns or villages within the area would support the theory that industrialisation was associated with a decline in religious practice, but others would not. In fact, the overall level of church-going was higher than in the surrounding rural districts – mainly because of the exceptional strength of Methodism among Black Country miners and nailers. The most that one can say is that certain kinds of economic and social change provided the preconditions for subsequent changes in religion.[34]

Antonius Liedhegener's study of the Westphalian cities of Bochum and Münster illustrates the fact that in the same environment Catholicism and Protestantism could develop in very different ways. In the period from 1845 to 1930, the administrative and commercial centre of Münster grew from 20,000 to 100,000 people, while Bochum with its mines and factories advanced from 5,000 to 300,000. During this time Protestant communicant statistics showed the predicted decline – from 60 per cent to 30 per cent in Münster and from 45 per cent to 20 per cent in Bochum. But when one looks more closely it becomes more difficult to explain the decline simply as an inevitable consequence of industrialisation and urban growth. In the first place it is striking that the course of Protestant decline follows a very similar pattern in the two cities, in spite of the differences in their ecomomy and the fact that the rate of demographic growth was much greater in Bochum than in Münster. Secondly, periods of rapid population growth were not always marked by a decline in religious practice: after a sharp drop in the years 1850–80, the Protestant communicant rate stabilised in the 1880s, although the population continued to grow very fast. Above all, these dramatic economic and social changes had little effect on the level of religious practice by Catholics. In 1925, Easter communicants were over 60 per cent of the Catholic population in Münster and over 50 per cent in Bochum. Unfortunately, we do not have a run of figures, but it is clear that any decline must have been very limited. Impressionistic evidence, suggests that the Catholic Church in Bochum was relatively weak in the 1840s and 1850s, but that its hold over its members began to grow from the 1860s with the construction of the all-embracing Catholic milieu.[35]

The theory that the rising standard of living in the later nine-teenth century was linked with growing religious apathy has been powerfully argued by A. D. Gilbert. He sees religion as something which people 'turn to', when they can see no human solution to their problems. He stresses the role of medical advances in reducing the number of crisis-points in most people's lives.[36] This theory seems at first sight very plausible, but it does not fit the facts. In England throughout the nineteenth century the social group most actively involved in organised religion was also the most prosper-ous, namely the upper middle class. In France during the second half of the nineteenth century religious involvement by the bour-geoisie was increasing, while working-class involvement was dimin-shing. The motives for religious involvement cannot be reduced to the search for help, and there are plenty of examples of those who saw their prosperity as a divine reward rather than as something which made religion unnecessary.[37]

Rather than there being any one master-factor that explains the decline in church-going during this period, there were a number of factors which potentially contributed to this trend, including economic and social upheavals associated with industria-lisation or urbanisation; the radicalisation of particular sections of the population, as a result of dramatic political events or the intensification of class conflict; the expanding role of the state in areas like education and welfare, displacing the churches from their former spheres of influence; the spread of urban influences to the countryside; and new intellectual and cultural developments, ranging from Darwinism to the cult of Wagner. It is essential to realise, however, that these developments did not affect religious practice in any uniform way: their significance in the very different environments of England, France and Germany, or on members of different social classes or religious denominations, or on those com-ing from different regions within those countries, could be vastly different.

Industry, Cities, Class Conflict

To begin with the first of the developments mentioned above: industrialisation and urbanisation in the nineteenth century often were associated with the decline of religious practice. The relation-ship is clearest in Germany. Statistics for the various German

states and provinces in the years 1891–5 showed a strong positive
correlation between the Protestant communion rate and the proportion of the population living in rural areas, and also a positive
correlation, though somewhat weaker, between the communion
rate and the proportion of the economically active employed in
agriculture.[38] As already indicated, the low rates of religious practice in many Germany towns preceded the rapid growth of population in the nineteenth century. However, it is evident that the
massive shifts of population from countryside to cities and industrial
regions in the second half of the nineteenth century presented the
churches with enormous logistical problems, as well as other major
challenges. Almost every growing city faced a shortage of churches
and clergy at some point in the nineteenth century. In the extreme
case of Berlin, the ratio of Protestant clergy to Protestant population, which had been 1:3000 in 1800, had grown to 1:4300 in 1850,
and 1:9593 in 1890. By the latter date the largest of many 'giant
parishes', Holy Cross in Luisenstadt, contained some 128,000 people. In 1891, when the national average was 1 pastor for 1887
Protestants, other great cities, while falling short of the situation in
Berlin, still showed very unfavourable ratios, for instance 8166 in
Hamburg, 5977 in Dresden, 5605 in Leipzig, 5324 in Chemnitz and
4146 in Bremen.[39]

   As well as long-term shortages of clergy, churches and parish
centres, many other factors might contribute to the decline of religious participation in areas with rapidly growing population,
whether cities, or newly developing industrial regions. For instance,
immigrants to cities or industrial regions sometimes remained
highly mobile, and found it difficult to form close relations with a
particular pastor or congregation.[40] The fact that much rural religion was closely linked with the fertility of the land, protecting
animals from disease or the cult of local saints, and that conformity
was maintained through the force of local custom, meant that
migrants to the city might be inclined to drop practices that seemed
irrelevant to their new situation. Studies of a number of predominantly Catholic cities, including Cologne, Düsseldorf and Marseilles,
which were growing fast during the second half of the nineteenth-
century, have shown that the church was relatively successful
in retaining the loyalty of workers born in the city, but was much
less able to attract those who came in from the countryside.[41]
Moreover, the nineteenth century city offered a highly pluralistic
environment, in which a vast range of leisure possibilities, as well as

political movements and rival systems of belief, offered numerous alternatives to the church.

The establishment of factories or mines in areas previously dominated by agriculture or domestic industry could have similar consequences, including, for instance, a large influx of population, antagonism between the newcomers and the long-settled local population, new work-rhythms (often including Sunday work), and the development of a youth culture, as young people earning relatively high wages could afford to ignore the moral prohibitions imposed by the church or by their parents. These newly industrialising communities frequently underwent a decline in church-going and other forms of religious observance.

The tendency in this period for church-going to be lower in towns than in rural areas, and lower in those small towns and villages that were industrialised than in those dominated by agriculture, was most pronounced in Protestant regions of Germany. But it can also be seen to a lesser degree in England, France, and Catholic regions of Germany. However, these tendencies should not be exaggerated. Most towns had a vigorous religious life, involving a substantial proportion of the population, even if the proportion involved was seldom as great as in the more devout rural areas.[42] Nor did rapid urban growth necessarily lead to any precipitous religious decline. Where established churches were able to respond to the needs of growing cities by, for instance, recruiting clergy, building churches, and providing educational, charitable and recreational facilities, they often succeeded in at least stabilising the situation. Hilaire cites the example of the textile districts round Roubaix and Tourcoing, one of the few industrial areas of France where the parochial network kept pace with the growth in population.[43] The Church of England, which had suffered considerable losses in the period c.1790–1840, made great and at least partly successful efforts in the period from about 1840 to 1890 to rebuild its position in the cities and industrial districts.[44] An even greater part in the religious life of Victorian cities was played by the Nonconformist chapels,[45] which were very successful in recruiting those alienated from the established church in the first half of the century and which, in spite of Anglican revival in the second half of the century, continued to maintain their share of the population. During the period 1851 and 1881 when the population of many English cities doubled, the proportion of church-goers remained more or less the same. Robin Gill who has examined figures for twenty-eight large towns, found a slight drop in average attendance from 37 per cent to 35 per cent in those years – though the average conceals considerable differences, including for instance, a large drop in Nottingham, and significant increases in Bolton, Bradford and Sheffield.[46] In both England and Prussia, the Catholic Church, in spite of the difficulties caused by the poverty of most Catholics in the former case, and by state persecution in the latter, succeeded in establishing numerous strong urban parishes.[47]

Rather, therefore, than assuming some kind of economic determinism, it is necessary to look both at how the various churches responded to the challenges presented by social change, and at the political context within which these changes took place. A good example is offered by the Pas-de-Calais in France, a mainly agricultural area which began to be transformed by coal-mining in the 1850s. Up to the 1870s it seems that the church was experiencing difficulties in the mining parishes, but as yet it had no effective rivals apart from the drinking places. The miners set great store by the rites of passage, especially religious burial, and by certain saints' days. They also came in large numbers to missions, and their precautions against accidents included the employment of priests to bless mines: in one mine that had gone without a single accident for five years in the 1850s, the fact was popularly attributed to the fact that the Bishop of Arras had blessed it. However, attendance at mass was generally low, whether because of tensions between the miners and the farmers, who were the mainstay of most congregations, because old-established parish churches were often inconveniently sited for the miners, because of Sunday work, or because those who were not working felt like relaxing in a bar. Wherever a peasant and a mining population lived side by side, the former were always more frequent church-goers. But as yet there was no open antagonism between church and miners.

This began to develop in the later 1870s with the advance of the anti-clerical republicans, and became acute with the growing strength of socialism and the major strikes in the 1890s. From about 1876 'the magic words of Liberty and Equality began to strike a chord with miners subjected to an extremely hierarchical system of paternalism'. The basic reason for the alienation of the miners from the church seems to have been the close relationship between the church and the mining companies. There were two elements in this: financial dependence and the church's paternalist social ideology. The dependence arose from the fact that many of the mining parishes or chaplaincies were financed substantially or entirely by the companies, which also supported, as part of their system of comprehensive paternalism, many schools staffed by religious orders. The church's need for such support became especially acute after the coming to power of the anti-clerical republicans, when the church's budget was cut, and it became impossible even to maintain the existing network of parishes, let alone to extend it. Those chaplains who became outspoken in support of the miners were dismissed. Successive bishops of Arras and many of the local clergy criticised specific abuses, but without questioning the authority of the companies. In their view, the answer was not democracy or socialism, but a more genuine paternalism.[48]

According to Hilaire, up to about 1890 industrialisation generally seemed to go hand in hand with dechristianisation in France, but from then on, because of a change of tactics by some of the clergy, the picture is more varied. He cites the example of the textile districts round Roubaix, Tourcoing and the Lys valley, close to the border with Belgium. In the first half of the twentieth century this was among the most Catholic of French industrial districts. This was partly because of the success, already mentioned, with which the church extended the parochial network to keep pace with the growing population. But equally important was a move away from reliance on paternalist employers. 'Democratic priests', inspired by Leo XIII's social encyclical, *Rerum Novarum*, were impressed by the way in which the Socialists had set up a mass of organisations providing for their members' every need. They decided to meet the enemy on their own ground by setting up Catholic trade unions, co-ops, benefit societies, youth groups, etc. as well as by speaking out on social and economic questions.[49]

The Pas-de-Calais can also be compared with the Deerness Valley in county Durham, where mines began to be sunk in about 1860. As a result, this thinly populated rural area experienced a rapid growth in mumbers, with workers coming from London, Lincolnshire and Ireland as well as the surrounding countryside. Initially the valley had a rather wild reputation, in which fighting and heavy drinking featured prominently. There were no Anglican churches in the area until 1874, and the Church of England never established a strong local presence. By the early twentieth century about a third of the households in the area still had no connection with a church or chapel. However, from very early days the Methodists, with their flexible system of small local chapels and lay preachers, were active in the area, and by the early twentieth century Methodism had something of the status of the locally established religion. About 40 per cent of households were said to be connected with a Methodist chapel, and moreover most of the local leaders of the Liberal Party, the miners' union and the Co-op were Methodists – the majority being Primitive Methodists, the most proletarian branch of the movement. There was an excellent fit between Methodism and the Liberal politics which were locally dominant until about 1910. Both placed great stress on respectability, self-help and education; both insisted on the rights and dignity of the worker, including the right to organise. They also – and this is where they came under attack from the growing socialist movement – believed that these were quite compatible with the capitalist system, and that trade unionists should work not to overthrow the existing order, but to bring about reconciliation between capitalist and worker, based on mutual recognition of the rights and interests of the other.

With declining profits and more aggressive styles of management in the early twentieth century, leading to growing working-class militancy, the formation of local branches of the Independent Labour Party (ILP), and participation in the national miners' strike in 1912, the result was not mass alienation from Methodism, but a split within local Methodism between those who remained faithful to the old liberalism and those who were moving towards socialism. To some extent it was a generational split, with most of the leaders of local Methodism remaining Liberal until after the First World War, while the younger generation were joining the ILP. The disputes were often bitter, but Methodism and the other branches of English Nonconformity, with their relatively democratic structures, and their dependence on lay preachers, were much more flexibile and susceptible to local opinion than French Catholicism. As against the polarisations so characteristic of France in the nineteenth century and the first half of the twentieth, the result was a confusion typical of England, with some Methodists staying Liberal, but most going Labour, some socialists staying Methodist, while others left in protest at the excessive moderation of the chapels. In the long run the role of Methodists in the trade unions declined, while the role of Roman Catholics increased. This was not for political reasons, but because of a combination of high rates of social mobility by Methodists and their strong temperance views, which were hard to reconcile with the tendency for union meetings to be held in working men's clubs, where the main activity was drinking.[50]

So the economic and social changes associated with industrialisation and urbanisation need to be placed in a specific political and religious context, and to be seen in terms of the social conflicts which they unleashed. Of the three major emancipatory currents of the nineteenth century, at least the first two had major consequences for religious practice. The first of these currents was liberal and democratic, spear headed by the progressive middle class. The second was socialist and mainly working class. The third was feminist. The women's movement of the later nineteenth and early twentieth centuries raised religious issues of many kinds, but does not seem to have had much immediate effect on religious practice.[51] However, both the liberal and democratic movements and later the socialist and working-class movements had great and immediate effects.

This is very clearly so in France, where the religious alienation of particular towns, districts or occupational groups is closely linked with politics, as are returns to the church or continuing Catholic loyalty elsewhere. The result was that during the period from about 1850 to 1960 France was highly differentiated religiously, with areas of very high and very low religious practice – sometimes in different districts of the same town or the same rural department.[52] Two examples will illustrate the crucial role of politics. The Creuse, an overwhelmingly rural department on the western edge of the Massif Central, had at the mid-twentieth century the lowest level of Catholic practice of any department in France. It was also a department noted for strongly radical traditions. The latter seem to have their roots mainly in the system of migrant labour, already well established in the early nineteenth century, whereby a large part of the male population left during the months of spring and summer to work as masons in Paris. Masons from the Creuse took part in the Parisian revolutions of 1830 and 1848 and in the Commune of 1871 – and a large number of them were arrested after the fall of the Commune. These radical loyalties they brought back to the family farm, and on the long winter evenings, when villagers elsewhere in France were entertaining one another with stories about wicked witches, cruel bandits or powerful saints, the people of the Creuse were learning about Paris and its revolutions. Already in 1849 they were voting heavily for the Democrat-Socialists, and under the Third Republic the department was a bastion first of the Radicals, and later of the Socialists and Communists. The first official recognition of the decline of religious practice came from the

Bishop of Limoges in 1875. But from 1880 onwards, and even more after the Separation of Church and State in 1905, the decline was rapid and dramatic. Alienation from the church reached its most extreme form in hamlets of small farmers where the force of neighbourly opinion often imposed a secular orthodoxy. In larger villages there were generally some dissenters who insisted on going to mass. Although anti-clericalism, with its focus on such issues as financial disputes and male sexual jealousy, preceded political radicalisation and to some extent continued independently of it, it is evident that political events played a decisive part in the dechristianisation of the Creuse, and that political idealism offered a powerful alternative faith for those alienated from Catholicism. Pérouas notes a strong strand of the 'mystical' and the 'millenarian', 'both socialist and Christian' in the rhetoric of the Radicals and Socialists of the Creuse. Jesus Christ was seen essentially as a poor man, who came to challenge the rich and powerful, especially the priests.[53]

The converse of this increasingly tight interlocking of Left-wing politics and anti-Catholicism was a strengthening of loyalty to the church among political conservatives, and sometimes politically-influenced conversions of those formerly hostile to the church. A classic example of the latter is the religious evolution of the bourgeoisie of Rouen, noted in the early nineteenth century for its indifference or hostility to the church, and by the late nineteenth century for its piety.[54] Under Napoleon, the bourgeoisie of France's fifth largest city had a reputation for irreligion. While a quarter of the women were said to receive communion, it was claimed that only 2 per cent of the men did so 'and among the latter, no magistrates, public officials or men of influence'. Under the Restoration, 'Voltairian' philosophy and bitter anti-clericalism reached a high point – partly in reaction to an ultra-conservative aristocratic archbishop. The chief institutions of the anti-clerical bourgeoisie were the Masonic lodges, of which there were six by 1848. Their favourite paper, the liberal *Journal de Rouen*, 'made a long-term speciality of anti-clerical quarrels, the Jesuits, the congregation, the fanaticism of the young priests and the obscurantism of their flocks'.[55] After public processions were suspended, following the revolution of 1830, the continuation of the ban became a touchstone for this paper, and thirty years later it was still thundering against the clergy. Meanwhile, however, many of its readers were changing their views. There was already a devout group within the bourgeoisie, drawn especially from the older families, whose fortunes had been made before 1789. Under the Second Empire these strongly Catholic families would provide a model for others, and a base for Catholic organisations. Already in the 1840s there were signs that previously irreligious members of the bourgeoisie were interested in the idea that religion could provide a basis for social cohesion, if it could be detached from the reactionary extremism of the Restoration years. In this respect the appointment from 1844 of a series of politically moderate archbishops helped.

Once again, the years 1848–51 marked a turning-point. The panic induced by the June Days in Paris, and more generally the fears provoked by the massive radicalisation of considerable sections of the working class, the peasantry and the lower middle class during these years, led to a major crisis of conscience on the part of the wealthy bourgeoisie. In particular they took advantage of the great expansion of Catholic secondary education following the Falloux law to provide their children with the religious schooling which they had never received themselves.[56] As in so many other religious revivals of the nineteenth century, it was women who led the way; but their husbands, and more especially their sons, followed. When in 1860 an elderly merchant who had remained a faithful disciple of Voltaire, came to write his spiritual testament, he expressed regret at the new spiritual climate in the city, and anxiety that when he was dying someone might send for a priest. In the latter part of the century, an important minority of the bourgeoisie (usually drawn from lower down the scale of wealth and status) remained true to the older liberal and anti-clerical traditions. But by 1892 the religious situation seemed to have changed so far that when a Parisian preacher came to deliver some Lent sermons he declared himself 'overwhelmed' by the sight of a congregation of several thousand, of whom two-fifths were men. The new religious atmosphere was reflected in domestic piety (families gathering to chant the Ave Maria together), in conservative politics (often inextricably bound up with Catholic faith), and in active support for charities of all kinds. Chaline comments that 'this world, otherwise so hard in matters of business, and so concerned about its own interests, could show an astonishing generosity, sacrificing large amounts of time and money'. He cites the example of the banker, Paul Le Picard, a leading member of the St Vincent de Paul Society, regarded as a saint by some, and by most as a bit mad.[57]

In Germany the relationship between political and religious loyalties was less clear-cut than in France, but it was nonetheless important. In Berlin in the later part of the nineteenth century, for instance, a major factor in the city's irreligious atmosphere was the fact that most of the population were supporters of the Social Democrats or the Left Liberals, and saw the Protestant church as a stronghold of conservatism. Conversely, those groups that were closest to the church, such as aristocrats, the military, state officials and the lower middle class, tended to be politically conservative.[58]

Church-going in Berlin had been in decline since at least the later eighteenth century, so the growth of liberal and socialist politics cannot be seen as a major cause of the decline. On the other hand, this can be argued with much more plausibility in Saxony or some west German industrial districts, where the level of religious practice was still relatively high around the middle of the nineteenth century. For instance, in the 1820s and 1830s the Wuppertal was still noted as a stronghold of Protestant revivalism, with Pietist textile employers like the Engels family and equally devout weavers. Friedrich Engels, who was born in Barmen in 1820, complained that when he was growing up the only interests of the workers were religion and drink. By the 1850s, however, while the interest in drink remained very much alive, there were frequent comments on the decline of working-class religion. Clergymen blamed the burgeoning urban leisure world, with its theatres, concerts, dancing halls and brothels, as well as numerous pubs. A more fundamental factor seems to have been the increasingly tense relations between employers and workers, which made it difficult to bring members of different classes together in the same church. In the 1820s and 1830s it seems that patriarchal relations between merchants and weavers had still been a reality. In the 1840s relations were deteriorating, especially in those branches of the textile industry where domestic production was giving way to workshop and factory. In May 1849, while Pietist merchants remained among the most loyal subjects of the Prussian monarchy, many workers took part in an insurrection which controlled the town of Elberfeld for a week.[59] In 1855 and 1857 there were major strikes. The 'old Wuppertal traditons' survived to some extent among locally born domestic textile workers, but they became increasingly marginal in the 1860s and 1870s with immigration from other parts of Germany, and the beginnings of socialist propaganda. The history of a working-class parish later recalled that 'At that time there was no section of society in which it was harder to declare yourself a Christian. Many gave up going to church in order to avoid the continual banter'. Ironically, by this time the 'old Wuppertal traditions' were in decline among the elite too, as they moved out of the town into a new suburb of large houses with extensive gardens, and eagerly threw off many of the constraints imposed by the old Calvinist asceticism on the full enjoyment of their wealth. However the church, even if no longer dominated by the elite, remained strongly conservative, as well as passionately patriotic and royalist.[60]

In England, there certainly were Liberals who were secularists or religious sceptics, but they were greatly outnumbered by those Liberals who were Nonconformists. If anything, the advance of Liberalism was likely to be associated with an intensification of religious life. The relationship between religion and the rise of organised labour and of socialism is a much more complicated question, and indeed remains controversial, in spite of the many books and articles already devoted to the subject.

The only mass movement of the English working class in which anti-clericalism was a major theme was the agricultural labourers' movement of the early and middle 1870s ('The Revolt of the Field'). Whereas in the towns the high degree of religious pluralism had considerably diluted the power of the Anglican clergy, there were many villages in which the parson was the most powerful figure, or second in importance only to the squire. While some Anglican clergy supported the labourers' movement, there were a great many who opposed it. For instance, Nigel Scotland in a study of Gloucestershire, found three clergymen who declared their support for the union, but he concluded that 'Gloucestershire clergy, like the majority of their contemporaries elsewhere in the country, showed themselves for the most part to be either hostile or at best apathetic to the labourers' side of the dispute'.[61] The clergy naturally became one of the movement's major targets. Denunciations of 'priestcraft' and 'clerical tyranny' were constant themes in the movement's press.[62] While opposition from squires and farmers was only to be expected, the labourers believed that the clergy 'ought' to have been on their side, and when the vicar preached submission to those set in authority, or condemned the 'interference' of the union, they saw this as an example of gross hypocrisy. At least in some areas the 1870s showed a significant drop in rural church-going. In the diocese of Oxford, for instance, the episcopal visitation of 1875 found many incumbents complaining of the 'slanders' of the union, or of the decline in church-going since the onset of the labourers' movement. In one parish the vicar claimed that 'three years ago the church was full, but now there are many empty benches'. A study of rural life published in 1913 stated that there were many rural parishes where tradition continued to hold that the clergy had stood against the people in the time of crisis, and had condoned the victimisation of activists that had followed the decline of the union. Clive Field studied episcopal visitations in the Oxford diocese from 1738 to 1936. He concluded that the decline in Anglican church-going began in the 1870s, and that the main initial reason was the alienation of male labourers because of clerical opposition to the union.[63]

However, in spite of occasional secularist voices[64] the union's rhetoric was predominantly Christian, and most commonly Methodist. The outstanding leader of the movement, Joseph Arch, was a Primitive Methodist preacher, and Scotland's study of officials of the two main agricultural unions in Norfolk, Suffolk and Lincolnshire during the years 1872–96 shows that slightly over half can be identified as Methodists. Union meetings often began with hymns, and special services conducted by one of the many union leaders who was also a local preacher, were held on Sunday afternoons, sometimes in a chapel, but often in the open air, or even a skittle alley. However, many chapels drew their membership from a wide social band, including, for instance, farmers and shopkeepers, as well as labourers and craftsmen. Ministers and lay leaders might respond to the deep divisions of opinion within their membership by trying to impose some kind of 'No Politics' rule, whereby preachers were required to steer away from controversial issues, and no meeting could be allowed on chapel premises which might be seen as 'taking sides'.[65] So the effect of the events of the 1870s on rural church-going was overwhelmingly negative so far as the Church of England was concerned – but limited in scale, because so many union members had long since gone over to Dissent. In the short run they were likely to strengthen the Nonconformist identity of many labourers, while sometimes placing strains on loyalty to their chapel in those cases where the minister and lay officals were unsupportive. In the longer run the chapels may have suffered from the disillusionment that set in with the decline of the union.

In south Wales, the Labour Party's greatest stronghold in the twentieth century and one of the greatest strongholds of Nonconformity in the nineteenth century, it has been argued that increasing working-class militancy, often reflected in conversion to some form of socialism, was a major factor in the decline of the chapels and that, in particular, the miners' strike of 1898 marked a turning-point.[66] But even in south Wales, more recent research suggests that the decline of working-class participation in the chapels was more long drawn out and gradual, and that relationships between the chapels and the growing forces of Labour and socialism were many-sided.[67] In England it would be very much harder to argue that political events played a major role in the decline of church-going during the period from the later 1880s until the First World War. In most parts of urban and industrial England the level of working-class religious involvement was already considerably lower than in south Wales, so that the number of those whose church-going habits were likely to be challenged by political radicalisation was smaller. Equally important was the highly pluralistic character of English urban religion, and the very varied response of the English churches to the advances of the labour movement in this period. There was certainly an important secularist strand in English labour and socialist organisations, but even in London, often regarded as the stronghold of working-class secularism, it was far from being the only strand. In many parts of the country, the Nonconformist strand was very important. And in certain localities, such as Liverpool, Manchester and the East End of London, Roman Catholics or Jews played a major role. If Anglicans tended to be seriously under-represented, there were major individual exceptions to the rule, including most notably George Lansbury, for many years the leading Labour figure in the East End of London, later editor of the *Daily Herald*, and finally leader of the Labour Party. There were also a number of locally influential socialist Anglican clergymen.[68]

While direct relationships between the rise of Labour politics and the decline in church-going were limited, it can more plausibly be argued that changes in class relationships, which might be summarised as 'the decline of paternalism' did have an important role.[69] During the period from the 1850s to the 1880s large paternalist employers had exercised a dominant influence on life in many parts of industrial England. Often they were men deeply involved in the lives of the communities where they made their money, sitting on the town council, belonging to a local church, patronising cricket clubs and garden shows, and cultivating personal relationships with their workforce. By a combination of carrots, sticks, and sometimes personal charisma, they were often able to have considerable influence on the political and religious behaviour of their workforce. By

the 1890s all this was beginning to change. Where the older generation of employers had lived close to the works and prided themselves on knowing by name most of the people who worked there,
the younger generation were buying country houses, adopting the
style of life of the wealthier gentry, and detaching themselves as
much as possible from the urban smoke. The trend towards more
impersonal and 'rational' styles of management was in any case
inevitable as family firms were increasingly transformed into limited
liability companies with their offices in London.

Meanwhile, especially after the highly publicised strikes in the
later 1880s and early 1890s, trade union organisation was spreading
to previously unorganised sections of the labour force, and the
Social Democratic Federation (1884) and Independent Labour
Party (1893) were popularising the socialist critique of capitalism.
A more independent-minded workforce was not necessarily less
religious – indeed a striking feature of the British socialist movement is the fact that so many of its pioneers came from a strongly
religious background and delivered their socialist message in a
language shaped by religion. But the working class of the early
twentieth century was much less willing to follow the religious or
political lead given by their employers. Britain to some extent
developed a Labour sub-culture of the kind which developed
much more fully in Germany and France.[70] Besides political parties
and trade unions, it included the co-ops and the Women's Co-
operative Guild, and also Labour Churches and Socialist Sunday
Schools. However, by comparison with, for instance, Germany, the
British labour sub-culture was more limited in scale and less exclusive. The Labour Churches (which were fading by 1914) and the
Socialist Sunday Schools offered one option for those who had
rejected the churches and wanted a formal alternative. But there
was plenty of scope for socialists either to remain religiously neutral
or to retain links with one of the churches.

The Role of the State

The third and fourth of the factors impinging on changes in
religious practice between 1848 and 1914, namely the growing
power of the state and the increasing influence of the towns on
the countryside, will be considered together, since in France the
chief example of the latter was the increasing presence of the state

in the countryside, especially after 1880. In all three countries the later nineteenth and early twentieth centuries saw a decline in urban/rural differences, as improved communications generally, and newspapers and political organisations in particular, rendered rural areas increasingly open to urban influences. In many cases the result was that rural religious practice declined, moving closer to urban levels. In Germany, where a series of excellent studies of local Protestantism were undertaken in the early twentieth century, the general conclusion was that all but the most remote villages had come under extensive urban influences, and that these were generally associated with a decline of religious practice.[71]

The process has been studied in considerable detail in the rural areas immediately to the east of Göttingen, in what was the kingdom of Hanover, until its annexation by Prussia in 1866. This was an area of above average levels of religious practice, with the great majority of the population receiving communion at least once in the year and about 15% attending church on an average Sunday at the end of the nineteenth century. However, the number both of communicants and of church-goers was declining, and the hard-to-please orthodox Lutheran clergy who predominated in Hanover were not impressed with the general level of piety. One of their chief bugbears had for long been the prevalence of Sunday work on the farms. But from the 1870s onwards more specifically urban influences entered into their complaints. From 1872 onwards the frequency of Sunday dances was a regular theme in their reports. From 1884 they were complaining about irreligious newspapers, and in 1888 they were noting the practice of going from village to village on Sundays, seeking out those where dances were being held. From 1890 the *Vereine*, a characteristic feature of urban life in nineteenth century Germany, were becoming extensively established in the villages, and the Social Democrats were beginning to win large numbers of votes in elections – though pastors stressed that in their area Social Democratic voters still went to church, and socialist propaganda did not include attacks on religion. However, in 1904 they reported that anti-religious ideas were beginning to get a hearing. About the same time there were frequent complaints of people from Göttingen coming out to the villages on Sundays, with all that this might imply in terms of the spread of urban mores.[72]

In France the state had a major role in these processes, as one of the most important instruments for the breaking down of rural isolation was the secular school. Roger Thabault in an account of his native village of Mazières-en-Gâtine showed how this might come about. In Mazières the church was still a very powerful force at mid-century, but by the 1880s it was declining in the face of what Thabault describes as 'a new religion', the faith in progress. The new era began about 1860 with the increasing involvement of the population in production for the market and consequently greater access to new ideas, and it progressed further in the 1870s with the politicisation of the village by a strongly anti-clerical bourgeois land-owner who successfully challenged the authority of the seigneur, replacing the latter as mayor. But the culmination of this phase was the arrival of a passionately republican school-teacher, who filled the younger generation with a belief in the possibility of a better life, and who successfully warded off a challenge from the priest – when the latter refused absolution to those parents who sent their children to the secular school, most ignored the threat. Apart from republican politics, patriotism and belief in education, the new faith in progress was also associated with a more rationalistic mentality, reflected in the practice of birth control and the declining influence of magic.[73]

The state's interventions in religious matters could, however, be counter-productive. I shall return to this theme in the latter part of the chapter.

The End of England's Victorian Era

As suggested earlier, intellectual and cultural changes are unlikely to have been a major factor in the decline of church-going in France and Germany during the second half of the nineteenth century, but they may have had a role in England. Trends in English church membership and attendance have been subjected to intensive analysis. From the 1850s to the later 1880s the overall level remained fairly stable, though with some variations between areas and denominations. A modest drop in attendance at churches of the Church of England and the major Nonconformist denominations was largely compensated for by the growth of attendance in some more plebeian Nonconformist denominations, which suggests that attendance may have been growing in this period in the working class. From the late 1880s to the First World War, there was a substantial drop in church attendance and a smaller drop in church membership.[74] The biggest drop of attendance was in the middle and upper classes. Figures for London showed that although wealthier areas still had the highest level of attendance, the gap was narrowing. In 1886–87, the wealthiest districts had an average rate of attendance on the census Sunday of 36.3 per cent and the poorest had an average of 20.2 per cent. By 1902–3 the averages were 26.3 per cent for the wealthiest districts asnd 18.5 per cent for the poorest.[75] Anglican congregations were shrinking fastest, though the Nonconformists also suffered significant losses, while trends in Roman Catholic attendance are less clear.

The reasons for this decline continue to be hotly disputed by historians and no consensus has yet been reached. Some of the factors which especially affected members of the working class have already been mentioned. The decline of middle and upper class church-going can best be seen as resulting from a combination of factors, including the intellectual and cultural, as well as the social. Among these were the growth of religious doubt, partly becuase of new scientific developments, but more especially because of changes in moral susceptibilities, which made many aspects of existing Christian orthodoxy harder to accept; the growing preoc-cupation with leisure, and the associated reaction against 'puritan' taboos and restrictions; and the decline of the social paternalism of which religious institutions and ideology had often been an integral part. Victorian social elites had frequently gone to church as a social duty, more or less independently of whatever religious convictions they had. By the early twentieth century, the church no longer seemed so important to the functioning of society; landowners and industrialists were less willing to accept that society and its needs had any claims on their time or money, and a less deferential working class was in any case not so inclined to follow whatever lead their 'masters' tried to give. The change was neatly summed up by an Anglican writer in 1911, comparing 'The Old Squire' with 'The New Squire'. The former 'does not ask whether he needs the comforts of religion, he is sure that society needs religion, and if society needs religion he, as one of the first in the social organisa-tion, must be there at his post'. The latter lived in the country because it was a pleasant place to live, and he meant to enjoy it; it was no concern of his whether the children went to school or their parents went to church.[76]

The survey of church attendance in London in 1902–3 showed that the largest congregations were still to be found in the wealthy suburbs, with large concentrations of the professional and business classes. In a group of wealthy suburbs the median level of attendance was 37 per cent of the adult population, and a maximum of 43 per cent was reached in the very affluent south-eastern district of Black-heath. In these districts both Dissent and the Church of England were very strong. There had been some decline in church-going in this group since the 1880s, and Dissent had also suffered from the defection of wealthy families to the Church of England. But at least until the 1880s, levels of church-going in the upper-middle and middle-middle class were very high, and in spite of the important political differences between the mainly Conservative Anglicans and the heavily Liberal Dissenters, they were relatively similar in their religious practices. Even those middle-class families which tried to avoid church-going found it hard to escape the constraints of the English Sunday, which was gaining in rigour during the first half of the nineteenth century, reaching a high point around the 1850s. Though in poorer districts the sabbath was widely ignored, whether in the interests of work or of pleasure, theatres and shops catering for a middle-class clientele were closed; public opinion prescribed not only that public worship should be the main form of Sunday activity, but that those who abstained from worship should not publicly advertise the fact by engaging in other forms of public activity. Even outside the hours of service, sport, as much as work, was taboo.[77]

The decline of middle-class religious practice, which did not become marked in England until the 1890s, took a distinctive form. Certainly the influence of Darwinism and biblical criticism played a part. But more important was the reaction against 'puritanism', against 'cant' or what came to be called 'Victorianism'. By contrast with France and Germany, the role of politics in all of this was rather small. Certainly there had been throughout the Victorian period a section of the middle-class intelligentsia which adopted a French-style secular Liberalism, associated especially with the *Westminster Review* or later the *Fortnightly Review*, and at the end of the century there was a section of the intelligentsia whose rebellion was associated with the adoption of socialism. Some successful businessmen, who were moving from Nonconformist to Anglican or agnostic in religion, were also moving from Liberal to Conservative in politics. But for the most part, the emphasis was on individual emancipation and the rejection of puritanical restraints. This was reflected in moves from town house to country mansion, purchases of yachts or race-horses,

and increasing numbers of foreign holidays. The latter were now
often taken at such places as Biarritz and Monte Carlo, rather than
the Swiss lakes and mountains, favoured by those who were rich,
but not ostentatiously so, and who were held back by taboos on
gambling and drink from the haunts of aristocracy and royalty.
For many tens of thousands of more ordinary middle-class families
these years were seeing a more gradual lifting of restraints – for
instance golf or cycling on Sundays, outings to the theatre, the dropping of family prayers and other forms of what were coming to be
seen as excessive piety, and a diminishing interest in sermons and
religious controversy.[78]

As in France and Germany, declining religious interest in the
prosperous middle class had a delayed impact on other classes. By
the late nineteenth century, churches and chapels were beginning
to experience a labour shortage. Recruitment to the Anglican ministry had peaked in 1886. For most Nonconformist denominations
the peak came in the early twentieth century, with the more middle-
class denominations being hit first.[79] By the early twentieth cenrury
there was also a shortage of voluntary church-workers, which
made it hard to maintain the big range of charitable activity typical
of the mid-and late-Victorian years.[80] Meanwhile, the decline of the
religiously based paternalism which had been especially characteristic of the period from ther 1850s to the 1880s meant that employers were increasingly inclined to leave workers to their own devices,
eschewing both the concern for workers' welfare and the forms of
moral discipline which had formerly been common. And when
private golf and tennis clubs opened on Sundays it became harder
to maintain sabbatarian restrictions on the public facilities used by
the mass of the people.

So, while French middle-class critiques of religion tended to stress
political themes, sometimes mixed up with the cult of science, and in
Germany political themes were also prominent, mixed with faith in
education and reverence for the German classics, in England questions of the individual's right to self-development, freed from moral
restrictions, came to the fore.[81]

Resistance to the Secularising State

Those areas in which the level of religious practice remained
more or less the same, or actually increased, during the period

1848–1914 were mainly those where unpopular interventions by the state had generated strong local solidarities. The most extreme example of such a situation was the annexation of Alsace-Lorraine by the German Empire after the Franco-Prussian war. While those parts of Lorraine which remained in France saw a major decline in religious practice during the Third Republic, the areas which became part of Germany showed an increase. The main reason for this seems to be that the church became the main symbol of local identity and hostility to Germany.[82] Meanwhile, the Third Republic's secularisation of the schools and attacks on the religious orders provoked determined opposition in some areas, further strengthening their Catholic loyalties. In 1902 soldiers and police-men were sent to close the thirty-seven schools run by the locally-based *Filles du Saint-Esprit* in the Breton department of Finistère; They met with violent resistance. There was also much resentment at a government decree banning religious instruction in the Breton language. The memory of these events was a major factor in turning the voters in the direction of Christian Democracy, and away from the pro-government republicans, who had been the previous ben-eficiaries of the decline of royalism. It also no doubt helped to maintain the department's high level of Catholic practice – in 1909, 83 per cent of the population aged over 14 were Easter communicants.[83]

A similar phenomenon was seen in Prussia and other German states, where state attacks served to increase the solidarity of the Catholic minority. Unfortunately, until the First World War statistics of religious practice seem to be less readily available for German Catholics than for French Catholics or German Protestants. So the trends have to be deduced on the basis of the much more fragmentary evidence that is available. In 1915 nationwide Catholic communicant statistics were published for the first time (see table 4).[84] These suggested that levels of practice by German Catholics were generally higher than in the case of French Catholics or German Protestants, and much less regionally varied. If Easter communicants as a percentage of the total Catholic population are compared with communions at any time of the year as a percentage of the Protestant population, the Catholic percentage was nearly always higher, and sometimes the difference was very considerable. For instance in Prussia the Catholic commu-nicant rate was 57 per cent and the Protestant rate 33 per cent; in Württemberg it was 63 per cent and 42 per cent; in Saxony 55

Table 4 Trends in Catholic religious practice in Germany

Easter communicants as a percentage of all Catholics			
	1915	*1920*	*1925*	*1930*
Germany	58		57	62
Prussia	57	54	55	60
Hesse-Darmstadt	51	53	54	56
Baden	57	60	61	62
Palatinate	53	57	57	57
Bavaria	63	64	67	67
Württemberg	63	64	66	67
Saxony	53	27	24	32
Thuringia	40	34	35	38
Brunswick	32	28	26	30
Oldenburg	62	67	65	70
Bremen	31		29	35
Lübeck	38	26	36	37
Berlin / Brandenburg		31	31	32

Source: Annemarie Bürger, *Religionszugehörigkeit und soziales Verhalten* (Göttingen, 1964), pp. 358–9.

per cent and 36 per cent; and in Baden 57 per cent and 47 per cent. The margin was only narrow in Bavaria (excluding the Palatinate) where it was 63 per cent and 61 per cent, and in Hesse where it was 51per cent and 48per cent. Somewhat more detailed figures of Catholic Easter communicants are available for 1924, when the national average was 57 communicants for every 100 Catholics. Since about a quarter of the population were children too young to be eligible, this would suggest that as many as three-quarters of Catholics aged 14 and over were doing their Easter duties. If accurate, this is a remarkable figure, and indeed one expert contemporary observer suggested that some of the figures had been inflated. He specifically mentioned Bavaria, where the very high figure reported seemed too good to be true.[85] The maximum figures tended to be in heavily Catholic rural regions, with intermediate levels in towns and industrial regions, like the Ruhr, where the presence of Catholics and Protestants in fairly equal numbers had fostered the development of a strong group-consciousness and an extensive Catholic subculture. Some Catholic cities like Cologne had below average-figures, and the lowest rates were found in

Protestant cities and industrial zones, where the Catholic community had been eroded by high rates of mixed marriages and where the relative weakness of the Catholic subculture meant that Catholics were susceptible to the pressures of a mainly socialist or Protestant environment. In cities like Cologne or Munich where a major part of the bourgeoisie was Catholic, something of the same working-class alienation from the church which was found in most Protestant areas had taken place, but the Catholic Church in Cologne or Munich retained a much larger working-class following than did the Protestant Church in, say, Hamburg or Berlin.[86]

It is impossible to say with any degree of certainty how these generally high levels of Catholic practice in the 1920s compared with the situation fifty or a hundred years earlier. However, research by Jonathan Sperber on the Rhineland and Westphalia suggests that the period between about 1850 and 1880 was a time of rising religious practice, after a relatively low period in the first half of the century. Evidence for this includes an increase in the proportion of wills containing bequests for religious purposes, a rise in the number of people taking part in pilgrimages, and more favourable comments by priests, in their reports to their bishops, on church attendance and observance of Catholic morality.[87] The solidest evidence concerns wills. The main statistical study of Catholic piety during the period 1700–1840 shows that in the Westphalian and Rhineland cities of Cologne, Aachen and Münster there was a decline in the use of religious languages in wills, and that there were also other possible signs of secularisation, such as a decline in the proportion of books within private libraries which were on religious subjects.[88] But a comparison between two mainly rural districts of Westphalia and the Rhineland shows a clear though unspectacular increase in the proportion of wills including religious bequests or using religious language between the periods 1801–49 and 1850–72. However, Sperber's chronology has been contested by Jürgen Herres, using communicant statistics from Mainz, as well as more impressionistic evidence from Cologne of non-church-going. In Mainz no less than 87 per cent of those eligible to receive communion at Easter 1847 had done so; but there was then a continuous decline until 1875, when it was 55 per cent, followed by a modest increase in the later 1870s. According to Herres, membership of Catholic organisations in Rhineland towns remained low in the 1850s and 1860s, and the Catholic revival of the later nineteenth century was primarily a response to the *Kulturkampf*.[89]

Thomas Mergel's work on the Catholic bourgeoisie of the Rhineland is consistent with Sperber in its chronology, though Mergel, like Herres, is primarily concerned to emphasise the limits of clerical and ultramontane influence and of the Catholic milieu. Mergel emphasises the disruption of Catholic religious life caused by the secularising measures imposed by Napoleon during the French occupation, and the religious ignorance or indifference of many of the Catholic bourgeoisie in the early decades of the century. He goes on to suggest that the shock produced by the 1848-9 revolutions had an effect rather similar to that in France in leading some of the previously indifferent to reassess the importance of religion as a potential source of social stability. He has a particularly telling quotation from the diary of a Bonn publisher, reviewing in May 1849 the changes in his thinking that the events of the past year had brought about. He had modified his earlier democratic views, feeling that the people were not yet ready for democracy, but that they needed 'an education for freedom' 'through the awakening of the moral sense', which could only come about through religion.[90] Accordingly many members of the bourgeoisie supported the big Jesuit and Redemptorist missions of the 1850s and other efforts to stimulate popular devotion, even if their own preference was for a quieter style of piety. As in France, women led the way in the move towards stricter religious observance, and they had at least some success in bringing their husbands and sons with them.[91] During the Prussian *Kulturkampf* in the 1870s massive numbers of Catholics took part in such demonstrations of collective piety and communal loyalty as the pilgrimage to the Marian shrine at Kevelaer, near the Dutch border. Pilgrims had averaged 36,000 a year between 1816 and 1824, but had risen to about 100,000 in 1861. In 1872 the total was estimated as 400,000.[92]

Meanwhile, the Centre Party won an overwhelming majority of the votes cast by Catholics in the northern Rhineland and Westphalia.[93] Although by the early twentieth century, the Centre was losing some of its working-class support to the Social Democrats in such former strongholds as Cologne and Düsseldorf,[94] there is a remarkable degree of continuity in the levels of support for the Party during the period of the Empire. In spite of fluctuations in the intervening years, the Centre was very successful in rallying the Catholic vote whenever the Catholic community felt itself under attack. In 1874 at the peak of the Prussian *Kulturkampf*, an estimated 45 per cent of the whole Catholic electorate across Germany had voted for the Centre, including 56 per cent of those who actually voted. In 1907, it is again estimated that 45 per cent of the whole Catholic electorate voted Centre, and 54 per cent of those actually voting.[95] These figures are particulary impressive when one bears in mind that Germany had a multi-party system, with five other major parties, and numerous minor parties or regional parties. The voting figures provide indirect evidence that the Catholic subculture was maintaining its strength over time during the later years of the Empire.

There is other evidence pointing in the same directioon. One is the very large membership of Catholic *Vereine* – a term which encompasses specifically Catholic organisations of many kinds, ranging from confraternities to football teams. Mooser estimates that between a third and a half of all German Catholics belonged to a church-related organisation in the period around 1900.[96] The figures were particularly high in Westphalia and the Rhineland. In the diocese of Paderborn in 1913, 46 per cent of Catholics belonged to a *Verein*, including 63 per cent in the very proletarian Ruhr town of Gelsenkirchen. A micro-study of one Gelsenkirchen parish, St Josef, Schalke, found that approximately half the parishioners attended the mission in 1906, that the combined membership of the parish's 33 *Vereine* in 1913 amounted to 56 per cent of the parochial population (including some people who belonged to two or more organisations), and that in 1925–7, 51 per cent of those aged 14 and over belonged to at least one *Verein*, while 42 per cent regularly attended mass.[97]

In spite of a growing body of research on German Catholicism during the second half of the nineteenth century, some aspects of the story remain unclear. It is evident that throughout this period levels of religious practice by German Catholics were high. It is also evident that the Catholic Church in Germany succeeded in retaining the loyalty of an impressively wide range of social groups. The reasons for this success are, however, much less clear, and the chronology remains vague. As Margaret Lavinia Anderson has pointed out, historians have focused more on the intentions and activities of the clergy than on the responses to these initiatives by the people, the meaning of their Catholicism to them, or the initiatives taken by the people themslves.[98]

Certainly, a fundamental aspect of the story is the relationship of Catholics to the Protestants who formed a numerical majority in all the German states except for Bavaria and Baden, who often were economically more powerful even where most of the population was Catholic, and who after 1871 clearly dominated the newly-established German Empire from every possible point of view.[99] When Catholics and Protestants lived in close proximity there was a sense of difference, and often tension, which could easily escalate into minor violence.[100] In towns like Augsburg, with a long-standing system of 'parity' between the faiths, Catholics and Protestants had learnt to live in peace, but they had largely continued to live separately.[101] The redrawing of the map of Germany by the victorious powers in 1815 meant that the majority of Catholics were placed under Protestant rule, while a much smaller number of Protestants in Franconia and the Palatinate were placed under Catholic Bavaria. The minority community was not always badly treated, but it came under periodic official attack, in, for instance, both Prussia and Bavaria in the 1830s, and above all in Prussia in the 1870s. While periodic attacks by the state on Catholic institutions and upon the leaders of the Catholic community played a crucial part in stimulating Catholic group-consciousness, the ridicule of Catholics and Catholicism in the press and the disdain of those in positions of authority at a more local level provided a constant source of irritation.[102] In Prussia, Baden and Hesse-Darmstadt the state was in periodic conflict with the Catholic Church from the 1830s onwards. Events such as the imprisonment of the Archbishop of Cologne in 1837 had an enormous impact on many Catholics. But most traumatic of all was the *Kulturkampf* in Prussia in the 1870s, not only because of the injustice of many of the laws enacted, but also because of the brutal and arbitrary way in which they were enforced, and the evident contempt with which many ministers, politicians and agents of the state regarded their Catholic fellow-citizens.

The formation of a highly organised subculture in the later nineteenth century was not unique either to Catholics (as opposed to other Germans) or to *German* Catholics (as opposed to those in other countries). In fact, Social Democrats and Protestants in Germany moved in a similar direction, and the tendency to form a 'Catholic ghetto' in the later nineteenth century was seen in many other countries, including the Netherlands, Switzerland and the United States.[103] However, there were few countries where it developed as far as in Germany, and in Germany only the Social Democrats developed a similarly extensive network of organisations held together by a similarly strong sense of group solidarity. This reflected the sense of exclusion and marginalisation that both Catholics and Social Democrats experienced in Imperial Germany – though it did nothing to bring them any closer together. In fact the Catholic and Social Democratic sub-cultures of the later nineteenth and early twentieth centuries had many important points of common, in spite of their mutual antagonism. The major difference perhaps was that the Catholics were more successful at appealing to women, while the Social Democrats appealed much more strongly to men. Catholics and socialists shared a strongly dualistic perception of the world,[104] which provided a rationale for the attempt to provide specifically Catholic or Social Democratic organisations to meet their members' every need; a militant style, expressed in mass rallies, marches through the streets, and suitably aggressive sermons or speeches; and a rich symbolism and iconography, including a heavy use of flags and banners, and a tendency for cults to develop around their heroes, martyrs and leaders.[105]

The leaders themselves had important points in common, in spite of obvious differences. Where the Protestant pastor tended to be set apart from the mass of his parishioners by the fact that he was a member of the educated bourgeoisie, Catholic priests and socialist leaders typically came from a lower middle class or upper working class background. They seldom came from extreme poverty, but typically they were local men, speaking the local dialect and not too far removed socially from their followers. This certainly does not mean that the relationship was problem-free. Some degree of tension is inherent in the relationship between clergy and laity, and the authoritarian style of leadership widely adopted by Catholic priests of the second half of the nineteenth century was guaranteed to bring about periodic conflict both with individuals and with groups within the parish. But, as Blaschke shows, the priest was widely regarded as the symbol of the Catholic community, and also as the acceptable face of authority – a formidable figure in some ways, but one who was trusted in a sense that, for instance, a state official or a lawyer was not.[106] The ways in which this potential closeness to the people was put into practice varied greatly. Blaschke quotes accounts of Bavarian peasants and Rhineland workers going to the parish priest to seek advice or comfort. Anderson stresses the role of the priest as confessor, and suggests that intransigent preachers might be much more understanding in dealing with individual cases. She also notes examples of priests who were popular because of their ability to socialise with their parishioners.[107]

The best-known example of the 'popular priest' in this era was the 'red curate' (*roter Kaplan*) who acted as a spokesman for his working-class parishioners. The pioneers in the early 1870s seem to have been two young priests, Cronenberg in Aachen and Laaf in Essen who played a prominent part in the formation of Catholic workers' associations and non-sectarian unions. Laaf went on to stand unsuccessfully for the Reichstag against the sitting Centre Party deputy. Cronenberg, like so many other troublesome junior clergy, ended up by being transferred to an out-of-the-way parish.[108] On the other hand, those 'red curates' who retained the support of their bishop were in danger of becoming too moderate for many of their parishioners. This was what happened in the Saar mining district in the later 1880s, where priests played an important part in the formation of the union, and Catholic newspapers initially had a big role in publicising the miners' grievances, but where the increased militancy of the miners soon left most of the clergy lagging behind.[109] So the influence of these radical priests was often short-lived, but the repeated appearance of new generations of such priests was a reflection of the frequent closeness of priests to people.

The social profile of German Catholic congregations in the later nineteenth century was similar to that of Protestantism: the aristocracy, the peasantry and the lower middle class were the most devout groups, while levels of involvement in the church were lower in the upper middle class and the urban working class.[110] The latter two groups were susceptible to the more secular ideas and mores widely current among their Protestant neighbours. However, at all social levels Catholics practised their religion to a greater degree than Protestants, and the difference was particularly striking in the case of the working class.

A comparison here can be made between the Protestant village of Berkheim in Württemberg and the Catholic villages of the northern Saarland.[111] From about the 1850s both began to see the temporary migration of most of the adult male population to nearby centres of industry. In the case of Berkheim they migrated daily to the factories and building sites of Esslingen, leaving early in the morning and returning late at night, so that only Sunday was fully spent in the home village. The Saarlanders, who went to work in the mines, spent Monday to Saturday in lodgings, and were at home only on Saturday evening and Sunday. In Berkheim, most of the men celebrated Sunday by sleeping in the morning, and then spending the rest of the day drinking with other men. On the other hand,

Sunday was for the Saarland miners 'a return to paradise' and to 'the bosom' not only of their wives, but of the church. Mallmann persuasively argues that the first generation of miners had a foot in two worlds. They went to church, they took part in pilgrimages and observed various saints' days, but they also ignored many of the church's moral prohibitions, and they went on strike, in spite of the dire warnings issued by the arch-conservative Bishop of Trier. Yet it seems from what Mallmann later says, that the strongly Catholic ethos of the Saar miners continued long beyond the first genera- tion. So, once again, rather than positing some kind of economic determinism, we need to focus on the religious, political and cul- tural context within which economic changes took place. In nine- teenth-century Germany, Catholicism was more successful than Protestanism in retaining working-class support in times of rapid social change, because it was more deeply rooted in popular culture, because the clergy were closer to the pople, because Catholics as a disadvantaged minority had developed a strong group-conscious- ness, and because the Catholic Church was less clearly identifed with political conservatism. Equally, the success with which Social Democracy had established itself in mainly Protestant towns and regions meant that the Protestant churches faced a formidable rival which posed much less of a threat to Catholicism. In a strongly confessionalised environment, Social Democratic propagandists started with a big disadvantage in their attempts to win Catholics.

Some sections of German Catholicism either had traditions of anti-clericalism, or at least resistance to clerical interventions in politics, or were moving in that direction in the later nineteenth century. This tended to be true of those Catholics who were politic- ally Liberal, such as the bourgeoisie of Rhineland towns like Cologne, Bonn or Düsseldorf, or the rural population of the south- ern Black Forest in Baden, which helped to turn that state into a Liberal stronghold.[112] In the late nineteenth century there were similar trends in Bavaria. The southern kingdom had a history of anti-clericalism among state officials, going back to the early nine- teenth century and Montgelas, a bureaucratic reformer in the tradi- tion of the Enlightened Absolutism of the eighteenth century. In the 1890s a large section of rural Catholics left the Centre Party and joined the Bavarian Peasants' League, which combined appeals for high tariffs and other measures to improve the economic position of the peasantry with strong attacks on the clergy, who were said to be getting richer while the peasants got poorer, and who were accused of neglecting peasant interests because of their preoccupation with strengthening the position of the church.[113] Meanwhile, the Catholic Church was experiencing in the working-class suburbs of Munich some of the problems that the Protestant churches were facing, albeit in more acute form, in the great cities of north Germany. Reports from Catholic pastors in the working-class suburbs of Munich in the 1880s and 1890s were full of complaints of shrinking congregations, blasphemy and unbelief, and immorality – not to mention *Pfaffenspott* (sneering at the clergy), a very expressive German word which, like the similar term *Pfaffenfresser* (literally 'priest-eater'), has no idiomatic English equivalent. How literally all this should be taken is debatable. Prostitutes and their clients were highly visible, while families who stayed at home saying the rosary were not; it is highly probable that visible evils, because of the pain they caused to the unwilling observer, were given a prominence out of all proportion to their actual significance. Nonetheless it is undeniable that Social Democracy, which most Catholic priests regarded as an unmitigated evil, was advancing rapidly.[114] In fact, during the period 1890 to 1912, the Social Democrats usually gained over half the votes cast in Munich in Reichstag elections.[115]

However, when one compares this situation with that in France, or indeed with that in many parts of north Germany, the limits of this anti-clericalism become apparent. The orators of the Bavarian Peasants' League repeatedly stressed that in attacking the clergy they were not attacking the Catholic religion, and levels of Catholic practice in the Bavarian countryside seem to have remained high. In Munich the 46 per cent of Easter communicants in 1887[116] was low by the standards of rural Bavaria, but would have seemed impressive in a French city. Moreover, in Munich, Social Democracy and Catholicism were far from being mutually exclusive options, whatever the clergy and some party militants expected. In other parts of Germany it was common for rank-and-file party comrades to continue to go to church, and in the more devout regions of the country, the party tried to steer clear of religious controversy, in order not to alienate such supporters. In Munich, the party secretary was himself a practising Catholic.[117] Certainly some Catholics, both in Bavaria and in other parts of Germany, rejected the church and the Catholic faith entirely after joining the Social Democrats. But this situation was less common in Germany than in France. A combination of the powerful confessional identity felt by most German Catholics and the strength of the all-embracing Catholic

'milieu' which the clergy built upon this foundation meant that
there were relatively few who broke away entirely.

Catholic Revival in France

In one of the later scenes from Roger Martin du Gard's *Jean Barois*,
set around 1910, the aging hero is harangued by two conservative
and nationalist Catholic students. Barois, who has been gradually
losing confidence in the republican and freethinking principles
which he has for most of his life espoused, finds that his worst
suspicions are confirmed when the young men claim that the present generation of students is predominantly Catholic.[118] After
many years of decline, the Catholic Church in France was staging
a partial recovery. The Separation of Church and State in 1905
presented the French church with major financial problems. But
the challenge also had a revitalising effect. The years leading up to
the First World War saw a great upsurge of new Catholic organisations and movements. The years immediately before the War may
also have seen a modest increase in the number of Catholics going
to mass, though in view of the drastic regional differences, it is
difficult to generalise.[119]

There were three aspects to this Catholic revival. The church was
in some respects benefiting from its freedom from state control.
The crisis facing the church was stirring loyal Catholics to be more
active and public in the practice of their faith and to launch new
forms of apostolate. And the church was being more successful in
attracting men – especially young middle-class men.

Under the Concordat the creation of a new parish had needed
state authorisation, and this was very often refused. In its first years
of involuntary freedom after 1905, the Catholic authorities seized
the opportunity of building many new churches and forming many
new parishes, and this continued on a bigger scale in the inter-war
years.[120] Catholic consciousness was raised by the many Catholic
newspapers founded in this period, and by the congresses held in
sixty dioceses between 1907 and 1914, and attended by the laity of
both sexes, as well as by priests. The period also saw numerous
conferences for the study of contemporary social problems, as well
as a more sluggish growth of Catholic trade unions and peasant
organisations. But the fastest growth was in organisations for
women and for youth. The biggest of these was the Patriotic League

of Frenchwomen (*Ligue patriotique des Françaises*), founded in Paris in 1902 as part of the oppositon to the measures against the religious orders, which were then being pushed through. Though it had a Jesuit chaplain, the League was led by aristocratic women. As well as supporting Catholic political campaigns, they were also highly active at the local level in founding Catholic libraries, study groups, clubs, holiday camps and so on. By the eve of war the League had about 600.000 members. It harnessed the energies of large num- bers of devout middle-class and upper-class laywomen, who in turn were often successful in mobilising working-class and peasant women. As one report from the Pas-de-Calais claimed: 'in a parish where twenty women went to mass, the league is organised and now two hundred go'.[121] There was also a huge growth in Catholic organisations for youth, whether focused on sport and gymnastics, or more general. These had some success in attracting young work- ing men, and they were even more successful with students – long regarded as one of the most outspokenly anti-clerical elements in French society. At one of the greatest anti-clerical strongholds, the *École Normale Supérieure*, a third of the students were taking part in the retreat organised by the Catholic chaplain at Easter 1914. The rapid growth of the (obviously much smaller) Protestant student federation during the same period reflected a general rise in reli- gious interest in the student milieu.[122]

This partly reflected a change in the French intellectual climate that had first been apparent about 1890, and which reached its culmination in the years immediately before the First World War.[123] In reaction against what they regarded as the aridity of positivism and the vindictiveness of the incessant attacks on the church by anti-clerical politicians, an important section of the intel- ligentsia had rediscovered Catholicism. The first high-profile con- version was that of the literary critic Ferdinand Brunetière, who wrote a much debated article in 1895 in which he declared that science had in some respects failed and that morality needed a religious basis. A number of other prominent literary figures announced their conversion at about the same time, and there was a bigger wave of conversions from about 1905. The most prominent personality in this Catholic renaissance was the poet Charles Péguy, who had been an ardent Dreyfusard and Socialist. Another less famous writer who converted at about the same time, Ernest Psi- chari, carried particular symbolic potency in Catholic eyes, because he was the grandson of Ernest Renan. A number of characteristic themes occurred in these conversions. Science was seen as having excluded important areas of the world and of human experience. Catholicism was regarded as providing a better basis for morality than positivism. Positivism was also seen as being naive in its optimism, while Catholicism was regarded as being more realistic in its acceptance of human sinfulness and of the the inescapable place of suffering in human life. There was also a cultural and political dimension to the appeal of Catholicism. Catholicism was valued because of its role in art, architecture and literature, and even more because of its central place in French history and its close association with French national identity. Péguy was typical here: his Catholic conversion was followed by the adoption of a romantic nationalism, which found expression in the cult of Joan of Arc.

This was the beginning of a period of partial recovery for French Catholicism. The 1920s, 1930s and 1940s were rich in new ideas and initiatives. So far as the statistics of Catholic practice are concerned, the period from about 1910 to 1960 frequently saw a stabilisation. While average levels of attendance at mass or participation in communion often changed little during that period, the average concealed a difference between the trend for women and for men. Although women remained the more devout sex, the gap between female and male piety was narrowing. In some towns the proportion of men who were Easter communicants was twice as high in 1960 as it had been fifty years ealier; but since in the meantime the proportion of women who were communicants had dropped, the overall average remained about the same.[124]

Conclusion

All three countries saw a significant drop in the proportion of the population going to church or taking part in communion between the mid-nineteenth century and the First World War. However, this by no means happened everywhere, and there are considerable differences in the timing and extent of this decline. So far as this aspect of secularisation is concerned, the attempt to find a general explanation fails. Instead we need to focus on the interaction between a complex mix of factors, the balance of which differed from country to country, and the impact of which on members of different social classes and different religious confessions could vary greatly.

6   Identity

'Unbelief is growing, and Catholicism is growing too. And it is Catholicism that is worse. The worship of idols is worse than unbelief'. Thus Aunt Adelheid in Theodor Fontane's novel *Der Stechlin* (1898). Ever on the look-out for nuances of language or manner that might betray a lack of Lutheranism, she objects to her nephew Woldemar using the word 'confess' (*beichten*) because it is 'Catholic'.

Aunt Adelheid is a comic portrait of a pious Lutheran aristocrat of the most rigid kind. But she only takes to the level of absurdity a sensitivity to confessionally-influenced differences that is common to most of the characters in Fontane's novels. Published in the 1880s and 1890s, the books mainly describe everyday life, and especially conversation, in aristocratic and bourgeois circles in Berlin, Brandenburg and Pomerania. The great majority of the characters are Protestants (though often far from pious), living in a mainly Protestant environment, but they are well aware of who among their acquaintances is or might be a Catholic or a Jew, and of the possible confessional significance of their names, the words they use or their cultural tastes. When Adelheid's brother, Dubslav von Stechlin, is on his death-bed, he decides not to see a doctor at all when he finds that the old doctor with whom he is familiar is not available: the old man's place has been taken by a young Jewish doctor, who 'smacks of Social Democracy', holds his cane in a strange way and wears a red tie. The heroine of *L'Adulterà* (1882), on first hearing of her future lover, Ebenezer Rubehn, has an immediately negative reaction, because his name sounds Jewish. She has equally negative feelings about the paintings of Murillo, because of their Catholicism, in which she sees something akin to witchcraft.[1]

216

To be a Christian or a Jew, Catholic or Protestant, Lutheran or Reformed, Anglican or Dissenter, Methodist, Baptist or Quaker, was to share a history, distinctive customs and rites, symbols and heroes, which continued to shape people's view of the world and their own place in it, even if they gave up practising their faith or believing in the doctrines associated with it. In England around the middle of the nineteenth century there would have been some people, but not very many, who refused to claim any of these forms of identity. And most of those would have claimed some explicitly non-religious identity, such as that of Positivist, Secularist or Socialist (meaning, in the 1840s, a follower of Robert Owen). In France there were certainly some who would have called themselves Positivists, Socialists or Voltairians, but the great majority would have identified themselves as Catholics, except for the small numbers of Protestants and Jews. In Germany it was difficult to disclaim any kind of religious label. Every citizen was regarded by the state as a member of the religious community into which they had been born, and official documents of many kinds recorded this affiliation. Transfers to another religious community had to be formally registered at the relevant government office, and could be subject to state restrictions. Until the 1870s few states allowed for the possibility of a person having no religion at all. When in 1873 the option of being without religious affiliation (*konfessionslos*) became available in Prussia, that choice had to be formally registered.[2]

The second half of the nineteenth century saw two important developments. The first was the emergence of a significant minority of those whose identity was emphatically secular, and who had consciously rejected their Catholic, Protestant or Jewish inheritance. The second was the increasing importance of nationalism and of membership of political parties as shapers of identity. These two developments to some extent overlapped, since membership of the various socialist parties often conferred a strong sense of identity and, at least in Germany and France, and to a lesser extent in England, this identity tended to be strongly secular. Membership of the English Secular Societies, or of the Freethought organisations in France and Germany, could also provide the basis for a new identity, which was emphasised by the introduction of secular rites of passage. These new secular identities developed furthest in France, and by the later nineteenth century the divide between Catholic and *laïc* was the deepest in French society, eclipsing in most regions of the country older divisions such as those between Catholic and Protestant. In Germany, the historic divide between Protestant and Catholic remained fundamental, and newer political and nationalist identities were often strongly coloured by confessional differences. In England, the most important religious distinction was generally that between Anglicans and Protestant Dissenters.

Confessional Consciousness

Religious identities stamped themselves powerfully upon the individual, and could not easily be erased, except by the sometimes even stronger counter-imprint of a political or secularist identity. Few people were simply neutral. Church and school inculcated confessional consciousness; differences had developed over several centuries not only between religious buildings and forms of worship, but also to some extent in vocabulary, in reading habits, in artistic and musical tastes, and in diet. Each community had its cultural heroes, and an awareness of its collective achievements. Differences in ethos, encompassing different political loyalties or moral values also played a role.[3]

Christel Köhle-Hezinger has studied relations between Protestants and Catholics in Württemberg from 1803, when the homogeneously Lutheran state first acquired a numerous Catholic population, up to the 1970s. At the latter date, most people said that confessional conflict was a thing of the past, but not very far beneath the surface the sense of difference, sometimes exacerbated by prejudices and grievances, was still there. Three points were especially noted by Protestants as summing up the difference: Catholics *knelt* during their worship, which to Protestants seemed undignified; they venerated saints, whom Protestants saw as little better than heathen idols; and above all the central role of Mary in Catholic life embodied everything that Protestants regarded as 'sickly-sweet' and 'kitsch'. For Catholics, on the other hand, their self-perception strongly emphasised piety and devotion to the church. The Protestant Church was still seen by them as little more than an adjunct of the state – it could never inspire the kind of affection which they felt for their 'Mother' Church. Protestantism was also equated with secularisation and moral decline, and Protestants were accused of monopolising positions of power and using them to oppress Catholics.[4]

Schools clearly had an important role, since so much nineteenth-century schooling was organised on a denominational basis, and the inculcation of confessional consciousness was often one of the school's major objectives. In Germany the great majority of children went to confessional schools throughout this period, and the great majority also attended confirmation classes. In France, after the secularisation of public education in 1881, state schools became as important in inculcating loyalty to the republic as Catholic schools were in promoting loyalty to the church. At the same time, the great majority of children continued to go to catechism classes and to receive First Communion,[5] so that those who had felt the imprint both of the church and of the secular school might feel a conflict of identities. In England up to the 1870s most elementary schooling was organised on denominational lines, and even after the establishment of non-sectarian Board Schools a large proportion of children continued to attend Anglican, Catholic or Wesleyan schools. Meanwhile, the overwhelming majority of working-class children went to Sunday School. Many of these had originally been non-denominational, but by the second half of the nineteenth century, they were generally attached to a church or chapel, and the recruitment of future church-members was one of their main purposes.[6] Middle-class children were usually sent to church services or went with their parents, and Budde's research on middle-class autobiographies would suggest that the overwhelming majority were brought up as members of a religious denomination.[7] All of this could be very superficial, but it meant that most people had some form of religious attachment which might be activated in appropriate circumstances.

This happened most readily to the members of religious minorities, and those living in situations of fierce inter-denominational competition. French Protestants and English Nonconformists were conscious from an early age of their descent from martyrs, and in the case of the Nonconformists various forms of disadvantage kept their sense of separate identity alive through most of the nineteenth century. Alan Bartlett's interview with a woman born in a Primitive Methodist family in 1927 in a working-class area of south London brings out well the various dimensions of this separate identity. She noted that 'We were always aware of being Nonconformists and a comparative minority group as children.' This meant having certain strongly defined beliefs, which made them different from the Church of England, which they saw as a superficial religion, mainly consisting of 'ritual' and going to church 'in order to look good', and also from non-church-going relatives and neighbours, since as Methodists they did not drink, did not use pawn-shops, and observed Sunday as a special day. It also gave them a special sense of history. They were 'very aware of the way people had fought for their freedoms; their freedom to worship in the way they wanted to, and the persecutions they had had'. This also led to a special attitude to authority: they were 'very law abiding', but their role-models were 'radical people who were prepared to give up things in order to do what they saw as the will of God'.[8] The Nonconformist self-image was sustained by memories of imprisonments or distraints for non-payment of church rates and tithes, and of the humiliations and injustices inflicted by squire and parson in An-glican-dominated 'close' villages. By the early twentieth century, Nonconformists had achieved respectability, prosperity, and often power. But with the campaign of Passive Resistance to the 1902 Education Act, many of them took a temporary step back into their heroic past.[9] Even those Dissenters who no longer relished appearances in court and visits from the bailiff were conscious of having a distinctive lifestyle. As a Tyneside Methodist, born in 1905, said, when asked about class differences in the area where she grew up: 'we didn't drink and we didn't gamble and we didn't buy on the never-never and we didn't swear. So I suppose that's a kind of class strata in its way too'.[10]

In the extreme case of the Jews, where confessional identity was informed not only by discrimination, but by abuse or even violence, as well as by awareness of a unique history, even the least devout frequently had a keen sense of loyalty to their co-religionists. A combination of factors, both internal and external, assisted the maintenance of a very strong sense of difference. The importance in Jewish life of domestic rituals was especially significant at a time when public religious observances were in decline. In Germany in the later nineteenth century, the lighting of candles and the meal together on the sabbath eve was general even in otherwise comple-tely unobservant families, and the kosher kitchen continued to be common. Distinctively Jewish dishes were popular, like the *Schalet*, a meal of noodles, eggs, raisins and flour, which was supposed to be prepared on Friday, cooked very slowly, and eaten on Saturday. By 1900, many housewives were turning to quick-cooking recipes which involved working on the sabbath – but it still had to be *Schalet*. Distinctive foods and domestic rituals were also an important aspect of other Jewish festivals, and helped stamp a sense of Jewishness on the growing child.[11]

Equally important, however, were the external factors that emphasised the Jewishness even of those who would have happily forgotten it. As Todd Endelman comments, summarising developments in England over two centuries – 'To be a Jew was to be regarded as different – a basic fact which no amount of acculturation could alter'.[12] The same was true in France,[13] although the Third Republic was favourable to Jews, and it was even more true in Germany. The assiduity of the German states in collecting statistics means that discrimination can be quantified in a way that would be impossible elsewhere. Figures for German universities in 1909–10 showed that 27 per cent of Christian members of Medical Faculties had been promoted to Professor, but only 12 per cent of 'baptised Jews' and 5 per cent of Jews. Figures for Faculties of Philosophy were comparable. However, in Faculties of Law, while Jews had by far the lowest percentage, 'baptised Jews' did marginally better than Christians.[14] In 1907,when 0.9 per cent of the economically active were Jewish, no Jews at all were officials of the various German royal and ducal courts, less than 0.1 per cent of officers in the army and navy were Jewish, and about 0.2 per cent of middle and lower state and municipal officials. On the other hand, Jews comprised 14.7 per cent of lawyers, 8.1 per cent of journalists and writers, and 6.0 per cent of doctors.[15] Such sharply defined patterns of employment contributed strongly to the formation of stereotypes both hostile and favourable, and to the perception by Jews themselves that there were social territories where they could flourish, and others which were no-go areas. Even those who had no religious belief at all often wanted their sons to be circumcised and to be bar mitzvah, and were bitterly opposed to their son or daughter marrying a gentile.[16] In Germany in the later nineteenth century, such people were known as *Trotzjuden* (Jews in spite), 'who in spite of their unbelief would not leave the Jewish community (*Gemeinde*), because they saw it as disreputable and opportunistic to leave an oppressed community'.[17] Admittedly, the reverse response was also quite common during this period – the 'self-hate' of those who felt a desperate need to escape from everything Jewish – an identity which no longer had any meaning for them, yet seemed to dominate their life.

In areas where Protestant and Catholic lived close to one another, in comparable numbers, and with histories of mutual antagonism – for instance, in the Rhineland, Lancashire, or south-eastern France – the sense of loyalty to one's own camp and the tendency towards hostile stereotyping of the others were also strong. Something similar existed in the many parts of England where church and chapel were locked in battle – though the antagonism was seldom quite as sharp as that between Catholic and Protestant.

Wherever in nineteenth-century Europe concentrated communities of Protestants and Catholics lived side by side or in neighbouring villages there were significant tensions between them. Wahl's study of Baden and Alsace and the various studies of Lancashire show many parallels in spite of major differences between the two environments and the nature of the Protestant and Catholic communities within them. (Most obviously, Lancashire Catholics in the later nineteenth century were predominantly Irish-born or of Irish descent, so that sectarian relations also included an important ethnic dimension, which was absent in Baden or Alsace.) In both cases the strength of sectarian identity was reflected in widespread hostility to mixed marriages. In Baden only 9 per cent of weddings in the period 1869–73 were confessionally mixed, and Wahl comments that 'for both communities the mixed marriage was regarded as a betrayal'.[18] In Lancashire mixed marriages were probably more common, though no such precise figures are available. But the couple generally met with intense opposition from one or both sides. Many Catholics saw such marriages as treachery, and Protestants, though their *esprit de corps* tended to be weaker, often regarded marriage with a Catholic as degrading. Interviews by oral historians with those brought up in Lancashire in the later nineteenth or early twentieth centuries have produced many examples of people shunned by relatives for several years or even permanently, because they married someone of the wrong religion, of disputes over the baptism of the resulting children, or of harassment by clergy or nuns of Catholics who 'turned'. (In the case of Protestants the opposition generally came from family rather than clergy.)[19]

Mutual stereotyping was rife. In Württemberg, where the local Pietist traditions reinforced the image of Catholics as showy, a 'Catholic hat' meant one with flowers, a feather, or some other form of extravagant display.[20] In Baden, where Protestants were on average more economically successful than Catholics, they made fun of the numerous Catholic saints' days, claiming that Catholics

were lazy, as well as being 'primitive beings'. Catholic farmers
complained of unfair competition from Protestants who worked
non-stop, including Sundays, and accused them of being pagans.
In Preston Protestants claimed that the local custom whereby
Catholics concentrated in particular places of work applied even
to the town's brothels, the prostitutes being of course Catholics,
which could be told from the fact that they turned out to kneel
on the pavement when religious processions passed down the
Manchester Road. Sectarian preconceptions were often revealed
more or less unconsciously. Thus a Barrow woman, who had
worked as a cleaner in a convent, was impressed by the fact that 'it
was spotlessly clean although they were Catholics', and a Preston
Catholic mentioned that his mother always went to 'a Catholic
doctor'.[21] Of course, rival versions of history played an important
part in defining communities, and separating them from other
communities. In Alsace and Baden 1789 and 1871 were still hotly
debated between those of rival confessions, as well as older controversies concerning, for instance, the St Batholomew's Day Massacre
or the conquests of Gustavus Adolphus. In Lancashire the bitterest
divisions between Catholic and Protestant surrounded the relationship between England and Ireland, including such issues as Catholic memories of the Famine and Protestant memories of murders
committed by the Fenians.[22]

With the great migration of the rural poor in search of better
wages in cities and industrial regions, there was a mixing of populations. Protestants moved to Catholic cities like Cologne, Catholics to
Protestant cities like Berlin or Frankfurt. Large new Jewish communities were established in Manchester and Leeds. Industrial
regions like the Ruhrgebiet attracted a vast influx of immigrants,
speaking many different languages and belonging to many different
religious denominations. In these situations, competition for jobs
helped to keep confessional consciousness at a high level. In Lancashire, and in some other parts of England in the early twentieth
century, it was common to find concentrations of Catholics, Protestants, or members of the same Protestant denomination working
together, whether because employers gave preference to members
of their own church, or because foremen recruited workers
through a church network, or sometimes (in the case of city employees) because councillors did favours for members of their own
religious or ethnic group.[23] Economic factors also played an important part in relations between Christians and Jews. In Baden Jewish

money-lenders controlled rural credit until the 1880s, after which their position was challenged by various credit organisations, mostly founded on a Catholic or Protestant basis, and thus further sustaining confessional identities.[24] The various anti-Semitic groups that emerged in the 1870s gave a major part in their propaganda to claims that Jewish money-lenders were exploiting the problems faced by landowners and farmers in the current agrarian crisis by charging exorbitant rates of interest.[25] Similarly, urban anti-Semitism appealed to small businessmen and master craftsmen by depicting big business as Jewish.[26]

The later nineteenth century saw the development of strongly defined confessional subcultures in most west European countries. This took extreme forms in The Netherlands, but it was also well-developed in Germany. It was a time when the identity of large sections of the population was defined most clearly by the organisations that they belonged to. It was a time when membership of certain organisations precluded membership of many others, so that organisations helped to define clear boundaries within the local community. It was also a time of pilgrimages and of regional, national and international congresses, when thousands of Catholics, Protestants, Freethinkers or Socialists would converge on a favourite shrine or a chosen city, to demonstrate their numbers, discuss common problems and gather strength for future struggles. Equally important was the local headquarters, large enough both to proclaim the presence of the organisation and to contain a wide range of facilities and activities. An account of the opening, in October 1898, of the clubhouse of the Catholic Workers' Association in south Cologne conveys something both of the symbolic significance attached to such buildings, and of the spirit of the organised Catholicism of the time. The celebrations began with a church service, after which 'an imposing festive procession' moved through the southern part of the city, with members of thirty-four Catholic Workers' Associations taking part, thirty-eight flags flying, and three bands playing. When they reached the clubhouse the crush was so great that not everyone could hear the numerous speeches. Those who squeezed in found that two very familiar themes predominated: loyalty to the Pope and attacks on Social Democracy.[27]

During this period Catholics, Protestants, Socialists and, less often, Freethinkers, set up organisations for girls and for boys, for young women, for mothers, for working men, for cyclists and for

footballers, as well as choirs and theatrical groups, and much else
besides.[28] There were certainly those who tried to maintain a dual
identity – to be, for instance, a Catholic *and* a Socialist – or who tried
to enjoy the sport or the singing while ignoring the ideology,
though leaders and rank-and-file militants made life difficult for
such people. But even for those whose involvement in their church
and its associated organisations was very limited, religion often
played a major part in shaping people's perceptions of who they
were, and who they were not.

This was reflected, for instance, in the pervasive anti-Catholicism,
which was a general feature of west European Protestantism at
this time, most notably in Germany. Shulamit Volkov suggests that
anti-Semitism in Imperial Germany acted as a 'cultural code'[29] –
that is, Jews were taken as symbols of certain trends in contemporary German society (for instance Liberalism or the development
of big business), and advocacy of anti-Semitism was also indirectly
a way of advocating such things as nationalism, imperialism and
a strong state. Equally, it should be noted that the adoption of anti-
Semitism by some Protestants, such as Adolf Stoecker, was a way
of pursuing battles within the Protestant churches. Protestant anti-
Semites belonged most commonly to the conservative wing of the
church, and in attacking Jews as embodiments of Liberalism,
city life and 'modernity', they were indirectly attacking their liberal
co-religionists.[30] Similar points can be made in respect of anti-
Catholicism, with the difference that the most fervent anti-Catholics
were liberal Protestants, who used attacks on the Pope, the Jesuits
and the Centre Party as an indirect means of attacking conservatives
within their own church.[31] But again, as Volkov points out, anti-
Semitic organisations may be less significant than the much wider
diffusion of anti-Semitic attitudes, and the same is no doubt true
of anti-Catholicism. The unreflecting attitude of superiority with
which German Protestants frequently faced their Catholic
compatriots was reflected in the use of the word 'Catholic' to
mean something stupid or absurd.[32] Large or highly ornate
churches were rejected as 'Catholic', as were those Lutherans who
wanted Protestant bishops. Protestants repeatedly claimed that
German intellectual, cultural and economic achievements were products of Protestantism.[33]

Thomas Nipperdey refers to the many 'Protestant agnostics' of
this era – 'Because they had been born Protestant, they remained
anti-Catholic, and because they were anti-Catholic, they felt

themselves to be "Protestant".[34] In England, anti-Catholicism was almost equally pervasive, both at popular and elite levels. It could take an evangelical form – which in its more extreme form included the belief that the Pope was literally the anti-Christ, and in its more moderate form simply asserted that Catholicism was a travesty of Christianity. It could take a liberal form, which focused on Catholic denial of the rights of conscience, or a rationalist form, which accused Catholicism of superstitition and opposition to the progress of science. It could take a quasi-pornographic form, homing in on allegations of debauchery in convents and seduction through the confessional.[35] The extreme form of evangelical anti-Catholicism declined, as this particular form of Protestantism declined, after about 1860. More generally anti-Catholicism as a force in English society was declining by the 1870s.[36] This is not to say that the English generally became more tolerant, or more appreciative of Catholicism – merely that other issues increasingly seemed more important. And here perhaps we have a form of secularisation.

Religion and Political Identity

Religion also fed into other forms of identity in such ways that even those whose religious interest was low encountered religion indirectly. The clearest indication of the continuing importance of confessional identities throughout this period lies in voting statistics. Some political parties deliberately sought the votes of particular religious communities by promising to defend their interests or redress their grievances. They might also take up wider issues that were known to be of particular concern to that denomination. And politicians, by highlighting their own religious beliefs and affiliations, struck a chord with the many voters who wanted to be represented by someone with whom they could personally identify. In some cases the affinities between a particular religious community and a particular poltical party were so close that the two kinds of loyalty became mutually reinforcing. Studies in all three countries demonstrate the crucial importance of religious variables in the elections of the period c.1870–1914, when the electorates were socially broad (though still exclusively male). While social class was also a major factor, religious factors were even more important.

In France the biggest division within the electorate was between practising Catholics, who predominantly voted for Right-wing parties, and non-practising Catholics or non-Catholics, who mainly voted for the Left. In Germany the most important dividing-line was that between Protestants and Catholics. In England, the most important division was that between Anglicans and Nonconformists. This is not to deny that differences within these various confessional categories were also important. For instance, the growing attraction of socialist parties to working-class voters in the years before 1914 posed a threat to the German Centre Party, which was losing working-class Catholics, and to the British Liberal Party, which was losing working-class Nonconformists, and to the French Radicals, who were losing working-class Freethinkers. But religious factors continued to have a bigger influence on the overall pattern of voting than any other.

Sperber's analysis of German elections between 1871 and 1912 leads him to conclude that confessional differences were 'the primary factor dividing the German electorate', and that this remained so right through this period.[37] The clearest indication of this lies in the very different patterns of turn-out between Catholic and Protestant voters. While the latter showed a gradual long-term increase – apparently in keeping with theories that participation increases with such factors as urbanisation, advances in communications and rises in educational levels – Catholic rates of voting fluctuated wildly according to the issues at stake in particular elections. Whereas Catholic turnout fluctuated between 60 and 70 per cent in normal years, it reached 80 per cent in the election of 1874, fought at the height of the *Kulturkampf*. It did so again in 1887 and 1907, when the government was beating the patriotic drum – which always led some politicians and journalists, especially those belonging to the National Liberal Party, in an anti-Catholic direction. In the 1907 election, for instance, the main issue was the government's request for more money to put down an uprising in South-West Africa. They were supported by the Conservatives and Liberals, and opposed by the Social Democrats, while the Centre was more ambivalent, supporting the principle of German imperialism, while criticising its practice. The Centre Party's hesitations were eagerly exploited by Liberal spokesmen. The Progressives claimed that 'as long as a part of the nation receives its orders for the settlement of political affairs from the Vatican, we will find ourselves in a state of civil war', and the *Dortmunder Zeitung* celebrated the dissolution of the Reichstag by declaring: 'May a whiff of Luther's anger and Luther's courage run through our nation: away from servitude to Rome and to truth and freedom'.[38] The main victors were the Liberals, who registered a large increase in their vote, with middle-class Protestants being especially responsive to their sectarian rhetoric. On the Catholic side the appeals to Catholic loyalty met a big response from working-class voters, who had been gradually shifting towards the Social Democrats, but on this occasion showed a strong preference for the Centre.

There was certainly a significant minority of Catholics who ignored such appeals, and who were susceptible to appeals on grounds of nationalism or class. Catholic workers, especially in such big cities as Munich and Cologne, showed a growing interest in the Social Democrats, while the Catholic middle class included a substantial Liberal element, and the anti-clerical Bavarian Peasants' League was a rival to the Centre among Bavarian farmers. But overall, the most striking point is the continuing willingness of Catholics to vote as Catholics. In 1890, according to Sperber's figures, Catholics of all social classes showed a clear preference for the Centre Party, whereas Protestants divided on class lines, middle-class Protestant votes being overwhelmingly Liberal, about half the Protestant working-class voters choosing the Social Democrats, and Protestant farmers being about evenly split between Liberals and Conservatives. During the period 1903–12 Catholics of all classes still showed a majority voting for the Centre, and Protestant farmers were still split between Liberals and the Right, but with the Right now in a majority, while Social Democrats now had a clear (though not overwhelming) majority among Protestant working-class voters. But Sperber's most sensational finding is that half of the Protestant middle-class vote was now going to the Social Democrats. Sperber sees this mainly in terms of the Socialists' role as an urban party, championing the urban consumer against the rural producer. But he also suggests that the Social Democrats did particularly well in constituencies where the main opposition came from the Centre Party. He suggests that this might be because the Social Democrats were perceived as a 'Protestant' party: if forced to choose, the middle-class Protestant would rather vote 'red' than 'black'.[39]

Religious factors clearly had a major influence on French voting patterns too. The basis of an electoral geography which lasted right through the Third and Fourth Republics, and well into the Fifth, was laid in two formative periods: the 1790s and the years of the Second Republic (1848–51), during which the basic division between a Catholic Right and an anti-clerical Left was established.

In the 1960s levels of religious practice were still the best predictors of how a person would vote,[40] and in the election of 1974
the regional pattern of political loyalties, established over a century
before, remained visible. Only in the 1980s did this pattern fade.[41]
While the importance of religious factors during the Third
Republic is obvious, it is not so clear whether religion was itself the
key factor, or whether it was dependent on something else. Jean-
Louis Ormières, summarising the origins of one of the basic divides
within French society, that between the 'reds' and the 'whites', and
also the older divide between 'blues' and 'whites', examines a series
of such allegedly fundamental factors. According to the oldest of
these theories, 'white' (conservative and Catholic) traditions flourished in areas of large-scale property, where monarchist aristocrats
could lay down the law, while 'blue' (going back to the 'patriots' of
the 1790s) or 'red' (radical and socialist) traditions reflected the
independence of the small property-owner. Other historians have
suggested that areas of subsistence farming are more likely to be
'white' than those well integrated into the market, that 'red' areas
are those where class conflict is most intense, or that 'blue' and 'red'
areas are those that have undergone greater degrees of modernisation. Some historians have rejected all such general explanations,
arguing that the various traditions are products of a multiplicity of
local factors, including, for instance, rivalries between neighbouring
villages or powerful families. The latter approach, while useful at
the level of the individual commune or canton, does not help to
explain how whole regions have come to be dominated by a particular tradition. And the former approaches all seem to work for
some areas, but not for others. Ormières concludes that 'the religious attitude of the populations concerned appears fundamental'[42]
– though this still leaves open one of the biggest problems of
modern French history, that of why attitudes to the Catholic Church
have, at least since the 1790s, varied so widely from one part of
France to another.

Again, the two formative periods appear to be the 1790s and the
Second Republic. For instance, it was in the 1790s that deep-rooted
traditions of Catholic conservatism were established in most of Brittany and the Vendée, and in the years 1848–51 that such rural
departments as the Creuse and the Var, and the working-class suburbs of such cities as Marseilles and Toulouse, became established as
radical strongholds. And this radicalism went with an increasing
alienation from the church. This alienation had its counterpart in

the increasing politicisation of the clergy, which reached a decisive stage in the years 1860–80. By about 1880, according to Langlois,[43] it is possible to speak of a division of rural France into two camps, one 'clerical' and the other 'anti-clerical', each bound together primarily by either closeness to or distance from the Catholic Church. In the west, where the great majority of the population still went to mass on Sunday and received communion at Easter at the beginning of this century, there was a distinction between 'blue' areas, where clerical interventions in politics were resented and parents sent their children to a secular school, and 'white' areas, which were much more amenable to clerical guidance in matters of education and politics. The 'blue' areas often saw a decline in religious practice after the First World War, but in the 'white' areas there was no serious decline until the 1960s.[44]

During the period 1880–1914 religious questions carried an unequalled resonance for French voters. There certainly were some working-class radicals who argued that there was nothing to choose between Catholics and anti-clerical republicans and that the battle between church and state was a giant red herring, devised to distract the attention of the people from more important issues.[45] But red herring or not, religious questions aroused more people more deeply than anything else could. The division of the population into two hostile camps is described with peculiar vividness in the reminiscences of a teacher who recalled entering his first post in the early years of this century in a village near Toulouse, and going one evening to pay his respects to the priest – only to be politely rebuffed in the following words:

Castelmayran is divided into two fiercely opposed clans, the republicans and the clericals; they keep their distance from one another, and they have sworn an eternal hatred. One side goes to the Café Bayrou and the other to the Café Bouché: young left-wingers have their own dance-hall and so do the young right-wingers. Each clan has its own grocer and its own butcher... Everyone here is classified, stamped; people only associate with their own side; they run away from the others. We, the priest and the teacher, are regarded as implacable enemies. You certainly have all my sympathy, but in our own interests we will not meet again. If someone caught you entering the presbytery I would lose all my reputation with my own congregation; they would try to get the bishop to move me. For your part the republicans would hate you, and would make such difficulties that whether you liked it or not you too would have to leave.[46]

The emotions which the church evoked in many republicans of this era are indicated in the climactic moment of Zola's novel *Paris* (1898). Guillaume Froment, the hero's brother, is an anarchist and also a scientist, whose research on explosives leads him to invent a device of immense destructive power, which he believes can be used for the benefit of humanity. After considering, and rejecting, the possibility that it might contribute to the cause of international peace, he decides to blow up a major building in Paris. However, he hesitates between various symbols of the capitalist order. Should it be the Opera House, the Stock Exchange, the Palace of Justice, or the Arc de Triomphe? But in the end he rejects all of these and selects the Basilica of Sacré Coeur de Montmartre. Moreover he decides to destroy it at a moment when ten thousand pilgrims are likely to be inside:

'If I have chosen the basilica of the Sacred Heart', he continued, 'it is because I found it near at hand and easy to destroy. But it is also because it haunts and exasperates me, because I have long since condemned it. As I have often said to you, one cannot imagine anything more preposterous than Paris, our great Paris, crowned by this temple raised to the glorification of the absurd. Is it not outrageous that common sense should receive such a smack after so many centuries of science, that Rome should claim the right of triumphing in this insolent fashion, on our loftiest height in the full sunlight? The priests want Paris to repent and do penitence for its liberative work of truth and justice. But its only right course is to sweep away all that hampers and insults it in its march towards deliverance. And so may the temple fall with its deity of falsehood and servitude! And may its ruins crush its worshippers, so that like one of the old geological revolutions of the world, the catastrophe may resound through the very entrails of mankind, and renew and change it!'[47]

In the event, the hero talks Guillaume out of his murderous scheme. Both are convinced that in the long run the church will be destroyed, not by explosives, but by the irresistible force of science and humanity's drive for freedom. Yet in the short term the church and clergy seem frighteningly powerful. The extraordinary resentment and bitterness with which anti-clerical militants regarded the church thus arose partly from a sense of the effrontery of the clergy – they are doomed, so why won't they admit it? But it also arose from a realistic appraisal of the great influence which Catholicism still had. The ten thousand pilgrims who were to be blown up with the church were one illustration of this. No other institution or organisation could bring together such huge crowds including both women and men, young and old, and drawn from all social classes. The cult of the Sacred Heart evoked the tenderness and compassion of Jesus, and also his vulnerability. It was closely associated with Lourdes, the place of miracles, where sufferers of all kinds claimed to have found answers to their prayers. In its combination of splendour and mystery, the basilica had an emotional power that it shared with many other Catholic churches – bringing a link with the distant past, access to the divine, and a bond with hundreds of fellow-worshippers.[48]

In England the most significant cleavage in the electorate was that between Anglican and Nonconformist. Antagonisms between Protestant and Catholic may have run deeper, but since Catholics made up only 5 per cent of the population, there were only a few areas, most notably Liverpool and some other parts of Lancashire, where Catholics were sufficiently numerous to have a major influence on voting patterns. In those areas the Conservatives were regarded as the Protestant party and benefited from a large 'Orange' vote by working-class Protestants, which continued until after the Second World War, while Catholics mainly voted Liberal or, later, Labour.[49] At least up to 1918, the Liberals attracted the votes of religious minorities generally, including not only Catholics, but also Nonconformists, Jews and Secularists. But it was the Nonconformists who were by far the largest and most politically significant of these groups. Already, in the period 1832–67, middle-class Dissenters were a major element in the Whig/Liberal/Radical electorate.[50] With the enfranchisement of a large part of the urban and rural working class in 1867 and 1884, a further large swathe of Nonconformist voters flocked to the Liberal banners. A computer-based analysis of elections from 1885 to 1910 suggests that throughout this period religious variables (especially those indicating the strength of Nonconformity) were the best predictors of the result. Only in 1918 did class become the key variable.[51]

In Britain, as in France, during the later nineteenth and early twentieth centuries the electoral system was structured round the opposition between conservatives (in Britain the Conservative Party and the Liberal Unionists) and progressives (Liberals and Labour), with Catholicism (in France) and the Established Churches (in Britain) as the most significant unifying force on the conservative side and religious dissent on the progressive side. In both countries there were militant socialists who wanted to get away from older religious feuds and to fight the class war. But, as elsewhere in Europe, socialism grew out of liberalism, and inherited important aspects of its cultural baggage. In France the Socialists inherited and maintained with varying degrees of enthusiasm the anti-clerical traditions of French republicanism, and in Britain, the Independent Labour Party was strongly influenced by the background of Protestant Dissent from which so many of its members had come. In Britain some problems arose from the fact that in appealing to the various religious minorities the Liberals brought together groups which were actually very different and in some repects scarcely compatible, including Roman Catholics and Secularists, as well as Protestant Dissenters.[52] Similarly in France the republican cause brought together atheists, deists, and devout Protestants and Jews. But since all agreed on hammering the Catholics, the fact that they did so from very different standpoints seldom caused major problems. In any case it often helped that French anti-clericals were inclined to philo-Protestantism.[53]

Religious identities were most intense and least problematic where they were intertwined with ethnicity, as they were for Irish Catholics, East European Jews or Welsh Nonconformists. For many people, on the other hand, religious identities were potentially in competition or even contradiction with other identities, such as those of class. Nonetheless, there were a number of factors which ensured that in Britain, as elsewhere, religious identities remained a crucial influence on voting in this period. One factor was simply that the section of society that was least involved in any kind of organised religion, namely the poorer sections of the urban working class, was also the group least likely to be able to vote under the restrictive franchise operating before 1918. Hereditary loyalties also played a part in ensuring that some of those who were no longer active members of their religious community voted in the way that they had been brought up to vote. The influence of employers could be important. Some landowners or farmers and some factory-owners expected their employees to vote for their political party and attend a church of their denomination,[54] though by the early twentieth

century, with the decline of employer paternalism and with increasing worker militancy, this situation was much less common than it
had been in the mid-Victorian period. Religion was an important
part of the public persona of many candidates for Parliament or
local councils and played a part in voters' ability to identify with
them. Analysis of the religious affiliations of candidates in the
elections of 1900, 1906 and 1910 shows that 64 per cent of Anglicans were standing as Conservatives or Liberal Unionists, and 91
per cent of Nonconformists stood as Liberals or Labour.[55] In some
communities the interpenetration of religious and political loyalties
was self-understood. This was most clearly the case in the many
villages where the dominant landowner was closely linked with the
parish church and the clergyman was an active supporter of
the Conservative cause. Here religious Dissent was unmistakably a
defiance of the powers that be, and a natural preparation for Liberal
and later Labour politics.[56] More generally, religious communities
often had a prevailing ethos which had clear political implications.
Nonconformists saw themselves as democratic, egalitarian, morally
upright, sturdily independent, and tended to regard Liberal or
Labour politics as a natural expression of these values. Anglicans,
on the other hand, tended to lay more stress on the virtues of
patriotism, loyalty to the Crown, respect for authority, and a com-
mon-sense, unpuritanical approach to morality, and this readily led
them in a Conservative direction.[57]

Religion and Nationalism

The growing importance of nationalism and imperialism in the later
nineteenth and early twentieth century also potentially diminished
the importance of religious or confessional factors: nationalism
could provide a bridge across the various confessional divides,
uniting believer and unbeliever, Catholic and Protestant; equally,
for the most fervent nationalists, there was a tendency for nationalism to take on the character of a new faith, replacing older forms.
The latter tendency developed furthest in Germany, where some
nationalists, regarding Christianity as an embarrassment and Judaism as an abomination, harked back to the old Teutonic gods.
Another current of thought drew upon racialist ideas to give a
'scientific' basis to the competition between peoples, and rejected
Christianity and Judaism as lacking any such scientific foundation.[58]

However, these tendencies should not be overstated. Many forms of nationalism contained a strong religious ingredient, and rival versions of nationalism were often an aspect of religious conflict.

The association between Protestantism and first English, and later British, national identity was of very long standing. The Reformation, the Spanish Armada, the Glorious Revolution, the wars against Louis XIV and Napoleon were all central events in a national history which was recognised by Anglican and Dissenter alike, and in which the central theme was the battle for English Protestant freedom against foreign Catholic despotism – admittedly, by the time of Napoeon, France had come to be associated in English Protestant minds even more with irreligion than with Catholicism. But it was a central tenet of nineteenth-century English Protestantism that Catholicism and irreligion tended to go together as different sides of the same coin, and that both were associated with despotism, while Protestantism went together both with freedom and with genuine piety. With the union of England and Scotland in 1707 and then of Britain and Ireland in 1801, religion was clearly a central factor both in the acceptance of the Union by most Scots, Welsh and Protestant Irish, and in its rejection by most Catholic Irish.[59]

Five definitions of British national identity occur continually throughout the nineteenth century and into the twentieth: Britain was Christian, Protestant, prosperous, civilised and free. Of course the importance attached to the various points varied over time and varied as between members of different political parties, social classes or religious communities. Thus in 1857, the leader of Manchester's Reform Synagogue, in declaring his conviction that the British nation had a 'Divine mission to carry civilization, liberty and prosperity to the uttermost bounds of the earth', naturally omitted reference to Christianity.[60] But the most striking point is how many people bought the whole package, and how many saw these five characteristics as inter-related, with Protestantism acting as the linchpin. Britain was more truly Christian than, for instance, France or Italy, the later Bishop of Durham, Hensley Henson, claimed in a debate at the Church Congress in 1898. This was because the free and rational Protestant faith was acceptable to the modern age, whereas the 'extreme and perverted sacerdotalism of the Roman Catholic Church' had led to 'the great and ever waxing alienation from the Church of the best conscience and intellect of the Latin races'. That Britain also owed her civilisation, freedom and prosperity to her Protestantism was strongly implied by J. E. C. Welldon, the Headmaster of Harrow and recently appointed Bishop of Calcutta, in a sermon on 'National Success and Christianity' at the same Congress and in a subsequent letter to the *Spectator*, an influential weekly review. In the sermon he stated that 'wherever there was a country that was stationary and retrogressive it was Catholic, wherever there was a people which was progressive and Imperial it was Protestant'. The decline of Spain, he claimed, was due to its Catholicism and 'The unique greatness of the British Empire dated from the Reformation'. Elaborating his argument in response to criticism, he went on to say that 'If it were necessary to look for an assurance of the divine favour towards the Christian nations that have shaken off the yoke of Rome, I should find it not so much in their success, as in the principles by which the success has been mainly won, in the love of truth, intellectual feedom, religious equality, the right of private judgement, and the sense of personal, direct responsibility to God, which produce a more robust and virile type of national character than has been, or can be, the product of sacerdotal authority.'[61]

In 1898 views of this kind were beginning to be to some extent controversial. They came under attack not only from Roman and Anglo-Catholics, but from some advocates of a broad religious tolerance, and also from a growing body of opinion which saw the roots of national character and achievement in race, rather than religion. Figures like Welldon and Henson were fighting to defend conceptions both of religion and of nationhood which they felt to be under attack. In 1850 or 1860 these would have been regarded as commonplaces. Many historians have demonstrated the pervasiveness of anti-Catholicism both in England and in Britain generally in the middle of the nineteenth century, and the ways in which it shaped many people's understandings of what it meant to be English or British. In the later nineteenth and early twentieth centuries religiously-based conceptions of the nation and the empire, whether (most commonly) specifically Protestant, or sometimes more broadly Christian, were still very widespread. They were certainly promoted in the schools. In the public schools, Anglicanism, cricket and the empire were all essential ingredients, and were often so completely mixed together that it was difficult to imagine one without reference to the others.[62] A study of the history textbooks used in the elementary schools of the later Victorian and Edwardian period notes that the teaching was intended to instil a strong sense of national identity, often with a strong Protestant dimension:

writers compared the state of religion and civil liberty attained in England with that elsewhere and concluded that the English were 'uniquely blessed by providence'.[63] The writers of these textbooks tended to justify the British Empire on the grounds that it brought civilisation and humanitarian reforms to peoples previously noted for their barbarism and cruelty. This kind of argument prepared the ground for the teaching of the Sunday School, where the encounters of Protestant missionaries with crocodiles, cannibals and Catholics were described in thrilling detail.[64]

Imperialism and Protestantism were linked through the frequent claim that Britain had a God-given mission to spread true religion and good government across the world and to impose humanitarian reforms, such as the abolition of the slave trade. These links were also reflected in and reinforced by the cults surrounding various national heroes of the period. John MacKenzie, in a study of the four most revered 'Heroes of Empire', General Sir Henry Havelock, David Livingstone, General George Gordon and T. E. Lawrence, shows that, in the case of the first three, devout Protestantism was an essential part of their public persona and the myths surrounding them. All three died in distant parts of the globe, two of them violently, and all of them came to be seen as martyrs. Havelock held religious services for his troops and was regarded as a second Cromwell – a comparison which seems to have made his brutal suppression of the Indian uprising more acceptable. Livingstone, besides being, of course, a missionary and a self-educated former factory worker (which added to his heroic stature and made him a favourite role-model to be offered to Sunday School children), was a vigorous opponent of the slave trade, as was Gordon. Gordon was also known as a keen Bible-reader, who devoted his spare time to running clubs for boys.[65] The 'Irish Question' also served to confirm the Protestant identity of a large part of the British public, though the Liberal adoption of Home Rule in 1886 and the Ulster crisis of 1912 tended to make anti-Catholic nationalism more of a specifically Conservative and Unionist phenomenon, rather than a sentiment that was spread widely across the political spectrum.

None the less, by the later nineteenth century the links between Protestantism and English or British national identity were being slowly eroded. This was partly because of the influence of more secular conceptions of the nation, and partly because of changes within Protestantism. To begin with the second of these:

anti-Catholicism was in gradual decline from about 1870 onwards. Both theological and social factors played a part in this. Theological factors included the decline of the ultra-evangelicalism that contributed strongly to the great revival of militant anti-Catholicism in the 1830s and 1840s. Whereas in Germany the most virulent anti-Catholics tended to be liberal Protestants and secularists who saw Catholicism as an affront to liberty of conscience and the authority of science, in England the cause was spearheaded by evangelicals who condemned Catholics for placing the Virgin Mary alongside Jesus Christ and putting the authority of the Pope above that of the Bible – indeed, these evangelicals frequently claimed that the Pope was the anti-Christ whose overthrow would herald the Second Coming. By the last third of the nineteenth century, the growing force in the Church of England were the Anglo-Catholics, sympathetic to many aspects of Roman Catholicism (and some of them eventually converts); on the Nonconformist side the main trend was towards a more liberal theology, within which anti-Catholicism generally took milder forms and was much less central.

In spite of the continuing strength of militant anti-Catholicism on Merseyside, there was also a gradual process in most parts of England whereby Catholics came to be accepted, however reluctantly, as a permanent part of English society, and anti-Catholic agitators came to be seen as ridiculous and potentially dangerous 'fanatics'. The respect enjoyed by such Catholic leaders as Cardinals Newman and Manning helped in this process. And a final stage was brought about by the First World War, fought in the name of Catholic Belgium, with the wholehearted support of the Catholic hierarchy, with Catholic military chaplains gaining a reputation for bravery and devotion. In 1926 a bill to remove most of the remaining Catholic disabilities passed through Parliament with very little opposition, one of the main arguments in favour being Catholic patriotism during the war. Equally important, though, was the increasing willingness from about the 1880s onwards for Protestants to criticise aspects of their own culture and traditions, and to accept the possibility that wisdom could come from other sources, including to some extent Catholicism. Thus even the most fervent British Protestants were beginning to recognise the superior record of Catholic nations, such as France and Italy, in art and the achievements of Austrian and German Catholics (as well as German Protestants and Jews) in music.[66]

At the same time wholly or largely secular ideas of national identity were challenging those rooted in Christianity. The two crucial developments here in the later nineteenth century were the increasing importance of the Empire within perceptions of Britain and the British people, and the influence of racial ideas. The Empire, as already argued, was frequently justified as an instrument for the spread of the gospel; but the definition of Britain as primarily an imperial power could be presented as an alternative to the older definition of Britain as a Protestant nation. More especially, racial ideas were often seen by their advocates as being in explicit contradiction to religious ideas. Increasingly from the 1860s onwards, it was being argued by British patriots that superior racial inheritance, rather than true religon, was the key to Britain's greatness, and that the Empire should be justified primarily on the grounds that the conquered peoples were 'inferior races'. Lorimer notes that by the end of the nineteenth century assumptions concerning the depth and funadamental nature of racial differences were so much of a contemporary orthodoxy, that even a Liberal like Lord Bryce when appealing in 1902 for more humane and responsible treatment of 'inferior races' took it for granted that they were 'inferior'.[67] A characteristic example of the way in which explanations of national differences based on assumptions about race had partly replaced the older explanations based on religion was an editorial in the *Spectator* in 1898, on 'The Relationship between Religion and National Success', where the editor criticised the views, quoted above, expressed by Bishop Welldon at the Church Congress:

> The North of Ireland is more prosperous than the South of Ireland because the North of Ireland is occupied, or at all events directed, by men of the Scoto-English breed, who are restless in poverty, who love order, and who are nearly as industrious as the worst race under heaven, the Chinese. Fill Ireland with ultra-Catholic Flemings and Ireland would be filled with a people making money every day, using her streams, her meadows, her fish, and above all her many facilities for manufactures. England is great because of the blood of her people, their energy, their freedom, and their industry, not because of their creed. . . . We are not contending, be it understood, for a moment, that Protestant-ism is not a more nutritive creed than Romanism. We fully believe that it is nearer to ultimate truth and, moreover, that owing to the

love of liberty that it has of late years developed, it allows the separate qualities of any race which adopts it to grow and strengthen to the fullest degree of which the inherent powers of the race may admit. Catholicism, where it is genuine, confines the human intelligence too much, and produces a submissiveness in the inner character which is apt to militate against either personal or national success.[68]

Race had thus become the master-factor, while religion, though not unimportant, had a secondary role. Equally significant, and symptomatic of changes in a section of the educated public, was the change in the language with which the role of religion was understood. Catholicism was treated with a degree of disdain, but without the vituperation that was so common a few decades earlier, and with a recognition that Catholic Belgians and Rhinelanders called in question the assumption that Catholicism went with backwardness. Meanwhile, Protestant Christianity was no longer 'the truth', but merely nearer to the truth than Catholicism, and 'the love of liberty' was not inherent in Protestantism, but a recent development. So the significance of religion in general and Protestantism in particualar was being relativised from several directions at once.

Religious and racial language were not necessarily mutually exclusive: as racial categories became increasingly widely accepted in the later nineteenth century, the two were often mixed together in a confused way. Howver, racial theories were generally justified on the grounds that they had a scientific basis which religion was seen to lack, or were presented in conjunction with explicitly anti-Christian Social Darwinist arguments.[69] Overseas missions were a particular field of conflict. For the supporters of Protestant missions, it was axiomatic that Christianity was the panacea which could ultimately overcome every social evil, and which could enable even the most degraded of peoples to rise and ultimately achieve equality with the most advanced. For propagandists of race this showed an alarming ignorance of racial differences and their scientific basis. Africans, for instance, were often seen as innately inferior. Indeed, it was sometimes argued that Islam was better suited to their needs than was Christianity.[70] Missionaries also found themselves in conflict with colonial administrators, though more often for pragmatic reasons of conflicting interests than for ideological reasons. Missionaries who wanted to evangelise everyone everywhere were blocked by administrators who needed to retain the support of non-Christian native elites. And attempts by missionaries to defend the rights of native Christians brought them into conflict with colonial authorities who placed British political and economic interests first.[71]

In Germany the enthusiasm evoked by the Prussian victory over France in 1870, the establishment of the German Empire in 1871, the subsequent acquisition of German colonies in Africa, and the apparently unstoppable economic and cultural progress of the new state all contributed to a mood of exalted nationalism, which seemed to take on the character of a new religion. Numerous nationalist writers identified the 'nation' and the 'people' as 'holy'. They gave the individual German a new kind of immortality, because the German people were 'eternal', binding together the living with countless generations now dead or yet to be born. The nation had an absolute claim on its members, and to die for the fatherland was the highest form of martyrdom.[72] This message was also emphasised by the many grandiose war memorials erected after 1871, on which the standard inscription was 'To the fallen in memory, to the living im recognition, to the future generations for emulation'. Patriotic monuments became a ubiquitous part of the environment in these years, and such events as the Kaiser's Birthday and the festivities organised by war veterans and other patriotic groups became a familiar part of the calendar.[73] Nationalist ideas were also heavily emphasised in the schools. By the 1890s proponents of this nationalism were sometimes consciously rejecting Christianity in the name of *völkisch* ideas: Christianity was just a phase in the long history of the the German people, whose greatness lay within the soul of the race. From this point of view, Christianity was often seen as an artifical source of division within the German people. The need was for a more authentically 'German' faith, which would unite all true Germans, and also separate them more clearly both from those outside, and from the alien elements within the German nation. These typically included both Judaism and 'Roman' Catholicism, and, according to Altgeld, anti-Catholicism was more central to pre-1914 ultra-nationalism than anti-Semitism. They were more lukewarm towards Protestantism, which provoked less hostility, but was often regarded with little real enthusiasm.[74]

However, nationalism as a new religion was less typical than nationalism expressed in terms drawn from the old religion, or the old religion reinterpreted in the light of nationalism. The German Empire, established in 1871, had an unmistakably Protestant character, which posed big problems for the large Catholic minority. Many Catholics had hoped for a different kind of Germany – one dominated by Catholic Austria, rather than Protestant Prussia. There were also many Bavarian Catholics who, at least initially, did not want a united German state at all, and would have preferred their Catholic kingdom to retain its independence. In addition, those Catholics who were Polish or French nationalists were equally hostile to Prussia and to Germany, and wanted nothing to do with either. With the exception of the Poles, most Catholics were gradually reconciled to the German Empire. In Alsace-Lorraine, for instance, this was reflected in the growing importance from the 1890s of the Centre Party and of national Catholic organisations like the *Volksverein für das katholische Deutschland* – Alsace-Lorrainers were coming to see themselves primarily as Catholics rather than primarily as French.[75]

By the 1890s nationalism was common to members of all religious denominations and those at most points in the political spectrum. Yet to a large extent it served to underline the deep differences within German society, since each group adhered to a different version of nationalism. For Protestants the leitmotiv of German history was the struggle for freedom, directed against the papacy and against France. The fight against the papacy could be traced back to the time of the medieval emperors, but its high-point was the revolt of Martin Luther, from whom all that was best in Germany stemmed. The French enemy came to the fore with Louis xiv's seizure of Protestant Strasbourg and with the conquests of Napoleon. But German renewal came with the great rising of the German people against French rule, culminating in the victory of 1813, and then most decisively with the second victory over the French in 1870, and the establishment of the Empire. In Protestant eyes these were victories for Protestantism, but, even more importantly, they were signs that the Germans were a chosen people, who would continue to enjoy God's favour as long as they remained faithful to him. Sedan Day, commemorating the Prussian victory over the French on 2 September 1870, was a major festival in Protestant regions of Germany, marked both by special religious services and by patriotic speeches and displays, as well as by vast amounts of beer-drinking and sausage-eating. But for long it was ignored by many Catholics.[76]

There was also a form of secular Protestantism which saw the *beginning* of everything worthwhile in German history in the Reformation, but which saw Luther's work as completed by the Enlightenment and the Romantics. The heroes of secular Protestantism were such figures as Frederick the Great, Lessing, Goethe, Schiller and von Humboldt, most of whom were unbelievers, but all of whom were Protestants by birth. Protestants both of the devout and of the more secular kind were inclined to be disparaging of Catholic cultural achievements and, for instance, to exclude Catholic authors from the canon.[77] Equally, of course, historical writing was a field of fierce confessional contention. To a large extent Protestant and Catholic readers took their knowledge and understanding of history from different writers. The most prestigious chairs of History were occupied by Protestants, Bismarck-worshipping National Liberals, like Heinrich von Treitschke and Heinrich von Sybel, whose routine dismissals of Catholicism as a retrograde force condemned by history were accepted by many readers as authoritative statements by the leaders of their profession. Catholic historians, like Johannes Janssen, did not gain the same official recognition, but it was their vision of the past which shaped that of most Catholics.[78]

Meanwhile, Jews tended to prefer a version of German history rather similar to that of the more secular liberal Protestants. Their starting-point tended to be the Enlightenment – naturally without the references back to Luther that were obligatory for Protestants, however secular. Some eighteenth-century writers were very highly regarded by Jews, notably Lessing because of his sympathetic presentation of the Jewish hero in his *Nathan the Wise*. But the greatest of all Germans was Schiller, who embodied a way of being German with which Jews readily identified themselves. His cult reached unprecedented heights among middle-class Jews.[79] Catholics, however, argued that Germany's greatest days were those of the Holy Roman Empire, before the tragic split brought about by the Reformation. They exalted the virtues of local and confessional loyalties over against the claims of the all-powerful modern state, of which Prussia was the embodiment. As Helmut Walser Smith argues, 'nationalism is not simply a unified story that people tell about themselves, but rather consists of stories – separate, but overlapping, and often in competition – that groups within the nation tell about the nation to which they belong. These stories typically appear inclusive even when they are not; indeed, that is a central paradox of nationalist ideologies: that they represent a generalized claim from the vantage, and often the interests, of a particular group'.[80] Of these 'groups', it was still those defined by religion that had the greatest influence on the different ways that the German nation was imagined.[81]

In France there were two rival versions of nationalism, one Catholic and the other republican, each claiming unique validity. One of the most powerful symbols of French identity, Joan of Arc, was claimed by both sides. A very influential definition of her role in French history was that of Jules Michelet, the great liberal anticlerical historian, writing in the 1840s. In his *History of France*, she became the founder of the French nation, the first to realise that France could be more than 'a combination of provinces, a vast chaos of fiefs'. She was a daughter of the people, and through her the deepest, though hitherto unconscious, desire of the people became a reality. In this version, according to Winock,[82] 'God was not denied, but relativised'. But soon, more overtly polemical versions of her story took over. For Catholics she was a saint, chosen by God to lead the French people. The campaign by French Catholics to secure her canonisation was launched in 1869, though it only finally achieved its goal in 1920. In the years around the end of the nineteenth century, when the battle to 'own' Joan of Arc was at its height, she had a triple significance for French Catholics. She symbolised the union of Catholicism and patriotism, at a time when a fervent nationalism, focused especially on the 'lost provinces' of Alsace and Lorraine, was widespread in the Catholic community. As the 'maid' she embodied the Catholic virtue of purity, so much derided by republicans. And as one who took the supernatural seriously she was a standing rebuke to contemporary scepticism. Some Catholics were also among those ultra-nationalists who drew anti-Semitic messages from her career. She was a daughter of the soil, unlike the nomadic and essentially urban Jew; she was a patriot over against Jewish cosmopolitanism; an idealist as against Jewish materialism; and she belonged to a superior race.[83] Republicans, however, celebrated her as a heretic, and emphasised the role of the church in her trial and execution, and socialists laid particular stress on her poverty and her identification with the poor. In the end, no one version was able to drive out the others, and her value as a national symbol during and immediately after the First World War lay in the fact that every section of a divided national community was able to find in her something to inspire them – as was pointed out by the deputy who in 1920 successfully proposed the institution of a national holiday in her honour.[84] Napoleon was another disputed figure. French patriots of all kinds could take pride in his military triumphs. On the other hand, Catholics might equally see him either as the restorer or as the persecutor of the church, and republicans might see him as betraying the Revolution, or as continuing its work.[85]

Otherwise, the two versions of French history were completely different, and the development under the Third Republic of two rival school systems led to these two rival stories being systematically developed and taught to the younger generation within each camp. For Catholics France was 'the eldest daughter of the Church', and the nation was greatest when it was most Catholic. The highest point of French history was reached in the thirteenth century when a saint, Louis IX, sat on the throne. Catholics also attached special significance to the fact that it was a French nun whose visions of the Sacred Heart of Jesus had laid the basis for the worldwide cult, and that the most influential of the many nineteenth-century Marian apparitions took place in France, notably those in Paris in 1830, at La Salette in 1846, and Lourdes in 1858. Mary, they believed, had a special predilection for the French people – a preference which gained added meaning when one considered how much the French people – or at least a powerful faction among them – had done to anger her.[86]

For republicans, however, France's finest hour was 1789, and all that was best in France stemmed from the events of that year. But they shared with the Catholics their faith in the sacredness of the French nation and their conviction that the French people had a worldwide mission. Kselman quotes a poem of 1877 in which Victor Hugo reviewed the disasters that had befallen France in the last decade, leading him to ask 'O France! Will you die?' He replied that this would be impossible because of France's God-given mission to fight against kings and priests, bringing liberty to the world.[87] In the later nineteenth century, Catholics and republicans could find common ground in their determination to win back Alsace and Lorraine and in their enthusiasm for the Empire. Indeed, anti-clerical French governments could be quite enthusiastic about Catholic missions, so long as they could be seen as spreading French culture at a safe distance from France.[88] More often, though, Catholic and republican nationalists were in conflict with one another. During the Franco-Prussian war, Catholics were accused of being too ready to make peace, and some of the more conspiracy-minded republicans even suspected that Catholic priests were in league with the enemy.[89] The Dreyfus Affair brought such mutual suspicions to a high point. By now the army, once a republican stronghold, was strongly influenced by a form of Catholic nationalism, which identified Frenchness so much with Catholicism, that the patriotism of Freemasons and Protestants, as well as of Jews, was open to question.[90]

Conclusion

So both in England and in Germany the most widely held version of national history and identity at the end of the nineteenth century was still one that had Protestantism at its centre. This view was propagated through the schools, through wide sections of the press, and by many of the most influential historians, as well as through the Protestant pulpit. On the other hand, in Germany there was a rival Catholic version, sustained through the powerful Catholic 'milieu', and adhered to by most Catholics. In both countries, ideas of nationality rooted in concepts of 'race' and of inherited racial characteristics passed on over many hundreds of years, were partly displacing older religiously-based concepts. However, the predominant tendency was for religious and racial ideas to mix together, sometimes the one and sometimes the other predominating. In France, there was a more clear-cut separation between two versions of national identity, which at least the more fervent proponents of each regarded as mutually incompatible. In one, France was 'the eldest daughter of the Church' and in the other the land of 'liberty, equality, fraternity' and of Voltaire and Rousseau. The latter view was propagated through the universities and the state school system. But the former view had the support of the vast resources of the church, which remained by far the most powerful cultural influence in many parts of the country, and a major presence almost everywhere else. And in spite of the anathemas which fervent Catholics and republicans heaped upon one another, there was also a third group of those who remained to some degree both Catholic and republican, and who were able, according to circumstances, to adopt either identity. Thus, Faury concludes his fine study of clericalism and anti-clericalism in the Tarn by noting that although a large part of the rural population voted republican, politicians tended to be remote figures, whereas they often retained close personal ties with their priest: 'born in the district, often of modest origins, not ashamed to use the Occitan language, he remains their spiritual confidant, and the one who presides at the times of great joy and of great distress in the family'.[91]

7 Religion and Popular Culture

She lit a candle, and went to a second and third bed under the wall, where she awoke her young sisters and brothers, all of whom occupied the same room. Pulling out the washing-stand so that she could get behind it, she poured some water from a jug, and made them kneel around, putting their hands together with fingers exactly vertical. While the children scarcely awake, awe-stricken at her manner, their eyes growing larger and larger, remained in this position, she took the baby from her bed.... Tess then stood erect with the infant on her arm beside the basin, the next sister held the Prayer-Book open before her, as the clerk at church held it before the parson; and thus the girl set about baptizing the child....

'What's his name going to be?'

She had not thought of that, but a name suggested by a phrase in the book of Genesis came into her head as she proceeded with the baptismal service, and now she pronounced it:

'SORROW, I baptize thee in the name of the Father, and of the Son, and of the Holy Ghost.'

She sprinkled the water and there was silence.

'Say "Amen", children.'

The tiny voices piped in obedient response 'Amen!'

Tess Durbeyfield, a young Dorset farm-worker has given birth to an illegitimate child. The child was very frail, and within a week of birth he is dying. When she realises that there is no hope, Tess is plunged into further despair by the realisation that he has not been baptised. She wants to send for the parson, but her father, humiliated by the shame that Tess has brought on the household, will have none of it, and when the parson does call, he refuses him entry. As Tess lies in bed that night she is terrified by the thought that her baby will go to hell. She accepted that 'if she should have to burn for what she had done, burn she must, and there was an end of it. Like all village girls she was well grounded in the Holy Scriptures, and had dutifully studied the histories of Aholah and Aholibah, and knew the inferences to be drawn therefrom'. But she is determined to save her beloved child from such a fate. So there and then she performs the rite herself, and when she finished, she 'poured forth from the bottom of her heart the thanksgiving that follows, uttering it boldly and triumphantly'.[1]

Rites of Passage

The interpenetration of Christianity and the popular culture of nineteenth-century Europe was seen nowhere more vividly than in the hold which the Christian rites of passage exercised on the imaginations of so many people. And, in case Hardy's account of Tess's fears and the way she resolved them might seem fanciful, it is worth noting the words of a Berlin clergyman writing in 1880 of his experiences in an impoverished working-class parish. 'In summer, the number of emergency baptisms is large. Death knocks on the door of culpable negligence and causes terror. Post-haste they send for the clergyman. He must quickly – but immediately – make good what laziness has spoiled. They demand vehemently that, in spite of other urgent business, the emergency baptism should be carried out at once'.[2]

Tess lived in a rural region of southern England, where the Church of England was an inescapable part of daily life, where most of the people had spent at least part of their childhood at Sunday School and in a church day school, where a considerable proportion continued to attend church regularly as adults, and where the clergy were well known to the great majority of the population. It is more remarkable that the emotions surrounding the rite of baptism continued to influence large numbers of people in the giant parishes of Berlin, where the direct influence of the clergy and of conformist pressures were much weaker. In devoutly Catholic communities, such emergency baptisms were less likely to be needed, as the great majority of infants were baptised within eight days of birth.[3] The Protestant church in Prussia encouraged its members to have their children baptised within a month of birth. In 1905 the pastor of another working-class parish in Berlin noted that fewer than one in ten of his parishioners had done this, but the great majority of childen *were* eventually baptised.[4] Many kinds of consideration influenced the people who sat loose to the strict requirements of their church, but did none the less eventually bring their children to the font. Fear for the fate after death of the unbaptised child was certainly one such factor. So intense could this fear be, that French babies who had been born dead, or who died before they could be baptised, were sometimes taken to a Marian shrine. There are several reports between 1820 and 1890 of the children being miraculously resuscitated for the few seconds needed in order to perform the rite.[5] Equally important in the case of children still living, but taken suddenly ill, was the hope that baptism might help them to recover. The pastor from 1886 to 1915 of one of the poorest parishes in Berlin noted the prevalence of this belief. He told the parents that all was in the hands of the heavenly father and baptism would not of itself save the child; but when the child did get better the parents were very grateful to him. There was also a more general feeling that the child needed the best possible start in life and that to be unbaptised was to be unlucky.[6]

In the eyes of Catholics, Christian baptism, marriage and burial took on a further dimension because of the belief that it was these rites which set apart human beings, endowed with immortal souls, from the beasts that perish. Animal imagery therefore readily entered into Catholic accounts of those who neglected or rejected these ceremonies. One French priest in 1903 advised those who were thinking of a purely civil marriage to decide which species they belonged to.[7] A secular burial was referred to as an *enfouissement* (a term normally used for animals) or *encrottement* ('throwing in the muck') rather than an *enterrement*, the term used for human beings.[8] During one civic funeral in a small town near Orléans, a group of girls belonging to a confraternity came to the cemetery and made pig-like grunts during the ceremony.[9]

In France First Communion was generally regarded as an essential threshold to cross on the path to adulthood – as well as an incomparable opportunity for one's daughter to outshine all the neighbours' daughters. Threats to refuse First Communion were therefore a very powerful weapon for the clergy in the battles with anti-clerical teachers and mayors in the 1880s and 1890s. During the 'battle of the manuals' in 1883, parents in the Tarn were put under heavy pressure to withdraw their children from schools where manuals deemed anti-Catholic were in use. At one village the children reported that 'the priest and his assistant told us that we would not make our solemn communion if we went on reading this bad book, which ought to be burnt, if we were not going to grow up into thieves and murderers who would be buried like rotting dogs'.[10]

In England one of the ceremonies with strongest popular resonance was the churching of mothers after childbirth, officially an act of thanksgiving, but popularly regarded as a rite of purification. Whereas the baptism of infants was strongly promoted by the clergy, and those neglecting the rite could come under heavy pressure to comply, the churching of the mother was not insisted upon by the clergy, and it owed its popularity entirely to popular demand. Some clergymen found that refusing to church a mother who had been married in a registry office or had never been married at all was a very effective means of expressing disapproval.[11] Because of the lack of clerical interest, evidence on this rite is sparse, but two east London clergymen interviewed in the 1890s both stated that churchings were at least as numerous as baptisms in their parishes.[12] Until she had been churched, the mother was regarded as unclean, and many people would not allow her into their house. A folklorist, commenting in 1866 on customs current in the north of England, wrote:

> As to the mother's churching, it is very uncanny for her to enter any house before she goes to church and she carries ill luck with her. It is believed also that if she appears out-of-doors in these circumstances and receiving any insult or blow from her neighbours she has no remedy at law.[13]

Religious Symbols in Daily Life

Christian rites were part of the taken-for-granted daily experience even of those who did not regard themselves as religious, *fromm*, *kirchlich* or *dévot*. The popular culture of west European countries in the second half of the nineteenth century was saturated with symbols, rituals, beliefs, drawn ultimately from Christianity, even if in some instances the relationship now seemed fairly tenuous. They coloured the day-to-day habits of pious and impious alike, as well as shaping much of the environment within which even the declared unbeliever had to live.

For instance, beliefs concerning likely sources of good and bad luck drew heavily on Christianity, even when the purposes for which the luck was needed had little to do with Christianity, or were even positively unChristian. In Zola's *The Earth*, set in the 1860s, the wife of a small farmer goes for an abortion to a witch in another village, who tells her:

> Well, what a man had done a man could undo, all he had to do was to have the woman and while having her make the sign of the cross on her stomach and say three aves backwards. And then if there was a baby it would go away like wind.[14]

A somewhat similar suggestion comes from one of the characters in *L'Assommoir*, which is set at about the same time in a working-class/ lower middle-class environment in Paris – 'You swallow a glass of holy water every night, making three signs of the cross with your thumb. It goes off like a bit of flatulence'.[15] Whether or not Zola invented these particular remedies, there is no doubt that he was close to the spirit of much folk wisdom. Ralph Gibson quotes a series of examples from the Perigord with a very similar flavour. If you could get a 'dry mass', without consecration of the wine, to be said for an enemy it would cause him or her to 'dry up'. Similar ideas – though without the malicious intent – were involved in women requesting priests to bless a wedding ring laid on an envelope containing a rat's tail. Once the blessing had been pronounced this would enable a sorcerer to 'tie the knot' on the woman's husband as a measure of contraception.[16] Jim Obelkevich shows how the rural population of nineteenth-century Lincolnshire found in everything connected with the church 'a vague reservoir of spiritual potency' which could be tapped for all sorts of purposes. Good Friday was regarded as a particularly good day for planting; Sunday was also a lucky day, but failure to wear new clothes on Easter Sunday would bring bad luck; worms taken from the churchyard at midnight were used in a remedy for ague; you should cross yourself after seeing a magpie in order to avert bad luck; and so on.[17] Very similar conclusions are suggested by a study of superstition in Berlin and the surrounding area published in 1899. The author declared, 'Yes, in Berlin and the Province of Brandenburg too, superstition accompanies humanity from the cradle to the grave, and like a luxuriant climbing-plant grows around all life's relationships'.[18] Many of the examples related in some way, however tenuous, to Christian rites or celebrations. Various examples were given of beliefs connected with baptism, Christmas, Sunday and Friday – the ill-omened reputation of which clearly originates from the fact that Jesus was killed on that day, though many of those who felt fearful on Friday probably did not know why. The way in which 'superstition' drew on the resources of specific religious cultures was illustrated by the fact that in the 1890s one of the collections of magical remedies sold by colporteurs (travelling book sellers) in Berlin had a Protestant, a Catholic and a Jewish version. A typical remedy was the following, recommended to Protestants, and to be repeated three times: 'Tumour, tumour, tumour, I command you in the name of Jesus Christ that you harm N.N. as little as Jesus Christ was harmed by the nails that the Jews hit into him.' Catholics were recommended to stop bleeding by repeating the following catchy rhyme nine times: 'Jesus Christ trägt sein Kreuz, warum, darum, weil er will. Blut steh still.' ('Jesus Christ carries his cross. Why? For this reason: because he wants to. Blood stand still.') If the examples given are typical, the differences between the Protestant and the Catholic books was not very great. Both they and the Jewish version reflect the familiarity of religious phraseology and biblical episodes, and the ways in which they could provide an entrance ticket to a world of hidden lore and supernatural power, which could be conjured up in any of life's crises.[19]

The presence of religious symbols in every area of daily life was most evident in a Catholic culture, such as that of France or much of southern and western Germany. Wayside shrines, crosses and small statues of the Virgin or other saints were extremely numerous in town and country alike, and their number was increasing in the nineteenth century. In the relatively devout diocese of Arras there was by 1900 an average of three Calvaries and one wayside chapel per commune.[20] The annual calendar was shaped by the liturgical calendar. The principal holidays were the Christian festivals of Christmas and Easter, together with the festival of the patron saint of the parish. In the diocese of Arras the agricultural year began on St Eloi's day, when the horses were fed blessed bread, and other saints' days provided the occasion for ceremonies associated with other animals or crops.[21] Crucifixes, pictures of saints and scenes from the Bible hung on the walls of countless homes,[22] and at least until the anti-clerical attacks of 1879 and after, on those of public buildings, such as schools, hospitals and court-rooms. According to Eugen Weber, the pictures sold to peasant families by colporteurs in the mid-nineteenth century so often depicted religious figures or scenes that they were known as 'saints', even if they actually portrayed a battle or an animal.[23] Such pictures were pinned or sewn to a hat or clothes, nailed to a wall or bedboard or stuck up in a stable.

Above all, it was the saints who entered into every area of life in Catholic communities. The Virgin Mary in all her countless manifestations was of course supreme, but numerous other saints had a large following, whether concentrated on a particular town, parish or professional group, or more widely dispersed. Saints symbolised the identity of a community, they provided protection both to individuals and to collectivities, and they offered help in emergencies. At the broadest public level, saints could act as figure-heads for a political cause. And at the most intimate personal level they were confidants for their devotees. And of course they could act as role-models. So the saints entered into the lives of Catholics at many different levels. I will mention here three ways in which the popular culture of Catholic communities was shaped by relations with the saints.

First, processions, or other forms of celebration, in honour of their patron saint were major events in the annual calendar of many communities, including not only parishes, but, for instance, occupational and regional or national communities. Thus miners marked St Barbara's day (4 December) by going to church in the morning and then enjoying an enormous celebration, for which they had saved for weeks beforehand.[24] In Catholic and royalist Brittany in the early years of the present century, there was little enthusiasm for Bastille Day, but the Sunday following 13 May was observed as an alternative national day, in honour of Joan of Arc.[25] There were also innumerable annual celebrations associated with local communities, which typically began with religious celebrations in the morning, followed by eating and drinking in the afternoon and dancing in the evening. In the Pas-de-Calais in the nineteenth century, according to Hilaire, the people generally recognised not only 'sacred places, objects and persons', but also 'sacred times, when work stops, when festivity and liturgy go together, when custom permits certain excesses'. Thus if not all of the people were regularly practising Catholics, nearly all of them were 'festive

Christians'.[26] Secondly, in times of individual or collective crisis it was normal to turn for help to the saints. Certain saints were specialists in the cure of particular diseases or in providing help with specific problems. And Mary was omnicompetent. In the nineteenth century, St Roch, a specialist in plagues, was particularly sought after during cholera epidemics. Throughout the year there was a constant stream of the sick, and of those who were praying for them, both to local shrines and to the big national shrines like Lourdes in the French Pyrenees or Altötting in Bavaria. During epidemics, or at other times of collective crisis, huge crowds would process through the streets, often ending at a local shrine.[27] And thirdly, individuals and households maintained a constant devotion to a particular favoured saint, whose picture hung on the wall or a medallion of whom they wore.[28]

Within Protestant cultures the sacred was less readily visible. The Reformation had abolished the saints, the primary point of contact between the human and the supernatural, and had also reduced both the number and the significance of the sacraments. Consequently, the interconnections between the religious and the magical were less extensive than in Catholic cultures. Nonetheless, here too religion was deeply rooted in popular culture. One aspect of this has been already mentioned, namely popular attachment to the Christian rites of passage. Christianity also influenced the patterning of time, though less extensively than in Catholic cultures. Christmas and Easter certainly remained important, and Obelkevich has shown how in Lincolnshire a number of saints' days retained some significance in the agricultural year, although they no longer had any religious meaning except for some High Anglicans.[29] In Protestantism the major distinction was between Sunday, the Protestant sabbath, and weekdays. In Germany the efforts of Protestant clergymen to promote sabbath observance never had a lot of success, but in nineteenth-century England 'keeping Sunday as Sunday' became a religious norm for many and a requirement of respectability for many more.[30]

One of the most important fields for the interpenetration of religion and popular culture was the Bible. In Protestant cultures the Bible was regarded as the supreme authority. The need for everyone to read it for themselves had provided a major incentive for the setting up of schools by the parish or by other religious agencies. Rival intepretations of the Bible had played, and continued to play, a major part in the schisms to which Protestant churches were prone, and Protestant propagandists attributed benefits of every kind to the availablity and regular study of the Scriptures. In Catholicism, tradition was placed alongside scripture as one of two supreme authorities, and moreover, scripture was only authoritative as interpreted by the church. But in Catholic France, as much as in Protestant England or north Germany in the nineteenth century, the Bible still had a place in countless homes, including many in which it was the only book or one of a very small number of books.[31] The Bible was often the first book that a person had read – whether they were self-taught, or had learnt in a Sunday School or day school – and it frequently continued to exercise an enormous hold over the imagination even of those who subsequently questioned its authority.[32] For many generations of rebels against religious authority, the Bible had given them the confidence to declare with Luther 'Here I stand'. Equally important in the nineteenth century was the encouragement that the Scriptures gave to political radicals. A survey of British Labour MPs in 1906 found that, when asked which book had exercised the greatest influence on them, the Bible was the work most often cited.[33] The Bible, especially the Old Testament, was also a rich source of dramatic stories, striking personalities, and memorable phrases. Particularly calculated to seize the imagination were the illustrated Bibles, with their unforgettable representations of such scenes as the Israelites escaping through the parted waters of the Red Sea or David killing Goliath. In France the Bible was sometimes read at the *veillées* – gatherings of country people on winter evenings, which were prime occasions for the passing on of local traditions and folktales. According to one memoirist from the Massif Central, recalling the 1850s, 'We loved the Bible. There were extraordinary stories which pleased us enormously'.[34] In Protestant households biblical scenes and texts frequently decorated the walls, taking the place of the saints favoured by Catholics. Bibles could have quasi-magical uses too. Soldiers would carry them as a kind of amulet, and many people sought guidance by opening the Bible at random.[35]

Hymns also came to play a very big part in the lives of Protestants. In nineteenth-century England there was no more universally popular art-form. Women sang hymns while they worked: in the Yorkshire industrial village of Pudsey in the years around 1830 it was said that someone passing a burling-shed 'would be apt to think that there was either a concert or some religious service going on. They knew all the last Whitsuntide school tunes, and most of the old

substantial ones, such as Luther's Hymn, etc. There is most exquis-
ite harmony, and not a mere rehearsal, for they are singing daily.'[36]
A century later a south London working-class housewife sang
hymns 'all the time, the way some people sing pop-songs nowadays'
– as her daughter later recalled.[37]

Men may not have sung hymns while they worked, but they sang
them when they were drunk. There is an hilarious account of such a
scene in *The Ragged Trousered Philanthropists*, which is set in Hastings,
'Mugsborough'. Most of the characters in the novel work for a
building firm called Rushton & Co., and one warm summer's day
the firm takes its employees for the 'Annual Beano', a trip into
the country involving large amounts of eating and drinking. On
the journey back, the bosses travel in the front vehicle, and each
of the following brakes contains a particular clique of workers, for
instance, heavy drinkers in one, church-goers in another, and in the
last brake, some who were 'steady workers' and were neither syco-
phants, nor heavy drinkers, nor church-goers, and so received
slightly less scathing treatment from Tressell than the others. As
night falls and conversation flags, one character, described only as
'the religious maniac' starts singing Sankey hymns. Soon the other
church-goers join in the choruses, and though the occupants of the
last brake at first find this amusing, they too know at least the
choruses. Soon they are joining in, and the only sounds coming
from the brakes are the strains of 'Pull for the Shore' and 'Where is
my Wandering Boy?'[38]

The association of religion and music was also represented in the
innumerable choral societies, with their strongholds in northern
textile towns, such as Huddersfield, a predominantly upper working class and lower middle class membership, and a preference for
oratorios – above all, Handel's *Messiah*.[39] According to Walvin, 'the
crowds drawn by Handel's music surpassed those at all other forms
of organised leisure' in the 1850s and 1860s.[40]

Obelkevich, in his study of nineteenth-century Lincolnshire, has
shown how prominent a part beliefs about the Devil played in the
mind of much of the rural population. He notes various stories,
some of which clearly show the imprint of some branch of Christianity. The overlap with Primitive Methodism is strongest. Early
Primitive Methodism had a very strong sense of the presence and
constant activity of the Devil, very much like that which Obelkevich
indicates among the mass of the local population. For instance,
Obelkevich quotes a story of a tailor who regarded Sunday as no

different from any other day, and who was measuring up a cus-
tomer one Sunday morning when he noticed that he had a cloven
hoof. The tailor became a Baptist and never worked on Sunday
again.[41] A somewhat similar story was told in the Yorkshire industrial village of Pudsey in the first half of the nineteenth century: one
young man joined the Methodists and became a local preacher after
being confronted by an apparition of his dead mother while walking
home drunk one night. 'This affair was looked upon both by the
young man himself and others not only as a direct interposition of
Divine Providence, but as a proof of the existence of apparitions.'[42]

Patterns of Change

In the years around 1900, there is evidence both of continuities in
the relationship between religion and popular culture and of significant changes. On balance it is the continuities that seem most
significant during the period up to the First World War.

To begin with the evidence for change, this appears to have come
from several directions: first, some aspects of popular culture were
weakened by universal education, the spread of literacy, and
attempts by teachers to inculcate a rationalistic mentality; secondly,
there are signs that within many of the churches clergy and lay
activists were tending to distance themselves from aspects of popular culture; thirdly there is the influence of political radicals, often
strongly committed to 'enlightenment'; and fourthly there is the
development towards the end of the nineteenth century of new
forms of popular culture, spreading out from the cities, as a result
of which newspapers, novels, commercial entertainment, professional sport, etc., tended to take the place of many more traditional
forms of amusement and sources of wisdom.

Certainly some contemporary observers claimed that the popular
outlook was changing. Joseph Lawson's *Progress in Pudsey*, written in
the 1880s, celebrated fifty years of mental as well as material progress, which he credited especially to the beneficial effects of compulsory education. Other favourable factors had included gas-
lighting (making people less ready to fear the presence of evil
spirits); parks, gardens and cricket, all of which had contributed to
a decline in heavy drinking and in cruel or violent sports; pianos,
which had enriched home life; and the spread of a more liberal

theology. According to his account, superstitions of every kind had abounded in the first half of the century, and were closely embedded both in the ale-house culture and in the Methodist chapels which were the main alternatives to the pub. Lawson, who would appear to have been a Unitarian, argued that the new popular culture was not necessarily less religious, but it was religious in different ways.

> People still believe in Providence, but it is a more reliable one, more rational, one that can be depended upon – not fickle, variable, one thing to-day and another to-morrow, snatching a child here and another there without any apparent reason or cause. Providence now is seen to have fixed methods; so that people studying its arrangements and conforming thereto, health, life and happiness can be enjoyed.[43]

Somewhat similar trends were noted, though with more ambivalence, in the diaries of Henry Winn, a Lincolnshire village shopkeeper and Anglican Sunday School teacher. Winn commented that the people among whom he had grown up in the 1820s and 1830s 'had a nearer apprehension of the spiritual world' and were 'far more poetical', whereas the people of the later nineteenth century were more 'practical'. Obelkevich, who draws on Winn's observations, sees a 'depersonalisation' of 'superstition'. Witches and wise men faded from the scene, and belief in ghosts declined, and 'Superstition subsided to the level of luck, its impersonal lowest common denominator'. He explains these changes in terms not so much of any spread of rationalism or education as of changes in social relations: partly the dominant influence of 'new-style' farmers who were hostile to such 'superstititions', and partly the change of mentality associated with the development of a society marked by more impersonal class relations in place of the more intimate rural community of former years.[44]

Eugen Weber, in his account of 'The modernisation of rural France 1870–1914', gives many examples of the ways in which this was undermining popular Catholicism. According to Weber, 'phosphates, chemical fertilisers and schooling had spelled the beginning of the end' for much of rural religion and the priests themselves had delivered the *coup de grâce* by their attacks on superstitious or licentious forms of devotion – since these also tended to be those which were most fun, and which the people regarded as most relevant to their needs. Newspapers had played a part too – '*Le Petit Parisien* is the Holy Scripture of the countryside', declared a Catholic in 1913.[45] And radical politics helped to undermine the authority of the priest – though Weber plays down this factor, arguing that purely local disputes were more important in generating anti-clericalism. In support of these generalisations, he gives examples of declining pilgrimages and processions, obsolete saints, and priests snubbed by their parishioners.[46]

While Weber's argument is vividly presented and richly documented, I think he overstates his case, and that the relationship between religion and popular culture remained more vital than he suggests, both in France and in other parts of western Europe. Certainly Weber's account is so heavily weighted towards evidence of religious decline that one would never guess from reading him that in 1947, when Canon Boulard drew up his famous 'Religious Map of Rural France',[47] there were still large areas where practising Catholics made up the majority of the population. Weber's account also presents the church as a passive victim of uncontrollable forces, overlooking the fact that many priests were actively seeking ways of responding to these challenges.[48]

A more differentiated analysis is offered by Gérard Cholvy, who suggests that in France during the second half of the nineteenth century there was a decline in what he terms 'natural religion', while what he calls 'popular religion' continued to flourish.[49] By the former he means practices associated especially with healing for human beings or animals and supernatural assistance in making the crops grow, finding marriage partners, ensuring or preventing fertility, et cetera, many of which drew partly on Christian symbols and rituals, but were only loosely connected with Christianity, and may often have had pre-Christian origins. By the latter he means forms of Christian devotion which have been adapted to the needs and cultural styles of the common people. According to Cholvy, the growth of ultramontane piety in the second half of the nineteenth century and the increasing willingness of the clergy to accept or even welcome those forms of 'superstition' that seemed to reflect a genuine faith led to a growing rapprochement in the more strongly devout regions of France between 'official' and 'popular' Catholicism. While newer forms of 'popular religion' associated especially with devotion to Mary or the Sacred Heart multiplied, many older practices, including the cults of local saints now disowned by the church, declined. They seem to have declined least in areas like the

Limousin, where the relative weakness of the Catholic Church meant that it was less able to replace the older beliefs and practices with more modern forms. In the Limousin many priests were complaining that their parishioners had little religion, but plenty of 'superstition'.[50] They would come in large numbers to church when relics were being displayed, and numerous chapels, fountains and wells associated with local saints attracted a regular flow of visitors. People who very seldom attended normal services at their parish church would come at other times to pray beside the statue of a favourite saint. In 1895 when the bishop and the local council agreed on the demolition of a small chapel which was thought to be dangerous, the local people had no objection to the removal of the altar, but there was fierce opposition to the removal of the statues of St Blaise and St Hilaire. In areas where many of the local population minimised contact with the priest, the preferred intermediary with the supernatural world was likely to be a wise woman, who claimed God-given powers, and who might herself be on good terms with the clergy.[51]

Thus even in regions of France, and indeed of England and Germany, where few people were regular church-goers or where anti-clericalism was widespread, many forms of 'popular' religion continued to be widely practised. The clearest example of this is the continuing popularity of the Christian rites of passage.

The emergence of a self-consciously secularist section of the population was reflected in the introduction of secular rites of passage. Funerals, and to a lesser extent baptism and confirmation, were the main fields for experimentation by those seeking secular alternatives to established religious rites. Secular funerals were pioneered by French political exiles in the 1850s. In France itself, they became more numerous in the 1860s and 1870s, and first became widespread in the 1880s. By the early twentieth century they accounted for 20 per cent of the funerals in Paris, and as many as 40 per cent in some left-wing strongholds, such as the mining villages of the Nord and the Pas-de-Calais.[52] They provide the best indicator of the extent of alienation from the Catholic Church at this time. For instance, in Paris there were big differences between the various districts of the city, the maximum level of 39 per cent being reached in the proletarian 20th *arrondissement*, while the minimum of 7 per cent was recorded in the bourgeois 16th.[53] Some of the big secular funerals of the later nineteenth century were national events. For instance, in 1885 Victor Hugo, France's most famous writer, and a republican hero, was buried with secular rites, providing a highly visible model for many more obscure sceptics and anti-Catholics.[54] In some republican municipalities the mayor took on the character of a secular priest, presiding at baptisms, weddings and funerals, and providing both the required ceremony and solemnity, and appropriate moral messages.[55]

In Germany the secular funeral was a socialist speciality, and had a particularly important role during the years of the Anti-Socialist Law between 1878 and 1890. The death of a prominent activist provided the occasion for a procession through the streets, followed by a graveside oration by one of the *Redner* (speakers) who specialised in celebrating the achievements of departed comrades and drawing inspiring lessons from their struggles.[56] In England the secular funeral remained a rarity. Indeed, some of the differences between France and England in this period may be symbolised by the fact that while Victor Hugo received a secular burial in the Panthéon in 1885, three years earlier, England's most famous agnostic, Charles Darwin, was given a Christian burial in Westminster Abbey.[57]

In France during this period secular funerals acquired great symbolic significance. In many small towns and villages the first secular funeral was a great event – noted with horror by pious Catholics.[58] Conversely, for those who had devoted a large part of their lives to fighting against the Catholic Church, it was often a matter of great concern that their corpse would not be polluted by the touch of a priest after their death. They therefore left strict instructions in their wills that they must receive a secular funeral, and it was the principal function of the numerous Freethought societies established during the early days of the Third Republic to ensure that these wishes were respected.[59] Bitter disputes often ensued as the widow, or other relatives of the deceased, tried to secure a Catholic burial. In some instances, a death-bed conversion was alleged. The death of the Positivist leader, Littré, in 1881 was followed by controversy between, on the one hand, his former colleagues and, on the other, his devout wife and the priest who had attended him at her request. An alternative repertoire of symbols evolved. For instance, a secularist gravestone clearly had to get rid of the cross, though there was no consensus as to what should replace it – flowers, clasped hands and urns were all used. Since most of those receiving secular funerals had been committed republicans, and many of them were members of the Radical or Socialist parties, the *Marseillaise* or the *Internationale* could take the place of Christian hymns, and for the Socialist a red flag took the place of the crucifix.

Secular baptisms were also mainly a French phenomenon, though they remained relatively unusual – partly because of objections from wives, who often remained attached to the traditional forms, even when their husbands had broken away. In a few radical strongholds such as Ivry, a working-class suburb of Paris, or in some villages in the Creuse, the ceremony was performed by the mayor. More often it was organised by the local Freethought society. Occasionally a senior member of the family would perform the baptism. In some of the latter cases, wine would be used in place of water, and the mood would be ribald and blasphemous. In the former cases the mood would be every bit as reverent as in a church, with republican or socialist rhetoric taking the place of the Catholic rubric.[60] In the Creuse village of Saint-Priest-la-Plaine, which stood at the heart of what was probably the most militantly secularist area in western Europe, 13 per cent of babies received a secular baptism in the period 1905–34, as against 39 per cent receiving a Catholic baptism and 48 per cent who were involved in no formal ceremony at all.[61] This 13 per cent may well be a record, and in most places the number of secular baptisms was very small indeed.

The secular confirmation, or *Jugendweihe*, was a German speciality – reflecting the importance in Germany of the religious confirmation, received by the overwhelming majority of adolescents in the later nineteenth and early twentieth century. It was first devised by the Free Parishes, as a humanist alternative to the Protestant or Catholic ceremony, and was later taken up by the Social Democrats, and then by the Communists, as a result of which it became quite widespread in the 1920s. But it was still rare in the pre-1914 period.

The most notable common feature of all these secular rites was their relative rarity. The secular funeral did attract more support than the others, and became quite an important aspect of life in the Third French Republic. A substantial proportion of couples did dispense with the religious marriage ceremony, but without adopting a ritualised secular alternative. Overall, the challenge mounted by the various secular rites to the well-established religious rites was fairly weak, and their appeal was mainly to political militants, whose devotion to the cause of their party was often of a 'religious' intensity and exclusivity. The appeal of the new rites thus remained much narrower than that of those which they sought to replace.

264   SECULARISATION IN WESTERN EUROPE, 1848–1914

The older rites carried with them the huge weight of tradition and they had come over the course of time to be invested with a multiplicity of meanings. Apart from relatively small numbers of political militants there were few people in this period who entirely rejected them. However, the popularity of these rites varied: there were many people who practised some but not others, and various short-term factors could affect the way in which people chose to celebrate the great turning-points of life. At certain times a more casual neglect of the rites of passage was also quite common, especially among the urban poor.

For instance, in Berlin there was a considerable drop in the numbers of baptisms and church marriages in the 1870s, after the introduction of civil registration, but numbers rose again in the 1880s and 1890s. Then after about 1900, numbers of religious marriages and funerals dropped, while baptisms and confirmations remained at a high level.[62] The best account of the varying degrees of popular attachment to the rites of passage in Berlin is Kniffka's study of the working-class borough of Friedrichshain in the 1920s. He found that approximately 90 per cent of babies were being baptised – though this fell to about 80 per cent in the Communist stronghold of Stralau. About 90 per cent of adolescents were being confirmed, while 7 per cent received a *Jugendweihe*. On the other hand, only 35 per cent of couples were being married in church. Since the civil ceremony was in any case compulsory, they claimed that church weddings were 'a beautiful but over-expensive duplication'. The degree to which short-term factors could affect large numbers of people's choices was indicated by the funeral statistics. Sixty per cent of those in Friedrichshain in 1920 had been accompanied by a religious ceremony, but by 1926 the proportion had shot up to an astonishing 98 per cent. Kniffka attributes the increase to two factors: the economic upturn and the lifting by the Protestant church of its previous ban on cremations.[63]

Responses to a questionnaire sent to south London clergy in the 1880s suggested that in working-class parishes many children had not been baptised.[64] However, this cannot be seen as reflecting a long-term decline. Across England as a whole the ratio of Anglican baptisms to live births was rising in the later nineteenth and early twentieth century – from 62 per cent in 1885, 64 per cent in 1895, to 66 per cent in 1905, peaking at 72 per cent in 1924.[65] Bartlett's intensive study of Bermondsey, a strongly working-class district of south London, suggests that numbers of baptisms were increasing during the period 1880–1914, having by the early twentieth century a 'normality', which they had not had a generation earlier. He associates this with growing stability, and a process by which migrants from the countryside put down roots in the locality, became integrated into networks of neighbours and kin, and often in the process established links with local churches – seldom through regular attendance at services, but more often through personal acquaintance with the clergy, membership of church organisations, and the traditions established by the fact that family-members had been christened, married or buried there.[66] This is certainly the kind of situation discovered by Sarah Williams at a slightly later period in the neighbouring borough of Southwark. As one woman told her: 'We had a church, St Mary Magdalene, that was our church, we was all christened there, my Mum was married there, we was all christened and we all went to church. I was in the Brownies, then in the Guides and my brothers in the Band of Hope.'[67]

In England and Wales there *is* a steady increase in the proportion of civil weddings during this period, from 5 per cent in 1854 to 22 per cent in 1913.[68] But the pattern becomes much more confusing when one looks at specific regions. In some areas there is a steady long-term increase; but in others the proportion of civil ceremonies peaked in the 1880s and subsequently declined. In some parts of northern and south-western England the decline seems to reflect the integration of isolated rural communties into the customs of the wider society or increasing stability in what had been rather chaotic new communties of miners or quarrymen. Even in London, where there is a pattern of gradually increasing levels of civil marriage, this can only partly be seen as reflecting increasing secularisation. It also reflects the fact that at least in working-class areas, the marriage ceremony was often regarded relatively casually, and taken much less seriously than for instance, a funeral.[69]

The importance attached to the various rites of passage differed as between different religious traditions, countries and social environments. Thus, for instance, the importance attached to the religious marriage ceremony was greatest among Catholics, for whom the secular ceremony was not a wedding at all, and couples married in this way were in mortal sin. At the other extreme were some of the British free churches, which saw marriage as a civil rather than a religious contract, and regarded the civil ceremony as an entirely acceptable alternative to a wedding in church or chapel.[70] Anglican and Lutheran views were somewhere between these extremes, though tending more to the former than the latter. Thus in the later nineteenth century north-west Wales had a civil marriage rate of around 50 per cent, which in a Catholic context would have suggested extreme irreligion. In fact this was one of the most devout regions in western Europe, and the local marriage customs seem primarily to have reflected the predominantly Calvinistic Methodist beliefs of the population. In France, while both the church and public opinion maintained a strong conformist pressure, ensuring that relatively few people rejected or neglected any of the Christian rites of passage, it seems to have been First Communion which enjoyed the deepest level of popular attachment. An added factor here certainly was the element of peer-group pressure and emulation which did not enter in the same way into the other rites. It was a big occasion for the child and for his or her class-mates, and however hesitant the parents might be the child seldom wanted to be left out. Recalling his own First Communion about 1890, the author, Henri Ghéon, wrote: 'They tell you it's the most beautiful day of your life. And it's true.' In Zola's *L'Assommoir* the normally totally irreligious Coupeau finds himself for once overcome with emotion at his daughter's First Communion:

> Everything looked heavenly, he was touched to the heart. There was in particular a psalm, something smooth and sweet, while the children took the sacrament, which seemed to trickle down his neck, sending a shiver all along his spine. All around him too there was a general display of damp handkerchiefs. It was a great occasion, a unique occasion. Only when he came out of church, and went for a drink with Lorilleux, who had not been at all impressed and laughed at him for it, he accused the 'crows' of burning wizard's herbs in order to make fools of men.[71]

During the years 1879–1914 in France there were numerous cases of anti-clerical municipalities or prefects banning processions and pilgrimages, yet even in towns where most people voted for the Left there was considerable popular resistance. Weber quotes one example. In a village in the Haute-Vienne in 1885 the priest, complying with an order by the prefect, refused to follow the traditional practice of ringing the church-bells to avert storms. The anti-clerical municipal council then realised that this was an excellent opportunity to win popularity while discrediting the priest, so they ordered that the bells be rung in defiance of both prefect and priest, and they spread rumours that the new regulation was the work of bishops, priests and nobles who wanted poor men to have their crops ruined.[72] Similarly, at the time of the cholera epidemic which hit southern France in 1884, the mayor of Aix lifted the prohibition on processions which the council had imposed just a few years before, and in Marseilles a banned procession was revived and there was a boom in pilgrimages to local shrines.[73] In other parts of the south the patronal festival and its procession were so widely supported that the local council exempted them from the general ban. In one such parish in 1907 it was noted that 'Not a single man does his Easter duties, but it is a curious fact that they all take part in the processions.'[74]

A study of a Breton rural parish in the 1980s, in an area with strong radical and anti-clerical traditions, illustrates both the continuing popularity of such patronal festivals and some of the reasons for this popularity in areas otherwise noted for detachment from the church. In La Feuillée, the major religious celebration of the year is the festival of St John the Baptist, the patron of the parish, on 24 June. After mass, the parishioners process round the village, headed by a small boy dressed in a sheepskin and sandals to represent John the Baptist and leading a lamb, decorated with pink cloth roses, which represents Christ:

> Whereas the regular Sunday mass at La Feuillée attracts fifteen or twenty faithful, most of them women, a congregation of two hundred or more attends the pardon mass. Moreover at least one-third of those who come to the pardon ceremony are men, generally the more vocally anti-clerical of the two sexes. Their presence in church is less an endorsement of Catholic doctrines than a statement of allegiance to the community. Attachment to the pardon stems from the perception that it epitomizes parish identity. As one twenty-one year old man enthuses, 'The little lamb, that's us, that's La Feuillée'.[75]

Badone's analysis of local folktales shows how the tellers continue to attribute various supernatural powers to the clergy – though clerical trickery is also seen as extending to fooling the populace through fake manifestations of these powers. With their proclivity for strange supernatural occurrences and the frequent occurrence within them of priests, monks and the devil, they are very much in the tradition of the nineteenth-century *veillées*.[76]

These examples relate to long-established traditions, surviving the anti-clerical onslaught of the later nineteenth century. But that period also saw the emergence of new saints, canonised by the people long before any official decision by the church, and new places of pilgrimage, widely popular long before any form of organisation was imposed. The two most important pilgrimage-sites of twentieth-century France both have their origins in the second half of the nineteenth century, and they also illustrate contrasting aspects of popular Catholicism. Lourdes, which now attracts some five million visitors annually, is primarily the greatest of the healing shrines, though at various times it has also been associated with French nationalism and/or right-wing politics. Lisieux, which attracts about one million visitors annually, owes its popularity more to the number of admirers of St Thérèse and of her form of spirituality.[77] At Altötting, the chief Marian shrine in Bavaria, the porter Brother Conrad came to be regarded as a saint because of his generosity to the poor and love of children. After his death in 1894 he attracted numerous pilgrims in his own right. By the 1920s miracles were being reported and in 1934 he was canonised.[78] Another such modern saint was the Dortmund Franciscan, Jordan Mai, who died in 1922. He was first buried in a city cemetery, but after devotees had removed most of the earth covering his grave, his remains were transferred to a Franciscan church, which became a place of pilgrimage.[79]

The Virgin Mary first spoke to Bernadette Soubirous, a fourteen-year-old shepherdess, at the grotto near Lourdes in February 1858, and she appeared again on eighteen occasions. The first miraculous cures were being claimed in March 1858, and official recognition by the Bishop of Tarbes came in 1862. Many small groups of pilgrims had already visited the grotto: the first official diocesan pilgrimage took place in 1864 and the opening of the railway in 1866 was followed by the arrival of pilgrims from all over France. In the political crisis of the early and mid-1870s the National Pilgrimages of 1872 and 1873 took on the character of royalist demonstrations and subsequent major pilgrimages often included political under-tones. But the main theme was miraculous healings. An analysis of over 2000 people who claimed to have been cured in the period 1858–1908 showed that they came from every department in France, with the biggest numbers coming either from in and around the great cities of Paris, Lyon and Lille, or from south-western departments. But even the Creuse, which was both very poor and very far from devout, contributed two who had been cured, and some quite distant rural departments produced thirty or forty.[80]

The most remarkable and novel feature of Lourdes was the Authentification Bureau, through which the church aimed to meet the medical profession on its own ground and to silence the critics. Miracles were only claimed where a detailed case history was available and doctors were prepared to certify that there could be no natural explanation for the observed cure. Many cases of allegedly miraculous cures were rejected, either because insufficient information about the patient's medical history was available or because some other explanation for the cure seemed possible. The Bureau was certainly one of the most controversial aspects of Lourdes and some Catholics believed that the church was wrong to seek this kind of external stamp of approval. It could equally be argued, however, that evidence of this kind forced critics like the Parisian psychiatrist Dr Charcot and the novelist Zola to take Lourdes seriously, and indeed to go part of the way towards accepting Catholic claims. Zola, for instance, in his famous novel, *Lourdes*, admitted the genuineness of the cures achieved there, even if he denied that they had any supernatural cause. As for the psychiatrists Charcot and Bernheim, Kaufman writes that 'While their studies were structured on a discursive opposition between religion and science, their investigations were unable to separate religion from medicine as forms of legitimate therapeutic power.[81] Meanwhile the place that the shrine had rapidly acquired within popular culture was reflected in the huge trade in Lourdes-related goods. In the 1880s and 1890s there were numerous pedlars selling medallions, rosaries, crosses, pictures of the grotto, pieces of sacred rock from Lourdes, and of course Lourdes water. Other Lourdes-related products included the liqueur 'La Bernadette', with the slogan 'indispensable for pilgrims'.[82]

Returning to England and Joseph Lawson's record of 'Progress in Pudsey': there is no doubt that the increasingly respectable and often middle-class character of English Protestantism had weakened its links with popular culture. New religious movements, like the Salvation Army, were set up with the aim of bridging this gap, but they did not have the breadth of popular appeal that, for instance, Primitive Methodism had enjoyed fifty years before.[83] None the less, Lawson's list of beneficial changes includes two areas where the religious dimensions of popular culture continued to be conspicuous. One of these was music. In particular, the pianos, or small organs, which entered the parlours of so many working-class and lower middle-class homes in the latter years of the nineteenth century, provided the ideal accompaniment to the Victorian and Edwardian institution of family hymn-singing. The best known witness to the influence of hymns on those growing up at the turn of the century is D. H. Lawrence, who was born in 1885 in Eastwood, Nottinghamshire, the son of a miner and a school-teacher. In 1928, when he had moved a long way both from East-wood and from the Congregationalism of his childhood, he wrote a newspaper article on 'Hymns in a Man's Life', in which he claimed that the poetry of Shakespeare, Keats and Wordsworth was not woven as deep into his consciousness as 'the rather banal Noncon-formist hymns that penetrated through and through my child-hood'. After enthusiastically recalling both the 'undimmed wonder' stirred by hymns that evoked exotic biblical scenes and the militancy of mid-Victorian revival hymns, he concluded 'Here is the clue to the ordinary Englishmen – in the Nonconformist hymns.'[84]

In one of his poems, Lawrence recalled 'the old Sunday evenings at home, with winter outside, And hymns in the cosy parlour, the tinkling piano our guide'.[85] Many, perhaps most, of his contemporaries would have immediately recognised the scene. William Barnes, born in a working-class family in Keighley in 1900, recalled Sunday evening as the supreme moment of togetherness in the week:

> Well me father used to try and keep the Sabbath as the Sabbath. And we always finished up at night with this organ on Sunday you know, and everybody singing, and then they had to do an individual turn you know, and you'd always get to tell your dad what you'd learnt at Sunday School and what you'd been talking about – and that.

They sang 'hymns and all sorts', his father's favourite being 'The Rugged Cross', and tears ran down his cheek as they sang it. The 'all sorts' no doubt included more secular songs, such as those from the music-halls, and it was this unself-conscious mixing of sacred and profane which indicated that hymns had become a generally

RELIGION AND POPULAR CULTURE

accepted part of the popular culture of the day. It was equally reflected in the comment of a man brought up in a Liverpool working-class family about the same time, that they included hymns in their Sunday evening singsongs 'even though we were heathens'.[86]

Lawson's eulogy of cricket points to an area in which religion and popular culture had actually come closer together during the later part of the nineteenth century. In the earlier part of the century, the intense supernaturalism of much popular culture provided common ground with at least the more popular branches of contemporary religion, such as Methodism; on the other hand, recreation was one of the areas of most bitter dispute. Any form of sport that was associated with drunkenness, gambling or violence to human beings or animals was bitterly attacked by a large part of the religious world, and especially the various forms of popular evangelicalism, which tended to be the religious groups most active in working-class communities.[87] After every sport that fell into one or other of these categories had been eliminated, there was not much left. Recreation was thus a major site for conflict between religious groups and a significant section of the male population, including many members both of the working class and the aristocracy. The spread of cricket in the second half of the nineteenth century was one example of a more general spread of 'rational' forms of recreation, which did not normally involve gambling, were not necessarily sited at public houses, did not involve cruelty to animals, and the rules of which minimised or strictly regulated body-contact between the players. Beside cricket, the most important examples were football, rugby, athletics, cycling and boxing, though numerous other forms of sport emerged in their modern form about this time. Boxing at first sight seems the odd man out, because violence was of its very essence. However, it was regarded by its advocates as being primarily a test of skill, with gloves and limited numbers of rounds minimising the damage done, and thus quite different from the older and distinctly non-'rational' sport of prize-fighting. Churches and chapels played a major part in the diffusion of all these sports, and in doing so they tried to kill several birds with one stone. Sports clubs drew new members into the church's orbit and strengthened the bonds between those who already belonged; they drew people away from other less desirable forms of amusement; and in the eyes of many Christians of the time, they embodied a broader conception of the gospel – one which was optimistic and life-affirming, and in which the church was required to care for 'the whole man', body, as well as mind and soul.[88]

In the longer term sport often became a rival to religion and the churches – competing for time and energy, and inspiring similar degrees of passionate commitment. In the shorter term religion and sport were frequently allies, enabling religion to establish a strong footing in areas of popular culture that had previously been alien. In Liverpool many of the pioneers of football were clergymen, and in 1885, twenty-five out of 112 teams in the city were attached to a church. In Birmingham, where the game advanced more rapidly, churches and chapels played an equally conspicuous part, with eighty-three out of 344 clubs in 1880 having a religious affiliation.[89] There were similar developments at a slightly later date in Germany and especially in France, where some Catholics saw sport as offering a unique opportunity to re-establish the church's popular base.[90]

The most detailed account of changes in popular religion during the early twentieth century is a study by Sarah Williams of South-wark, a working-class district in south London, based primarily on interviews with residents born in the period 1892–1921. She concludes that 'adaptation and continuity were the predominant characteristics of this period rather than dislocation from earlier patterns of belief', and that 'a distinct pattern of urban popular religion was consolidated at the end of the nineteenth century in tandem with the stabilisation of urban popular culture'.[91] As Williams notes, this popular religion has often been defined, whether by Victorian clergy or by modern historians, in terms of what it did *not* include – notably regular attendance at church services. It would be far more illuminating, she suggests, to see it as a form of religion in its own right, and to focus on what it *did* include. Major aspects, she suggests, were the 'intermingling of folk and orthodox religious idioms', including both extensive use of charms, folk remedies and spells, and widespread practice of certain church-based rituals; identification with local religious buildings and personnel; prayer and hymn-singing; and belief in 'practical Christianity'.[92]

A very similar picture emerges from Richard Sykes's recent study of the Black Country between 1914 and 1965. Sykes took more account than Williams of denominational distinctions (mainly between Anglicans and Methodists) and distinctions between those working-class people (relatively numerous in the Black Country) who continued to attend church as adults, and those who largely gave up when they left Sunday School. But he concluded that, at least until the 1950s and 1960s these distinctions were not reflected in widely different beliefs about the supernatural. Non-church-goers prayed, sang hymns, were churched, insisted on their children being christened, and regarded neighbourly help as a religious duty.[93] In a scene reminiscent of Yorkshire in the 1830s, one of Sykes's informants described the women in Dudley tailoring factories in the 1930s and 1940s singing hymns as they worked. The hymns were sometimes mixed with contemporary popular favourites – 'But a lot of the time it used to be mostly hymns because everybody seemed to know more hymns.'[94] Both church-goers and non-church-goers carried lucky charms, consulted fortune-tellers and believed in ghosts. Emphasising that the overwhelming majority of working-class children attended Sunday School at least up to the 1930s, and that church-goers and non-church-goers alike had access to an orally transmitted culture of folktales and 'superstitions', he highlighted the large areas of common beliefs and practices shared by most working-class families regardless of their religious affiliation or non-affiliation.[95]

Conclusion

While Williams identifies certain areas of change during the period 1880–1939, she suggests that these were 'complex and amorphous and cannot simply be identified with "decline"'.[96] She argues that the biggest changes have come since the Second World War. Sykes, who explored the extent and causes of this decline more fully, reached the same conclusion.[97] Unfortunately, no similarly detailed studies have been undertaken in other parts of western Europe for the period. But the weight of the available evidence suggests that Williams is right to put the main stress on continuity, even though she may be overstating her case. She emphasises the role of women in passing on the various forms of popular belief, both 'folk' and 'church-related' to the next generation, and the fact that many men, without contesting such beliefs regarded them as belonging to the female sphere.[98] Two-thirds of her interviewees were women, which probably accentuates the bias of her evidence towards the elements of continuity. Sources of change would seem to include the promotion of rationalism and the cult of science both by schools and by radical political parties; the availability of technological solutions to problems previously addressed through religion or magic; and the

declining authority of the clergy, together with diminishing knowledge of Christian doctrines, rituals and literature. Yet in all these
cases, change came only very gradually, and in particular the influence of rationalist modes of thinking must not be exaggerated.
Doctors may have come to be much more widely used, but the
number of pilgrimages to Lourdes has also increased. Faith in the
ability of the Party to solve economic and political problems does
not preclude calling on fortune-tellers or saints to help with more
intimate and personal needs. And the alternative to belief in God is
not necessarily a belief in science – it may equally be astrology,
magic, or simply luck.[99]

8 1914

On 28 July 1914 Austria-Hungary declared war on Serbia. When Serbia's Russian allies mobilised, Germany declared war first on Russia on 1 August, then two days later on Russia's ally, France. The quickest way to France was through Belgium, so a few hours later Germany invaded Belgium. On the evening of 4 August Britain joined the war in defence of France and Belgium. And so began the Great War, which was to leave some eight million people dead, and which would become in the memories of subsequent generations the supreme example of the horror and futility of war.

In Germany, the Emperor lost no time in claiming God's support for the national cause, and the clergy, both Protestant and Catholic, were almost unanimous in giving their blessing. On Sunday, 2 August, Wilhelm II told the crowd gathered outside the royal palace: 'Go to church and pray to God that he will grant victory to the German army and the German cause.' As King of Prussia and supreme bishop of the Prussian church, he announced that 5 August would be a day of prayer when all Protestant churches would be open for special services. In many other parts of Germany the following Sunday was also declared a day of prayer.[1] The bitter divisions between liberals and conservatives in the German Protestant churches were for the time being pushed to one side, as preachers and theologians from both parties united to declare that God was with the Germans in their fight, and that self-sacrifice in the national cause was a religious duty.[2] The Catholic clergy, if less conspicuous as patriotic preachers, were none the less unequivocal in their support.[3]

France entered the war with a government of a totally different complexion. The Socialist Viviani headed a predominantly Radical

Cabinet, many of whom were militant anti-clericals. There could be no direct calls by the French Head of State for divine assistance. None the less, President Raymond Poincaré declared a 'sacred union', in which anti-clericals and Catholics would unite to repel the invader, all France's internal wars being suspended for the duration of the Great War. The reality never quite matched the rhetoric, since the more militant Catholics believed that the war was a divine punishment for French national apostasy, and the more militant anti-clericals responded that the Catholics *wanted* France to be invaded.[4] But, for the most part, the fervent patriotism and hatred of the invader that was shared by those at all points in France's religious and political spectrum did provide common ground for believer and unbeliever, Catholic, Protestant and Jew, and in many instances led to a real improvement in relations between members of these different groups.[5] The clergy were as willing as their counterparts in Germany to declare that the national cause was God's cause, and, in a more limited way, the war enabled Catholics to return to public positions – though it was not until October 1915 that a practising Catholic was included in the cabinet.[6] In Christian Germany, the clergy were excluded from bearing arms – much to the disgust and disappointment of many among them. In secularist France, priests, pastors and rabbis were liable to conscription, and by the end of the war 4618 Catholic priests, monks and seminarians, as well as ninety-one Protestant pastors and theology students, had been killed.[7] Here perhaps was the most effective refutation of the charges of lack of patriotism levelled by republicans against Catholics, and the most powerful argument against the persistent marginalisation of Catholics. In view of the meagre number of chaplains provided by the French state, combatant priests also found themselves supplementing their military duties by providing spiritual services to their fellow-soldiers.[8]

In pluralist England the relationship between church and state was less clearly defined than in Germany or France. A Conservative government would have had little hesitation in calling on the support of the Church of England. The Liberal government, which had been in power since 1905, had some of its greatest strongholds in Presbyterian Scotland and Nonconformist Wales, and included several agnostics, as well as some Jews, among its leading members.[9] There could be no question of the government itself decreeing a national day of prayer, as had last happened during the Indian

Mutiny – though in 1918 King George V would designate Sunday, 6 January as a day of prayer and thanksgiving throughout his dominions. Neither was there any of the religious warfare that continued beneath the surface of the 'Sacred Union' in France. Moral support for the national cause was gratefully received from whatever quarter it might come, and different members of the government specialised in winning the support of different constituencies. Particularly significant here was David Lloyd George, the Welsh Nonconformist Chancellor of the Exchequer, who, like many of his co-religionists, had opposed the Boer War, and who was uniquely qualified to drum up Nonconformist support for the war against Germany.[10] In England, too, priests, pastors and rabbis generally gave their support to the war, and there were many who joined the Anglican Bishop of London, Winnington-Ingram, in declaring that it was a 'holy war' and that those who died in it were 'martyrs'.[11] The position was, however, complicated by the existence of a number of smaller Nonconformist denominations, most notably the Quakers, who were committed to pacifism,[12] and by traditions of anti-militarism within many of the larger Nonconformist churches. On Sunday 2 August there were still numerous Nonconformist preachers who declared that Britain could and should stay out of the war.[13] Admittedly, two days later the invasion of Belgium had completely changed the situation, and the following Sunday most of them were insisting that Britain had a moral obligation to come to 'Little' Belgium's aid. But, in the eyes of many super-patriots, sermons in support of the war were often less wholehearted and unqualified than they should have been.[14] The identification between Christianity and the national cause was more ambiguous than in Germany. In England religious factors played a major part in the admittedly very limited opposition to the war, and support for the war was more often based on purely secular arguments.

While governments differed in the ways in which they drew upon religious support, there seem to have been considerable similarities in the ways in which the people in the three countries responded religiously to the outbreak of war. Reports of a 'return to the altars' were most widespread in France. But many similar reports came from Germany in the later months of 1914, and some from England, though here the evidence is less clear. In Berlin the Protestant church authorities noted in September 1914 that the war had 'united all classes and social strata of our people.... Even in those circles that were formerly indifferent or hostile to the church, and especially in the working class world, it has led to a desire for the church, which has found expression in high attendance at all places of worship in Berlin'. In the Social Democratic stronghold of 'red' Wedding, a crowd was said to have 'stormed' a church, and demanded a service when none was planned. Official statistics showed that Protestant communions in Berlin were 32 per cent higher in 1914 than in the previous year.[15] In Hamburg it was reported that the average size of congregations had doubled during the autumn of 1914.[16] Admittedly, these two cities had some of the lowest levels of church attendance in the Western world, and in other more pious regions of Germany, the increase was more modest. In Berlin and Hamburg, where non-religious funerals had for long been quite common, the proportion of funerals conducted by a clergyman also increased considerably during the war years.[17]

In France there were even more numerous reports of crowded services and increasing numbers of communicants, whether in Paris and Lyon, in remote villages, or at the front.[18] In France there was also a great increase in the popularity of local pilgrimages. Fewer people had the opportunity to get to Lourdes or La Salette, but many soldiers visited the shrine of a local saint before going to the front; mothers, sisters, wives continued going there to pray for their return; and, if they did return, the soldiers would go to give thanks. Many years after, one of the survivors described a typical scene – the place being Carcassonne, which had been one of the pace-makers in the forcible dechristianisation of the 1880s:

> After long embraces we separated, and then we went directly to the church of Saint Vincent, where they showed me, at the end, a chapel with a Virgin holding a branch. It was Our Lady of Perpetual Help. Above her head on the wall there flew a large tricolour, and all around were marble plaques, nailed onto the wall or placed on a big marble table, and engraved with messages of gratitude, offered by relatives of the soldiers at the front who were their husbands or sons. My mother had bought a photo of the Virgin and she told me to place it among the flowers and pieces of marble. We said the Lord's Prayer, and every time she came into town she came and knelt in front of the Virgin and prayed for me.[19]

In England there were some reports of unusually crowded services in the early months of the war, and especially large numbers

either going to special services of intercession or going into
churches to pray silently.[20] However, such reports were less frequent than in France or Germany and, in contrast to Germany,
church membership (in the case of Nonconformists) and Easter
communicants (in the case of Anglicans) dropped consistently, albeit
slowly, in the years 1914–17.[21] (The only exceptions were slight
increases in Congregationalist membership in 1915 and Quaker
membership in 1916.) The biggest decline was suffered by the
Quakers, who lost nearly 5 per cent of their members between
1914 and 1915, the main reason for this clearly being the pacifist
stance of the Society of Friends, which had never been asserted so
unequivocally before – even during the Boer War it had been possible for some Quakers to support the British government's policy.[22]
On the other hand, the Anglicans, who generally supported the war,
saw a 1 per cent decline in the number of Easter communicants, and
the almost equally pro-war Wesleyans, Primitive Methodists and
Baptists suffered losses of around 0.5 per cent. The London Congregationalist preacher W. E. Orchard, who was a pacifist, had an
obvious axe to grind, but he may have identified an important
paradox when he wrote that:

> The public are difficult to satisfy. They came to church in the early
> days of the war to hear what the Christian preacher had to say,
> and then came no more. If we had said that the war was wrong
> and unchristian, they would have hanged us and burned our
> churches about our ears. But somehow they treated us even
> worse when they heard what we had to say: that this was a
> Christian war and our one loyalty to the Kingdom of God
> demanded its prosecution at any price to a victorious conclusion.
> Why did they not continue with us? Because they could hear that
> very well elsewhere – in secular gatherings and the Press – with-
> out the complications that Christianity seemed to bring in.[23]

Many English clergymen were in fact open to charges of incon-
sistency that could not be levelled at their French or German
counterparts. In German Protestantism, especially, there was a
powerful tradition of patriotic preaching, going back to the time
of the War of Liberation against Napoleon, and reinforced by the
experiences of the wars of 1864–71, in which Prussian victories had
been widely interpreted as signs of divine favour. This tradition
had been intensified by the various nationalist movements of the

period preceding the war, in which Protestant pastors often played an active part.[24] Nationalism was equally central to the thinking of large numbers of French Catholics in the later nineteenth and early twentieth centuries, and the fact that the French were actually defending their soil from foreign invasion meant that doubts about the morality of war were even less likely than elsewhere to receive a serious hearing.[25] In England, however, the churches had been much more divided in their attitude to questions of war and peace, as had been shown by the Boer War. A substantial minority of Nonconformist ministers, and a smaller minority of Anglican clergy, had opposed the war.[26] While this opposition was primarily due to doubts both about the justice of the British cause and about the treatment of Afrikaner civilians by the British forces, it also reflected a more generalised critique of militarism and of the role of business interests in profiting from war. This critique was frequently heard in the Nonconformist chapels, and sometimes extended to a more generalised pacifism, usually justified by reference to a mixture of the New Testament and radical or socialist politics.[27] It may be that long years of hearing sermons about peace had left many people with rather mixed feelings about the role of the churches in war-time. They may themselves have felt that they had a duty to fight; yet at the same time they saw the incongruity in a Christian minister justifying killing. This certainly was the position of the poet Wilfred Owen[28] and of the Liberal politican Charles Masterman, who was British Director of Propaganda, yet felt that the only two Christian leaders or bodies to emerge with credit from the war were the Pope and the Society of Friends.[29]

In Britain there was a small, but nonetheless vocal, opposition to the war, which had two major concentrations of support in the Independent Labour Party and the Society of Friends, as well as more scattered support among liberal intellectuals, socialists generally, and members of non-pacifist churches.[30] The critique took three main forms, liberal, socialist and Christian, though these categories were by no means mutually exclusive. The liberal critique, represented in the Union of Democratic Control, focused on the dangers of secret diplomacy, and on the need for parliamentary control over foreign policy. Rather than advocating a refusal to fight, members of the UDC concentrated on the search for an early peace, and on preventing future wars. A more uncompromising line was taken by such bodies as the No Conscription Fellowship, a predominantly socialist organisation with strong

Quaker input, the Fellowship of Reconciliation, an inter-denominational body of Christian pacifists formed in December 1914, or the
Society of Friends itself. Though some of these protesters were
imprisoned, and some – including several Nonconformist ministers
– lost their jobs, they remained fairly much in the background
until 1916, when the introduction of conscription gave them
their chance to make a public stand for their beliefs, and also
presented them with the probability of prison and the possibility
of death[31] if they refused to compromise with authority. An analysis
of the religious affiliations of one group of several thousand
Conscientious Objectors showed that 95 per cent of those whose
affiliation was known were Protestant Dissenters, though there
were also considerable numbers whose objections were primarily
political.[32]

The boom in church-going in the early months of the war seems
to have reflected partly specific needs, partly a more generalised
search for strength and reassurance, partly an indentification of
the national cause with the cause of God. Just as personal crisis
would often lead to the reawakening of a partly dormant religiosity,
it seems that collective crisis may have had the same effect. But in
France, there were also many reports of conversions of unbelievers
at the front. It is well known that such traumatic experiences as
war, imprisonment, serious illness or bereavement often lead to a
drastic reconsideration of views of the world, often including
discovery of religious faith by those who had been unbelievers or
loss of faith by those who had believed. A British report, *The Army
and Religion*, published at the end of the war, noted that the
same incident could have precisely the opposite effect on the
religious beliefs of two different individuals. As one chaplain said:
'The War affects men in many contradictory ways. I have had
more than one case of officers previously religious who have
chucked religion altogether', the main reason apparently being
the feeling that God should not have allowed the war to happen.
What is striking about the French experience during the First
World War is the degree to which conversions of sceptics to
Catholicism seem to have outnumbered rejections of Catholicism
by those who had previously believed.[33] So far as intellectuals are
concerned, this probably was a continuation of the rediscovery of
Catholicism which had been going on for several years before the
war.[34] The strongly nationalist flavour of the Catholicism of the
time, and the sense that Catholicism embodied the central defining

tradition in French culture, was an important aspect of its appeal, and was clearly further enhanced after the outbreak of war.[35]

According to Annette Becker, Catholicism was to the ordinary soldier above all the religion of the miraculous.[36] One such miracle in many French eyes was their victory at the battle of the Marne, fought at a time when the French government had already withdrawn to Bordeaux in the face of the possible fall of Paris. Catholics attributed special significance to the fact that victory came on the day of the feast of the birth of the Virgin Mary, and they saw this as further evidence that she was fighting on their side. But the war was also full of minor miracles. Just as the disasters of August 1914 prepared the way for the extraordinary gratitude with which the French experienced the successes of September, the appalling carnage all around enhanced the relief of those who had escaped, and the need for them to make appropriate expressions of thankfulness. As Becker writes:

> To remain at the front, to live in the middle of death, the soldiers had need of multiple means of assurance. Those provided by the affection of their family, by the fatherland, by religious faith, and by superstition. Far from cancelling one another out, they reinforced one another in the horror of the conflict. Families in any case had recourse to everything in their power that might give spiritual help to the soldiers at the front. They would even baptise during the war children who had not been baptised at birth in order to preserve their father at the front.[37]

So the soldiers and their families drew upon a wide repertoire of sources of strength, reassurance and protection, some of which were explicitly Christian, some of which used Christian symbols in a way that many Christians regarded as 'superstitious' and some of which drew on forms of belief largely or wholly independent of Christianity. Thus British soldiers were said to pray before battle and to give thanks to God afterwards, and French soldiers would write to their parish priest asking for his prayers. English soldiers who never received communion at other times would do so while at the front – a chaplain commented: 'In some it means everything that we would wish it to mean; in others it is indubitably a superstitious feeling. They believe that having taken Communion they will be safe.'[38] French soldiers would visit Marian shrines close to the front, sometimes leaving messages for the Virgin.[39] In

Bavaria the tradition was maintained in wartime of bringing to the Marian shrine a painting depicting the kind of protection that was sought – and at the end of the war, paintings of soldiers returning to their village were presented in thanksgiving.[40] Catholic soldiers carried medallions of the Sacred Heart and Protestant soldiers carried Bibles; both Catholics and Protestants carried crucifixes. English soldiers also carried rabbits' feet and lucky coins. And grieving parents and wives found fresh hope through Spiritualism, which gained many new followers during the war. This eclecticism led one observer of the British Army to comment, 'The soldier has got religion. I am not so sure that he has got Christianity.'[41]

Conclusion

The upsurge of religious activity in the early part of the war led one French observer to comment that 'the dechristianisation of the peasant soul, even in those villages where the church seems to be abandoned, is extremely superficial'.[42] The same kind of comment could also be made of Germany or of an overwhelmingly urbanised England. By 1914 a significant minority of the population had become converts to a new world-view, based most commonly on scientism, socialism, or a combination of the two. But for the much larger number of those whose beliefs were more fluid and eclectic, Christianity generally remained a significant influence on their understanding of the world, and one that came to the fore in times of crisis. There were large numbers of people who were suspicious of the church and clergy, seldom went to church, and had relatively little knowledge of Christian doctrine, but who believed in God, regarded themselves as Christians, and were familiar with a wide range of Christian ideas and symbols, which might remain largely dormant in 'normal' times but were readily drawn upon in times of crisis.

As regards the various dimensions of secularisation discussed earlier, the response to the outbreak of war suggests that religion of various kinds remained deeply embedded in popular culture, most especially in a Catholic environment, as in France or Bavaria, where processions, pilgrimages, visits to shrines, and the cult of the saints generally, related closely to basic human needs for protection, assurance and the search for miracles. In matters of religious practice, the increase, at least in the early part of the war (certainly in France and

Germany, and more questionably in England), indicated that between the strongly committed church-goers and the decided non-church-goers there was a considerable number of those whose religious practice was more contingent. It should be noted, however, that in the case of Protestant north Germany church-going remained very much a minority activity, even at the height of the war-time boom. In terms of the secularisation of religious belief, the effects of the war seem ambiguous. Certainly it raised in a particularly acute way the age-old questions of the relationship between God and evil. It raised equally pressing questions about the realism of the widespread assumption that humanity was about to enjoy an era of continuous progress through the application of science and political action. It placed huge numbers of people in situations of desperate need where questions concerning God, the soul and immortality acquired an urgency which they might not have had before. Questions of religious identity, on the other hand, may have lost some of their importance during the war, as military units brought together men of widely differing religious beliefs and affiliations, united only on the basis of common nationality, and religious differences between the combatant nations were of very marginal relevance to the conflict. There was, in fact, a strand of French Catholic patriotic rhetoric which blamed German national sins on the influence of Lutheranism[43] (just as some English preachers accused the Germans of being rationalists and atheists rather than real Protestants).[44] But it was an essential part of the rhetoric of the *Union Sacrée*, accepted by most Catholics, that Protestants, Jews, Freethinkers and Catholics were all part of the one great French nation and were all fighting as one to defend the sacred soil of the fatherland: some manifestations of this unity became part of national folklore, most notably an incident where, in the absence of any priest, a rabbi had held the crucifix in front of a dying Catholic soldier.[45]

The relationship between religion and the experience of war would go through many subsequent phases – including the mounting war-weariness of 1916 and 1917, the joy and relief of victory or the trauma of defeat in 1918 and 1919, the search for a return to 'normality' in the 1920s, growing criticism of the war, of militarism, and of exalted patriotism from the later 1920s, and the revival of *völkisch* nationalism in Germany. But they raise many new issues that are more appropriately dealt with at the beginning of a book on the religious history of the twentieth century, rather than at the end of a book on the religious history of the nineteenth century.

Conclusion

Six aspects of the social role of religion, and six possible areas of secularisation, have been considered in this book: individual belief; formal religious practices; the place of religion in public institutions; its part in public debate; its significance as an aspect of identity; and its relationship with popular culture.

The clearest evidence of secularisation during this period is in the first two areas. In all three countries, there was a substantial decline in the proportion of the population attending church services or participating in communion – though the pattern of decline was very uneven. There was also a rise in the proportion of professed unbelievers, and a range of alternative systems of belief became widely available, challenging the dominant influence of the various religions.

In the third and fourth areas the results of the changes in these years were more mixed. By the early twentieth century there were major differences between the parts played by religion in the public institutions of the three countries. These differences were more significant than any common tendency. The clearest evidence of secularisation was in France. But while the state was being secularised, Catholics were setting up a range of counter-institutions. These were often quite successful. In England, the strength of the Nonconformists, with their agenda of 'religious freedom', as well as the 'New Liberal' programme of expanding the national and local state, led to a creeping secularisation, but without a supporting secularist ideology. And in Germany the role of religion and the churches in the fields of education and welfare remained very extensive. Furthermore, the introduction of church taxes laid the basis for the continuing institutional strength of the churches in the twentieth century – often contrasting with the smallness of Sunday congregations. The different balance of political forces in the three countries led to very different relationships between church and state. In public debate there is clear evidence of secularisation, in as much as religion no longer provided a common language. At least in France and Germany, it became part of the ideological weaponry of particular parties, providing an essential link between these parties and their supporters, but cutting them off from other sections of the electorate. So the role of religion in public debate certainly narrowed. But it remained central for certain political groups, mainly on the Right.

In the fifth and sixth areas, the evidence for secularisation is much less. Religious identities were sometimes supplanted by, for instance, nationalist or socialist identities, and they continued to be modified by, for instance, social class. But the beliefs, experiences, symbols, relationships derived from religion remained uniquely potent as shapers of identity, especially since the majority of the population continued to be subject to religious influences from an early age. Moreover, newer sources of identity often had a religious component. In particular, nationalism and religion, though potentially rivals, frequently intermingled, producing nationalist religions and religiously shaped nationalisms. As for popular culture: the weakening of the relationships between Protestantism and popular culture has been one of the most important aspects of twentieth-century secularisation in England and Germany – and one of the biggest points of difference from the United States. But this process had not gone very far by 1914, and the links between Catholicism and popular culture remained close.

Returning to the discussion in the Introduction of the various possible ways of 'telling the story' of religion in modern western Europe: I believe that one of the ways of telling this story must be in terms of secularisation. But, rather than one simple story-line, we need a narrative in which a variety of plots and sub-plots are intertwined. One of these plots would turn on the emergence of new 'Religions of Humanity', and their efforts to devise new rituals and moral principles and to sell them to a mass public. Another would focus on the response of Christians and Jews to the secularist challenge, and the battle within church and synagogue between modernisers and traditionalists.

If one of these stories is to be given pride of place it should be not secularisation, but pluralism. One of the most significant turning-points in Europe's religious history was the introduction of a degree of toleration from the later seventeenth century onwards. As the religious controls were gradually lifted, an increasingly wide range of possibilities opened up, including deism, scepticism and atheism, as well as many alternative forms of Christianity and Judaism. In the eighteenth century, revealed religion faced powerful intellectual challenges. But the secularisation of society only became a realistic possibility from the 1790s onwards, as liberal and radical political movements mobilised wide sections of the population to attack the *ancien régime*. Liberal, radical, and later socialist political movements were bitterly opposed to established churches, which they saw as major strongholds of the old order; followers of these movements often had a profound, in some respects 'religious', faith in the possibility of achieving far-reaching and beneficial social changes through political action. By the middle of the nineteenth century, established religion also faced a powerful challenge from the growing influence of scientists, many of whom made immense claims for the authority and potential of science. In the second half of the century, west European societies were the scenes of fierce ideological competition. It was not simply a matter of 'religious' versus 'secular', but of rival forms of religion and rival forms of secularity, each battling on several fronts.

There were several salient aspects of this pluralism. In the first place, both radical politics and the cult of science had a very powerful attraction, at least for certain sections of the population. Where people were giving up going to church or synagogue, or abandoning their belief in God, it was not only because of 'doubt' or 'apathy'. More often it was because of the attraction of rival systems of belief. Secondly, church and synagogue were not passive in the face of these attacks. They fought back vigorously, and sometimes successfully. For instance, one of the most striking signs of the vitality of the churches in this period was the great wave of overseas missionary activity, which turned Christianity into a worldwide religion, even as it was losing ground in some of its old European strongholds. Thirdly, secularisation has come about for different reasons in different countries and at different times, and there is no master-factor – whether 'science', 'modernisation' or any other – which can account for this pattern. This explains the fact that at each stage some sections of Christianity have been more successful than others in resisting trends towards secularisation – but that the 'success-story' of one generation is often the 'failure' of the next. For most of the nineteenth century the English free churches were remark-ably successful in recruiting sections of the liberal middle class and the self-educating working class that were strongly inclined towards secularism in France and Germany. The relative success of Non-conformity and the relative slowness of secularisation in England up to about 1890 suggest the primacy of political factors in secularisa-tion in the nineteenth century. However, the English free churches ran into increasing problems after about 1890, for reasons that varied from the political (their moderate radicalism alienated the increasing numbers both of socialists and of Liberal Unionists or Conservatives in their ranks), to the theological (similar polarisa-tions between fundamentalist and liberal views of the Bible), to the cultural (their puritanism was going out of fashion). From about 1890 to 1960 it was the Roman Catholic Church which succeeded in retaining high levels of support in many (though by no means all) parts of western Europe, at a time when most branches of Protest-antism were losing ground. The greater popular appeal of Catholi-cism in this period seems to have had three main dimensions: the greater closeness of priests and nuns (drawn from more modest backgrounds and more readily 'available' than their highly edu-cated and middle class Protestant counterparts) to the people; the success with which the church built up an extensive organisational network, entering the lives of Catholics at many levels, and tending to enclose them within a Catholic world; and the degree to which Catholicism, with its faith in the miraculous and its cult of the saints, met needs which Protestantism could not. However, it is also worth noting that Catholicism was quite successful in this period in attract-ing such groups as artists and writers, who were often in reaction against the apparent cultural barrenness of both Protestantism and Positivism. Since the 1960s, as Catholicism, and also socialism, have been weakened by the dominant trends towards individualism and privatisation, it is evangelical Protestantism which has been the most expansive branch of Christianity.

In nineteenth- and twentieth-century Europe (and no doubt in earlier centuries, too) there have been many people who are neither fervent believers nor convinced unbelievers. Their religious ideas may well be more complex and ambivalent, but in matters of public religious profession and practice they have accepted the prevailing conventions. I referred earlier to Samuel Butler's comments on the church-going farmers in his father's parish, and to Nietzsche's account of the 'religiously indifferent' German bourgeois of his time. A later example of the same phenomenon was the 'nominal atheism', which was said by Soviet sociologists to be characteristic of Russian cities in the 1960s and 1970s. Such people, numerous as they are, seldom play a decisive role in religious history. This role has more often been played by smaller groups of the strongly committed, who are prepared to pioneer new ways by defying prevailing orthodoxies. But the practices of the less committed provide a good indicator of the relative strength of religious and secular influences, and of varying kinds of religion and of secularity. Judging by this criterion, the balance between the religious and the secular forces in these countries in the early twentieth century was fairly even – though each, of course, had their strongholds in particular regions or social milieux. The mass of the people still observed the Christian rites of passage (or most of them) – and secularist or socialist alternatives had relatively little success. They sent their children to Sunday School, catechism or confirmation class. They believed in God, they prayed (at least in times of crisis), and their view of the world, however unorthodox in the eyes of the clergy, was shaped more by religion than by secular thought. Religious language continued to be widely used both by public figures and in everyday life, in spite of the growing influence of the alternative languages of science, of the various professions, or of the political Left. On the other hand, in most regions of England, France and Germany, regular church-going was becoming a minority activity – a matter of personal choice, rather than a requirement of 'respectability'. The influence of the clergy was narrowing with the growing size and power of the professions, and predominantly secular universities had become established as the main arbiters of intellectual orthodoxy. This fine balance between the forces of religion and secularity remained characteristic of western Europe until the 1960s. Only then did the balance tip more decisively in a secular direction.

Notes

Notes to the Introduction

1. Entry on 'secularisation' in the *Oxford English Dictionary* (Oxford, 1989); W. E. H. Lecky, *History of the Rise and Influence of the Spirit of Rationalism in Europe*, 2 vols (London, 1893), vol. II, pp. 99–100 (1st edn 1865). A very useful summary of the development of concepts of secularisation from Comte to the present day, with the emphasis on the debates among sociologists since the 1960s, is provided by Olivier Tschannen, *Les théories de la sécularisation* (Geneva, 1992).
2. Ibid., pp. 96–111.
3. For Comte and his contemporaries, see D. G. Charlton, *Secular Religions in France, 1815–1870* (Oxford, 1963); T. R. Wright, *The Religion of Humanity* (Cambridge, 1986).
4. Tschannen, op. cit., pp. 119–36; W. S. F. Pickering, *Durkheim's Sociology of Religion* (London, 1984), pp. 445–7.
5. Dietrich Bonhoeffer, *Letters and Papers from Prison* (English translation, London, 1959), p. 91.
6. Thomas Luckmann, *Das Problem der Religion in der modernen Gesellschaft* (Freiburg, 1963) (English translation published in 1967 as *The Invisible Religion*); Bryan Wilson, *Religion in Secular Society* (London, 1966) and *Contemporary Transformations of Religion* (Oxford, 1976); Peter Berger, *The Sacred Canopy* (New York, 1967) (published in the UK in 1973 as *The Social Reality of Religion*).
7. E.g., Rodney Stark and William Sims Bainbridge, *The Future of Religion: Secularization, Revival and Cult Formation* (Berkeley, CA, 1985); Laurence R. Iannacone, 'The Consequence of Religious Market Structure: Adam Smith and the Economics of Religion', *Rationality and Society*, 3 (1991), pp. 156–77; Roger Finke, 'An Unsecular America', in Steve Bruce (ed.), *Religion and Modernization: Sociologists and Historians Debate the Secularization Thesis* (Oxford, 1992), pp. 145–69.

8. This I take to be the position of David Martin, in his *A General Theory of Secularization* (Oxford, 1978), which assumes the theory, but tries to present it in a more nuanced fashion, with more sensitivity to national and confessional differences, as well as in those works where he has been more directly critical of the theory, such as *Tongues of Fire: The Explosion of Protestantism in Latin America* (Oxford, 1990). A similar stance is adopted by Grace Davie, *Religion in Britain since 1945: Believing without Belonging* (Oxford, 1994); Michael Hornsby-Smith, 'Recent Transformations in English Catholicism: Evidence of Secularization?', in Bruce (ed.), op. cit., pp. 118–44; Jose Casanova, *Public Religions in the Modern World* (Chicago, IL, 1994).

9. See Bruce's own contributions to Bruce (ed.), op. cit., pp. 8–30, 170–94, and for the fullest statement of his position, Steve Bruce, *Religion in the Modern World: From Cathedrals to Cults* (Oxford, 1995).

10. As James Obelkevich wrote, in one of the most influential of such studies: 'Popular Christianity in south Lindsey was no mere derivative or debased version of the clerical faith. Its libretto was not written by bishops or by Fellows of Oriel or by Regius Pofessors of Divinity. What villagers understood by Christianity was never preached from a pulpit or taught in Sunday School, and what they took from the clergy they took on their own terms' (*Religion and Rural Society: South Lindsey, 1825–1875* (Oxford, 1976), p. 279). The tendency more recently has been to make less sharp distinctions between official and popular religion, and to place more emphasis on the influence of the clergy. According to Philippe Boutry, *Prêtres et paroisses au pays du Curé d'Ars* (Paris, 1986), p. 454: 'In the countryside of the Ain during this century faith is defined above all by the observation of the rules and rites of the church: never perhaps was the conformity of religious practices to the injunctions of the clergy so complete or immediate. To go in search of a "popular religion" seen as autonomous, even as in rupture with the teaching of the clergy, would be to underestimate or to ignore the imprint of the church on the overall religious behaviour of the faithful, and the deep attachment of the rural populations to Catholic rites and dogmas.... The seven sacraments form the basis and the point of reference of rural Christianity in the 19th century: which does not exclude from the point of view of the faithful either incomprehensions or conflicts.' While Boutry is more sceptical of the concept of 'popular religion', the concern with understanding 'the religion of the people' remains central.

11. Here I am borrowing the terminology of Jeffrey Cox, especially as presented in 'Master Narratives of Religious Change', a paper presented at the conference 'The Decline of Christendom in Western Europe *c.* 1750–2000' (Paris, 1997) which acknowledges the power of the secularisation 'story', while also identifying some of its weaknesses,

and more tentatively proposing an alternative. Some of the same points are made briefly in Jeffrey Cox, 'Religion and Imperial Power in Nineteenth-Century Britain', Richard Helmstadter (ed.), *Freedom and Religion in the Nineteenth Century* (Stanford, 1997), pp. 339–42.

12. For a summary see Hugh McLeod, *Religion and the People of Western Europe, 1789–1989* (Oxford, 1997), pp. 135–54.

13. Accounts which place the main stress on intellectual factors, while also taking account of others, are Owen Chadwick, *The Secularization of the European Mind in the Nineteenth Century* (Cambridge, 1975); Mary Heimann, 'Christianity in Western Europe from the Enlightenment', in Adrian Hastings (ed.), *A World History of Christianity* (London, 1999), pp. 458–507; Franz Schnabel, *Deutsche Geschichte im 19. Jahrhundert*, vol. 4: *Die religiösen Kräfte* (Freiburg im Breisgau, 1937); and Thomas Nipperdey, *Deutsche Geschichte, 1800–1866* (Munich, 1983), pp. 440–51. An account in entirely intellectual terms (though he notes the influence of political context on theology and philosophy) is Martin Schmidt, 'Die Entchristlichung in der neuzeitlichen Kirchengeschichte im deutschsprachigen Gebiet', *Zeitschrift für Kirchengeschichte*, 79 (1968), pp. 342–57.

14. Alfred Kelly, *The Descent of Darwin: The Popularization of Darwinism in Germany, 1860–1914* (Chapel Hill, NC, 1981).

15. Roger Thabault, *Mon village* (Paris, 1945).

16. See Frank M. Turner, *Contesting Cultural Authority: Essays in Victorian Intellectual Life* (Cambridge, 1993), which interprets the 'conflict between science and religion' as a successful campaign by scientists to establish their professional status and sphere of intellectual jurisdiction at the expense of the clergy.

17. A. D. Gilbert, *Religion and Society in Industrial England: Church, Chapel and Social Change, 1740–1914* (London, 1976). See also Bonnie G. Smith, *Ladies of the Leisure Class: The Bourgeoises of Northern France in the Nineteenth Century* (Princeton, NJ, 1981), where the greater religiosity of women than men is explained in terms of a lesser degree of exposure to industrial society and its ways of thinking. See also the excellent study of Bavaria, Werner Blessing, *Staat und Kirche in der Gesellschaft* (Göttingen, 1982).

18. See especially Stephen Yeo, *Religion and Voluntary Organisations in Crisis* (London, 1976). A similar position was adopted by Callum G. Brown in his work in the later 1980s and early 1990s on the links between urbanisation and secularisation. While denying that there was any necessary relationship between the two, he suggested that there was a link during the phase which set in around the end of the nineteenth century. See his articles 'Did Urbanization Secularize Britain?' *Urban History Yearbook*, 1988, pp. 1–14, and 'The Mechanism of Religious Growth in Urban Societies: British Cities since the Eighteenth Cen-

tury', in Hugh McLeod (ed.), *European Religion in the Age of Great Cities* (London, 1995), pp. 239–62.

19. Helen Meller, *Leisure and the Changing City, 1870–1914* (London, 1976), chs 8–9; James Walvin, *Leisure and Society, 1830–1950* (London, 1978), ch 7.

20. Callum G. Brown, 'The Secularisation Decade: The Haemorrhage of the British churches in the 1960s', a paper presented at the Conference 'The Decline of Christendom in Western Europe, 1750–2000' (Paris, 1997). See also Callum G. Brown, *Religion and Society in Scotland since 1707* (Edinburgh, 1997), pp. 158–207.

21. Peter van Rooden, 'Secularization, Dechristianization and Rechristianization in The Netherlands', in Hartmut Lehmann (ed.), *Säkularisierung, Dechristianisierung, Rechristianisierung im neuzeitlichen Europa* (Göttingen, 1997), pp. 131–53.

22. See, e.g., Wade Clark Roof and William McKinney, *American Mainline Religion* (New Brunswick, NJ, 1987); Robert Wuthnow, *The Restructuring of American Religion* (Princeton, NJ, 1988).

23. Wuthnow, op. cit., pp. 167, 300. For some west European statistics, see McLeod, *Religion and the People*, p. 177.

24. I have discussed some of these points more fully in Hugh McLeod, 'Dechristianization and Rechristianization: the Case of Great Britain', *Kirchliche Zeitgeschichte*, 11 (1998), pp. 21–32.

25. Following R. Laurence Moore, *Selling God: American Religion in the Marketplace of Culture* (New York, 1994).

26. Jeffrey Cox, *English Churches in a Secular Society* (Oxford, 1982). A more extreme version of this argument is presented in the work of some American sociologists, see e.g. Roger Finke and Rodney Stark, *The Churching of America, 1776–1990: Winners and Losers in our Religious Economy* (New Brunswick, NJ, 1992); Rodney Stark and Laurence R. Iannacone, 'A Supply-side Reinterpretation of the Secularization of Europe', *Journal for the Scientific Study of Religion*, 33 (1994), pp. 230–52. Similar ideas, though in highly nuanced form, appear in David Hempton, *Religion and Political Culture in Britain and Ireland* (Cambridge, 1996), which stresses the significance of the differential ability of British and Irish churches to 'reflect and propagate the social, political and cultural aspirations of their members' (p. 178). Another 'supply-side' interpretation is Robin Gill, *The Myth of the Empty Church* (London, 1993).

27. E.g., Bruce, *Religion in the Modern World*, pp. 37–8 takes it as axiomatic that the explanation for secularisation must be sociological, while Owen Chadwick, *Secularization*, p. 14, insists that 'without the intellectual enquiry the social enquiry is fated to crash'.

28. Typical of much of the work published in 1960s and 1970s would be the classic series of textbooks on modern European history by Eric Hobs-

bawm. In *The Age of Revolution, 1789–1848* (London, 1962), there is a useful chapter on religion, albeit with a heavy emphasis on secularisation. In *The Age of Capital, 1848–1875* (London, 1975), religion is limited to five pages, prefaced by the comment (p. 271) that 'Compared to secular ideology, religion in our period is of slight interest, and does not deserve extended treatment'. General works published in the 1980s and 1990s have tended to take religion much more seriously. See, e.g., Thomas Nipperdey, *Deutsche Geschichte, 1800–1866* (Munich, 1983); David Blackbourn, *The Fontana History of Germany, 1780–1918: The Long Nineteenth Century* (London, 1997); José Harris, *Private Lives, Public Spirit: A Social History of Britain, 1870–1914* (Oxford, 1993).

29. E.g. Carl Strikwerda, *A House Divided: Catholics, Socialists and Flemish Nationalists in Belgium* (Lanham, MD, 1997); Mark Smith, *Religion and Industrial Society: Oldham and Saddleworth, 1740–1865* (Oxford, 1995). For overviews of the literature on urban and working-class religion, see Hugh McLeod (ed.), *European Religion in the Age of Great Cities* (London, 1995); idem, *Piety and Poverty: Working-Class Religion in Berlin, London and New York, 1870–1914* (New York, 1996).

30. As examples of work on women's religion in nineteenth century Europe: Leonore Davidoff and Catherine Hall, *Family Fortunes: Men and Women of the English Middle Class, 1780–1850* (London, 1987); Claude Langlois, *Le catholicisme au féminin* (Paris, 1984); Irmtraud Götz von Olenhusen et al., *Frauen unter dem Patriarchat der Kirchen: Katholikinnen und Protestantinnen im 19. und 20. Jahrhundert* (Stuttgart, 1995). See now Ruth Harris, *Lourdes: Body and Spirit in a Secular Age* (London, 1999), an important study, which appeared too late to be used in this book.

31. Anthony Steinhoff, 'Protestants in Strasbourg, 1870–1914: Religion and Society in late Nineteenth-Century Europe' (University of Chicago PhD thesis, 1996), pp. 1–9.

32. Edward Ross Dickinson, *The Politics of German Child Welfare from the Empire to the Federal Republic* (Cambridge, MA, 1996), p. 289.

33. Thomas Kselman, 'The Varieties of Religious Experience in Urban France', in McLeod (ed.), *Age of Great Cities*, p. 167.

34. Gérard Cholvy, *La religion en France de la fin du XVIIIᵉ à nos jours* (Paris, 1991), pp. 189–92; S. C. Williams, *Religious Belief and Popular Culture in Southwark, c.1880–1939* (Oxford, 1999), pp. 1–6.

35. Cholvy, *La religion en France*; Williams, *Religious Belief and Popular Culture in Southwark*, pp. 1–23; Lucian Hölscher, 'Secularization and Urbanization in the Nineteenth Century: An Interpretative Model', in McLeod (ed.), *Age of Great Cities*, pp. 263–88.

36. David D. Hall, 'Religion and Secularization in America: A Cultural Approach', in Lehmann (ed.), *Säkularisierung*, p. 118.

37. Thomas Kselman, *Death and the Afterlife in Nineteenth Century France* (Princeton, NJ, 1993), p. 135.

38. Boutry, *Prêtres et paroisses*, p. 649.
39. Cf. Bruce, *Religion in the Modern World*, pp. 35–7.
40. Ernst Rudolf Huber, *Deutsche Verfassungsgeschichte seit 1789*, 4 vols (Stuttgart, 1957–69), IV, pp. 646–7.
41. Hempton, *Religion and Political Culture* is a pioneering attempt to treat the religious history of the British Isles as a whole. However, he deals with Irish Catholic nationalism and with Ulster Protestantism in two completely separate chapters.
42. Sheridan Gilley and W. J. Sheils (eds), *A History of Religion in Britain: Practice and Belief from Pre-Roman Times to the Present* (Oxford, 1994), which covers the whole of Britain, generally treats England, Scotland and Wales in separate chapters – though some of the chapters which claim to be about Britain are largely or entirely about England.
43. As is done by Michael R. Watts, *The Dissenters*, Vol. 2: *The Expansion of Evangelical Nonconformity* (Oxford, 1995).
44. Alan Haig, *The Victorian Clergy* (Beckenham, 1984), pp. 192–204.
45. Overviews are provided by Owen Chadwick, *The Victorian Church*, 2 vols (London, 1966); Gerald Parsons *et al.* (eds), *Religion in Victorian Britain*, 5 vols (Manchester, 1988–96); Frances Knight, *The Nineteenth-Century Church and English Society* (Cambridge, 1995).
46. Gérard Cholvy and Yves-Marie Hilaire, *Histoire religieuse de la France contemporaine*, 3 vols (Toulouse, 1985–8), vol. I: *1800–1880*. A useful summary of church–state relations and of religious legislation is provided by C. T. McIntire, 'Changing Religious Establishments and Religious Liberty in France, 1787–1908', in Helmstadter (ed.), op. cit., pp. 233–301.
47. Nicholas Hope, *German and Scandinavian Protestantism, 1700 to 1918* (Oxford, 1995), pp. 316–53.
48. Nipperdey, *Deutsche Geschichte*, p. 405.
49. Frank Tallett, 'Dechristianizing France: The Year II and the Revolutionary Experience', in Frank Tallett and Nicholas Atkin (eds), *Religion, Society and Politics in France since 1789* (London, 1991), pp. 1–28.
50. Ralph Gibson, *A Social History of French Catholicism, 1789–1914* (London, 1989), chs 3–4; Langlois, *Le catholicisme au féminin*.
51. Roland Aminzade, 'Breaking the Chains of Dependency: from Patronage to Class Politics, Toulouse, France, 1830–1872', *Journal of Urban History*, 3 (1977), pp. 485–505.
52. Yves-Marie Hilaire, *Une chrétienté au XIXe siècle? La vie religieuse des populations du diocèse d'Arras, 1840–1914* (Lille, 1977).
53. Claude Langlois, 'La déchirure', in Timothy Tackett, *La Révolution, L'Église, la France: Le serment de 1791* (Paris, 1986), pp. 319–37.
54. Ibid., pp. 324–7.
55. Christiane Marcilhacy, *Le diocèse d'Orléans au milieu du XIXe siècle* (Paris, 1964), pp. 303–7.

56. Gibson, op. cit., pp. 195–9.
57. W. R. Ward, *Religion and Society in England, 1790–1850* (London, 1972); David Hempton, *The Religion of the People: Methodism and Popular Religion, c.1750–1900* (London, 1996).
58. Gunilla-Frederike Budde, *Auf dem Weg ins Bürgerleben* (Göttingen, 1994), pp. 378–400; Davidoff and Hall, *Family Fortunes*.
59. Edward Royle, *Victorian Infidels* (Manchester, 1974); Watts, op. cit., pp. 470–8; Hugh McLeod, *Religion and Society in England, 1850–1914* (London, 1996), p. 253; Gilbert, *Religion and Society*, ch. 5.
60. Hope, op. cit., ch 15; Schnabel, op. cit., p. 568. A good overview in English is R. M. Bigler, *The Politics of German Protestantism* (Los Angeles, 1972). There is a growing body of literature on the dissenting movements emerging in this period. See for instance, Jörn Brederlow, *'Lichtfreunde' und 'freie Gemeinden'* (Munich, 1976); Friedrich Wilhelm Graf, *Die Politisierung des religiösen Bewußtseins* (Stuttgart, 1978); Sylvia Paletschek, *Frauen und Dissens* (Göttingen, 1990). The Trier pilgrimage is the subject of considerable debate. For opposing interpretations, see Wolfgang Schieder, 'Kirche und Revolution. Zur Sozialgeschichte der Trierer Wallfahrt von 1844', *Archiv für Sozialgeschichte*, 14 (1974), pp. 419–54; Rudolf Lill, 'Kirche und Revolution', ibid., 18 (1978), pp. 565–75. For an overview of the growth of scepticism and alienation from the church among the middle class, see. Lucian Hölscher, 'Die Religion des Bürgers: Bürgerliche Frömmigkeit und protestantische Kirche im 19. Jahrhundert', *Historische Zeitschrift*, 250 (1990), pp. 595–630; Nipperdey, *Deutsche Geschichte*, pp. 440–51.
61. Eileen Yeo, 'Christianity in Chartist struggle, 1838–42', *Past & Present*, 91 (1981), p. 109.
62. Ibid., pp. 133–4.
63. Ibid., p. 139.
64. Ibid., pp. 112–13.
65. Edward Berenson, *Populist Religion and Left-Wing Politics in France, 1830–1852* (Princeton, NJ, 1984), pp. 52–4.
66. Gérard Cholvy, 'Expressions et évolution du sentiment religieux populaire dans la France du XIXe siècle au temps de la restauration catholique (1800–60)', *La piété populaire de 1610 à nos jours* (Paris, 1976), pp. 297–8.
67. Knight, op. cit., pp. 61–2; Boutry, op. cit., pp. 124–7.
68. Gibson, op. cit., p. 163.
69. Olive Anderson, 'The Incidence of Civil Marriage in Victorian England and Wales', *Past & Present*, 69 (1975), p. 55.
70. David Sorkin, *The Transformation of German Jewry* (Cambridge, 1987), pp. 113, 122–3.
71. Stefi Jersch-Wenzel, 'Population Shifts and Occupational Structure', in Michael A. Meyer (ed.), *German-Jewish History in Modern Times*, vol. 2: *Emancipation and Acculturation, 1780–1871* (New York, 1997), p. 57.

72. Michael A. Meyer, 'Jewish Communities in Transition', ibid., pp. 100–103.
73. Michael A. Meyer, *Response to Modernity: A History of the Reform Movement in Judaism* (Detroit, MI, 1995), pp. 53–61, 100–12, 121.
74. Aubrey Newman, 'The Office of Chief Rabbi: a Very English Institution', in Nigel Aston (ed.), *Religious Change in Europe, 1650–1914* (Oxford, 1997), pp. 289–308; Michael R. Marrus, *The Politics of Assimilation: A Study of the French Jewish Community at the Time of the Dreyfus Affair* (Oxford, 1971), pp. 68–71.
75. Geoffrey Alderman, *Modern British Jewry* (Oxford, 1992), pp. 38–50.
76. Gérard Cholvy and Yves-Marie Hilaire, *Histoire religieuse de la France contemporaine, 1800–1880* (2nd edn, Toulouse, 1990) pp. 216–19.
77. Shulamit Volkov, 'Die Verbürgerlichung der Juden in Deutschland', in Jürgen Kocka (ed.), *Bürgertum im 19. Jahrhundert: Deutschland im europäischen Vergleich*, 3 vols (Munich, 1988), vol. II, pp. 343–71; Alderman, op. cit., p. 103; Marrus, op. cit., p. 35.
78. See above, pp. 9–11.
79. Berger, *Social Reality of Religion*, p. 131.

Notes to Chapter 1   1848

1. Jonathan Sperber, *The European Revolutions, 1848–1851* (Cambridge, 1994), pp. 123–4; Roger Magraw, 'The Conflict in the Villages: Popular Anti-Clericalism in the Isère', in Theodore Zeldin (ed.), *Conflicts in French Society* (London, 1970), pp. 218–19.
2. Bernt Satlow, 'Die Revolution von 1848. Die Kirche und die soziale Frage', in Günter Wirth (ed.), *Beiträge zur Berliner Kirchengeschichte* (Berlin, 1987), pp. 177–8.
3. Rüdiger Hachtmann, ' "ein gerechtes Gericht Gottes": Der Protestantismus und die Revolution von 1848 – das Berliner Beispiel', *Archiv für Sozialgeschichte*, 36 (1996), p. 224.
4. Jean Faury, *Cléricalisme et anticléricalisme dans le Tarn* (Toulouse, 1980), pp. 23–4, 34–7; Gérard Cholvy, *Religion et société au XIXᵉ siècle: Le diocèse de Montpellier*, 2 vols (Lille, 1973), vol. I, pp. 646–53.
5. Though the degree of such support may vary from area to area: for instance Hachtmann (op. cit., pp. 234–9) stresses the prominence of Jews in the democratic movement in Berlin, while Sperber plays down the extent of radicalism among Jews in the Rhineland. See Jonathan Sperber, *Rhineland Radicals: The Democratic Movement and the Revolution of 1848–1849* (Princeton, NJ, 1991).
6. Ibid., pp. 276–9.
7. Andreas Holzem, *Kirchenreform und Sektenstiftung: Deutschkatholiken, Reformkatholiken und Ultramontane am Oberrhein, 1844–1866* (Paderborn, 1996), pp. 334–6, 406–21.

8. Ibid.
9. Ibid.; Sylvia Paletschek, 'Frauen und Säkularisierung Mitte des 19. Jahrhunderts', in Wolfgang Schieder (ed.), *Religion und Gesellschaft im 19. Jahrhundert* (Stuttgart, 1993), p. 303.
10. Ibid., p. 308. See also Catherine Prelinger, *Charity, Challenge and Change: Religious Dimensions of the Mid-Nineteenth-Century Women's Movement in Germany* (New York, 1987); Dagmar Herzog, *Intimacy and Exclusion: Religious Politics in Pre-revolutionary Baden* (Princeton, NJ, 1996) – the latter being more critical of the role of Dissent.
11. Stefan Dietrich, *Christentum und Revolution: Die christlichen Kirchen in Württemberg, 1848–1852* (Paderborn, 1996), pp. 406–11.
12. Martin Greschat, 'Die Revolution von 1848–9 und die Kirchen', in Helmut Baier (ed.), *Kirche in Staat und Gesellschaft im 19. Jahrhundert* (Neustadt a.d. Aisch, 1992), pp. 75–7.
13. Dietrich, op. cit., pp. 280–94.
14. Sperber, *Rhineland Radicals*, p. 282.
15. Jonathan Sperber, *Popular Catholicism in Nineteenth-Century Germany* (Princeton, NJ, 1984), pp. 99–102.
16. Hachtmann, op. cit., pp. 205–8; Hans-Jürgen Gabriel, 'Im Namen des Evangeliums gegen den Fortschritt. Zur Rolle der "Evangelischen Kirchenzeitung" unter E. W. Hengstenberg von 1830 bis 1849', in Wirth (ed.), *Beiträge*, pp. 154–76.
17. Faury, op. cit., pp. 32–3.
18. Gérard Cholvy and Yves-Marie Hilaire, *Histoire religieuse de la france contemporaire*, vol. I: *1800–80* (Toulouse, 1990). p. 229.
19. For the example of Oldenburg see Dietmar von Reeken, 'Protestantische Milieu und "liberale" Landeskirche?' in Olaf Blaschke and Frank-Michael Kuhlemann (eds), *Religion im Kaiserreich: Milieus – Mentalitäten – Krisen* (Gütersloh, 1996), pp. 290–4.
20. See Werner Ustorf, *Theologie im revolutionären Bremen: Die Aktualität Rudolph Dulons* (Bonn, 1992).
21. Hachtmann, op. cit., pp. 240–5.
22. Hermann Rückleben, 'Theologischer Rationalismus und kirchlicher Protest in Baden 1843–49', *Pietismus und Neuzeit*, 5 (1979), pp. 77–83; Dietrich, op. cit., pp. 412–14.
23. Sperber, *Rhineland Radicals*, p. 283.
24. Hachtmann, op. cit., pp. 234–9; Wolfgang Schwentker, *Konservative Vereine und Revolution in Preußen 1848/49* (Düsseldorf, 1988), pp. 216–19.
25. See, e.g., Gerhard Schäfer, 'Die evangelische Kirche in Württemberg und die Revolution 1848/9', *Pietismus und Neuzeit*, 5 (1979), pp. 39–65.
26. Sperber, *Rhineland Radicals*, p. 283.
27. See Werner Blessing, *Staat und Kirche in der Gesellschaft* (Göttingen, 1982), pp. 100–4.
28. Schwenkter, op. cit., pp. 18, 214–23.

29. Blessing, op. cit., pp. 138–45.
30. Ustorf, op. cit., p. 78; Hachtmann, op. cit., p. 249, note 159; K.Schmaltz, *Kirchengeschichte Mecklenburgs*, 3 vols (Schwerin and Berlin, 1935–52), III, pp. 359–67.
31. Magraw, 'Conflict in the Villages', pp. 219–24.
32. Holzem, *Kirchenreform*, pp. 422–4.
33. Ibid., p. 432; John Breuilly, *Labour and Liberalism in Nineteenth-Century Europe* (Manchester, 1992), p. 212.
34. Hachtmann, op. cit., pp. 249–55.
35. Holzem, *Kirchenreform*, p. 429.
36. Lucian Hölscher, *Weltgericht oder Revolution* (Stuttgart, 1989), pp. 171–3; Paletschek, 'Frauen und Säkularisierung', p. 315.
37. Jakob Petuchowski, 'Frankfurt Jewry: a Model of Transition to Modernity', *Yearbook of the Leo Baeck Institute*, 29 (1984), pp. 410–11; Robert Liberles, 'The So-Called Quiet Years of German Jewry, 1849–1869: A Reconsideration', *Yearbook of Leo Baeck Institute*, 41 (1996), pp. 65–74.
38. Margaret Lavinia Anderson, 'Piety and Politics: Recent Work on German Catholicism', *Journal of Modern History*, 63 (1991), pp. 681–716.
39. Sperber, *Popular Catholicism*, p. 95; Reilinde Meiwes, 'Religiosität und Arbeit als Lebensform für katholische Frauenkongregationen im 19. Jahrhundert', in Irmtraud Götz von Olenhusen et al. (eds), *Frauen unter dem Patriarchat der Kirchen: Katholikinnen und Protestantinnen in 19. und 20. Jahrhundert*. (Stuttgart, 1995), pp. 69–88.
40. Claude Langlois, 'Permanence, Renouveau et Affrontements', in François Lebrun (ed.), *Histoire des catholiques en France* (Toulouse, 1980), pp. 346–7; Cholvy and Hilaire, *Histoire religieuse*, vol. I: *1800–1880*, pp. 221–7; Faury, op. cit., pp. 63–6.
41. Jean-Pierre Chaline, *Les bourgeois de Rouen: Une élite urbaine au XIXe siècle* (Paris, 1982), p. 268.
42. Colin Heywood, 'The Catholic Church and the Business Community in Nineteenth Century France', in Frank Tallett and Nicholas Atkin (eds), *Religion, Society and Politics in France since 1789* (London, 1991), pp. 78–83.
43. Thus Faury, op. cit., pp. 47–63, with regard to the Tarn. However Philippe Boutry, *Prêtres et paroisses au Pays du Curé d'Ars* (Paris, 1986) pp. 357–8, sees 1860 as the turning-point in the Ain, after which there was a serious deterioration in relations between the clergy and civil authority.
44. Faury, op. cit., pp. 47–57. For the extreme case of the Legitimist bishop Pie of Poitiers, initially a luke-warm supporter of the Empire, but soon in constant conflict with representatives of the state, see Austin Gough, 'The Conflict in Politics', in Zeldin (ed.), *Conflicts*, pp. 94–168.
45. W. O. Shanahan, *German Protestants Face the Social Question* (Notre Dame, IN, 1954), ch. 3.

46. Ibid., pp. 241–54.
47. Richard J. Evans, *Rituals of Retribution: Capital Punishment in Germany, 1600–1987* (2nd edn, London, 1997), p. 918.
48. Ernst Christian Helmreich, *Religious Education in German Schools* (Cambridge, MA, 1959), pp. 41–6.
49. F. Lisco, *Zur Kirchengeschichte Berlins* (Berlin, 1857), pp. 286–7; Shanahan, op. cit., pp. 266–7.
50. Blessing, op. cit., pp. 100–4; Schäfer, op. cit., p. 62; Rainer Marbach, *Säkularisierung und sozialer Wandel im 19. Jahrhundert* (Göttingen, 1978), pp. 21–2.
51. Faury, op. cit., pp. 23–45.
52. Ibid., p. 37.
53. Ibid., p. 38.
54. Jacqueline Lalouette, *La libre pensée en France, 1848–1940* (Paris, 1997), p. 30; Cholvy, *Religion et société*, vol. I, p. 730.
55. Ibid., p. 732.
56. Ibid., p. 731.
57. Lalouette, op. cit., pp. 31, 333.
58. Ibid., pp. 38–9; Magraw, 'Conflict in the Villages', pp. 225–7; Faury, op. cit., pp. 72–83.
59. Edward Berenson, *Populist Religion and Left-Wing Politics in France, 1830–1852* (Princeton, NJ, 1984), pp. 227–38.
60. Thomas Kselman, *Miracles and Prophecies in Nineteenth-Century France* (New Brunswick, NJ, 1983), pp. 121–31.
61. Gérard Cholvy and Yves-Marie Hilaire, *Histoire religieuse de la France contemporaine, 1880–1930* (Toulouse, 1986), pp. 16–34; Oscar Arnal, *Ambivalent Alliance: The Catholic Church and the Action Française, 1899–1939* (Pittsburgh, 1985), pp. 17–18.
62. Hachtmann, op. cit., pp. 245–8.
63. Kelly, op. cit., pp. 17–23; Andreas Daum, 'Naturwissenschaften und Öffentlichkeit in der deutschen Gesellschaft: Zu den Anfängen einer Populärwissenschaft nach der Revolution von 1848', *Historische Zeitschrift*, 267 (1998), pp. 57–90.
64. For the religious attitudes of German Liberals, see Roísín Healy, 'The Jesuit as Enemy: Anti-Jesuitism and the Protestant Bourgeoisie of Imperial Germany, 1890–1917' (Georgetown University PhD thesis, 1999). For bourgeois religion more generally, Lucian Hölscher, 'Bürgerliche Religiosität im protestantischen Deutschland des 19. Jahrhunderts', in Wolfgang Schieder (ed.), *Religion und Gesellschaft* (Stuttgart, 1993), pp. 191–216. For the Schiller cult, see John Breuilly, 'The Schiller Centenary of 1859 in Hamburg' (unpublished paper).
65. V. L. Lidtke, 'August Bebel and German Social Democracy's Relation to the Christian Churches', *Journal of the History of Ideas*, 27 (1966), p. 249.

66. See Jochen-Christoph Kaiser, 'Sozialdemokratie und "praktische" Religionskritik: Das Beispiel der Kirchenaustrittsbewegung, 1878–1914', *Archiv für Sozialgeschichte*, 22 (1982), pp. 263–98.
67. K. E. Pollmann, *Lansdesherrliches Kirchenregiment und soziale Frage* (Berlin, 1973); H. Grote, *Sozialdemokratie und Religion* (Tübingen, 1968); Hugh McLeod, 'Religion in the British and German Labour Movements: a Comparison', *Bulletin of the Society for the Study of Labour History*, 50 (1986), pp. 25–36.
68. Ursula Krey, 'Mit Gott für König und Vaterland: Konservative Leitbilder im östlichen Westfalen um 1900', in Joachim Meynert, Josef Mooser and Volker Rodekamp (eds), *Unter Pickelhaube und Zylinder: Das östliche Westfalen im Zeitalter des Wilhelmismus, 1888–1914* (Bielefeld, 1991), pp. 235–58.
69. H. U. Faulkner, *Chartism and the Churches* (New York, 1918).
70. Michael R. Watts, *The Dissenters*, vol. 2: *The Expansion of Evangelical Nonconformity* (Oxford, 1995) p. 520.
71. Ibid., pp. 561–2; see also Edward Royle, *Victorian Infidels* (Manchester, 1974)
72. Watts, op. cit., pp. 524–5, 561.
73. Breuilly, op. cit., pp. 208–9, 252–5; J. P. Parry, *Democracy and Religion: Gladstone and the Liberal Party, 1867–75* (Cambridge, 1986), pp. 198–201; McLeod, 'Religion in Labour Movements', pp. 25–6.
74. Eugenio F. Biagini, *Liberty, Retrenchment and Reform: Popular Liberalism in the Age of Gladstone, 1860–1880* (Cambridge, 1992); Nigel Scotland, *Methodism and the Revolt of the Field* (Gloucester, 1981), p. 89.
75. F. Linden, *Sozialismus und Religion* (Leipzig, 1932), pp. 110–11; Gillian Rose, 'Locality, Politics and Culture: Poplar in the 1920s' (University of London PhD thesis, 1989), pp. 237–8, 278–9; Philip Williamson, 'The Doctrinal Politics of Stanley Baldwin', in Michael Bentley (ed.), *Public and Private Doctrine* (Cambridge, 1993), pp. 181–208.

Notes to Chapter 2   Institutions

1. For an overview, see G. I. T. Machin, *Politics and the Churches in Great Britain, 1832 to 1868* (Oxford, 1977). He sees in the 1850s 'the increase of State neutrality in religion'; 'the advances made by ecclesiastical movements were not spectacular, controversial episodes were perhaps less frequent' (p. 252).
2. Catholic priests had since 1836 been paid to minister to Catholic soldiers, but only in 1858 were there Catholic professional chaplains, appointed by the War Office, and on an equal footing with Anglicans and Presbyterians. Kenneth E. Hendrickson III, *Making Saints: Religion and the Public Image of the British Army, 1809–1885* (Cranbury, NJ, 1998), p. 63.

3. Frances Knight, 'The Bishops and the Jews 1828–1858', in Diana Wood (ed.), *Christianity and Judaism*, Studies in Church History 29 (Oxford, 1992), pp. 387–98.

4. Cf. Antony Lentin, 'Anglicanism, Parliament and the Courts', in Gerald Parsons *et al.* (eds), *Religion in Victorian Britain*, 5 vols (Manchester, 1988–96), vol. II, p. 103.

5. Machin, op. cit., p. 286; Owen Chadwick, *The Victorian Church*, 2 vols (London, 1966–70), vol. I, p. 482.

6. Ibid., pp. 162–6; Walter L. Arnstein, 'Queen Victoria and religion', in Gail Malmgreen (ed.), *Religion in the Lives of English Women, 1760–1930* (Beckenham, 1986), pp. 88–128.

7. 'Religious Worship (England and Wales)', *Parliamentary Papers* (1852–53) vol. 89, p. clviii.

8. Chadwick, op. cit., vol. I, pp. 238–49; vol. II, pp. 328–42.

9. Olive Anderson, 'The Growth of Christian Militarism in Mid-Victorian Britain', *English Historical Review*, 86 (1971), pp. 46–72. See also Hendrickson, op. cit., which identifies a similar long-term trend, but sees its origins in the 1840s.

10. Bob Bushaway, 'Popular Belief on the Western Front', seminar paper, University of Birmingham, 8 May 1997,

11. Peter van Rooden, 'Secularization, Dechristianization and Rechristianization in The Netherlands', in Hartmut Lehmann (ed.), *Säkularisierung, Dechristianisierung, Rechristianisierung im neuzeitlichen Europa* (Göttingen, 1997), pp. 147–51; J. H. Whyte, *Church and State in Ireland, 1923–1979* (2nd edn, Dublin, 1980), ch. 2.

12. I broadly agree with the interpretation offered by Edward Norman, 'Church and State since 1800', in Sheridan Gilley and W. J. Sheils (eds), *A History of Religion in Britain: Practice and Belief from Pre-Roman Times to the Present* (Oxford, 1994) pp. 279–90.

13. Jeffrey Cox, *English Churches in a Secular Society* (Oxford, 1982) pp. 182–207, 214.

14. Ibid., p. 182.

15. Peter Marsh, *Joseph Chamberlain: Entrepreneur in Politics* (New Haven, CT, 1994), pp. 49–58.

16. Cox, op. cit., pp. 151–76. For the Civic Gospel, advocated by Birmingham Nonconformist preachers of the 1860s and 1870s, such as George Dawson and R. W. Dale, see E. P. Hennock, *Fit and Proper Persons* (London, 1973); David Thompson, 'R. W. Dale and the "Civic Gospel"', in Alan Sell (ed.), *Protestant Nonconformity and the West Midlands of England* (Keele, 1996), pp. 99–118.

17. For the *Gemeinde* system as applied to German Jews, see Arthur Ruppin, *Soziologie der Juden*, 2 vols (Berlin, 1930–1), vol. II, pp. 191–8. For the introduction of the church tax from 1852 onwards in the various German states, see Nicholas Hope, *German and Scandinavian Protestantism,*

1700 to 1918 (Oxford, 1995), p. 486; John E. Groh, *Nineteenth-Century German Protestantism: The Church as a Social Model* (Washington, DC, 1982), pp. 389–402; Ernst Christian Helmreich, *The German Churches under Hitler: Background, Struggle and Epilogue* (Detroit, MI, 1979), pp. 37–9.

18. Edward Ross Dickinson, *The Politics of German Child Welfare from the Empire to the Federal Republic* (Cambridge, MA, 1996) pp. 56–8, 96–100.

19. Daniel R. Borg, *The Old-Prussian Church and the Weimar Republic* (Hanover, NH, 1984), pp. 83–97, 116–22. Also stressing continuities between Empire and Republic in the public role of religion is Geoffrey G. Field, 'Religion in the German Volksschule, 1890–1928', *Yearbook of the Leo Baeck Institute*, 25 (1980), pp. 64–6.

20. Dickinson, op. cit., ch. 5; Walter Lorenz, 'Personal Social Services', in Jochen Clasen and Richard Freeman (eds), *Social Policy in Germany* (Hemel Hempstead, 1994), p. 160.

21. A good overview is provided by John McManners, *Church and State in France, 1870–1914* (London, 1972).

22. C. T. McIntire, 'Changing Religious Establishments and Religious Liberty in France, 1787–1908', in Richard Helmstadter (ed.), *Freedom and Religion in the Nineteenth Century* (Stanford, CA, 1997), pp. 273–99.

23. Maurice Larkin, *Church and State after the Dreyfus Affair* (London, 1974), pp. 102–3.

24. Ibid., p. 129.

25. Ibid., pp. 214–15.

26. Ibid., pp. 193–4.

27. Michel Lagreé, 'Exilés dans leur patrie (1880–1920)', in François Lebrun (ed.), *Histoire des catholiques en France* (Toulouse, 1980), pp. 369–411. He begins by noting the 'kind of exile, the marginalisation' experienced by Catholics at this time, and adds that they created 'a countersociety, designed to resist the attacks of the time'.

28. Jacques Ozouf, *Nous les maîtres d'école* (Paris, 1973), pp. 209–11.

29. See Philippe Martin, 'Christianisation? Déchristianisation? Rechristianisation? La question de la sacralisation de l'espace dans la France catholique (XIXᵉ–XXᵉ siècles)', *Kirchliche Zeitgeschrchte*, 11 (1998), pp. 51–68, for a good overview with many specific examples.

30. Jacqueline Lalouette, *La libre pensée en France, 1848–1940* (Paris, 1997), pp. 283–93.

31. Michel Lagrée, *Religions et cultures en Bretagne, 1850–1950* (Paris, 1992), pp. 145–6.

32. Lalouette, op. cit., pp. 296–8.

33. Maurice Larkin, *Religion, Politics and Preferment in France since the 1890s: La Belle Époque and its Legacy* (Cambridge, 1995), pp. 45–6, 101, 163–4, 183.

34. Mona Ozouf, *L'École, L'Église et la République* (Paris, 1963), p. 273.

304   NOTES

35. Jean Baubérot, *La Morale laïque contre l'ordre moral* (Paris, 1997), pp. 218–20.
36. Ibid., pp. 143–51.
37. Jean Faury, *Cléricalisme et anticléricalisme dans le Tarn* (Toulouse, 1980), pp. 121–47.
38. Baubérot, op. cit., pp. 117–273.
39. Ibid., p. 69; Jacques and Mona Ozouf, *La république des instituteurs* (Paris, 1992), pp. 214–18.
40. Baubérot, op. cit., pp. 53–113.
41. Ozouf, *République des instituteurs*, pp. 214–18.
42. Gérard Cholvy and Yves-Marie Hilaire, *Histoire religieuse de la France contemporainé*, vol. I: *1880–1930*. (Toulouse, 1986), P. 63.
43. Lagrée, *Religions et cultures*, pp. 371–81.
44. Robert Anderson, 'The Conflict in Education: Catholic Secondary Schools (1850–70) – A Reappraisal', in Theodore Zeldin (ed.), *Conflicts in French Society* (London, 1970), p. 59.
45. See Rebecca Rogers, 'The Socialization of Girls in France under the Influence of Religion and the Church', in M. Kraul and C. Lüth (eds), *Erziehung der Menschen-Geschlechter* (Weinheim, 1996), pp. 139–58.
46. Anderson, op. cit., pp. 80–1.
47. Ralph Gibson, *A Social History of French Catholicism, 1789–1914* (London, 1989), pp. 200–202.
48. Larkin, *Religion, Politics and Preferment*, pp. 35–9.
49. Lagrée, *Religions et cultures*, pp. 381–2.
50. Ibid., pp. 397–403; Judson Mather, 'The Assumptionist Response to Secularization, 1870–1900', in Robert Bezucha (ed.), *Modern European Social History*, (Lexington, MA, 1971), pp. 59–89.
51. Ted Margandant, 'Primary Schools and Youth Groups in Pre-war Paris: Les "Petites A's"', *Journal of Contemporary History*, 13 (1978), pp. 323–36.
52. Richard Holt, *Sport and Society in Modern France* (London, 1981), pp. 190–211.
53. Lagrée, *Religions et cultures*, pp. 414–15.
54. Alfred Wahl, *Les archives du football: Sport et société en France, 1880–1980* (Paris, 1989), pp. 99–100.
55. Ibid., pp. 51–2; Lagrée, *Religions et cultures*, pp. 413–14.
56. Wahl, op. cit., pp. 100–5.
57. Lagrée, 'Exilés dans leur patrie', p. 391.
58. Cholvy and Hilaire, op. cit., pp. 153–4.
59. Émile Zola, *Lourdes* (1894) brings out very well the many-sided attractions of the pilgrimage. His main emphasis is on the sufferings of the sick, the triumph of those who are cured, the despair of some and the stoicism of others for whom no miracle comes, and the devotion shown by nuns, relatives and other carers. But he brings out many other dimensions – for instance, Lourdes as a political symbol, a marriage

market, a place to go on outings and meet friends or lovers, or simply a memorable experience.

60. A good overview is Ronald J. Ross, *The Failure of Bismarck's Kulturkampf: Catholics and State Power in Imperial Germany, 1871–1887* (Washington, DC, 1997).

61. See David Blackbourn, *Marpingen: Apparitions of the Virgin Mary in Bismarckian Germany* (Oxford, 1993).

62. Ronald J. Ross, 'The Kulturkampf: Restrictions and Controls on the Practice of Religion in Bismarck's Germany', in Richard Helmstadter (ed.), *Freedom and Religion in the Nineteenth Century* (Stanford, CA, 1997), pp. 175–84.

63. See the essay on 'Progress and Piety' in David Blackbourn, *Populists and Patricians: Essays in Modern German History* (London, 1987), pp. 143–67.

64. Marjorie Lamberti, *State, Society and the Elementary School in Imperial Germany* (New York, 1989), pp. 93–7.

65. For an overview, see Marjorie Cruickshank, *Church and State in English Education: 1870 to the Present Day* (London, 1963).

66. Ibid., pp. 44–5; N. J. Richards, 'Religious Controversy and the School Boards, 1870–1902', *British Journal of Educational Studies*, 18 (1970), p. 193.

67. Richards, op. cit.; J. E. B. Munson, 'The London School Board Election of 1894: a Study in Victorian Religious Controversy', *British Journal of Educational Studies*, 23 (1975), p. 8.

68. Cox, op. cit., pp. 186–90, 273–4.

69. K. D. Wald, *Crosses on the Ballot* (Princeton, NJ, 1983), pp. 222–34.

70. Cox, op. cit., p. 187.

71. J. S. Hurt, *Elementary Schooling and the Working Clases, 1860–1918* (London, 1979); Richard Sykes, 'Popular Religion in Dudley and the Gornals, *c*. 1914–1965' (University of Wolverhampton PhD thesis, 1999), p. 120.

72. Cf. Wald, p. 232. See also Jon Lawrence, *Speaking for the People: Party, Language and Popular Politics in England, 1867–1914* (Cambridge, 1998), p. 102, noting the predominance of Anglican schools in some strongly Radical areas of the Black Country.

73. J. R. de S. Honey, *Tom Brown's Universe: The Victorian Public School* (London, 1977), pp. 7, 284–5.

74. Ibid., pp. 308–9; A. G. L. Haig, 'The Church, the Universities and Learning in later Victorian England', *Historical Journal*, 29 (1986), pp. 187–201.

75. Desmond Bowen, *The Idea of the Victorian Church* (Montreal, 1968), pp. vii–viii.

76. Honey, op. cit., pp. 7, 284–5, 309–13. See also Adrian Hastings, *A History of English Christianity, 1920–1985* (London, 1986), p. 74.

77. Roald Dahl, *Boy* (Harmondsworth, 1986), pp. 144–6.

78. Chadwick, *Victorian Church*, vol. II, pp. 444, 449.
79. Haig, 'Church, Universities, Learning', p. 190.
80. V. H. H. Green, *Religion at Oxford and Cambridge* (London, 1964), p. 339.
81. Chadwick, *Victorian Church*, vol. II, pp. 450–2, 460–2; D. W. Bebbington, *Evangelicalism in Modern Britain: A History from the 1730s to the 1980s* (London, 1989), p. 186; Hastings, op. cit., p. 117.
82. Green, op. cit., pp. 322–4.
83. The uniquely high profile of the Church of England in Oxford and Cambridge in the twentieth century, and the growing presence of other denominations, is noted by Hastings, op. cit., pp. 65–6, 117, 140.
84. Field, op. cit., pp. 41–2.
85. Ernst Christian Helmreich, *Religious Education in German Schools*, (Cambridge, MA, 1959), pp. 47–9.
86. Ibid., pp. 45–6; Lamberti, op. cit., pp. 211–17.
87. Frank-Michael Kuhlemann, 'Zwischen Tradition und Modernität: Volksschule und Volksschullehrer im wilhelmischen Ostwestfalen', in Joachim Meynert, Josef Mooser and Volker Rodekamp (eds), *Unter Pickelhaube und Zylinder: Das Östliche Westfalen im Zeitalter desWilhelmismus, 1888–1914* (Bielefeld, 1991), p. 337.
88. Lamberti, op. cit., pp. 20–1.
89. Ibid., pp. 76–81.
90. Ibid., pp. 93–7.
91. Ibid., pp. 266–9.
92. Helmreich, *Religious Education*, p. 71.
93. Lamberti, op. cit., pp. 211–17.
94. J. A. Mangan, 'Social Darwinism and Upper-class Education in Late Victorian and Edwardian England', J. A. Mangan and James Walvin (eds), *Manliness and Morality: Middle Class Masculinity in Britain and America, 1800–1940* (Manchester, 1987), pp. 135–59.
95. Stephen Humphries, '"Hurrah for England": Schooling and the Working Class in Bristol, 1870–1914', *Southern History*, 1 (1979), pp. 182–4.
96. Werner Blessing, *Staat und Kirche in der Gesellschaft* (Göttingen, 1982), p. 223.
97. Ibid., pp. 199–200.
98. Christel Köhle-Hezinger, *Evangelisch–Katholisch: Untersuchungen zu konfessionellem Vorurteil und Konflikt im 19. und 20. Jahrhundert vornehmlich am Beispiel Württembergs* (Tübingen, 1976), pp. 287–90.
99. Hartmut Lehmann, '"God Our Old Ally": the Chosen people Theme in Late Nineteenth- and Early Twentieth-Century German Nationalism', in William R. Hutchison and Hartmut Lehmann (eds), *Many Are Chosen: Divine Election and Western Nationalism* (Minneapolis, MN, 1994), pp. 85–107.

100. Helmut Walser Smith, *German Nationalism and Religious Conflict: Culture, Ideology, Politics, 1870–1914* (Princeton, NJ, 1995), pp. 22–39.
101. Wolfgang Altgeld, *Katholizismus, Protestantismus, Judentum: Über religiös begrundete Gegensätze und nationalreligiöse Ideen in der Geschichte des deutschen Nationalismus* (Mainz, 1992), pp. 3–4.
102. Kuhlemann, op. cit., pp. 336–40.
103. Humphries op. cit., p. 184.
104. See J. Wigley, *The Rise and Fall of the Victorian Sunday* (Manchester, 1980).
105. Ibid., *passim*; Hugh McLeod, *Class and Religion in the Late Victorian City* (London, 1974), pp. 139–43. 220–2, 231–7.
106. Ibid., pp. 235, 267–8; John Lowerson, *Sport and the English Middle Classes* (Manchester, 1993), pp. 274–5; Tony Mason, 'Football', idem. (ed.), *Sport in Britain: A Social History* (Cambridge, 1989), p. 149; Cynthia Brown, *Northampton, 1835–1985: Shoe Town, New Town* (Chichester, 1990), p. 129; Jack Williams, *Cricket and England: A Cultural and Social History of the Inter-war Years* (London, 1999), pp. 153–4.
107. G. I. T. Machin, 'British Churches and the Cinema in the 1930s', in Diana Wood (ed.), *The Church and the Arts*, Studies in Church History 28 (Oxford, 1992), p. 483; Paddy Scannell and David Cardiff, *A Social History of British Broadcasting*, vol. 1: *1922–1939* (Oxford, 1991), p. 232.
108. For London, see Cox, op. cit., pp. 163–4; for Northampton, Brown, op. cit., p. 129; for Norwich, see Barry M. Doyle, 'Urban Liberalism and the "Lost Generation": Politics and Middle Class Culture in Norwich, 1900–1935', *Historical Journal*, 38 (1995), p. 626.

Notes to Chapter 3   The Pace-Setters

1. Gerard Cholvy and Yues-Marie Hilaire, *Histoire religieuse de la France antemporaine*, vol. I: *1800–1880* (Toulouse, 1990), pp. 199–201; Yves-Marie Hilaire, *Une chrétienté au XIXe siècle? La vie religieuse des populations du diocèse d'Arras*, 2 vols (Lille, 1977), vol. II, pp. 553–66; Hans Reif, *Westfälischer Adel* (Göttingen, 1979); R. M. Bigler, *The Politics of German Protestantism* (Los Angeles, CA, 1972), ch. 4; Hugh McLeod, *Class and Religion in the Late Victorian City* (London, 1974), pp. 200–1.
2. Diary of Edward Derrington, entry for 26 January 1838, Carrs Lane MSS, vol. 61 (Birmingham Central Reference Library); Geoffrey Robson, 'Religion and Irreligion in Birmingham and the Black Country' (University of Birmingham PhD thesis, 1997), p. 217. See also Geoffrey Robson, 'The Failures of Success: Working-class Evangelists in Early Victorian Birmingham', in Derek Baker (ed.), *Religious Motivation: Biographical and Sociological Problems for the Church Historian*, Studies in Church History, 15 (Oxford, 1978), pp. 381–91.

3. Carrs Lane MSS, vol. 61, entries for 18, 26 and 31 January 1838.
4. Ibid.
5. Eileen Yeo, 'Christianity in Chartist Struggle, 1838–42', *Past & Present*, 91 (1981) p. 132, note 63.
6. Alan Bennett Bartlett, 'The Churches in Bermondsey 1880–1939' (University of Birmnigham PhD thesis, 1987), pp. 137–9.
7. Mcleod, op. cit., p. 304.
8. Hugh McLeod, 'Class, Community and Region: The Religious Geography of Nineteenth-century England', in Michael Hill (ed.), *Sociological Yearbook of Religion in Britain*, 6 (1973), pp. 49–52.
9. Hugh McLeod, *Piety and Poverty: Working Class Religion in Berlin, London and New York, 1870–1914* (New York, 1996), p. 11.
10. Cholvy and Hilaire, op. cit., p. 198.
11. Fernand Charpin, *Pratique religieuse urbaine et formation d'une grande ville (Marseille 1806–1958)* (Paris, 1964), pp. 254–5, 288–92, 296–7, 299.
12. Lucian Hölscher, 'Säkularisierungsprozesse', in Hans-Jurgen Pühle (ed.), *Bürger in der Gesellschaft der Neuzeit* (Göttingen, 1991) pp. 243–9.
13. Lucian Hölscher, 'Statistische Erfassung kirchlicher Bindungen', in Kaspar Elm and Hans-Dietrich Loock (eds), *Seelsorge und Diakonie: Beiträge zum Verhältnis von Kirche und Großstadt im 19. und beginnenden 20. Jahrhundert* (Berlin, 1990), pp. 42–3.
14. Chester diocesan Visitation Returns, 1778 (Cheshire County Record Office, Chester). For similar comments see Alan Gilbert, *Religion and Society in Industrial England: Church, Chapel and Social Change, 1740–1914* (London, 1976), pp. 10–11; Clive Field, 'A Godly People? Aspects of Religious Practice in the Diocese of Oxford, 1738–1936', *Southern History*, 14 (1992), pp. 65–6.
15. Serge Bonnet, 'Verriers et bûcherons d'Argonne', F. Bédarida and J. Maitron (eds), *Christianisme et monde ouvrier* (Paris, 1975), p. 232.
16. See Donald M. Lewis, *Lighten their Darkness: The Evangelical Mission to Working Class London, 1828–1860* (London, 1986).
17. See, e.g., B. I. Coleman, 'The Church Extension Movement in London c.1800–1860' (University of Cambridge PhD thesis, 1968); Hilaire, *Une chrétienté?*, vol. II, pp. 549–53; Martin Greschat, 'Die Berliner Stadtmission', in Elm and Loock (eds), op. cit., pp. 451–75.
18. D. B. McIlhiney, 'A Gentleman in every Slum: Church of England Missions in the East End of London, 1837–1914' (Princeton Universioty PhD thesis, 1977), pp. 128–31.
19. Glenn Horridge, *The Salvation Army: Origins and early Days, 1865–1900* (Godalming, 1993). For discussion of some of the ways Salvationists related to the culture of working-class neighbourhoods, see Pamela J. Walker, 'A Chaste and Fervid Eloquence: Catherine Booth and the Ministry of Women in the Salvation Army', in Beverly Mayne Kienzle

and Pamela J. Walker (eds), *Women Preachers and Prophets through Two Millennia of Christianity* (Berkeley, CA, 1998), pp. 288–302.

20. McLeod, *Piety and Poverty*, ch. 6.

21. Paul Thompson, *Socialists, Liberals and Labour: The Struggle for London, 1885–1914* (London, 1967), p. 239.

22. McLeod, *Piety and Poverty*, pp. 9–19, 42.

23. Ibid., p. 21; C. Willard, 'Notre Dame de l'Usine', in Bédarida and Maitron (eds), op. cit., pp. 245–51.

24. Hartmut Zwahr, *Zur Konstitutierung des Proletariats als Klasse* (Berlin, 1978).

25. Theodore Koditschek, *Class Formation and Urban-Industrial Society: Bradford, 1750–1850* (Cambridge, 1991), p. 195.

26. Wolfgang Köllmann, *Sozialgeschichte der Stadt Barmen* (Tübingen, 1960), p. 157.

27. See McLeod, *Piety and Poverty* for data on lay leadership in Berlin Protestant parishes. The fullest investigations of this topic have been for Presbyterian congregations in Scottish cities: see A. A. McLaren, *Religion and Social Class: The Disruption Years in Aberdeen* (London, 1974); Peter Hillis, 'Presbyterianism and Social Class in Mid-nineteenth Century Glasgow: a Study of Nine Churches', *Journal of Ecclesisastical History*, 32 (1981), pp. 47–64. Obelkevich, *Religion and Rural Society: South Lindsey, 1825–1875*, (Oxford, 1976), pp. 195, 239, analyses the social composition of the Wesleyan and Primitive Methodist lay leadership in Lincolnshire, but no similarly systematic study of English urban congregations has been made. See, however, Simon Gunn, 'The Ministry, the Middle Class and the "civilizing mission" in Manchester, 1850–80', *Social History*, 21 (1996), pp. 25–6, which is more impressionistic, and Clyde Binfield, *Pastors and People* (Coventry, 1984), pp. 60–1, an intensive study of a Baptist church in Coventry.

28. Koditschek, op. cit., ch. 10.

29. See Charpin, op. cit.; W. Sewell, 'Social Change and the Rise of Working Class Politics in Nineteenth-Century Marseilles', *Past & Present*, 65 (1974), pp. 75–109; J. M. Phayer, *Sexual Liberation and Religion in Nineteenth-Century Europe* (London, 1977).

30. McLeod, *Piety and Poverty*, ch. 6.

31. Ellen Ross, 'Hungry Children: Housewives and London Charity', in Peter Mandler (ed.), *The Uses of Charity: The Poor on Relief in the Nineteenth-Century Metropolis* (Philadelphia, PA, 1990), pp. 169–71; F. K. Prochaska, 'Body and Soul: Bible Nurses and the Poor in Victorian London', *Historical Research*, 60 (1987), pp. 336–48; L. Strumhinger, '"A bas les prêtres! A bas les couvents!" The Church and the Workers in Nineteenth-Century Lyon', *Journal of Social History*, 11 (1978), pp. 546–7.

32. For prayer, see McLeod, *Piety and Poverty*, pp. 192–4.
33. Philip Nord, *The Republican Moment: Struggles for Democracy in Nineteenth-Century France* (Cambridge, MA, 1995), p. 48.
34. Ibid.
35. Ralph Gibson, *A Social History of French Catholicism, 1789–1914* (London, 1989), pp. 195–212.
36. Nord, op. cit., chs 2, 3 and 6.
37. Ibid., chs 4 and 5; Cholvy and Hilaire, *Histoire religieuse, 1880–1930*, pp. 36, 50.
38. Nord, op. cit., ch. 1; Maurice Larkin, *Religion, Politics and Preferment in France since the 1890s: La Belle Époque and its Legacy* (Cambridge, 1995), pp. 119–27.
39. Ralph Gibson, 'Why Republicans and Catholics Couldn't Stand Each Other in the Nineteenth Century', in Frank Tallett and Nicholas Atkin (eds), *Religion, Society and Politics in France since 1789* (London, 1991), pp. 113.
40. René Rémond, *L'anti-cléricalisme en France: De 1815 à nos jours* (2nd edn, Paris, 1992), p. 185.
41. Gibson, 'Republicans and Catholics', p. 115, citing an article in *Le Journal de Rouen*.
42. Jacqueline Lalouette, *La Libre Pensée en France, 1848–1940* (Paris, 1997), pp. 160–1.
43. Jacques and Nora Ozouf, *La république des instituteurs* (Paris, 1992) pp. 210–11.
44. E.g., in Berlin in the 1840s, the court and aristocracy favoured the Pietist clergy, while the city council supported the liberals see Walter Wendland, *Siebenhundert Jahre Kirchengeschichte Berlins* (Berlin, 1930), pp. 300–3.
45. Lucian Hölscher, 'Kirchliche Demokratie und Frömmigkeitskultur im deutschen Protestantismus', in Martin Greschat and Jochen-Christoph Kaiser (eds), *Christentum und Demokratie* (Stuttgart, 1992), pp. 191–5.
46. Gangolf Hübinger, 'Kulturprotestantismus, Bürgerkirche und liberaler Revisionismus im wilhelminischen Deutschland', in Wolfgang Schieder (ed.), *Religion und Gesellschaft in 19. Jahrhundert* (Stuttgart, 1993), pp. 273–4; Hölscher, 'Kirchliche Demokratie', pp. 200–3.
47. McLeod, *Piety and Poverty*, p. 23.
48. Arnold Horowitz, 'Prussian State and Protestant Church in the Reign of Wilhelm II' (Yale University PhD thesis, 1976), pp. 216–32.
49. Ibid., pp. 53–8; Hübinger, op. cit., pp. 295–9.
50. See Thomas Mergel, *Zwischen Klasse und Konfession: Katholisches Bürgertum im Rheinland, 1794–1914* (Göttingen, 1994).
51. E. Rolffs, *Das kirchliche Leben der evangelischen Kirchen in Niedersachsen* (Tübingen, 1917), pp. 600–1.

52. Gunilla-Friederike Budde, *Auf dem Weg ins Bürgerleben: Kindheit und Erziehung in deutschen und englischen Bürgerfamilien 1840–1914* (Göttingen, 1994), p. 380.

53. Ibid., p. 387.

54. *Jenseits von Gut und Böse* (1886), in F. Nietzsche, *Werke*, 3 vols (Munich, 1955), vol. II, pp. 618–19.

55. H. H. Gerth and C. Wright Mills (eds), *From Max Weber* (London, 1948), pp. 134–8, 142–3, 153–6.

56. Paul Drews, *Das kirchliche Leben der Evangelisch-Lutherischen Landeskirche des Königreichs Sachsen* (Tübingen, 1902), p. 365.

57. Wolfgang Ribbe (ed.), *Geschichte Berlins*, 2 vols (Munich, 1987), vol. II, pp. 680–3.

58. Henry Wassermann, 'Jews and Judaism in the Gartenlaube', *Yearbook of the Leo Baeck Institute*, 23 (1978), p. 51.

59. Alfred Kelly, *The Descent of Darwin: The Popularization of Darwinism in Germany, 1860–1914* (Chapel Hill, 1981) pp. 15–28; Karl Birker, *Die deutschen Arbeiterbildungsvereine, 1840–1870* (Berlin, 1973), pp. 58, 153–4, 183–6.

60. David Blackbourn, *Marpingen: Apparitions of the Virgin Mary in Bismarckian Germany* (Oxford, 1993), pp. 288–91.

61. Norbert Schloßmacher, 'Der Deutsche Verein für die Rheinprovinz', in Olaf Blaschke and Frank-Michael Kuhlemann (eds), *Religion im Kaiserreich: Milieus – Mentalitäten – Krisen* (Gütersloh, 1996), p. 479.

62. Lalouette, op. cit., pp. 245–8; Rémond, op. cit., pp. 190–1; Smith, *German Nationalism and Religious Conflict* (Princeton, NJ, 1995), pp. 26–37.

63. Smith, *German Nationalism*, p. 22.

64. Ibid., pp. 23–37.

65. Koditschek, op. cit., pp. 135–203, 257.

66. Simon Gunn, 'The Ministry, the Middle Class and the "Civilizing Mission"', pp. 25, 30.

67. E. P. Hennock, *Fit and Proper Persons* (London, 1973), pp. 61–79, 154–69; Peter T. Marsh, *Joseph Chamberlain: Entrepreneur in Politics* (New Haven, CT, 1994), pp. 41, 240, 273.

68. G. I. T. Machin, *Politics and the Churches in Great Britain, 1832–1868* (Oxford, 1977) p. 162.

69. Cox, *English Churches in a Secular Society*, pp. 161–2.

70. Frank M. Turner, *Contesting Cultural Authority: Essays in Victorian Intellectual Life* (Cambridge, 1993), p. 170.

71. Nord, op. cit., p. 37.

72. Ozouf, *République des instituteurs*, pp. 183–8.

73. Ibid., pp. 197–8.

74. Ibid., pp. 172–4, Annex 3.

75. On the wide-ranging role of the village school teacher, see Barnett Singer, *Village Notables in Nineteenth-century France: Priests, Mayors and Schoolmasters* (Albany, NY, 1983), p. 126 and *passim*.

76. N. J. Richards, 'Religious Controversy and the School Boards, 1870–1902', *British Journal of Educational Studies*, 18 (1970), pp. 183–4.

77. Hugh McLeod, 'White-Collar Values and the Role of Religion', in Geoffrey Crossick (ed.), *The Lower Middle Class in Britain, 1870–1914* (London, 1977), p. 80. Some Anglican-dominated Boards insisted on teachers being Anglicans. See Richards, op. cit., p. 194.

78. Cox, *English Churches in a Secular Society*, p. 188.

79. Marjorie Cruickshank, *Church and State in English Education: 1870 to the Present Day* (London, 1963).

80. J. E. B. Munson, 'The London School Board Election of 1894: a Study in Victorian Religious Controversy', *British Journal of Educational Studies*, 23 (1975), pp. 11–12.

81. Ernst Christian Helmreich, *Religious Education in German Schools* (Cambridge, MA, 1959), ch. 5; Jonathan Sperber, *Rhineland Radicals* (Princeton, NJ, 1991) pp. 85–6, 287–9.

82. Werner Blessing, *Staat und Kirche in der Gesellschaft* (Göttingen, 1982), pp. 175, 221–6; Ian Farr, 'From Anti-Catholicism to Anticlericalism: Catholic Politics and the Peasantry in Bavaria, 1860–1900', *European Studies Review*, 13 (1983), pp. 261–5.

83. Helmreich, pp. 96–7; Geoffrey G. Field, 'Religion in the German Volksschule 1890–1928', *Yearbook of the Leo Baeck Institute*, 25 (1980), pp. 48–52.

84. Johannes Tews, *Berliner Lehrer* (Berlin, 1907), pp. 76–7; see also McLeod, *Piety and Poverty*, p. 14.

85. Blessing, op. cit., pp. 217, 354, note 52.

86. Nord, op. cit., pp. 35–41. In Rennes, where levels of piety were generally high around the middle of the nineteenth century, the major exceptions were students in medicine and law: see Michel Lagrée, *Mentalités, religion et histoire en Haute-Bretagne au XIXe siècle* (Paris, 1977), pp. 327–38.

87. Pierre Guillaume, *Médecins, Église et foi* (n.p., 1990), pp. 105–8.

88. Theodore Zeldin, *France, 1848–1945*, 2 vols (Oxford, 1973–7), vol. I, p. 23.

89. Lucian Hölscher, 'Die Religion des Bürgers: Bürgerliche Frömmigkeit und protestantische Kirche im 19. Jahrhundert', *Historische Zeitschrift*, 250 (1990), pp. 611–12; Blackbourn, *Marpingen*, pp. 184–5.

90. A Preston working man, interviewed by an oral historian in the 1970s, described the typical members of the congregation at the Anglican church to which he had belonged in the 1920s as 'the doctors'. Hugh McLeod, 'New Perspectives on Victorian Working Class Religion: the Oral Evidence', *Oral History Journal*, 14 (1986), p. 39. However, by

comparison with the relatively detailed information that we have on working-class religious activity in Victorian/Edwardian England, information on the various sections of the middle class is more limited.

91. Catherine J. Kudlick, *Cholera in Post-Revolutionary Paris: A Cultural History* (Berkeley, CA, 1996), pp. 144–6.
92. Ibid., pp. 164–75.
93. R. J. Morris, *Cholera 1832* (London, 1976), pp. 203–4, 214.
94. Frank M. Turner, *Contenting Cultural Authority*, pp. 164–7.
95. Guillaume, op. cit., pp. 26–8.
96. See Judith R. Walkowitz, *Prostitution and Victorian Society* (Cambridge, 1980); Paul McHugh, *Prostitution and Victorian Social Reform* (London, 1980).
97. Baubérot, op. cit., pp. 303–4.
98. Lalouette, op. cit., pp. 276–82.
99. Émile Zola, *Lourdes* (English translation, Stroud, 1993), [first published 1894], pp. 27–8, 102. In Zola's *Doctor Pascal* (1893) the doctor as secular saint is the central character.
100. Louis Pérouas, *Refus d'une religion, religion d'un refus en Limousin rural, 1880–1940* (Paris, 1985), pp. 163–5.
101. Guillaume, op. cit., pp. 80–8.
102. Olivier Janz, 'Zwischen Bürgerlichkeit und kirchlichem Milieu: Zum Selbstverständnis und sozialen Verhalten der evangelischen Pfarrer in Preußen in der zweiten Hälfte des 19. Jahrhunderts', in Blaschke and Kuhlemann (eds), op. cit., pp. 388–9, gives many examples of the contacts of clergy with doctors and those of similar standing – though his main concern is to indicate a growing distance between clergy and bourgeoisie.
103. Alan Haig, *The Victorian Clergy* (Beckenham, 1984), pp. 32, 35–48.
104. Gibson, op. cit., pp. 68–76.
105. Karl Marx and Friedrich Engels, *On Religion* (Moscow, 1957), p. 37.
106. Judson Mather, 'The Assumptionist Response to Secularization, 1870–1900', in Robert Bezucha (ed.), *Modern European Social History* (Lexington, MA, 1971), p. 60.
107. See the contributions by Madeleine Rebérioux on Le mur des Fédérés (I, pp. 535–58) and by François Loyer on Sacré-Coeur (III, pp. 4253–70) to Pierre Nora (ed.), *Les lieux de mémoire*, 3 vols (2nd edn, Paris, 1997).
108. See numerous examples in Rémond, op. cit., pp. 171–223.
109. Lalouette, op. cit., p. 219.
110. See V. L. Lidtke, *The Alternative Culture* (New York, 1985).
111. See Horst Ermel, *Die Kirchenaustrittsbewegung im Deutschen Reich 1906–14* (Dissertation, Cologne University, 1971).
112. Lucian Hölscher, *Weltgericht oder Revolution* (Stuttgart, 1989), pp. 142–56.

314 NOTES

113. Jochen Loreck, *Wie man früher Sozialdemokrat wurde* (Bonn, 1977), pp. 145–56.
114. Wolfgang Emmerich (ed.), *Proletarische Lebensläufe*, 2 vols (Reinbek bei Hamburg, 1974), vol. I, pp. 284–5.
115. Mcleod, *Piety and Poverty*, pp. 163–9.
116. Karl-Heinrich Pohl, 'Katholische Sozialdemokraten oder sozialdemokratische Katholiken in München: Ein Identitätskonflikt', in Blaschke and Kuhlemann (eds), op. cit., pp. 233–53; Karl Ditt, *Industrialisierung, Arbeiterschaft und Arbeiterbewegung in Bielefeld, 1850–1914* (Dortmund, 1982), p. 239; Loreck, op. cit., p. 155.
117. E. Rolffs, *Das kirchliche Leben der evangelischen Kirchen in Niedersachsen* (Tübingen, 1917), pp. 447, 533–7.
118. P. Glaue, *Das kirchliche Leben der evangelischen Kirchen in Thüringen* (Tübingen, 1910), p. 366; Drews, op. cit., p. 354.
119. Edward Royle, *Radicals, Secularists and Republicans: Popular Freethought in Britain, 1866–1915* (Manchester, 1980), pp. 232–9; Leonard Smith, *Religion and the Rise of Labour* (Keele, 1993), pp. 130–8.
120. For Chartist critiques of the established church, see H. U. Faulkner, *Chartism and the Churches* (New York, 1918), pp. 31–5, 108–9; for Secularist views, Royle, *Radicals*, p. 295.
121. Royle, *Radicals*, p. 129.
122. *New Statesman and Society*, 30 September 1994.
123. Robert Tressell, *The Ragged Trousered Philanthropists* (London, 1955) [first published 1914], pp. 176–88, 491–2. P. S. A.s (Pleasant Sunday Afternoons) were special services for working men provided by many Nonconformists chapels *c*. 1900.
124. See Eric Hobsbawm's essay, 'Religion and the Rise of Socialism' in his collection *Worlds of Labour* (London, 1984), pp. 33–48.
125. Zeldin, op. cit., vol. I, p. 764.
126. The *calotte* (a priest's skull-cap) came to be used in nineteenth-century France as an abusive term for the clergy. People deemed too friendly to the clergy were dubbed *calotins*. There was even an anti-clerical journal called *La Calotte*. See Rémond, op. cit., p. 214.
127. Roger Martin Du Gard, *Jean Barois* (Paris, 1921) [first published 1913], p. 67.
128. Mary Ryan, 'A Woman's Awakening: Evangelical Religion and the Families of Utica, New York, 1800–1840', in Janet Wilson James (ed.), *Women in American Religion* (Philadelphia, PA, 1980), pp. 90–1; Olwen Hufton, 'The Reconstruction of a Church 1796–1801', in Gwynne Lewis and Colin Lucas (eds), *Beyond the Terror: Essays in French Regional and Social History 1794–1815* (Cambridge, 1983), pp. 39–41.
129. Claude Langlois, *Le catholicisme au féminin* (Paris, 1984), pp. 310–11.
130. Clive Field, 'Adam and Eve: Gender in the English Free Church Constituency', *Journal of Ecclesiastical History*, 41 (1993), pp. 63–79.

The best statistical study of the gender composition of Nonconformist congregations in the later nineeenth century is Rosemary Chadwick, 'Church and People in Bradford and District 1880–1914' (University of Oxford DPhil thesis, 1986).

131. Gibson, op. cit., p. 181.
132. Geneviève Gadbois, '"Vous êtes presque la seule consolation de l'Église"', in Jean Delumeau (ed.), *La religion de ma mère* (Paris, 1992), p. 321.
133. Gibson, op. cit., p. 174.
134. Ibid., p. 181.
135. P. Pieper, *Kirchenstatistik Deutschlands* (Freiburg im Breisgau, 1899), p. 233.
136. McLeod, *Piety and Poverty*, pp. 25–6, 159–60.
137. Royle, *Radicals*, p. 130; Lalouette, op. cit., p. 93.
138. McLeod, *Piety and Poverty*, pp. 160, 163; Rickie Burman, '"She looketh well to the ways of her household": the Changing Role of Jewish women in Religious Life *c*.1880–1930', in Gail Malmgreen (ed.), *Religion in the Lives of Englishwomen, 1760–1930* (Beckenham, 1986), pp. 234–57; Marion Kaplan, *The Making of the Jewish Middle Class: Women, Family and Identity in Imperial Germany* (New York, 1991), pp. 64–84.
139. Richard J. Evans, *Kneipengespräche im Kaiserreich* (Hamburg, 1989), pp. 171–2; Lalouette, op. cit., pp. 334–45; Mary Hartman, *Victorian Murderesses* (New York, 1976), pp. 206, 239.
140. Hufton, 'Reconstruction', p. 22, notes that while open conflict between devout women and irreligious men took place for the first time during the Revolution, clear differences in levels of piety were already apparent. For instance, in one village near Paris in 1780 all widows and spinsters and nearly all married women received Easter communion, but only about 45 per cent of adult men did so.
141. Jules Michelet, *Du Prêtre, de la Famille, de l'Église* (Paris, 1845), pp. v–vi.
142. Gibson, op. cit. p. 182; Lalouette, op. cit., pp. 335–7.
143. Imbke Behnken and Pia Schmid, 'Religion in Tagebüchern von Frauen – zwei Fallstudien', in Kraul and Luth (eds), op. cit., pp. 63–77.
144. Eberhard Bethge, *Dietrich Bonhoeffer* (English translation, London, 1970), pp. 20–1.
145. Kaplan, op. cit., pp. 73–4.
146. Monika Richarz, *Jüdisches Leben in Deutschland*, 3 vols (Stuttgart, 1979), vol. II, pp. 298–9.
147. Ibid., II, pp. 360–2.
148. Ellen Ross, 'Survival Networks: Women's Neighbourhood Sharing in London before World War I', *History Workshop Journal*, 15 (1983), pp. 4–27, emphasies the separation between the worlds of women and of men.
149. Smith, *Ladies of the Leisure Class*, ch. 5.

150. This is stated most explicitly in Luckmann, op. cit., p. 30.

151. Hugh McLeod, *Religion and the People of Western Europe, 1789–1989* (Oxford, 1997), pp. 101–10.

152. Paul Thompson, with Tony Wailey and Trevor Lummis, *Living the Fishing* (London, 1983).

153. Roger Magraw, 'Popular Anti-clericalism in Nineteenth-Century Rural France', in James Obelkevich, Lyndal Roper and Raphael Samuel (eds), *Disciplines of Faith* (London, 1987), p. 361.

154. Herwart Vorländer, *Evangelische Kirche und soziale Frage in der werdenden Industriegroßstadt Elberfeld* (Düsseldorf, 1963), pp. 74–5.

155. Faury, op. cit., pp. 272–3.

156. Michelet, op. cit., pp. v–vi.

157. Gibson, op. cit., pp. 160–1.

158. Faury, op. cit., p. 271.

159. E.g. George Eliot, *Scenes from Clerical Life* (Harmondsworth, 1973) [first published 1858], p. 275.

160. For Germany, see Mary Lee Townsend, *Forbidden Laughter* (Ann Arbor, MI, 1992), pp. 150–3.

161. Reproduced on the cover of Evans, *Rituals of Retribution*.

162. Jane Rendall, *The Origins of Modern Feminism* (London, 1985), p. 148; McLeod, *Piety and Poverty*, pp. 165–7; Bartlett, op. cit., pp. 193–5.

163. Philippe Boutry and Michel Cinquin, *Deux pélérinages au XIXe siècle: Ars et Paray-le-Monial* (Paris, 1980), pp. 29–58.

164. See Paul Seeley, 'O Sainte Mère: Liberalism and the Socialization of Men in Nineteenth-Century France', *Journal of Modern History*, 70 (1998), pp. 862–91.

165. For England, Adrian Hastings, *A History of English Christianity, 1920–1985* (Londary, 1986), pp. 561–3; for Germany Andreas Holzem, 'Dechristianisierung und Rechristianisierung: Der deutsche Katholizismus im europäischen Vergeleich', *Kirchliche Zeitgeschichte*, 11 (1998), p. 74.

166. Possibly the best of the many discussions of this theme is an intensive local study, Philippe Boutry, *Prêtres et paroisses au pays du Curé d'Ars* (Paris, 1986). Useful overviews include Olaf Blaschke, 'Die Kolonialisierung der Laienwelt: Priester als Milieumanager und die Kanale klerikaler Kuratel', in Blaschke and Kuhlemann (eds), op. cit., pp. 93–138; Singer, op. cit.

167. See for instance Josef Mooser, 'Arbeiter, Bürger und Priester in den konfessionellen Arbeitervereinen im deutschen Kaiserreich, 1880–1914', in Jürgen Kocka (ed.), *Arbeiter und Bürger im 19. Jahrhundert* (Munich, 1986), pp. 103–4.

168. See two contributions to Ellen Badone (ed.), *Religious Orthodoxy and Popular Faith in European Society* (Princeton, NJ, 1990) – Badone, 'Breton Folklore of Anticlericalism', (pp. 140–62), and Lawrence

J. Taylor, 'Stories of Power, Powerful Stories' (pp. 163–84); Eliot, op. cit., p. 275; Obelkevich, *Religion and Rural Society*, pp. 277–8.

169. Boutry and Cinquin, op. cit., pp. 61, 64; McLeod, *Piety and Poverty*, p. 195.

170. Émile Zola, *The Earth* (English translation, Harmondsworth, 1980) [first published 1887], pp. 337–8.

171. Boutry, *Prêtres et paroisses*, pp. 360–1.

172. Ibid., p. 359.

173. Ibid., p. 362.

174. Lalouette, op. cit., pp. 245–50; Faury, op. cit., pp. 435–6; Rémond, op. cit., p. 190.

175. D. F. Summers, 'The Labour Church and Allied Movements of the late 19th and early 20th Centuries' (University of Edinburgh PhD, 1958) summarises (pp. 687–90) the varying and mutually incompatible theological tendencies within the movement. The Ashton, Birmingham and Bradford branches were among those seriously divided by these rival tendencies, and the Glasgow branch framed a constitution designed to avoid religious controversy (pp. 325–7, 330–40, 367–9, 395).

176. Stephen Yeo, 'The Religion of Socialism', *History Workshop Journal*, 4 (1977) p. 36.

177. Nord, op. cit., ch. 5.

178. This was a constant theme of John Trevor, founder of the British Labour Churches. Summers, op. cit., p. 5.

179. Jeffrey Cox, *English Churches in a Secular Society* (Oxford, 1982), p. 232.

180. Ibid., p. 235.

181. Ibid., pp. 233–5; McLeod, *Class and Religion*, pp. 254–5.

182. Arnold Ruppin, op. cit., II, pp. 176–7; Paula Hyman, 'The Social Contexts of Assimilation: Village Jews and City Jews in Alsace', in Jonathan Frankel and Steven J. Zipperstein (eds), *Assimilation and Community: The Jews in Nineteenth-century Europe* (Cambridge, 1992), pp. 116–20.

183. Jacob Borut and Oded Heilbronner, 'Leaving the Walls of Anomalous Activity: the Catholic and Jewish Rural Bourgeoisie in Germany', in *Comparative Studies in Society and History*, 40 (1998), pp. 494–7.

184. Michael R. Marrus, *The Politics of Assimilation* (Oxford, 1971) pp. 54–5; Anne J. Kershen and Jonathan A. Romaine, *Tradition and Change: A History of Reform Judaism in Britain, 1840–1995* (London, 1995), pp. 71–9; Bill Williams, *The Making of Manchester Jewry, 1740–1875* (Manchester, 1976), pp. 92–3.

185. Rickie Burman ' "She looketh well to the ways of her household": The changing role of Jewish women in religious life, *c.*1880–1930', in Malmgreen (ed.), op. cit., pp. 245–6; Volkov, 'Verbürgerlichung', pp. 358–9.

318   NOTES

86. Geoffrey Alderman, *Modern British Jewry* (Oxford, 1992), pp. 86, 142–51.
187. Lloyd P. Garner, *The Jewish Immigrant in Britain, 1870–1914* (2nd edn, London, 1973), pp. 192–7.
188. Burman, op. cit., pp. 248–52.
189. David Sorkin, *The Transformation of German Jewry* (Oxford, 1987), pp. 122–3.
190. Volkov, 'Verbürgerlichung', pp. 354–8; Jacob Katz, 'German Culture and the Jews', in Jehuda Reinharz and Walter Schatzberg (eds), *The Jewish Response to German Culture* (Hanover, NH, 1985), pp. 88–9; Gerhard Besier, *Religion, Nation, Kultur: Die Geschichte der christlichen Kirchen in den gesellschaftlichen Umbrüchen des 19. Jahrhunderts* (Neukirchen-Vluyn 1992), pp. 62–3.
191. Volkov, 'Verbürgerlichung', pp. 359–61, p. 365.
192. Michael A. Meyer (ed.), *German-Jewish History in Modern Times* (New York, 1997) vol. 2, p. 323.
193. Todd M. Endelman, *Radical Assimilation in English Jewish History, 1656–1945* (Bloomington, IN, 1990), p. 81.
194. Ibid., pp. 94–113.
195. Ibid., pp. 128–40.
196. Todd M. Endelman, 'The Social and Political Context of Conversion in Germany and England, 1870–1914', in idem (ed.), *Jewish Apostasy in the Modern World* (New York, 1987), p. 85.
197. Katz, op. cit., p. 98.
198. Michael A. Meyer, *Jewish Identity in the Modern World* (Seattle, 1990), pp. 39–40; Endelman, 'Conversion', pp. 85–6.
199. Endelman, *Radical Assimilation*, pp. 98–113.
200. See, e.g., W. J. Fishman, *East End Jewish Radicals, 1875–1914* (London, 1975).
201. David Feldman, 'Immigrants and Workers, Englishmen and Jews: Jewish Immigrants in the East End of London 1880–1906' (University of Cambridge PhD thesis, 1985), pp. 316–24.
202. Paul Weindling, 'Jews in the Medical Profession in Britain and Germany', Michael Brenner et al. (eds), *Two Nations: British and German Jews in Comparative Perspective* (Tübingen, 1999), p. 403.
203. Meyer, *Jewish Identity*, pp. 19–20.

Notes to Chapter 4   Belief

1. Friedrich Saß, *Berlin in seiner neuesten Zeit und Entwicklung* (Berlin, 1983) [first published 1846], pp. 111–12.
2. For discussions of the literature of religious doubt, see Joseph N. Moody, *The Church as Enemy: Anticlericalism in Nineteenth Century French*

Literature (Washington, DC, 1968); Robert Lee Wolff, *Gains and Losses: Novels of Faith and Doubt in Victorian England* (New York, 1977).

3. Basil Willey, *More Victorian Studies: A Group of Honest Doubters* (London, 1956); James R. Moore, 'The Crisis of Faith: Reformation Versus Revolution', in Gerald Parsons, James R. Moore and John Wolffe (eds), *Religion in Victorian Britain*, 5 vols (Manchester, 1988–96), vol. II, pp. 220–37.

4. Timothy Hands, *Thomas Hardy: Distracted Preacher?* (London, 1989).

5. Thomas Hardy, *Tess of the d'Urbervilles* (London, 1912) [first published 1891], p. 153.

6. Frank M. Turner, 'The Victorian Crisis of Faith and the Faith that was lost', in Richard J. Helmstadter and Bernard Lightman (eds), *Victorian Faith in Crisis: Essays on Continuity and Change in Nineteenth-Century Religious Belief* (Basingstoke, 1990), pp. 9–38.

7. Gérard Cholvy and Yues-Marie Hilaire, *Histoire religieuse de la France cantemporarine*, vol. II: *1880–1930* (Toulouse, 1986), pp. 142–50.

8. See Bernard Lightman, 'Robert Elsmere and the Agnostic Crisis of Faith', in Helmstadter and Lightman (eds), op. cit., pp. 283–311.

9. Thomas Mergel, *Zwischen Klasse und Konfession* (Göttingen, 1994) pp. 281–2.

10. Moore, op. cit., pp. 228–32; George Gissing, *Born in Exile* (London, 1970) [first published 1892], p. 119.

11. Thomas Kselman, *Death and the Afterlife in Nineteenth Century France* (Princeton, NJ, 1993), p. 182; Wolfgang Emmerich (ed.), *Proletarische Lebensläufe*, 2 vols (Reinbek bei Hamburg, 1974) vol. I, p. 285.

12. Geoffrey Robson, 'Working Class Evangelists in Early Victorian Birmingham,' in Derek Baker (ed.), *Religious Motivation: Biographical and Sociological Problems for the Church Historian*, Studies in Church History, 15 (Oxford, 1978), p. 390.

13. Alfred Kelly, *The Descent of Darwin: The Popularization of Darwinism in Germany, 1860–1914* (Chapel Hill, NC, 1981), pp. 123–4.

14. The best discussion of this theme is Stephen Yeo, 'The Religion of Socialism', *History Workshop Journal*, 4 (1977), pp. 5–56.

15. Leonard Smith, *Religion and the Rise of Labour* (Keele, 1993), p. 41.

16. Sheridan Gilley, 'Catholics and Socialists in Glasgow, 1906–1912', in Kenneth Lunn (ed.), *Hosts, Immigrants and Minorities* (Folkestone, 1980), p. 186; Hugh McLeod, 'Religion in the British and German Labour Movements', *Bulletin of the Society for the Study of Labour History*, 50 (1986), p. 27.

17. See examples in Smith, op. cit., pp. 129–59.

18. Dieter Dowe, 'The Workingmen's Choral Movement in Germany before the First World War', *Journal of Contemporary History*, 13 (1978), p. 275.

19. Erich Schmidt, *Meine Jugend in Groß-Berlin* (Bremen, 1988), pp. 26–7.

20. D. G. Charlton, *Secular Religions in France, 1815–1870* (Oxford, 1963), pp. 47–53, 87–95; T. R. Wright, *The Religion of Humanity* (Cambridge).
21. Theodore Zeldin, *France 1848–1945* (Oxford, 1973–7), vol. I, pp. 624–5.
22. Charlton, op. cit., pp. 87–95.
23. Owen Chadwick, *The Secularization of the European Mind in the Nineteenth Century* (Cambridge, 1975), ch. 7; Kelly, op. cit., pp. 21–8.
24. Kelly, op. cit., pp. 36–56; Hugh McLeod, *Piety and Poverty* (New York, 1996) p. 27.
25. Kelly, op. cit., p. 132.
26. Émile Zola, *Paris* (English translation, Stroud 1993) [first published 1898], pp. 485–6. For Zola's 'reverence for science', see F. W. J. Hemmings, *Émile Zola* (2nd edn, Oxford, 1965), pp. 20–21, 55.
27. Turner, op. cit., p. 170.
28. Thomas Nipperdey, *Deutsche Geschichte, 1800–1866* (Munich, 1983), p. 496.
29. Eugen Weber, *Peasants into Frenchmen* (London, 1977), pp. 354–6.
30. Thomas Nipperdey, *Religion im Umbruch* (Munich, 1987), p. 142.
31. Arnold Horowitz, 'Prussian State and Protestant Church in the Reign of Wilhelm II' (Yale University PhD thesis, 1976), p. 218.
32. James Obelkevich, 'The Religion of Music', in James Obelkevich, Lyndal Roper and Raphael Samuel (eds), *Disciplines of Faith* (London, 1987), p. 562.
33. Theodor Fontane, *L'Adulterà* (1882), ch. 7.
34. Nipperdey, *Religion*, p. 141.
35. Lucian Hölscher, 'Bürgerliche Religiosität im protestantischen Deutschland des 19. Jahrhunderts', in Wolfgang Schieder (ed.), *Religion und Gesellschaft im 19. Jahrhundert* (Stuttgart, 1993), pp. 208–13. The cult of Goethe and Schiller caused considerable misgivings among conservative Protestants. See Christel Köhle-Hezinger, *Evangelisch-Katholisch* (Tübingen, 1976), p. 288.
36. John Breuilly, 'The Schiller Centenary of 1859 in Hamburg' (unpublished paper). I am very grateful to John Breuilly for allowing me to read this paper.
37. Gangolf Hübinger, 'Kulturprotestantismus, Bürgerkirche und liberaler Revisionismus im Wilhelminischen Deutschland', in Schieder (ed.), op. cit., p. 280.
38. Richard Aldington, *Death of a Hero*, unexpurgated edition (London, 1965), p. 222.
39. Richard Aldington, *Life for Life's Sake* (London, 1968) [first published 1941], p. 78.
40. Mrs Humphry Ward, *Robert Elsmere* (London, 1952) [first published 1888], pp. 90–1.

41. Kselman, *Death and the Afterlife*, pp. 150–9.
42. Logie Barrow, *Independent Spirits: Spiritualism and English Plebeians, 1850–1910* (London, 1986), pp. 4–29.
43. Frank Turner, *Between Science and Religion: The Reaction to Scientific Naturalism in Late Victorian England* (New Haven, CT, 1974), pp. 108–11; Barrow, op. cit., pp. 126–7, 213–17; H. Freimark, *Moderne Geisterbeschwörer und Wahrheitssucher*, Großstadt-Dokumente 38 (Berlin, n.d.), p. 51. See also S. C. Williams, *Religious Belief and Popular Culture in Southwark, c. 1880–1939* (Oxford, 1999), p. 82. For the role of wise men in nineteenth-century rural England, see Obelkevich, op. cit., pp. 287–91, 309–10.
44. Turner, op. cit.
45. Mark Bevir, 'Annie Besant's Quest for Truth: Christianity, Secularism and New Age Thought', *Journal of Ecclesiastical History*, 50 (1999), pp. 83–7.
46. Chushichi Tsuzuki, *Edward Carpenter, 1844–1929: Prophet of Human Fellowship* (Cambridge, 1980).
47. Nipperdey, *Religion* p. 143; see also Andreas Daum, 'Naturwissenschaften und Öffentlichkeit in der deutschen Gesellschaft: Zu den Anfängen einer Populärwissenschaft nach der Revolution von 1848', *Historische Zeitschift*, 267 (1998), pp. 85–6, which notes a tendency among German popular-scientific writers 'to sacralise nature itself, and to give nature-worship the character of a substitute religion'.
48. Edward Royle, *Radicals, Secularists and Republicans* (Manchester, 1980) pp. 132–6.
49. Ibid., p. 133.
50. See Susan Budd, *Varieties of Unbelief* (London, 1977).
51. Jacqueline Lalouette, *La libre pensée en France, 1848–1940* (Paris, 1997), pp. 25–44.
52. Ibid., pp. 99–103.
53. Frank Simon-Rits, 'Kulturelle Modernisierung und Krise der religiösen Bewußtseins', in Olaf Blaschke and Frank-Michael Kuhlemann (eds), *Religion im Kaiserreich* (Gütersloh, 1996) pp. 460–1.
54. Ibid., pp. 463–5; Lucian Hölscher, *Weltgericht oder Revolution* (Stuttgart, 1989), pp. 169–73.
55. Jochen-Christoph Kaiser, 'Sozialdemokratie und "praktische" Religionskritik', *Archiv für Sozialgeschichte*, 22 (1982), p. 284.
56. Simon-Rits, op. cit., p. 468.
57. C. F. G. Masterman, *The Condition of England* (London, 1909), pp. 88–9.
58. Thomas Kselman, 'The Varieties of Religious Experience in Urban France', in Hugh McLeod (ed.), *European Religion in the Age of Great Cities* (London, 1995), pp. 175–9.
59. W. L. Courtney (ed.), *Do We Believe?* (London, 1905), pp. 2–13.
60. Ibid., pp. 96–7.

61. Ibid., pp. 136–7.
62. Ibid., p. 245.
63. Williams, op. cit., pp. 85–6 and *passim*.
64. Michael Watts, *The Dissenters*, vol. 2: *The Expansion of Evangelical Nonconformity, 1791–1859* (Oxford, 1995), pp. 103–10; Barrow, op. cit., p. 12.

Notes to Chapter 5   Going to Church

1. Lucian Hölscher, 'Die Religion des Bürgers', *Historische Zeitschrift*, 250 (1990) pp. 597–603; R. Gibson, *A Social History of French Catholicism, 1789–1914* (London, 1989) pp. 1–2; Jean Delumeau, *Le catholicisme entre Luther et Voltaire* (Paris, 1971), pp. 308–16; G. V. Bennett, 'The Conflict in the Church', in Geoffrey Holmes (ed.), *England after the Glorious Revolution* (London, 1969), pp. 157–65.
2. Lucian Hölscher, 'Möglichkeiten und Grenzen der statistischen Erfassung kirchlicher Bindungen', in Kaspar Elm and Hans-Dietrich Loock (eds), *Seelsorge und Diakonie: Beiträge zum Verhältnis von Kirche und Großstadt im 19. und beginnenden 20. Jahrhundert* (Berlin, 1990), pp. 39–59.
3. Samuel Butler, *The Way of All Flesh* (London, 1966) [first published, 1903], p. 94.
4. Thomas Wright, *The Great Unwashed* (London, 1868), as quoted in Gerald Parsons, James R. Moore and John Wolffe (eds), *Religion in Victorian Britain*, 5 vols (Manchester, 1988–96), 3, pp. 321–2; Sarah C. Williams, *Religious Belief and Popular Culture in Southwark, c.1880–1939* (Oxford, 1999).
5. E.g., Roger Magraw, 'Popular Anticlericalism in Nineteenth-Century Rural France', in James Obelkevich, Lyndal Roper and Raphael Samuel (eds), *Disciplines of Faith* (London, 1987), p. 361.
6. For discussion of reasons for low rates of participation in communion in England, see James Obelkevich, *Religion and Rural Society: South Lindsey 1825–1875* (Oxford, 1976), pp. 137–43, 271–2; Frances Knight, *The Nineteenth-Century Church and English Society* (Cambridge, 1995), pp. 35–6, 53–7, 81, 95, 203.
7. For instance, Antonius Liedhegener, *Christentum und Urbanisierung: Katholiken und Protestanten in Münster und Bochum, 1830–1933* (Paderborn, 1997), pp. 584–6, partly attributes the decline of Protestant practice, at a time when the Catholic figures remained fairly stable, to the fact that Protestant teaching tended to relativise the church, leading to an attitude of religious individualism.
8. Michael R. Watts, *The Dissenters*, vol. 2: *The Expansion of Evangelical Nonconformity* (Oxford, 1995), pp. 682–712; Ralph Gibson, *A Social History of French Catholicism, 1789–1914* (London, 1989), pp. 174–6;

Lucian Hölscher, *Weltgericht oder Revolution* (Stuttgart, 1989), p. 143; Lucian Hölscher and Ursula Männich-Polenz, 'Die Sozialstruktur der Kirchengemeinden Hannovers im 19. Jahrhundert. Eine statistische Analyse', *Jahrbuch der Gesellschaft für niedersächsische Kirchengeschichte*, 88 (1990), pp. 159–217.

9. Todd M. Endelman, *Radical Assimilation in English Jewish History, 1656–1945* (Bloomington, IN, 1990), pp. 94–7; L. P. Gartner, *The Jewish Immigrant in Britain, 1870–1914* (London, 1973), pp. 192–7; David Feldman, 'Immigrants and workers, Englishmen and Jews' (University of Cambridge PhD thesis, 1985), pp. 287–9; Hugh McLeod, *Piety and Poverty* (New York, 1996) pp. 160, 163.

10. Michael A. Meyer, *Response to Modernity* (Detroit, MI, 1995), pp. 53–61; Michael R. Marrus, *The Politics of Assimilation* (Oxford, 1971), p. 57; Elaine R. Smith, 'Jews and Politics in the East End of London', in David Cesarani (ed.), *The Making of Modern Anglo-Jewry* (Oxford, 1990), pp. 142–4.

11. Yves-Marie Hilaire, *Une chrétienté an XIXe siècle?* (Lille, 1997) II, p. 575.

12. E. Rolffs, *Das kirchliche Leben der evangelischen Kirchen in Niedersachsen* (Tübingen, 1917), pp. 567–8.

13. Alan D. Gilbert, *Religion and Society in Industrial England* (London, 1976), pp. 98–103.

14. Hölscher, *Weltgericht*, p. 148; idem., 'Secular Culture and Religious Community in the City: Hannover in the 19th Century', *Hispania Sacra*, 42 (1990), p. 407; idem., 'Säkularisierungsprozesse', in Hans-Jurgen Pühle (ed.), *Bürger in der Gesellschaft der Neuzeit* (Göttingen, 1991), p. 244.

15. Jürgen Boeckh, 'Predigt in Berlin', in Elm and Loock (eds), op. cit., p. 312; Franz Schnabel, *Deutsche Geschichte im 19. Jahrhundert*, vol. 4: *Die Religiösen Kräfte* (Freiburg im Breisgau, 1937), pp. 570–1.

16. Hölscher, 'Säkularisierungsprozesse', pp. 243–9.

17. Wolfgang Ribbe, 'Zur Entwicklung und Funktion der Pfarrgemeinden in der evangelischen Kirche Berlins bis zum Ende der Monarchie', in Elm and Loock (eds), op. cit., pp. 233–63.

18. Hölscher, 'Säkularisierungsprozesse', pp. 241–52.

19. Rudolf Schlögl, *Glaube und Religion in der Säkularisierung* (Munich, 1995).

20. During the Revolution, the area round La Rochelle was said to be the first in France where some parents gave up baptising their children, and during the Second Empire the proportion of adolescents missing their First Communion and of couples having an exclusively civil wedding, appears to have been among the highest in France. F. Boulard, *Introduction to Religious Sociology* (English translation, London, 1960), pp. 29–31; Gérard Cholvy and Yves-Marie Hilaire, *Histoire religieuse de la France contemporaine*, vol. I: *1800–1880* (Toulouse, 1990), pp. 295–6.

21. Cholvy and Hilaire, ibid., pp. 27–8.
22. Gérard Cholvy, *Religion et société au XIXe Siècle: Le diocèse de Montpellier*, (Lille, 1973) i, p. 136; Michel Lagrée, *Mentalités, religion et histoire en Haute Bretagne au XIXe siècle* (Paris, 1977), pp. 79–83.
23. Gibson, *Social History of French Catholicism*, pp. 195–9.
24. Olwen Hufton, *Bayeux in the Late Eighteenth Century* (London, 1967), pp. 191–2.
25. Cholvy and Hilaire, op. cit., pp. 274–8.
26. See, e.g, McLeod, *Piety and Poverty*, pp. 104–5, citing examples from working-class areas of Berlin.
27. Philippe Boutry, *Prêtres et paroisses au pays du Curé d'Ars* (Paris, 1986), pp. 649–51.
28. Hölscher, *Weltgericht*, p. 143.
29. Gibson, *Social History of French Catholicism*, pp. 227–32.
30. See the contrasting regional profiles in Cholvy and Hilaire, *Histoire religieuse, 1880–1930*, pp. 185–218.
31. Hugh McLeod, *Religion and Society in England, 1850–1914* (Basingstoke, 1996), pp. 169–96.
32. Hugh McLeod, *Class and Religion in the Late Victorian City* (London, 1974), pp. 25–8. More scattered evidence suggests that religious belief and practice have continued to correlate positively with higher levels of education and social status. Mass Observation, *Puzzled People* (London, 1947), pp. 28–9, reported that in a sample of 500 interviewed in London, 66 per cent of those with secondary education, and 41 per cent of those with only elementary education, believed in some form of afterlife. A recent enquiry into the beliefs of MPs found that 54 per cent of Conservative MPs and 38 per cent of Labour MPs claimed to be practising a religion, which is considerably higher than the figure for the adult population as a whole (*New Statesman and Society*, 30 September and 7 October 1994). A survey of mass attendance by Catholics in England and Wales in 1968, suggested that the rate was highest (62 per cent) for the professional and managerial middle class and lowest (36 per cent) for the unskilled and semi-skilled working class (Ivan Reid, *Social Class Differences in Britain* (London, 1977), pp. 205–8).
33. See F. Boulard and J. Rémy, *Pratique religieuse urbaine et régions culturelles* (Paris, 1968).
34. Geoffrey Robson, 'Religion and Irreligion in Birmingham and the Black Country' (University of Birmingham PhD thesis, 1997), pp. 81, 95–6.
35. Liedhegener, op. cit.
36. Gilbert, op. cit., p. 186. See also Alan D. Gilbert, *The Making of Post-Christian Britain: A History of the Secularization of Modern Society* (London, 1980).

37. For the religious attitudes of nineteenth-century businessmen, see, e.g., Gibson, *Social History of French Catholicism*, pp. 199–216; Colin Heywood, 'The Catholic Church and the Business Community in Nineteenth-Century France', in Frank Tallett and Nicholas Atken (eds), *Religion, Society and Politics in France since 1789* (London, 1991), pp. 67–88; Jane Garnett, 'Evangelicalism and Business in Mid-Victorian Britain', in John Wolffe (ed.), *Evangelical Faith and Public Zeal: Evangelicals and Society in Britain, 1780–1980* (London, 1995), pp. 59–80; David Jeremy (ed.), *Business and Religion in Britain* (Aldershot, 1988); David Jeremy (ed.), *Religion, Business and Wealth in Modern Britain* (London, 1998).

38. Hugh McLeod, 'Protestantism and the Working Class in Imperial Germany', *European Studies Review*, 12 (1982), p. 325.

39. Paul Drews, *Das kirchliche Leben der Evangelisch-Lutherischen Landeskirche des Königreichs Sachsen* (Tübingen, 1902), P. 22; P. Pieper, *Kirchenstatistik Deutschlands* (Freiburg im Breisgau, 1899), pp. 150–54; Hugh McLeod, 'Introduction', in idem. (ed.), *European Religion in the Age of Great Cities* (London, 1995), p. 11.

40. Anthony Steinhoff, 'Protestants in Strasbourg, 1870–1914' (University of Chicago PhD thesis, 1996), pp. 760–3, 790–4.

41. Fernand Charpin, *Pratique religieuse urbaine et formation d'une grande ville (Marseille 1806–1958)* (Paris, 1964); Mary Nolan, *Social Democracy and Society: Working Class Radicalism in Düsseldorf, 1890–1920* (Cambridge, 1987); p. 51; Raymond Sun, ' "Before the Enemy is within our Walls": a Social, Cultural and Political History of Catholic Workers in Cologne, 1895–1912' (Johns Hopkins University PhD, 1991), pp. 259–61.

42. See, for instance, the overview in David Hempton, *Religion and Political Culture in Britain and Ireland* (Cambridge, 1996), ch. 6, and the intensive local study of Protestantism in Strasbourg in Steinhoff, op. cit.

43. Yves-Marie Hilaire, 'Les ouvriers de la région du Nord devant l'Église catholique (XIXᵉ et XXᵉ siècles)', in F. Bédarida and J. Maitron (eds), *Christianisme et monde ouvrier* (Paris, 1975), pp. 230–3.

44. Gilbert, op. cit., pp. 125–38. However, his claim (p. 138) that 'a higher proportion of the English population practised Anglicanism in 1914 than in 1830' (p. 138) is not a 'fact', but a guess based on what must be fairly tentative estimates (see pp. 28, 222).

45. Hempton, op. cit., pp. 128–42.

46. Robin Gill, *The Myth of the Empty Church* (London, 1993), pp. 136–7, 305.

47. See, e.g., the chapters by Gerard Connolly, Sheridan Gilley and Raphael Samuel in Roger Swift and Sheridan Gilley (eds), *The Irish in the Victorian City* (London, 1985); Steven Fielding, *Class and Ethnicity: Irish Catholics in England, 1880–1939* (Buckingham, 1993), chs 3–4; Liedhegener, op. cit.

48. Hilaire, *Une chrétienté?*, vol. II, pp. 629–61.
49. Hilaire, 'Les ouvriers du Nord', pp. 233–8.
50. Robert Moore, *Pit-men, Preachers and Politics* (London, 1974).
51. This statement is tentative, because the issue is ignored by most of the literature. Its potential interest and significance are indicated in a pioneering essay by Krista Cowman, '"We intend to show what Our Lord has done for women": The Liverpool Church League for Women's Suffrage, 1913–18', in R. N. Swanson (ed.), *Gender and the Christian Religion*, Studies in Church History 34 (Woodbridge, 1998), pp. 475–86.
52. Gibson, *Social History of French Catholicism*, ch. 6; Boulard and Rémy, op. cit., showed that in the 1950s and 1960s the differences *between* towns in levels of religious practice had diminished, but that the differences *within* towns between the practice of those belonging to different social classes remained large.
53. Louis Pérouas, *Refus d'une religion* (Paris, 1985), pp. 50–1, 59–65, 67–78, 130–6, 193–8.
54. Jean-Pierre Chaline, *Les bourgeois de Rouen: Une élite urbaine au XIXe siècle* (Paris, 1982), ch. 8.
55. Ibid., p. 265.
56. Cf. Robert Anderson, 'The Conflict in Education', in Theodore Zeldin, (ed.), *Conflicts in French Society* (London, 1970), p. 59.
57. Chaline, op. cit., pp. 273, 404.
58. McLeod, *Piety and Poverty*, pp. 5, 9–10, 86.
59. Jonathan Sperber, *Rhineland Radicals* (Princeton, NJ, 1991). pp. 365–80.
60. Herwart Vorländer, *Evangelische Kirche und soziale Frage in der werdenden Industriegroßstadt Elberfeld* (Düsseldorf, 1963), pp. 41–8, 52–4; Wolfgang Köllmann, *Sozialgeschichte der Stadt Barmen* (Tübingen, 1960), pp. 150–3, 198–212.
61. Nigel Scotland, *Agricultural Trade Unionism in Gloucestershire, 1872–1950* (Cheltenham, 1991), pp. 37–8.
62. Eugenio F. Biagini, *Liberty, Retrenchment and Reform: Popular Liberalism in the Age of Gladstone, 1860–1880* (Cambridge, 1992), pp. 248–51.
63. Pamela Horn, 'The Labourers' Union in Oxfordshire', in J. P. Dunbabin (ed.), *Rural Discontent in Nineteenth-Century Britain* (London, 1974), p. 97; Clive Field, 'A godly people? Aspects of Religious Practice in the Diocese of Oxford, 1738–1936', *Southern History*, 14 (1992) pp. 58–9, 65–6; E. N. Bennett, *Problems of Village Life* (London, 1913), pp. 129–31.
64. Owen Chadwick, *The Victorian Church* (London, 1966–70), vol. II, p. 156.
65. Nigel Scotland, *Methodism and the Revolt of the Field* (Gloucester, 1981), pp. 57–74.
66. E. T. Davies, *Religion in the Industrial Revolution in South Wales* (Cardiff, 1965), pp. 160–1.

67. Cyril Gwyther, 'Sidelights on Religion and Politics in the Rhondda Valley, 1906–26', *Llafur*, 3 (1980), pp. 36–43; Stuart Macintyre, *Little Moscows* (London, 1980); Kenneth O. Morgan, *Rebirth of a Nation: Wales 1880–1980* (Oxford 1981), pp. 193–9.

68. McLeod, *Piety and Poverty*, pp. 111, 115, 143–5, 156; A. Ainsworth, 'Religion in the Working Class Community and the Evolution of Socialism in Later Nineteenth Century Lancashire', *Histoire Sociale*, 10 (1977), pp. 354–80; Dan Weinbren, 'Building Communities, Constructing Identities: the Rise of the Labour Party in London', *London Journal*, 23 (1998), pp. 48–9; Geoffrey Alderman, *The Jewish Community in British Politics* (Oxford, 1983), pp. 105–7, 115; on the complex relationship between Catholics and the labour movement in Manchester see Fielding, op. cit., chs 5–6.

69. For a brief overview see Patrick Joyce, *Work, Society and Politics* (Brighton, 1980), pp. 331–42; for an extended discussion, Stephen Yeo, *Religion and Voluntary Organisations in Crisis* (London, 1976).

70. Stefan Berger, *The British Labour Party and the German Social Democrats* (Oxford, 1994), pp. 133–172.

71. Drews, op. cit., p. 89; P. Wurster, *Das kirchliche Leben der evangelischen Landeskirche in Württemberg* (Tübingen, 1919), pp. 78–88.

72. Rainer Marbach, *Säkularisierung und sozialer Wandel im 19. Jahrhundert* (Göttingen 1978), pp. 125–7, 131–48, 160.

73. Roger Thabault, *Mon village* (Paris, 1945), p. 193 and *passim*.

74. McLeod, *Religion and Society*, pp. 170–9.

75. McLeod, *Piety and Poverty*, p. 33.

76. W. Gascoyne-Cecil, 'The Old Squire and the New', in W. K. Lowther-Clarke (ed.), *Facing the Facts: The Englishman's Religion* (London, 1911), pp. 43–54.

77. McLeod, *Class and Religion*, pp. 220–2, 235–6 304; Gunilla-Frederike Budde, *Auf dem Weg ins Bürgerleben* (Göttingén, 1994), p. 386. See also McLeod, *Religion and Society*, p. 65, which suggests levels of middle-class church-going around the end of the nineteenth century which are still very high, though not as high as in Budde's sample: Paul Thompson and Thea Vigne interviewed some 500 men and women born in Britain between 1872 and 1909. Of those brought up in English middle-class families, 75 per cent stated that their mother had been a regular church-goer in their childhood, and 60 per cent that their father had been (see McLeod, *Religion and Society*, for full details).

78. McLeod, *Class and Religion*, ch. 8; idem., *Religion and Society*, ch. 4.

79. Chadwick, *Victorian Church*, vol. II, p. 249; Robert Currie, Alan Gilbert and Lee Horsley, *Churches and Churchgoers* (Oxford, 1977), pp. 203–12.

80. Alan Bennett Bartlett, 'The Churches in Bermondey, 1880–1939' (University of Birmingham PhD thesis, 1987), p. 178; J. N. Morris,

Religion and Urban Change: Croydon, 1890–1914 (Woodbridge, 1992), pp. 182–3.

81. McLeod, *Class and Religion*, pp. 239–42, 254–5.

82. Gibson, *Social History of French Catholicism*, p. 237.

83. Caroline Ford, *Creating the Nation in Provincial France: Religion and Political Identity in Brittany* (Princeton, NJ, 1993), pp. 73, 135–69.

84. Annemarie Burger, *Religionszugehörigkeit und soziales Verhalten* (Göttingen, 1964), pp. 350–9.

85. Johannes Schauff, *Das Wahlverhalten der deutschen Katholiken* (Mainz, 1975) [first published 1928], pp. 137–41.

86. See Werner Blessing, *Staat und Kirche in der Gesellschaft* (Göttingen, 1982), pp. 192–5; Sun, op. cit., p. 261, 506.

87. Jonathan Sperber, 'Roman Catholic Religious Identity in Rhineland-Westphalia, 1800–70', *Social History*, 7 (1982) pp. 305–18; idem., *Popular Catholicism*, pp. 64–73, 83–5, 91–8.

88. Schlögl, op. cit., pp. 80–109, 179–95.

89. Sperber, 'Roman Catholic Religious Identity'; Jürgen Herres, *Städtische Gesellschaft und katholische Vereine im Rheinland, 1840–1870* (Koblenz, 1996).

90. Thomas Mergel, *Zwischen Klasse und Konfession* (Göttingen, 1994), pp. 169–70.

91. Thomas Mergel, 'Die subtile Macht der Liebe: Geschlecht, Erziehung und Frömmigkeit in katholischen rheinischen Bürgerfamilien', in Irmtraud Götz von Olenhusen et al. (eds), *Frauen unter dem Patriarchat der Kirchen* (Stuttgart, 1995), pp. 29–30.

92. Sperber, *Popular Catholicism*, p. 64.

93. Ibid., p. 256.

94. Nolan, op. cit., p. 179.

95. Jonathan Sperber, *The Kaiser's Voters* (Cambridge, 1997), pp. 361–3. Many historians have suggested higher estimates of the proportion of Catholics voting Centre in 1874, and a substantial subsequent decline. This overlooks the fact that a far higher proportion of Catholics than Protestants voted in 1874, so that the extent of Catholic support for the Centre cannot be deduced by simply comparing the percentage of voters choosing the Centre with the percentage of Catholics in the electorate (ibid., p. 170).

96. Josef Mooser, 'Das katholische Milieu in der bürgerlichen Gesellschaft: Zum Vereinswesen des Katholizismus im späten Kaiserreich', in Olaf Blaschke and Frank-Michael Kuhlemann (eds), *Religion im Kaiserreich* (Gütersloh, 1996), p. 75.

97. Josef Mooser, 'Katholische Volksreligion, Klerus und Bürgertum in der zweiten Hälfte des 19. Jahrhunderts. Thesen', in Wolfgang Schieder (ed.), *Religion und Gesellschaft im 19. Jahrhundert* (Stuttgart, 1993), pp. 151–2; Hans-Jürgen Brand, 'Kirchliches Vereinswesen und Freizeitgestaltungen

in einer Arbeitergemeinde, 1872–1933', G. Huck (ed.), *Sozialgeschichte der Freizeit* (Wuppertal, 1980), pp. 211–13, 221.

98. Margaret Lavinia Anderson, 'The Limits of Secularization: On the Problem of the Catholic Revival in Nineteenth-century Germany', *Historical Journal*, 38 (1993), p. 651.

99. Christel Köhle-Hezinger, *Evangelisch-Katholisch: Untersuchungen zu Konfessionellem Vorurteil und Konflikt im 19. und 20. Jahrhundert vornehmlich am Beispiel Württembergs* (Tübingen, 1976) pp. 104, 128, 136, 265–78, 379, and *passim*, discusses the minority-consciousness and the sense of Protestant 'dominance' among Catholics in Württemberg, which was rife throughout the nineteenth century, and still to some extent persisted at the time of her research in the early 1970s.

100. See, e.g., Sperber, *Rhineland Radicals*, pp. 78–9.

101. Ilse Fischer, *Industrialisierung, sozialer Konflikt und politische Willensbildung in der Stadtgemeinde* (Augsburg, 1977), p. 225.

102. Köhle-Hezinger, op. cit., pp. 134–46; David Blackbourn, *Marpingen: Apparitions of the Virgin Mary in Bismarckian Germany* (Oxford, 1993), p. 295; Heinz Blankenberg, *Politischer Katholizismus in Frankfurt am Main, 1918–33* (Mainz, 1981), pp. 13–14; Mary Lee Townsend, *Forbidden Laughter* (Ann Arbor MI, 1992), pp. 139–48; Ronald J. Ross, *The Failure of Bismarck's Kulturkampf* (Washington, DC, 1998), pp. 25–6.

103. Hugh McLeod, 'Building the "Catholic Ghetto": Catholic Organisations 1870–1914', in W. J. Sheils and Diana Wood (eds), *Voluntary Religion*, Studies in Church History 23 (Oxford, 1986), pp. 411–44.

104. Olaf Blaschke, 'Die Kolonialisierung der Laienwelt: 'Priester als Milieumanager' und die Kanale klerikaler Kuratel', in Blaschke and Kuhlemann (eds), op. cit., p. 96; McLeod, *Religion and the People*, pp. 51–3.

105. McLeod, ' "Catholic Ghetto" ', pp. 424–7; Vernon L. Lidtke, *The Alternative Culture* (New York, 1985), pp. 112–14.

106. Blaschke, 'Priester als Milieumanager', pp. 98–101.

107. Ibid.; Anderson, 'Limits of Secularization', pp. 656–63. Anderson's article is partly a critique of Wolfgang Schieder and historians influenced by him. Schieder in turn has counter-attacked, emphasising the distance between priests and people, the tightness of episcopal control over the clergy, and the degree to which most initiatives within German Catholicism came 'from above'. See his paper 'Konfessionelle Erneuerung in den christlichen Parallelkirchen Deutschlands im 19. Jahrhundert', in Hartmut Lehmann (ed.), *Säkularisierung, Dechristianisierung, Rechristianisierung im neuzeitlichen Europe* (Göttingen, 1997), pp. 223–8.

108. E. D. Brose, 'Christian Labor and the Politics of Frustration in Imperial Germany' (Ohio State University PhD thesis, 1978), pp. 45–52.

109. Klaus Michael Mallmann, ' "Aus des Tages Last machen sie ein Kreuz des Herrn ..."? Bergarbeiter, Religion und sozialer Protest im

Saarrevier des 19. Jahrhunderts', in Wolfgang Schieder (ed.), *Volksreligiosität in der modernen Sozialgeschichte* (Göttingen, 1986), pp. 167–77.
110. Mergel, 'Die subtile Macht', pp. 22–3; Blessing op. cit., pp. 192–5.
111. Mallmann, op. cit.; W. von Hippel, 'Industrieller Wandel im ländlichen Raum', *Archiv für Sozialgeschichte*, 19 (1979), pp. 43–122.
112. Thomas Mergel, 'Ultramontanism, Liberalism, Moderation: Political Mentalities and Political Behavior of the German Catholic *Bürgertum*, 1848–1914', *Central European History*, 29 (1996), pp. 151–74; Oded Heilbronner, 'In Search of the (Rural) Catholic Bourgeoisie: The *Bürgertum* of South Germany', ibid., pp. 175–200.
113. Blessing, op. cit., pp. 23–7, 34–8; Ian Farr, 'From Anti-Catholicism to Anticlericalism: Catholic Politics and the Peasantry in Bavaria, 1860–1900', *European Studies Review*, 13 (1983).
114. Blessing, op. cit., pp. 194–5.
115. Karl-Heinrich Pohl, 'Katholische Sozialdemokraten oder sozialdemokratische Katholiken in München: Ein Identitätskonflikt', in Blaschke and Kuchemann, op. cit., p. 235.
116. Blessing, op. cit., p. 249, note 349.
117. Pohl, op. cit., p. 236.
118. Roger Martin du Gard, *Jean Barois* (Paris, 1921), p. 369.
119. Gibson, *Social History of French Catholicism*, pp. 231–2.
120. Yves-Marie Hilaire, 'Observations sur la pratique religieuse urbaine en France pendant la première moitié du XXe siècle', *Hispania Sacra*, 42 (1990), pp. 462–3.
121. Cholvy and Hilaire, *Histoire religieuse, 1880–1930*, p. 157. See also James F. McMillan, 'Women in Social Catholicism in late Nineteenth- and Early Twentieth Century France', in W. J. Sheils and Diana Wood (eds), *Women in the Church*, Studies in Church History 27 (Oxford, 1990), pp. 467–80.
122. Cholvy and Hilaire, *Histoire religieuse, 1880–1930*, p. 162.
123. Ibid., pp. 139–69; Richard Griffiths, *The Reactionary Revolution: The Catholic Revival In French Literature, 1870–1914* (New York, 1965); John McManners, *Church and State in France, 1870–1914* (London, 1972), ch. 12.
124. Hilaire, 'Observations', pp. 461–3.

Notes to Chapter 6   Identity

1. Theodor Fontane, *Romane und Gedichte* (Munich, n.d.), pp. 873, 968, 1022, 91–2, 101; Ronald J. Ross, *Beleaguered Tower: The Dilemma of Political Catholicism in Wilhelmine Germany* (Notre Dame, IN, 1976), p. 1.
2. Ernst Rudolf Huber, *Deutsche Verfassungsgeschichte seit 1789*, 4 vols (Stuttgart, 1957–69), vol. IV, pp. 714–15, gives details of the Prussian

law of 1873. For broader discussion of the extent of and reasons for leaving the church, see Horst Ermel, *Die Kirchenuastrittsbewegung im Deutschen Reich 1906–14* (dissertation, Cologne University 1971); Jochen-Christoph Kaiser, 'Sozialdemokratie und "praktische" Religionskritik: Das Beispiel der Kirchenaustrittsbewegung 1878–1914', *Archir für Sozialgeschichte*, 22 (1982).

3. Two useful discussions of the ways in which distinctive forms of worship and devotion helped to shape sharply defined religious identities are Anthony Steinhoff, 'Protestants in Strasbourg, 1870–1914' (University of Chicago PhD thesis, 1996), pp. 461–7 and *passim*; Norbert Busch, 'Frömmigkeit als Faktor des katholischen Milieus: Der Kult zum Herzen-Jesu', in Olaf Blaschke and Frank-Michael Kuhlemann (eds), *Religion im Kaiserreich* (Gütersloh, 1996), pp. 136–65.

4. Christel Köhle-Hezinger, *Evangelisch-Katholisch: Untersuchungen zu konfessianellem Vorurteil und Konflikt im 19 und 20. Jahrhundert vornehmhich am Beispiel Württembergs* (Tübingen, 1976), pp. 99–110.

5. Gibson, *Social History of French Catholicism*, pp. 165–6.

6. See Thomas Walter Laqueur, *Religion and Respectability: Sunday Schools and Working Class Culture, 1780–1850* (New Haven, CT, 1976); Hugh McLeod, *Religion and Society in England, 1850–1914* (London, 1996), pp. 78–82.

7. Gunilla-Frederike Budde, *Auf dem Weg ins Bürgerleben* (Göttingen, 1994), pp. 380, 397–8.

8. Hugh McLeod, 'New Persepctives on Victorian Working Class Religion: the Oral Evidence', *Oral History Journal*, 14 (1986), p. 43, citing interview no. 9 by Alan Bartlett in the Bartlett Oral History Collection, in Southwark Local History Library.

9. James Munson, *The Nonconformists* (London, 1991), pp. 207–8, 250, 263–76.

10. Hugh McLeod, 'White-Collar Values and the Role of Religion', in Geoffrey Crossick (ed.), *The Lower Middle Class in Britain, 1870–1914* (London, 1977), p. 75, citing interview no. 250, p. 50, in Paul Thompson and Thea Vigne, 'Interviews on Family Life and Work Experience before 1918', University of Essex Oral History Archive.

11. Marion Kaplan, *The Making of the Jewish Midde Class: Women, Family and Identity in Imperial Germany* (New York, 1991) pp. 69–79.

12. Todd M. Endelman, *Radical Assimilation in English Jewish History, 1656–1945* (Bloomington, IN, 1990), pp. 207–8.

13. Michael R. Marrus, *The Politics of Assimilation: A Study of the French Jewish Community at the Time of the Dreyfus Affair* (Oxford, 1971), pp. 41–5.

14. Peter Hönigmann, *Die Austritte aus der Jüdischen Gemeinde Berlin, 1873–1941* (Frankfurt am Main, 1988), p. 109.

15. Annemarie Burger, *Religionszugehörigkeit und soziales Verhalten* (Göttingen, 1964), p. 343.

16. Endelman, *Radical Assimilation*, pp. 86–92, 98–113.
17. Monika Richarz, *Jüdisches Leben in Deutschland*, 3 vols (Stuttgart, 1979), vol. II, p. 50. Similarly, Andrea Hopp, 'Von der "heiligen Gemeinde" zur Vielfalt der ethnisch-religiösen Minderheit: Die jüdische Gemeinde in Frankfurt am Main', in Blaschke and Kuhlemann (eds), op. cit., pp. 450–1, cites examples from the later nineteenth and early twentieth centuries of non-observant Jewish businessmen in Frankfurt who rejected baptism as 'dishonourable' and 'deserting the flag'.
18. Alfred Wahl, 'Confession et comportement dans les campagnes d'Alsace et de Bade', 2 vols (University of Metz doctoral thesis, 1980) vol. II, p. 784.
19. McLeod, 'New Perspectives', p. 43; Elizabeth Roberts, *A Woman's Place: An Oral History of Working Class Women, 1890–1940* (Oxford, 1984), pp. 73–4.
20. Köhle-Hezinger, op. cit., p. 134.
21. McLeod, 'New Perspectives', p. 42; Wahl, 'Confession', I, pp. 385–7, 614–5.
22. Wahl, 'Confession', I, pp. 618–21; Raphael Samuel, 'The Roman Catholic Church and the Irish Poor', in Roger Swift and Sheridan Gilley (eds), *The Irish in the Victorian City* (London, 1985) pp. 283–4.
23. McLeod, 'New Perspectives', pp. 38, 42; Hugh McLeod, *Piety and Poverty* (New York, 1996) pp. 143–4.
24. Wahl, 'Confession', vol. I, pp. 546–7.
25. Uriel Tal, *Christians and Jews in Germany: Religion, Politics and Ideology in the Second Reich, 1870–1914* (English translation, Ithaca, NY, 1975), pp. 242–3.
26. Jonathan Sperber, *The Kaiser's Voters* (Cambridge, 1997), p. 213.
27. E.-D. Broch, *Katholische Arbeitervereine in der Stadt Köln, 1890–1901* (Hamburg, 1977), pp. 98–102.
28. Hugh McLeod, ' "Building the Catholic Ghetto" ', in Sheils and Wood (eds), *Voluntary Religion*, Studies in Church History 23 (Oxford, 1986), pp. 424–6.
29. Shulamit Volkov, 'Antisemitism as a cultural code: Reflections on the history and historiography of antisemitism in Imperial Germany', *Yearbook of the Leo Baeck Institute*, 23 (1978) pp. 25–46.
30. Günter Brakelmann, Martin Greschat and Werner Jochmann, *Protestantismus und Politik. Werk und Wirkung Adolf Stoeckers* (Hamburg, 1982), pp. 41–5, 90–1, 96–104, shows that for Stoecker the greatest enemy was liberalism, and that his anti-Semitic agitation initially stemmed from his belief that the liberal press was run by Jews. For the use of Jews and Judaism in inter-Protestant polemic see the reports in the conservative *Kreuzzeitung*, on the Berlin church elections in 1894 and 1895, and in the liberal *Chronik der Christlichen Welt* on the elections in 1912. At a meeting in the Heilig-Kreuz parish (*Kreuzzeitung*, 20 September 1894) a

conservative speaker was accused by the liberals of being an anti-Semite, and the paper reported (13 October 1894) that conservatives were using the election slogan 'We will not vote for any Jews'. In 1912 leaflets distributed in Immanuel parish were said to refer to liberals as 'Jewish Protestants' (*Chronik der Christlichen Welt*, 3 April 1913).

31. Róisín Healy, 'Religion and Civil Society: Catholics, Jesuits and Protestants in Imperial Germany', in Frank Trentmann (ed.), *Paradoxes of Civil Society: New Perspectives on Modern Britain and Germany* (Oxford, 1999).

32. See the article on 'Konfession' in E. Hoffman-Krayer (ed.), *Handwörterbuch des deutschen Aberglaubens*, 9 vols (Berlin, 1927–38).

33. Köhle-Hezinger, op. cit., pp. 99–103; Helmut Walser Smith, *German Nationalism and Religious Conflict: Culture, Ideology, Politics, 1870–1914* (Princeton, NJ, 1995), pp. 22–37; Gangolf Hübinger, 'Kulturprotestantismus, Bürgerkirche und liberaler Revisionismus im wilhelminischen Deutschland' in Wolfgang Schieder (ed.), *Religion und Gesellschaft im 19. Jahrhundert* (Stuttgart, 1993), pp. 280–1.

34. Thomas Nipperdey, *Religion im Umbruch* (Munich 1987), pp. 153, 155.

35. There is an extensive literature on English anti-Catholicism in the nineteenth century. See especially John Wolffe, *The Protestant Crusade in Great Britain, 1829–1860* (Oxford, 1991); D. G. Paz, *Popular Anti-Catholicism in Mid-Victorian England* (Stanford, CA 1992).

36. See Hugh McLeod, 'Protestantism and British National Identity, 1815–1945', in Peter van der Veer and Hartmut Lehmann (eds), *Nation and Religion: Perspectives on Europe and Asia* (Princeton, NJ, 1999), pp. 44–70.

37. Sperber, *Kaiser's Voters*, p. 281.

38. Ibid., pp. 245–6.

39. Ibid., pp. 58–9.

40. E. Aver et al., 'Pratique religieuse et comportement electorale', *Archives des Sciences Sociales de la Religion*, 29 (1970), pp. 27–52.

41. Jean-Louis Ormières, 'Les rouges et les blancs', in Pierre Nora (ed.), *Les lieux de mémoire*, 3 vols (2nd edn, Paris, 1997), vol. II, pp. 2420–3.

42. Ibid., p. 2418.

43. Claude Langlois, 'La déchirure', in Timothy Tackett (ed.), *La Révolution, L'église, la France: Le serment de 1791* (Paris, 1986), pp. 319–37.

44. Michel Lagrée, *Religion et cultures – Bretagne, 1850–1950* (Paris, 1992), pp. 65–85.

45. Claude Langlois, 'Catholiques et laïcs', in Nora (ed.), op. cit., II, pp. 2327–9.

46. Jacques and Mona Ozouf, *La République des instituteurs* (Paris, 1992), p. 205.

47. Émile Zola, *Paris* (English translation, Stroud, 1993), p. 453.

48. For the cult of the Sacred Heart generally, see Busch, op. cit.; for the controversies surrounding the construction of the basilica in Montmar-

tre, see the overview by François Loyer, 'Le Sacré-Cœur de Montmartre', in Nora (ed.), op. cit., vol. III pp. 4253–69, and the full-scale discussion by Jacques Benoist, *Le Sacré-Cœur de Montmartre* (Paris, 1992).

49. P. J. Waller, *Democracy and Sectarianism: A Political and Social History of Liverpool, 1868–1939* (Liverpool, 1981).

50. Until 1872 open voting meant that it was possible to know how individuals voted. John Vincent, *Pollbooks: How Victorians Voted* (Cambridge, 1967), shows the very strong tendency of Anglican clergy and church employees to vote Conservative, and for Nonconformist ministers and Roman Catholic priests to vote Whig, Radical or Liberal.

51. K. D. Wald, *Crosses on the Ballot* (Princeton, NJ, 1983). This is not necessarily incompatible with views such as that of Peter F. Clarke, 'Electoral Sociology of Modern Britain', *History*, 57 (1972), pp. 49–53, who dates the transition from a religious-based to a class-based pattern of voting from 1910, since Wald's figures relate to the whole of Britain, while Clarke focuses on London and Lancashire, which he sees as pioneering trends that were not yet fully established elsewhere.

52. E.g. in Northampton, a town where both Nonconformity and Secularism were strong, Liberals were bitterly divided by the parliamentary candidacy of the Secularist leader, Charles Bradlaugh, who was defeated in 1874, but elected in 1880 and subsequently. Cynthia Brown, *Northampton 1835–1985: Shoe Town, New Town* (Chichester, 1990), pp. 64–6.

53. Philip Nord, *The Republican Moment: Struggles for Democracy in Nineteenth-century France* (Cambridge, MA, 1995), pp. 109–10.

54. Patrick Joyce, *Work, Society and Politics* (Brighton, 1980), chs 6–7; McLeod, 'New Perspectives', pp. 38–40; Henry Pelling, *Social Geography of British Elections, 1885–1910* (London, 1967) gives numerous examples of the exercise of 'influence'. See, e.g., his comments on the impact on the south Midlands of the switch from Liberalism to Unionism of many landlords (p. 122).

55. Wald, op. cit., p. 197.

56. Alan D. Gilbert, 'The Land and the Church', in G. E. Mingay (ed.), *The Victorian Countryside*, 2 vols (London, 1981), vol. I, pp. 46–50.

57. McLeod, *Religion and Society*, pp. 94–100. See also the discussion in Wald, op. cit., ch. 7.

58. Tal, op. cit., pp. 259–79.

59. See Linda Colley, *Britons: Forging the Nation, 1707–1837* (2nd edn, London, 1994).

60. Bill Williams, *The Making of Manchester Jewry, 1740–1875* (Manchester, 1976), p. 259. The following section is based on McLeod, 'Protestantism and British National Identity'.

61. *Spectator*, 1, 8, 22 October 1898.
62. See J. A. Mangan, *Athleticism and the Victorian and Edwardian Public School: The Emergence and Consolidation of an Educational Ideology* (Cambridge, 1981), and idem., *The Games Ethic and Imperialism* (Harmondsworth, 1986), which discuss such figures as H. H. Almond, headmaster of Loretto, a muscular Christian, sports enthusiast, and ardent imperialist.
63. V. E. Chancellor, *History for their Masters* (Bath, 1970), p. 112.
64. Susan Thorne, 'Protestant Ethics and the Spirit of Imperialism: British Congregationalists and the London Missionary Society, 1795–1925' (University of Michigan PhD thesis, 1990), pp. 291–5.
65. John M. MacKenzie, 'Heroic Myths of Empire', in idem. (ed.), *Popular Imperialism and the Military, 1850–1950* (Manchester, 1992), pp. 109–38; on Havelock and Gordon as Christian national heroes, see also Kenneth E. Hendrickson, *Making Saints: Religion and the Public Image of the British Army, 1809–1885* (Cranbury, NJ, 1998), chs 8–10.
66. McLeod, 'Protestantism and national identity'. See also discussions of the decline of anti-Catholicism in Wolffe, op. cit.; Paz, op. cit.; Walter L. Arnstein, *Protestant Versus Catholic in mid-Victorian England* (Columbia, MO, 1982); Christopher Ford, 'Pastors and Polemicists: the Character of Popular Anglicanism in South-east Lancashire, 1847–1914' (University of Leeds PhD thesis, 1991).
67. Douglas A. Lorimer, 'Race, Science and Culture: Historical Continuities and Discontinuities, 1850–1914', in Shearer West (ed.), *Victorians and Race* (Aldershot, 1996), pp. 12–33.
68. *Spectator*, 29 October 1898.
69. Christine Bolt, *Victorian Attitudes to Race* (London, 1971), pp. 7–9, 26–8; David Feldman, *Englishmen and Jews: Social Relations and Political Culture, 1840–1914* (New Haven, CT, 1994), pp. 82–115.
70. Bolt, op. cit., pp. 113–7.
71. Karen Fields, 'Christian Missionaries as Anti-colonial Militants', *Theory and Society*, 2 (1982), pp. 95–108; Thorne, op. cit., pp. 174–84.
72. Nipperdey, *Religion im Umbruch*, pp. 138–9; Peter Walkenhorst, 'Nationalismus als "politische Religion"?' in Blaschke and Kuhlemann (eds), op. cit., pp. 509–13.
73. Walkenhorst, 'Nationalismus als "politische Religion"?', pp. 514–16.
74. Ibid., pp. 521–4; Wolfgang Altgeld, *Katholizismus, Protestantismus, Judentum* (Mainz, 1992), pp. 1–4.
75. Sperber, *Kaiser's Voters*, p. 99.
76. Smith, *German Nationalism*, pp. 50–9; Hartmut Lehmann, ' "God, our old ally" ', in William R. Hutchison and Hartmut Lehmann (eds), *Many are Chosen* (Minneapolis, 1994) p. 90–1, 94, 107; Sperber, *Popular Catholicism*, pp. 225–7; Werner Blessing, *Staat und Kirche in der Gesellschaft* (Göttingen, 1982) p. 190.

77. Smith, *German Nationalism*, pp. 23–6.

78. Helmut Walser Smith, 'Catholics, the Nation and Nationalism in Nine-teenth-century Germany', paper read at conference 'Religion and Nationalism', University of Amsterdam, 1995; idem., *German National-ism*, pp. 26–37.

79. For Jewish conceptions of modern German history, see David Sorkin, 'The Impact of Emancipation on German Jewry', in Jonathan Frankel and Steven J. Zipperstein (eds), *Assimilation and Community: The Jews in Nineteenth-century Europe* (Cambridge, 1992), pp. 186–9; for Schiller, see Peter Freimark, 'Kuggel und Lockschen in Hamburg. Ein Beitrag zur jüdischen Schiller-Rezeption im 19. Jahrhundert', in Peter Freimark, Inas Lorenz and Günter Marwedel (eds), *Judentore, Küggel, Steuerkonten: Untersuchungen zur Geschichte der deutschen Juden vornehmlich im Hamburger Raum* (Hamburg, 1983), pp. 169–220; for more general discussion of German Jewish identity, Michael A. Meyer (ed.), *German-Jewish History in Modern Times* (New York, 1997).

80. Smith, 'Catholics, the Nation, and Nationalism', p. 27.

81. Walkenhorst, op. cit., pp. 516–20; Altgeld, op. cit., pp. 9–24.

82. Michel Winock, 'Jeanne d'Arc', in Nora (ed.), op. cit., vol. III, p. 4449.

83. Ibid., pp. 4456–7.

84. Gerd Krumeich, 'Jeanne d'Arc-Kult und politische Religiosität in Frankreich', in Schieder (ed.), op. cit., pp. 318–31; James F. McMillan, 'Reclaiming a Martyr: French Catholics and the Cult of Joan of Arc, 1890–1920', in Diana Wood (ed.), *Martyrs and Martyrologies*, Studies in Church History 30 (Oxford, 1993), pp. 359–70.

85. Yves Lambert, *Dieu change en Bretagne: La religion à Limerzel de 1900 à nos jours* (Paris, 1985), pp. 91–8; Austin Gough, 'The Conflict in Politics', in Theodore Zeldin (ed.), *Conflicts in French Society* (London, 1970), p. 102; Jean Baubérot, *La Morale laïque Contre l'ordre moral* (Paris, 1997), pp. 238–45.

86. René Rémond, 'La fille ainée de l'Église', in Nora (ed.), op. cit., III, pp. 4321–51; Thomas Kselman, 'Religion and French Identity: The Origins of the Union Sacrée', in Hutchison and Lehmann (eds.), op. cit., pp. 57–61.

87. Kselman, 'Religion and French Identity', p. 72.

88. Gérard Cholvy and Yves-Marie Hilaire, *Histoire religieuse de la france contemporainè*, vol. II: *1880–1930* (Toulouse, 1986), p. 219.

89. Jean Faury, *Cléricalisme et anticléricalisme dans le Tarn* (Toulouse, 1980), pp. 85–94.

90. Oscar Arnal, *Ambivalent Alliance: The Catholic Church and the Action Fran-çaise, 1899–1939* (Pittsburgh, PA, 1985), pp. 20–1.

91. Faury, op. cit., p. 493.

Notes to Chapter 7   Religion and Popular Culture

1. Thomas Hardy, *Tess of the d'Urbervilles* (London, 1891), ch. 14.
2. Eugen Baumann, *Der Berliner Volkscharacter in der Seelsorge* (Berlin, 1880), p. 61. See also Hugh McLeod, *Piety and Poverty* (New York, 1996) pp. 179–82, and the comments by Lincolnshire villagers in 1845 quoted by Frances Knight, *The Nineteenth-Century Church and English Society* (Cambridge, 1995), p. 32.
3. Gérard Cholvy and Yves-Marie Hilaire, *Histoire religieuse de la France contemporains*, vol. II: *1880–1930* (Toulouse, 1986), p. 206.
4. McLeod, *Piety and Poverty*, p. 180.
5. Judith Devlin, *The Superstitious Mind: French Peasants and the Supernatural in the Nineteenth Century* (New Haven, CT, 1987), pp. 64–6.
6. *Geschichte der St Pauls-Gemeinde zu Berlin N.* (Berlin, 1935), p. 50; McLeod, *Piety and Poverty*, pp. 179–82. For discussion of meanings given to baptism by working-class Londoners in the early twentieth century, see Alan Bennett Bartlett, 'The Churches in Bermondsey, 1880–1939' (University of Birmingham PhD thesis, 1987), pp. 182–8; Sarah C. Williams, *Religious Belief and Pupular Culture in Southwork c. 1880–1939* (Oxford, 1999), pp. 87–8, 93–4, 103–4.
7. Louis Pérouas, *Refus d'une religion, religion d'un refus en Limousin rural, 1880–1940* (Paris, 1985), p. 128.
8. Jacqueline Lalouette, *La libre pensée en France, 1848–1940* (Paris, 1997), pp. 346–7.
9. Ibid., p. 96.
10. Jean Faury, *Cléricalisme er anticléricalisme dans le Tarn* (Taulouse, 1980), pp. 147–8.
11. Knight, op. cit., p. 91.
12. McLeod, *Piety and Poverty*, p. 243, note 38.
13. Sarah Williams, *Religious Belief*, p. 91.
14. Émile Zola, *The Earth* (English translation, Harmondsworth, 1980), p. 429.
15. Émile Zola, *L'Assommoir* (English translation, London, 1995) [first published, 1877], p. 166.
16. Ralph Gibson, *A Social History of French Catholicism, 1789–1914* (London, 1989), p. 135.
17. James Obelkevich, *Religion and Rural Society: South Lindsey, 1825–1875* (Oxford, 1976), pp. 263–71.
18. Karl Julius Müller, *Aberglaube und Occultismus in Berlin und der Provinz Brandenburg* (Berlin, 1899), p. 13.
19. Ibid., pp. 8–10, 13–15.
20. Yves-Marie Hilaire, *Une chrétienté au XIXᵉ siècle?* (Lille, 1977), vol. I, pp. 374–8.

338   NOTES

21. Ibid., pp. 70–83.
22. See Helena Waddy Lepovitz, 'The Industrialization of Popular Art in Bavaria', *Past & Present*, 99 (1983), p. 109, for a photograph of a *Herrgottswinkel*, with its crucifix and paintings of the madonna and child, a typical feature of nineteenth-century Bavarian peasant homes.
23. Eugen Weber, *Peasants into Frenchmen* (London, 1977), pp. 456–7.
24. Hilaire, *Une chrétienté?*, vol. II, p. 633.
25. Yves Lambert, *Dieu change en Bretagne: La religion à Limerzel de 1900 à nos jours* (Paris, 1985), p. 36.
26. Hilaire, *Une chrétienté?* vol. I, pp. 80–1.
27. Gérard Cholvy, 'Expressions et évolution du sentiment religieux populaire dans la France du XIXe siècle au temps de la restauration catholique (1801–1860)', in *La piété populaire de 1610 à nos jours* (Paris, 1976), pp. 293–303; Thomas Kselman, *Miracles and Prophecies in Nineteenth-Century France* (New Brunswick, NJ, 1983), pp. 25–59.
28. Lambert, op. cit., pp. 49–50.
29. Obelkevich, *Religion and Rural Society*, pp. 265–71.
30. McLeod, *Piety and Poverty*, pp. 187–8; idem., *Religion and Society*, pp. 100–5.
31. Ibid., pp. 106–9; Edward Berenson, *Populist Religion and Left-Wing Politics in France, 1830–1852* (Princeton, NJ, 1984), p. 70; P. Wurster, *Das kirchliche Leben der evangelischen Landeskirche in Württemberg* (Tübingen, 1919), pp. 226–8. Wurster suggests, however, that the Bible was often mainly for show, and that prayer-books were more widely read. Hymn-books also played a big part in German Protestantism, in the home as well as in the church, and were a major focus of conflict between supporters of rival church parties. See Anthony Steinhoff, 'Protestants in Strasbourg, 1870–1914' (University of Chicago PhD thesis, 1996), pp. 541–55.
32. Cholvy and Hilaire, *Histoire religieuse, 1800–1880*, pp. 144–6; Thomas Walter Laqueur, *Religion and Respectability: Sunday Schools and Working Class Culture, 1780–1850* (New Haven, CT, 1976), pp. 116, 118–9, 160–1.
33. F. Linden, *Sozialismus und Religion* (Leipzig, 1932), p. 163.
34. Cholvy, 'Expressions et évolution', pp. 315–16.
35. Wurster, op. cit., pp. 258–61.
36. Joseph Lawson, *Letters to the Young on Progress in Pudsey during the last Sixty Years* (Stanningley, 1887), pp. 33–4.
37. Hugh McLeod, 'New Perspectives on Victorian Working Class Religion', *Oral History Journal*, 14 (1986), p. 35, quoting Bartlett, Interview no 9, p. 187.
38. Robert Tressell, *The Ragged Trousered Philanthropists* (London, 1955), p. 493.
39. James Obelkevich, 'The Religion of Music', in Obelkevich, Roper and Samuel (eds), *Disciplines of Faith*, p. 557.

40. James Walvin, *Leisure and Society, 1830–1950* (London, 1978), pp. 98, 102.

41. Obelkevich, *Religion and Rural Society*, pp. 276–7. For the role of 'superstition' in early Primitive Methodism, see Michael R. Watts, *The Dissenters* vol. 2: *The Expansion of Evangelical Nonconformity* (Oxford, 1995), pp. 106–7.

42. Lawson, op. cit., p. 50.

43. Ibid., p. 54.

44. Obelkevich, *Religion in Rural Society*, pp. 310–12, 331.

45. Weber, op. cit., p. 470.

46. Ibid., pp. 354–6.

47. For which, see, e.g., Gibson, op. cit., p. 171.

48. See, e.g., Michel Lagrée, 'Exilés dans leur patrie', in François Lebrun (ed.). *Histoire des catholiques en France* (Toulouse, 1980), pp. 383–97.

49. Cholvy, 'Expressions et évolution,' pp. 290–303.

50. Louis Pérouas, *Les Limousins, leurs saints, leurs prêtres, du XVᵉ au XXᵉ siècle* (Paris, 1988), p. 192.

51. Ibid., pp. 197–205; Gérard Cholvy, *Religion et société au XIXᵉ siècle: Le diocèse de Montpellier*, II (Lille, 1973), pp. 1538–40.

52. Hilaire, *Une chrétienté?*, II, pp. 795–801; Cholvy and Hilaire, *Histoire religieuse, 1880–1930*, p. 180.

53. François-André Isambert, *Christianisme et classe ouvrière* (Tournai, 1961), p. 74.

54. Avner Ben-Amos, 'Les funérailles de Victor Hugo', in Pierre Nora (ed.), *Les Lieux de mémoire*, 3 vols (2nd edn, Paris, 1997), vol. I, pp. 425–64.

55. Pérouas, *Refus d'une religion*, pp. 169–85.

56. Eduard Bernstein, *Die Geschichte der Berliner Arbeiter-Bewegung*, 3 vols (Berlin, 1907–10), vol. I, p. 353.

57. James R. Moore, 'Freethought, Secularism, Darwinism: The Case of Charles Darwin', in Gerald Parsons, James R. Moore and John Wolffe (eds), *Religion in Victorian Britain*, 5 vols (Manchester, 1988–96), vol. I, p. 313.

58. Lalouette, op. cit., p. 340.

59. Pérouas, *Refus d'une religion*, loc. cit.

60. Lalouette, op. cit., pp. 372–4.

61. Pérouas, *Refus d'une religion*, pp. 169–78.

62. Annemarie Burger, *Religionszugehörigkeit und soziales Verhalten* (Göttingen, 1964), pp. 343, 350–9; Lucian Hölscher, *Weltgericht oder Revolution* (Stuttgart, 1989), pp. 154–63.

63. Jörg Kniffka, *Das kirchliche Leben in Berlin-Ost in der Mitte der zwanziger Jahre* (dissertation, Westfälische Wilhelms-Universität, Münster, 1971), pp. 114–34.

64. Bartlett, op. cit., p. 183.

65. Owen Chadwick, *The Victorian Church*, II (London, 1970), pp. 221–2; *Facts and Figures about the Church of England*, 3 (London, 1965), p. 54.
66. Bartlett, op. cit., pp. 183–8.
67. Williams, *Religious Belief*, p. 97.
68. Olive Anderson, 'The Incidence of Civil Marriage in Victorian England and Wales', *Past & Present*, 69 (1975), p. 55.
69. McLeod, *Piety and Poverty*, p. 184.
70. Anderson, 'Civil Marriage', p. 61, note 14.
71. Zola, *L'Assommoir*, pp. 292–3; Fréderic Gugelot, 'Henri Ghéon: Ou l'histoire d'une âme en guerre', in Nadine-Josette Chaline, *Chrétiens dans la Première Guerre Mondiale* (Paris, 1993), p. 69.
72. Weber, op. cit., p. 361.
73. Kselman, op. cit., p. 30.
74. Cholvy, *Montpellier*, II, p. 1519; idem., 'La France contemporaine (XIX–début XXe siècles),' in B. Plongeron (ed.), *La religion populaire en occident chrétien* (Paris, 1976), pp. 160–1.
75. Ellen Badone, 'Breton Folklore', in Ellen Badone (ed.), *Religious Orthodoxy and Popular Faith in European Society* (Princeton, NJ, 1990), pp. 149–50.
76. Ibid., pp. 153–8.
77. Matthew J. Dowling, 'The Evolution of a Modern Pilgrimage: Lisieux, 1897–1939' (Yale University PhD thesis, 1995), pp. 7–14.
78. Helena Waddy, 'St Anthony's Bread: The modernized religious culture of German Catholics in the early twentieth century', *Journal of Social History*, 31 (1998), p. 357.
79. W. Brepohl, *Industrievolk im Wandel von der agraren zur industriellen Daseinsform dargestellt am Ruhrgebiet* (Tübingen, 1957), p. 285.
80. Kselman, op. cit., pp. 201–3.
81. Suzanne F. Kaufman, 'Miracles, Medicine and the Spectacle of Lourdes: Popular Religion and Modernity in Fin-de-Siècle France' (Rutgers University PhD thesis, 1996), p. 254.
82. Ibid., pp. 116–17, 124–5.
83. Gilbert, *Religion and Society in Industrial England*, p. 44.
84. Ian Bradley, *Abide with Me: The World of Victorian Hymns* (London, 1997), pp. 217–19. See also John Worthen, *D. H. Lawrence: The Early Years, 1885–1912* (Cambridge, 1991), pp. 380–1. On the day when Lawrence first met his future wife Frieda, he spent the evening singing hymns 'with gusto' with his former lover, Jessie Chambers, and her brothers and sister.
85. D. H. Lawrence, *Selected Poems* (Harmondsworth, 1972), p. 21.
86. Thompson and Vigne interviews (University of Essex Oral History Archive), no. 108, pp. 12, 14; no. 339, pp. 28, 33, 45.
87. Brian Harrison, 'Religion and Recreation in Nineteenth-Century England', *Past & Present*, 38 (1967), pp. 98–125.

88. Walvin, op. cit., ch. 7; John Lowerson, *Sport and the English Middle Classes* (Manchester, 1993); Norman Vance, *The Sinews of the Spirit* (Cambridge, 1985).

89. Walvin, op. cit., p. 87.

90. Jack Williams, 'Churches, Sport and Identities in the North, 1900–1939', Jeff Hill and Jack Williams (eds), *Sport and Identity in the North of England* (Keele, 1996), pp. 113–36; Willi Schwank, *Kirche und Sport in Deutschland von 1848 bis 1920* (Hochheim-am-Main, 1979); Michel Lagrée, 'Sport et sociabilité catholique en France au début du XXe siècle', in P. Arnaud and J. Camy (eds), *La naissance du Mouvement Sportif Associatif en France* (Lyon, 1986), pp. 327–35.

91. Sarah C. Williams, 'Religious Belief and Popular Culture: a Study of the South London Borough of Southwark c.1880–1939' (University of Oxford DPhil thesis, 1993), p. 305.

92. Ibid., pp. vi, 220–3, 291–2, 295.

93. Richard Sykes, 'Popular Religion in Dudley and the Gornals c.1914–1965' (University of Wolverhampton PhD thesis, 1999), pp. 116–19, 128–38, 175–84, 226–39.

94. Ibid., p. 138.

95. Ibid., pp. 185–207, 358–62.

96. Williams, 'Religious Belief and Popular Culture: a Study of the South London Borough of Southwark', pp. 316–17.

97. Sykes, op. cit., ch 7.

98. Williams, 'Religious Belief and Popular Culture: a Study of the South London Borough of Southwark', pp. 160–2.

99. Studies of popular belief in the post-1945 period which stress the continuing importance of the non-rational include Émile Pin, *Pratique religieuse et classes sociales* (Paris, 1956), pp. 400–1; Geoffrey Gorer, *Exploring English Character* (London, 1955), p. 269; N. Abercrombie et al., 'Superstition and Religion: the God of the Gaps', in David Martin and Michael Hill (eds), *A Sociological Yearbook of Religion in Britain*, vol. 3 (London, 1970), pp. 93–129; Stephen Wilson, 'Cults of Saints in the Church in Central Paris', in idem. (ed.), *Saints and their Cults* (Cambridge, 1983), pp. 233–60. Yves Lambert, who has conducted various surveys of religious belief (especially among young people) in contemporary France, argues that the decline of Catholic belief and practice has been associated with a rapid growth of 'alternative' forms of religiosity. See Yves Lambert, 'Vers une ère post-chrétienne?', *Futuribles*, 200 (1995), pp. 85–111.

Notes to Chapter 8   1914

1. Joachim Rohde, 'Streiflichter aus der Berliner Kirchengeschichte von 1900 bis 1918', in Günther Wirth (ed.), *Beiträge zur Berliner Kirchen-*

seschichte (Berlin, 1987), p. 230; Nicholas Hope, *German and Scandinavian Protestantisim, 1700 to 1918* (Oxford, 1995), p. 594.

2. A. J. Hoover, *The Gospel of Nationalism: German Patriotic Preaching from Napoleon to Versailles* (Stuttgart, 1986).

3. H.-J.Scheidgen, *Deutsche Bischöfe im Ersten Weltkrieg* (Cologne, 1991).

4. Annette Becker, *La guerre et la foi: De la mort à la mémoire, 1914–1930* (Paris, 1994), pp. 32–3.

5. Ibid., pp. 42–5.

6. Maurice Larkin, *Religion, Politics and Preferment in France Since the 1890s: La Belle Epoque and its Legacy* (Cambridge, 1995), pp. 39, 148–50.

7. Gérard Cholvy and Yves-Marie Hilaire, *Histoire religieuse de la France Contemporains*, vol. II: *1880–1930* (Toulouse, 1986), p. 257.

8. Jacques Fontana, *Les catholiques français pendant la Grande Guerre* (Paris, 1990), pp. 296–300.

9. On the religious tendencies of Asquith's government, see G. I. T. Machin, *Politics and the Churches in Great Britain, 1869–1921* (Oxford, 1987), pp. 274–5; Adrian Hastings, *A History of English Christianity, 1920–1985* (London, 1986), pp. 54–5. For the Day of Prayer, see Alan Wilkinson, *The Church of England and the First World War* (London, 1978), p. 61.

10. Alan Wilkinson, *Dissent or Conform? War, Peace and the English Churches, 1900–1945* (London, 1986), pp. 26–8.

11. Wilkinson, *Church of England*, pp. 217–18, 251–4.

12. A good discussion of the Quaker response to the war is Thomas C. Kennedy, 'The Quaker Renaissance and the Origins of the Modern British Peace Movement, 1895–1920', *Albion*, 16 (1984), pp. 243–72.

13. Wilkinson, *Dissent or Conform?*, pp. 23, 25, 30–1.

14. Stuart Paul Mews, 'Religion and English Society in the First World War' (University of Cambridge PhD thesis, 1973), pp. 59–63.

15. Hugh McLeod, *Piety and Poverty* (New York, 1996), p. 198.

16. Hope, op. cit., p. 591.

17. Ibid., p. 597.

18. Michel Lagrée, 'Exilés dans leur patrie', in François Lebrun (ed.), *Historie des catholiques en France* (Toulouse, 1980), pp. 400–1; Fontana, op. cit. pp. 25–8.

19. Becker, op. cit., p. 64.

20. Mews, op. cit., p. 50; McLeod, *Piety and Poverty*, pp. 199–200.

21. Robert Currie, Alan Gilbert and Lee Horsley, *Churches and Churchgoers* (Oxford, 1977), pp. 128, 143, 150, 157.

22. Kennedy, op. cit., pp. 246–7. It seems likely that the big drop suffered by the Quakers in 1914–15 was due to the departure of those Friends who rejected the Society's anti-war stance, and that the small increase in 1915–16 was due to the accession of pacifists from other churches. For the remainder of the war membership stabilised. During the Second

World War, by which time the Quaker anti-war position was clearly defined and well known, membership increased, though again most other churches suffered losses.

23. Mews op. cit., p. 54.
24. Hartmut Lehmann, ' "God our old ally" ', in Wiliam R. Hutchison and Hartmut Lehmann (eds), *Many are Chosen: Divine Election and Western Nationalism* (Minneapolis, 1994); von Reeken, op. cit., p. 315.
25. Fontana, op. cit., pp. 64–70. See ibid., pp. 169–221, for the resistance, and frequently open hostility, of French Catholics to the Pope's peace-making initiatives (and the delighted derision of French freethinkers).
26. Stephen Koss, *The Pro-Boers* (Chicago, 1973), pp. 33, 225–6, 230–1; Margaret Blunden, 'The Anglican Church During the War', in Peter Warwick (ed.), *The South African War: The Anglo-Boer War, 1899–1902* (Harlow, 1980), pp. 279–80. Though Anglican critics of the war were few, they included some of the most prominent figures in the church, such as bishop Percival of Hereford, the later bishops, Charles Gore and Edward Hicks, and Henry Scott Holland, Canon of St Paul's and later Regius Professor at Oxford.
27. For pacifism and anti-militarism in the Nonconformist chapels, see Wilkinson, *Dissent or Conform?* pp. 12–13, 21–3, 48–53.
28. Wilkinson, *Church of England*, pp. 114–15.
29. Lucy Masterman, *C. F. G. Masterman: A Biography* (London, 1939), p. 290.
30. John W. Graham, *Conscription and Conscience: A History, 1916–1919* (London, 1922), pp. 155–211.
31. John Rae, *Conscience and Politics* (London, 1970), p. 155. A more vivid and avowedly partisan account of the treatment of the first cohort of Conscientious Objectors is provided in Graham, op. cit., ch. 4. None of the death sentences imposed on thirty-two members of this group was carried out. However, a former CO told me that when he first refused to be conscripted he did so assuming that it would lead to his being executed, and he had a clear picture of this event in his mind. In the event, he spent most of the latter part of the war in prison, and was still alive seventy-six years later. Interview with Walter Griffin at his Birmingham home, 5 December 1992 (tape in my possession).
32. Rae, op. cit., pp. 250–1; Graham, op. cit., p. 352. Felicity Goodall, *A Question of Conscience: Conscientious Objection in the Two World Wars* (Stroud, 1997), p. 44, quotes an estimate that three-quarters of the 1000 COs in Dartmoor were objecting primarily on political grounds, and a quarter primarily on religious grounds – though, as she indicates, there were many who objected on both grounds, and others whose objections were more strictly on the grounds of individual moral conviction.
33. David Cairns (ed.), *The Army and Religion* (London, 1919), pp. 8, 26–30; Becker, op. cit., pp. 46–55.

344 NOTES

34. John McManners, *Church and State in France, 1870–1914* (London, 1972), pp. 112–17; Cholvy and Hilaire, *Histoire religieuse, 1880–1930*, pp. 142–6.

35. See, e.g., Frederic Gugelot, 'Henri Ghéon: Ou l'histoire d'une âme en guerre', in Nadine-Josette Chaline, *Chrétiens dans la Première Guerre Mondiale* (Paris, 1993), which analyses the wartime conversion of the writer Henri Ghéon, which seems to have had its two-fold roots in his discovery, in the pre-war years, of nationalism and of the art of Giotto and Fra Angelico. For a more general discussion of wartime conversions see Becker, op. cit., pp. 46–55 and *passim*.

36. Ibid., pp. 48, 69.

37. Ibid., p. 92.

38. Cairns, op. cit., p. 172.

39. Becker, op. cit., pp. 60–1.

40. Waddy, 'St Anthony's Bread', p. 350.

41. Becker, op. cit., p. 92; Wilkinson, *First World War*, p. 195; J. M.Winter, 'Spiritualism and the First World War', in R. W. Davis and R. J. Helmstadter (eds), *Religion and Irreligion in Victorian Society* (London, 1992), pp. 185–200; Cairns, op. cit., p. 9.

42. Becker, op. cit., p. 99.

43. Fontana, op. cit., pp. 52–3.

44. A. J. Hoover, *God, Germany, and Britain in the Great War: A Study in Clerical Nationalism* (New York, 1989), pp. 35–7.

45. Becker, op. cit., pp. 42–3.

Bibliography

Abercrombie, N. et al., 'Superstition and Religion: the God of the Gaps', in David Martin and Michael Hill (eds), *A Sociological Yearbook of Religion in Britain*, vol. 3 (London, 1970), pp. 93–129.

Ainsworth, A., 'Religion in the Working-Class Community and the Evolution of Socialism in Later Nineteenth-Century Lancashire', *Histoire Sociale*, 10 (1977), pp. 354–80.

Alderman, Geoffrey, *The Jewish Community in British Politics* (Oxford, 1983).

——, *Modern British Jewry* (Oxford, 1992).

Aldington, Richard, *Death of a Hero*, unexpurgated edition (London, 1965).

——, *Life for Life's Sake* (London, 1968; 1st edn 1941).

Altgeld, Wolfgang, *Katholizismus, Protestantismus, Judentum: Über religiös begrundete Gegensätze und nationalreligiöse Ideen in der Geschichte des deutschen Nationalismus* (Mainz, 1992).

Aminzade, Roland, 'Breaking the Chains of Dependency: from Patronage to Class Politics, Toulouse, France, 1830–1872', *Journal of Urban History*, 3 (1977), pp. 485–505.

Anderson, Margaret Lavinia, 'Piety and Politics: Recent Work on German Catholicism', *Journal of Modern History*, 63 (1991), 681–716.

——, 'The Limits of Secularization: on the Problem of the Catholic Revival in Nineteenth-Century Germany', *Historical Journal*, 38 (1993) pp. 647–70.

Anderson, Olive, 'The Growth of Christian Militarism in Mid-Victorian Britain', *English Historical Review*, 86 (1971), pp. 46–72.

——, 'The Incidence of Civil Marriage in Victorian England and Wales', *Past & Present*, 69 (1975), pp. 50–87.

Anderson, Robert, 'The Conflict in Education: Catholic Secondary Schools (1850–70) – A Reappraisal', in Zeldin (ed.), *Conflicts*, 51–93.

Arnal, Oscar, *Ambivalent Alliance: The Catholic Church and the Action française, 1899–1939* (Pittsburgh, PA, 1985).

Arnstein, Walter L., *Protestant versus Catholic in Mid-Victorian England* (Columbia, MO, 1982).

——, 'Queen Victoria and Religion', in Malmgreen (ed.), *Religion in the Lives of English Women*, pp. 88–128.

Aver, E. *et al.*, 'Pratique religieuse et comportement electorale', *Archives des Sciences Sociales de la Religion*, 29 (1970), pp. 27–52.

Badone, Ellen (ed.), *Religious Orthodoxy and Popular Faith in European Society* (Princeton, NJ, 1990).

Badone, Ellen, 'Breton Folklore of Anti-Clericalism', in idem (ed.), *Religious Orthodoxy*, pp. 140–62.

Barrow, Logie, *Independent Spirits: Spiritualism and English Plebeians, 1850–1910* (London, 1986).

Bartlett, Alan Bennett, 'The Churches in Bermondsey, 1880–1939' (University of Birmingham PhD thesis, 1987).

Jean Baubérot, *La morale laïque contre l'ordre moral* (Paris, 1997).

Baumann, Eugen, *Der Berliner Volkscharacter in der Seelsorge* (Berlin, 1880)

Bebbington, D. W., *Evangelicalism in Modern Britain: A History from the 1730s to the 1980s* (London, 1989).

Becker, Annette, *La guerre et la foi: De la mort à la mémoire 1914–1930* (Paris, 1994).

Bédarida, F., and Maitron, J. (eds), *Christianisme et monde ouvrier* (Paris, 1975).

Behnken, Imbke, and Schmid, Pia, 'Religion in Tagebüchern von Frauen – zwei Fallstudien', in Kraul and Luth (eds), *Erziehung*, pp. 63–77.

Ben-Amos, Avner, 'Les funérailles de Victor Hugo', in Nora (ed.), *Lieux de mémoire*, vol. I, pp. 425–64.

Bennett, E. N., *Problems of Village Life* (London, 1913).

Bennett, G. V., 'The Conflict in the Church', in Geoffrey Holmes (ed.), *England after the Glorious Revolution* (London, 1969), pp. 155–75.

Benoist, Jacques, *Le Sacré-Cœur de Montmartre* (Paris, 1992).

Berenson, Edward, *Populist Religion and Left-Wing Politics in France, 1830–1852* (Princeton, NJ, 1984).

Berger, Peter, *The Social Reality of Religion* (Harmondsworth 1972).

Berger, Stefan, *The British Labour Party and the German Social Democrats* (Oxford, 1994).

Bernstein, Eduard, *Die Geschichte der Berliner Arbeiter-Bewegung*, 3 vols (Berlin, 1907–10).

Besier, Gerhard, *Religion, Nation, Kultur: Die Geschichte der christlichen Kirchen in den gesellschaftlichen Umbrüchen des 19. Jahrhunderts* (Neukirchen-Vluyn, 1992)

Bethge, Eberhard, *Dietrich Bonhoeffer* (English translation, London, 1970).

Bevir, Mark, 'Annie Besant's Quest for Truth: Christianity, Secularism and New Age Thought', *Journal of Ecclesiastical History*, 50 (1999), pp. 62–93.

Biagini, Eugenio F., *Liberty, Retrenchment and Reform: Popular Liberalism in the Age of Gladstone, 1860–1880* (Cambridge, 1992).

Bigler, R. M., *The Politics of German Protestantism* (Los Angeles, 1972).

Binfield, Clyde, *Pastors and People* (Coventry, 1984).

Birker, Karl, *Die deutschen Arbeiterbildungsvereine, 1840–1870* (Berlin, 1973).

Blackbourn, David, *Populists and Patricians: Essays in Modern German History* (London, 1987).

——*Marpingen: Apparitions of the Virgin Mary in Bismarckian Germany* (Oxford, 1993).

——*The Fontana History of Germany, 1780–1918: The Long Nineteenth Century* (London, 1997).

Blankenberg, Heinz, *Politischer Katholizismus in Frankfurt am Main, 1918–33* (Mainz, 1981).

Blaschke, Olaf, 'Die Kolonialisierung der Laienwelt: Priester als Milieumanager und die Kanale klerikaler Kuratel', in Blaschke and Kuhlemann (eds), *Religion im Kaiserreich*, pp. 93–138.

Blaschke, Olaf, and Kuhlemann, Frank-Michael (eds), *Religion im Kaiserreich: Milieus – Mentalitäten – Krisen* (Gütersloh, 1996).

Blessing, Werner, *Staat und Kirche in der Gesellschaft* (Göttingen, 1982).

Blunden, Margaret, 'The Anglican Church During the War', in Peter Warwick (ed.), *The South African War: The Anglo-Boer War, 1899–1902* (Harlow, 1980).

Boeckh, Jürgen, 'Predigt in Berlin', in Elm and Loock (eds), *Seelsorge und Diakonie*, pp. 307–28.

Bolt, Christine, *Victorian Attitudes to Race* (London, 1971).

Bonhoeffer, Dietrich, *Letters and Papers from Prison* (English translation, London, 1959).

Bonnet, Serge, 'Verriers et bûcherons d'Argonne', in Bédarida and Maitron (eds), *Christianisme et monde ouvrier* (Paris, 1975), pp. 187–222.

Borg, Daniel R., *The Old-Prussian Church and the Weimar Republic* (Hanover, NH, 1984).

Borut, Jacob, and Heilbronner, Oded, 'Leaving the Walls of Anomalous Activity: The Catholic and Jewish Rural Bourgeoisie in Germany', *Comparative Studies in Society and History*, (1998), pp. 475–502.

Boulard, F., *Introduction to Religious Sociology* (English translation, London, 1960).

Boulard, F., and Rémy, J., *Pratique religieuse urbaine et régions culturelles* (Paris, 1968).

Boutry, Philippe, *Prêtres et paroisses au pays du Curé d'Ars* (Paris, 1986).

Boutry, Philippe, and Cinquin, Michel, *Deux pélérinages au XIXe siècle: Ars et Paray-le-Monial* (Paris, 1980).

Bowen, Desmond, *The Idea of the Victorian Church* (Montreal, 1968).

Bradley, Ian, *Abide with Me: The World of Victorian Hymns* (London, 1997).

Brakelmann, Günter, Greschat, Martin, and Jochmann, Werner, *Protestantismus und Politik: Werk und Wirkung Adolf Stoeckers* (Hamburg, 1982).

Brand, Hans-Jürgen, 'Kirchliches Vereinswesen und Freizeitgestaltungen in einer Arbeitergemeinde, 1872–1933', in G. Huck (ed.), *Sozialgeschichte der Freizeit* (Wuppertal, 1980), pp. 207–22.

Brederlow, Jörn, *'Lichtfreunde' und 'freie Gemeinden'* (Munich, 1976).

Brenner, Michael, Liedtke, Rainer, and Rechter, David (eds), *Two Nations: British and German Jews in Comparative Perspective* (Tübingen, 1999).

Brepohl, W., *Industrievolk im Wandel von der agraren zur industriellen Daseinsform dargestellt am Ruhrgebiet* (Tübingen, 1957).

Breuilly, John, *Labour and Liberalism in Nineteenth-Century Europe* (Manchester, 1992).

—— 'The Schiller Centenary of 1859 in Hamburg' (unpublished paper).

Broch, E.-D., *Katholische Arbeitervereine in der Stadt Köln, 1890–1901* (Hamburg, 1977).

Brose, E. D., 'Christian Labor and the Politics of Frustration in Imperial Germany' (Ohio State University PhD thesis, 1978).

Brown, Callum G., 'Did Urbanization Secularize Britain?', *Urban History Yearbook* (1988), pp. 1–14.

—— 'The Mechanism of Religious Growth in Urban Societies: British Cities Since the Eighteenth Century', in Hugh McLeod (ed.), *European Religion in the Age of Great Cities* (London, 1995), pp. 239–62.

—— 'The Secularisation Decade: The Haemorrhage of the British Churches in the 1960s', paper read at conference on 'The Decline of Christendom in Western Europe', Paris (1997).

—— *Religion and Society in Scotland since 1707* (Edinburgh, 1997).

Brown, Cynthia, *Northampton 1835–1985: Shoe Town, New Town* (Chichester, 1990).

Bruce, Steve, *Religion in the Modern World: From Cathedrals to Cults* (Oxford, 1995).

—— (ed.), *Religion and Modernization: Sociologists and Historians Debate the Secularization Thesis* (Oxford, 1992).

Budd, Susan, *Varieties of Unbelief* (London, 1977).

Budde, Gunilla-Frederike, *Auf dem Weg ins Bürgerleben* (Göttingen 1994).

Burger, Annemarie, *Religionszugehörigkeit und soziales Verhalten* (Göttingen, 1964).

Burman, Rickie, ' "She looketh well to the ways of her household": The Changing Role of Jewish women in Religious Life c.1880–1930', in Malmgreen (ed.), *Religion in the Lives of Englishwomen*, pp. 234–57.

Busch, Norbert, 'Frömmigkeit als Faktor des katholischen Milieus: Der Kult zum Herzen-Jesu', in Blaschke and Kuhlemann (eds), *Religion im Kaiserreich*, pp. 136–65.

Bushaway, Bob, 'Popular Belief on the Western Front', seminar paper, University of Birmingham, 8 May 1997.

Butler, Samuel, *The Way of all Flesh* (London, 1966) [first published, 1903].

Cairns, David (ed.), *The Army and Religion* (London, 1919).

Casanova, Jose, *Public Religions in the Modern World* (Chicago, 1994).

Chadwick, Owen, *The Victorian Church*, 2 vols (London, 1966–70).

—— *The Secularization of the European Mind in the Nineteenth Century* (Cambridge, 1975).

Chadwick, Rosemary, 'Church and People in Bradford and District, 1880–1914' (University of Oxford DPhil thesis, 1986).

Chaline, Jean-Pierre, *Les bourgeois de Rouen: Une élite urbaine au XIXe siècle* (Paris, 1982).

Chancellor, V. E., *History for their Masters* (Bath, 1970).

Charlton, D. G., *Secular Religions in France, 1815–1870* (Oxford, 1963).

Charpin, Fernand, *Pratique religieuse urbaine et formation d'une grande ville (Marseille, 1806–1958)* (Paris, 1964).

Cholvy, Gérard, *Religion et société au XIXe siècle: Le diocèse de Montpellier*, 2 vols (Lille, 1973).

—— 'Expressions et évolution du sentiment reliegieux populaire dans la France du XIXe siècle au temps de la restauration catholique (1801–60)', in *La piété populaire de 1610 à nos jours* (Paris, 1976), pp. 289–320.

—— 'La France contemporaine (XIX–début XXe siècles)', in B. Plongeron (ed.), *La religion populaire en occident chrétien* (Paris, 1976).

—— *La religion en France de la fin du XVIIIe à nos jours* (Paris, 1991).

Cholvy, Gérard, and Hilaire, Yves-Marie, *Histoire religieuse de la France contemporaine*, 3 vols (Toulouse, 1985–8), vol. 1: *1800–1880*; vol. 2: *1880–1930*; vol. 3: *1930–1985*.

Clarke, Peter F., 'Electoral Sociology of Modern Britain', *History*, 57 (1972), pp. 49–53.

Coleman, B. I., 'The Church Extension Movement in London *c*.1800–1860' (University of Cambridge PhD thesis, 1968).

Colley, Linda, *Britons: Forging the Nation, 1707–1837* (2nd edn, London, 1994).

Courtney, W. L. (ed.), *Do We Believe?* (London, 1905).

Cowman, Krista, '"We intend to show what Our Lord has done for Women": The Liverpool Church League for Women's Suffrage, 1913–18', in R. N. Swanson (ed.), *Gender and the Christian Religion*, Studies in Church History 34 (Woodbridge 1998), pp. 475–86.

Cox, Harvey, *The Secular City* (New York, 1965).

Cox, Jeffrey, *English Churches in a Secular Society* (Oxford, 1982).

—— 'Religion and Imperial Power in Nineteenth-Century Britain', in Richard Helmstadter (ed.), *Freedom and Religion*, pp. 339–72.

—— 'Master Narratives of Religious Change', paper read to conference on 'The Decline of Christendom in Western Europe' (Paris, 1997).

Cruickshank, Marjorie, *Church and State in English Education: 1870 to the Present Day* (London, 1963).

Currie, Robert, *Methodism Divided* (London, 1968).

Currie, Robert, Gilbert, Alan, and Horsley, Lee, *Churches and Churchgoers* (Oxford, 1977).

Dahl, Roald, *Boy* (Harmondsworth, 1986).

Daum, Andreas, 'Naturwissenschaften und Öffentlichkeit in der deutschen Gesellschaft: Zu den Anfängen einer Populärwissenschaft nach der Revolution von 1848', *Historische Zeitschrift*, 267 (1998), pp. 57–90.

Davidoff, Leonore and Hall, Catherine, *Family Fortunes: Men and Women of the English Middle Class, 1780–1850* (London, 1987).

Davie, Grace, *Religion in Britain since 1945: Believing without Belonging* (Oxford, 1994).

Davies, E. T., *Religion in the Industrial Revolution in South Wales* (Cardiff, 1965).

Delumeau, Jean, *Le catholicisme entre Luther et Voltaire* (Paris, 1971).

Devlin, Judith, *The Superstitious Mind: French Peasants and the Supernatural in the Nineteenth Century* (New Haven CT, 1987).

Dickinson, Edward Ross, *The Politics of German Child Welfare from the Empire to the Federal Republic* (Cambridge, MA, 1996).

Dietrich, Stefan, *Christentum und Revolution: Die christlichen Kirchen in Württemberg, 1848–1852* (Paderborn, 1996).

Ditt, Karl, *Industrialisierung, Arbeiterschaft und Arbeiterbewegung in Bielefeld, 1850–1914* (Dortmund, 1982).

Dowe, Dieter, 'The Workingmen's Choral Movement in Germany before the First World War', *Journal of Contempoary History*, 13 (1978), pp. 269–96.

Dowling, Matthew J., 'The Evolution of a Modern Pilgrimage: Lisieux, 1897–1939' (Yale University PhD thesis, 1995).

Doyle, Barry M., 'Urban Liberalism and the "Lost Generation": Politics and Middle Class Culture in Norwich, 1900–1935', *Historical Journal*, 38 (1995), pp. 617–34.

Drews, Paul, *Das kirchliche Leben der Evangelisch-Lutherischen Landeskirche des Königreichs Sachsen* (Tübingen, 1902).

Eliot, George, *Scenes from Clerical Life* (Harmondsworth, 1973) [first published 1858].

Elm, Kaspar, and Loock, Hans-Dietrich (eds), *Seelsorge und Diakonie: Beiträge zum Verhältnis von Kirche und Großstadt im 19. und beginnenden 20. Jahrhundert* (Berlin, 1990).

Emmerich, Wolfgang (ed.), *Proletarische Lebensläufe*, 2 vols (Reinbek bei Hamburg, 1974).

Endelman, Todd M., *Radical Assimilation in English Jewish History, 1656–1945* (Bloomington, IN, 1990).

—— 'The Social and Political Context of Conversion in Germany and England, 1870–1914', in idem (ed.), *Jewish Apostasy in the Modern World* (New York, 1987), pp. 83–107.

—— 'Jewish Self-Hatred in Britain and Germany', in Brenner, Liedtke and Rechter (eds), *Two Nations*, pp. 331–63.

Ermel, Horst, *Die Kirchenaustrittsbewegung im Deutschen Reich 1906–14* (dissertation, Cologne University, 1971).

Evans, Richard J., *Kneipengespräche im Kaiserreich* (Hamburg, 1989).

——, *Rituals of Retribution: Capital Punishment in Germany, 1600–1987* (2nd edn, London, 1997).

Facts and Figures about the Church of England, 3 (London, 1965).

Farr, Ian, 'From Anti-Catholicism to Anticlericalism: Catholic Politics and the Peasantry in Bavaria, 1860–1900', *European Studies Review*, 13 (1983), pp. 246–69.

Faulkner, H. U., *Chartism and the Churches* (New York, 1918).

Faury, Jean, *Cléricalisme et anticléricalisme dans le Tarn* (Toulouse, 1980).

Feldman, David, 'Immigrants and Workers, Englishmen and Jews: Jewish Immigrants in the East End of London, 1880–1906' (University of Cambridge PhD thesis, 1985).

—— *Englishmen and Jews: Social Relations and Political Culture, 1840–1914* (New Haven, CT, 1994).

Field, Clive, 'A Godly People? Aspects of Religious Practice in the Diocese of Oxford, 1738–1936', *Southern History*, 14 (1992), pp. 46–73.

—— 'Adam and Eve: Gender in the English Free Church Constituency', *Journal of Ecclesiastical History*, 41 (1993), pp. 63–79.

Field, Geoffrey G., 'Religion in the German Volksschule, 1890–1928', *Yearbook of the Leo Baeck Institute*, 25 (1980), pp. 41–71.

Fielding, Steven, *Class and Ethnicity: Irish Catholics in England, 1880–1939* (Buckingham, 1993).

Fields, Karen, 'Christian Missionaries as Anti-colonial Militants', *Theory and Society*, 2 (1982), pp. 95–108.

Finke, Roger, 'An unsecular America', in Bruce (ed.), *Religion and Modernization*, pp. 145–69.

Finke, Roger and Stark, Rodney, *The Churching of America, 1776–1990: Winners and Losers in our Religious Economy* (New Brunswick, NJ, 1992).

Fischer, Ilse, *Industrialisierung, sozialer Konflikt und politische Willensbildung in der Stadtgemeinde* (Augsburg, 1977).

Fishman, W. J., *East End Jewish Radicals, 1875–1914* (London, 1975).

Fontana, Jacques, *Les catholiques français pendant la Grande Guerre* (Paris, 1990).

Fontane, Theodor, *L'Adulterà* (1882), in idem., *Romane und Gedichte* (Munich, n.d.).

——, *Der Stechlin* (1898), in idem., *Romane und Gedichte* (Munich, n.d.).

Ford, Caroline, *Creating the Nation in Provincial France: Religion and Political Identity in Brittany* (Princeton, NJ, 1993).

Ford, Christopher, 'Pastors and Polemicists: the Character of Popular Anglicanism in South-east Lancashire, 1847–1914' (University of Leeds PhD thesis, 1991).

Frankel, Jonathan, and Zipperstein, Steven J. (eds), *Assimilation and Community: The Jews in Nineteenth-Century Europe* (Cambridge, 1992).

Freimark, H., *Moderne Geisterbeschwörer und Wahrheitssucher*, Großstadt-Dokumente 38 (Berlin, n.d.).

Freimark, Peter, 'Kuggel und Lockschen in Hamburg. Ein Beitrag zur jüdischen Schiller-Rezeption im 19. Jahrhundert', in Peter Freimark, Inas Lorenz and Günter Marwedel (eds), *Judentore, Küggel, Steuerkonten: Untersuchungen zur Geschichte der deutschen Juden vornehmlich im Hamburger Raum* (Hamburg, 1983), pp. 169–220.

Gabriel, Hans-Jürgen, 'Im Namen des Evangeliums gegen den Fortschritt. Zur Rolle der "Evangelischen Kirchenzeitung" unter E. W. Hengstenberg von 1830 bis 1849', in Wirth (ed.), *Beiträge*, pp. 154–76.

Gadbois, Geneviève, '"Vous êtes presque la seule consolation de l'Église"', in Jean Delumeau (ed.), *La religion de ma mère* (Paris, 1992), pp. 301–26.

Garnett, Jane, 'Evangelicalism and Business in Mid-Victorian Britain', in John Wolffe (ed.), *Evangelical Faith and Public Zeal: Evangelicals and Society in Britain, 1780–1980* (London, 1995), pp. 59–80.

Gartner, Lloyd P., *The Jewish Immigrant in Britain, 1870–1914* (2nd edn, London, 1973).

Gascoyne-Cecil, W., 'The Old Squire and the New', in W. K. Lowther-Clarke (ed.), *Facing the Facts: The Englishman's Religion* (London, 1911), pp. 43–54.

Gerth, H. H., and Mills, C. Wright (eds), *From Max Weber* (London, 1948).

Geschichte der St Pauls-Gemeinde zu Berlin N. (Berlin, 1935).

Gibson, Ralph, *A Social History of French Catholicism, 1789–1914* (London, 1989).

—— 'Why Republicans and Catholics Couldn't Stand Each Other in the Nineteenth Century', in Tallett and Atkin (eds), *Religion in France*, pp. 107–20.

Gilbert, Alan D., *Religion and Society in Industrial England: Church, Chapel and Social Change, 1740–1914* (London, 1976).

—— *The Making of Post-Christian Britain: A History of the Secularization of Modern Society* (London, 1980).

—— 'The Land and the Church', in G. E. Mingay (ed.), *The Victorian Countryside*, 2 vols (London, 1981), vol. I, 43–57.

Gill, Robin, *The Myth of the Empty Church* (London, 1993).

Gilley, Sheridan, 'Catholics and Socialists in Glasgow, 1906–1912', in Kenneth Lunn (ed.), *Hosts, Immigrants and Minorities* (Folkestone, 1980) pp. 160–200.

Gilley, Sheridan, and Sheils, W. J. (eds), *A History of Religion in Britain: Practice and Belief from Pre-Roman Times to the Present* (Oxford, 1994).

Gissing, George, *Born in Exile* (London, 1970) [first published 1892].

Glaue, P., *Das kirchliche Leben der evangelischen Kirchen in Thüringen* (Tübingen, 1910).

Goodall, Felicity, *A Question of Conscience: Conscientious Objection in the Two World Wars* (Stroud, 1997).

Gorer, Geoffrey, *Exploring English Character* (London, 1955).

Götz von Olenhusen, Irmtraud et al. (eds), *Frauen unter dem Patriarchat der Kirchen: Katholikinnen und Protestantinnen im 19. und 20. Jahrhundert* (Stuttgart, 1995).

Gough, Austin, 'The Conflict in Politics', in Zeldin (ed.), *Conflicts*, pp. 94–168.

Graf, Friedrich Wilhelm, *Die Politisierung des religiösen Bewußtseins* (Stuttgart, 1978).

Graham, John W., *Conscription and Conscience: A History, 1916–1919* (London, 1922).

Green, S. J. D., *Religion in the Age of Decline: Organisation and Experience in Industrial Yorkshire, 1870–1920* (Cambridge, 1996).

Green, V. H. H., *Religion at Oxford and Cambridge* (London, 1964).

Greschat, Martin, *Das Christentum vor der Moderne* (Stuttgart, 1980).

—— 'Die Berliner Stadtmission', in Elm and Loock (eds), *Seelsorge und Diakonie*, pp. 451–75.

—— 'Die Revolution von 1848–9 und die Kirchen', in Helmut Baier (ed.), *Kirche in Staat und Gesellschaft im 19. Jahrhundert* (Neustadt a. d. Aisch, 1992), pp. 67–81.

Griffiths, Richard, *The Reactionary Revolution: The Catholic Revival in French Literature, 1870–1914* (New York, 1965).

Groh, John E., *Nineteenth-Century German Protestantism: The Church as a Social Model* (Washington, DC, 1982).

Grote, H., *Sozialdemokratie und Religion* (Tübingen, 1968).

Gugelot, Fréderic, 'Henri Ghéon: Ou l'histoire d'une âme en guerre', in Nadine-Josette Chaline, *Chrétiens dans la Première Guerre Mondiale* (Paris, 1993), pp. 66–93.

Guillaume, *Pierre, Médecins, Église et foi* (n.p., 1990).

Gunn, Simon, 'The Ministry, the Middle Class and the "Civilizing Mission" in Manchester, 1850–80', *Social History*, 21 (1996), pp. 22–36.

Gwyther, Cyril, 'Sidelights on Religion and Politics in the Rhondda Valley, 1906–26', *Llafur*, 3 (1980), pp. 36–43.

Hachtmann, Rüdiger, ' "ein gerechtes Gericht Gottes": Der Protestantismus und die Revolution von 1848 – das Berliner Beispiel', *Archiv für Sozialgeschichte*, 36 (1996), pp. 205–55.

Haig, Alan, *The Victorian Clergy* (Beckenham, 1984).

—— 'The Church, the Universities and Learning in later Victorian England', *Historical Journal*, 29 (1986), pp. 187–201.

Hall, David D., 'Religion and Secularization in America: a Cultural Approach', in Lehmann (ed.), *Säkularisierung*, pp. 118–30.

Hands, Timothy, *Thomas Hardy: Distracted Preacher?* (London, 1989).

Hardy, Thomas, *Tess of the d'Urbervilles* (London, 1912) [first published 1891].

Harris, José, *Private Lives, Public Spirit: A Social History of Britain, 1870–1914* (Oxford, 1993).

Harris, Ruth, *Lourdes: Body and Spirit in a Secular Age* (London, 1999).

Harrison, Brian, 'Religion and Recreation in Nineteenth Century England', *Past & Present*, 38 (1967), pp. 98–125.

Hartman, Mary, *Victorian Murderesses* (New York, 1976).

Hastings, Adrian, *A History of English Christianity, 1920–1985* (London, 1986).

——*The Construction of Nationhood: Ethnicity, Religion and Nationalism* (Cambridge, 1997).

Healy, Roísín, 'The Jesuit as Enemy: Anti-Jesuitism and the Protestant Bourgeoisie of Imperial Germany, 1890–1917' (Georgetown University PhD thesis, 1999).

Healy, Róisín, 'Religion and Civil Society: Catholics, Jesuits and Protestants in Imperial Germany', in Frank Trentmann (ed.), *Paradoxes of Civil Society: New Perspectives on Modern Britain and Germany* (Oxford, 1999).

Heilbronner, Oded, 'In Search of the (Rural) Catholic Bourgeoisie: the *Bürgertum* of South Germany', *Central European History*, 29 (1996), pp. 175–200.

Heimann, Mary, *Catholic Devotion in Victorian England* (Oxford, 1995).

——'Christianity in Western Europe from the Enlightenment', in Adrian Hastings (ed.), *A World History of Christianity* (London, 1999), pp. 458–507.

Helmreich, Ernst Christian, *Religious Education in German Schools* (Cambridge, MA, 1959).

——*The German Churches under Hitler: Background, Struggle and Epilogue* (Detroit, MI, 1979).

Helmstadter, Richard (ed.), *Freedom and Religion in the Nineteenth Century* (Stanford, CA, 1997).

Helmstadter, Richard J., and Lightman, Bernard (eds), *Victorian Faith in Crisis* (Basingstoke, 1990).

Hemmings, F. W. J., *Émile Zola* (2nd edn, Oxford, 1965).

Hempton, David, *Religion and Political Culture in Britain and Ireland* (Cambridge, 1996).

——*The Religion of the People: Methodism and Popular Religion c.1750–1900* (London, 1996).

Hendrickson, Kenneth E. III, *Making Saints: Religion and the Public Image of the British Army, 1809–1885* (Cranbury NJ, 1998).

Hennock, E. P., *Fit and Proper Persons* (London, 1973).

Herres, Jürgen, *Städtische Gesellschaft und katholische Vereine im Rheinland, 1840–1870* (Koblenz, 1996).

Herzog, Dagmar, *Intimacy and Exclusion: Religious Politics in Pre-revolutionary Baden* (Princeton, NJ, 1996).

Heywood, Colin, 'The Catholic Church and the Business Community in Nineteenth-Century France', in Tallett and Atkin (eds), *Religion in France*, pp. 67–88.

Hilaire, Yves-Marie, *Une chrétienté au XIXe siècle? La vie religieuse des populations du diocèse d'Arras, 1840–1914* (Lille, 1977).

——'Les ouvriers de la région du Nord devant l'Église catholique (XIXe et XXe siècles)', in Bédarida and Maitron (eds), *Christianisme et monde ouvrier*, pp. 222–43.

——'Observations sur la pratique religieuse urbaine en France pendant la première moitié du XXe siècle', *Hispania Sacra*, 42 (1990), pp. 457–67.

Hillis, Peter, 'Presbyterianism and Social Class in Mid-nineteenth Century Glasgow: A Study of Nine Churches', *Journal of Ecclesisastical History*, 32 (1981), pp. 47–64.

Hippel, W. von, 'Industrieller Wandel im ländlichen Raum', *Archiv für Sozialgeschichte*, 19 (1979), pp. 43–122.

Hobsbawm, Eric, *The Age of Revolution, 1789–1848* (London, 1962).

——*The Age of Capital, 1848–1875* (London, 1975).

——*Worlds of Labour* (London, 1984).

Hoffman-Krayer, E. (ed.), *Handwörterbuch des deutschen Aberglaubens*, 9 vols (Berlin, 1927–38).

Hölscher, Lucian, *Weltgericht oder Revolution* (Stuttgart, 1989).

——'Secular Culture and Religious Community in the City: Hannover in the 19th Century', *Hispania Sacra*, 42 (1990), pp. 405–11.

——'Die Religion des Bürgers: Bürgerliche Frömmigkeit und protestantische Kirche im 19. Jahrhundert', *Historische Zeitschrift*, 250 (1990), pp. 595–630.

——'Möglichkeiten und Grenzen der Statistischen Erfassung kirchlicher Bindungen', in Elm and Loock (eds), *Seelsorge und Diakonie*, pp. 39–62.

——'Säkularisierungsprozesse', in Hans-Jurgen Pühle (ed.), *Bürger in der Gesellschaft der Neuzeit* (Göttingen, 1991), pp. 238–58.

——'Kirchliche Demokratie und Frömmigkeitskultur im deutschen Protestantismus', in Martin Greschat and Jochen-Christoph Kaiser (eds), *Christentum und Demokratie* (Stuttgart, 1992), pp. 187–205.

——'Bürgerliche Religiosität im protestantischen Deutschland des 19. Jahrhunderts', in Schieder (ed.), *Religion*, pp. 191–215.

——'Secularization and Urbanization in the Nineteenth Century: an Interpretative Model', in McLeod (ed.), *Age of Great Cities*, pp. 263–88.

——' "Weibliche Religiosität"? Der Einfluß von Religion und Kirche auf die Religiosität von Frauen im 19. Jahrhundert', in Kraul and Luth (eds), *Erziehung*, pp. 45–62.

Lucian Hölscher and Ursula Männich-Polenz, 'Die Sozialstruktur der Kirchengemeinden Hannovers im 19. Jahrhundert. Eine statistische

Analyse', *Jahrbuch der Gesellschaft für niedersächsische Kirchengeschichte*, 88 (1990), pp. 159–217.

Holt, Richard, *Sport and Society in Modern France* (London, 1981).

Holzem, Andreas, *Kirchenreform und Sektenstiftung: Deutschkatholiken, Reformkatholiken und Ultramontane am Oberrhein, 1844–1866* (Paderborn, 1996).

—— 'Dechristianisierung und Rechristianisierung: Der deutsche Katholizismus im europäischen Vergeleich', *Kirchliche Zeitgeschichte*, 11 (1998), pp. 69–93.

Honey, J. R. de S., *Tom Brown's Universe: The Victorian Public School* (London, 1977).

Hönigmann, Peter, *Die Austritte aus der Jüdischen Gemeinde Berlin, 1873–1941* (Frankfurt am Main, 1988).

Hoover, A. J., *The Gospel of Nationalism: German Patriotic Preaching from Napoleon to Versailles* (Stuttgart, 1986).

—— *God, Germany, and Britain in the Great War: A Study in Clerical Nationalism* (New York, 1989).

Hope, Nicholas, *German and Scandinavian Protestantism, 1700 to 1918* (Oxford, 1995).

Hopp, Andrea, 'Von der "heiligen Gemeinde" zur Vielfalt der ethnischreligiösen Minderheit: Die jüdische Gemeinde in Frankfurt am Main', in Blaschke and Kuhlemann (eds), *Religion im Kaiserreich*, pp. 435–54.

Horn, Pamela, 'The Labourers' Union in Oxfordshire', in J. P. Dunbabin (ed.), *Rural Discontent in Nineteenth-Century Britain* (London, 1974).

Hornsby-Smith, Michael, 'Recent Transformations in English Catholicism: Evidence of Secularization?' in Bruce (ed.), *Religion and Modernization*, pp. 118–44.

Horowitz, Arnold, 'Prussian State and Protestant Church in the Reign of Wilhelm II' (Yale University PhD thesis, 1976).

Horridge, Glenn, *The Salvation Army: Origins and Early Days, 1865–1900* (Godalming, 1993).

Howkins, Alun, *Poor Labouring Men: Rural Radicalism in Norfolk, 1870–1923* (London, 1986).

Huber, Ernst Rudolf, *Deutsche Verfassungsgeschichte seit 1789*, 4 vols (Stuttgart, 1957–69).

Hübinger, Gangolf 'Kulturprotestantismus, Bürgerkirche und liberaler Revisionismus im wilhelminischen Deutschland', in Schieder (ed.), *Religion*, pp. 272–89.

Hufton, Olwen, *Bayeux in the Late Eighteenth Century* (London, 1967).

—— 'The Reconstruction of a Church 1796–1801', in Gwynne Lewis and Colin Lucas (eds), *Beyond the Terror: Essays in French Regional and Social History, 1794–1815* (Cambridge, 1983), pp. 21–52.

Humphries, Stephen, '"Hurrah for England": Schooling and the Working Class in Bristol, 1870–1914', *Southern History*, 1 (1979), pp. 171–208.

Hurt, J. S., *Elementary Schooling and the Working Classes, 1860–1918* (London, 1979).

Hutchison, William R., and Lehmann, Hartmut (eds), *Many are Chosen: Divine Election and Western Nationalism* (Minneapolis, 1994).

Hyman, Paula, 'The Social Contexts of Assimilation: Village Jews and City Jews in Alsace', in Frankel and Zipperstein (eds), *Assimilation and Community*, pp. 110–29.

Iannacone, Laurence R., 'The Consequence of Religious Market Structure: Adam Smith and the Economics of Religion', *Rationality and Society*, 3 (1991), pp. 156–77.

Isambert, François-André, *Christianisme et classe ouvrière* (Tournai, 1961).

Janz, Olivier, 'Zwischen Bürgerlichkeit und kirchlichem Milieu: Zum Selbstverständnis und sozialen Verhalten der evangelischen Pfarrer in Preußen in der zweiten Hälfte des 19. Jahrhunderts', in Blaschke and Kuhlemann (eds), *Religion im Kaiserreich*, pp. 382–406.

Jeremy, David (ed.), *Business and Religion in Britain* (Aldershot, 1988).

—— (ed.), *Religion, Business and Wealth in Modern Britain* (London, 1998).

Jersch-Wenzel, Stefi, 'Population Shifts and Occupational Structure', in Meyer (ed.), *German–Jewish History*, pp. 50–89.

Joyce, Patrick, *Work, Society and Politics* (Brighton, 1980).

Kaiser, Jochen-Christoph, 'Sozialdemokratie und "praktische" Religionskritik: Das Beispiel der Kirchenaustrittsbewegung 1878–1914', *Archiv für Sozialgeschichte*, 22 (1982), pp. 263–98.

Kaplan, Marion, *The Making of the Jewish Middle Class: Women, Family and Identity in Imperial Germany* (New York, 1991).

Katz, Jacob, 'German Culture and the Jews', in Jehuda Reinharz and Walter Schatzberg (eds), *The Jewish Response to German Culture* (Hanover, NH, 1985), pp. 85–99.

Kaufman, Suzanne F., 'Miracles, Medicine and the Spectacle of Lourdes: Popular Religion and Modernity in Fin-de-Siècle France' (Rutgers University PhD thesis, 1996).

Kelly, Alfred, *The Descent of Darwin: The Popularization of Darwinism in Germany, 1860–1914* (Chapel Hill, NC, 1981).

Kennedy, Thomas C., 'The Quaker Renaissance and the Origins of the Modern British Peace Movement, 1895–1920', *Albion*, 16 (1984), pp. 243–72.

Kent, John, *Holding the Fort: Studies in Victorian Revivalism* (London, 1978).

Kershen, Anne J., and Romaine, Jonathan A., *Tradition and Change: A History of Reform Judaism in Britain, 1840–1995* (London, 1995).

Kniffka, Jörg, *Das kirchliche Leben in Berlin-Ost in der Mitte der zwanziger Jahre* (dissertation, Westfälische Wilhelms-Universität, Münster, 1971).

Knight, Frances, *The Nineteenth-Century Church and English Society* (Cambridge, 1995).

—— 'The Bishops and the Jews, 1828–1858', in Diana Wood (ed.), *Christianity and Judaism*, Studies in Church History 29 (Oxford, 1992), pp. 387–98.

Kocka, Jürgen (ed.), *Bürgertum im 19. Jahrhundert: Deutschland im europäischen Vergleich*, 3 vols (Munich, 1988).

Koditschek, Theodore, *Class Formation and Urban–Industrial Society: Bradford, 1750–1850* (Cambridge, 1991).

Köhle-Hezinger, Christel, *Evangelisch–Katholisch: Untersuchungen zu konfessionellem Vorurteil und Konflikt im 19. und 20. Jahrhundert vornehmlich am Beispiel Württembergs* (Tübingen, 1976).

Köllmann, Wolfgang, *Sozialgeschichte der Stadt Barmen* (Tübingen, 1960).

Koss, Stephen, *The Pro-Boers* (Chicago, 1973).

Kraul, M., and Lüth, C. (eds), *Erziehung der Menschen-Geschlechter* (Weinheim, 1996).

Krey, Ursula, 'Mit Gott für König und Vaterland: Konservative Leitbilder im östlichen Westfalen um 1900', in Meynert, Mooser and Rodekamp (eds), *Pickelhaube und Zylinder*, pp. 235–58.

Krumeich, Gerd, 'Jeanne d'Arc-Kult und politische Religiosität in Frankreich', in Schieder (ed.), *Religion*, pp. 318–31.

Kselman, Thomas, *Miracles and Prophecies in Nineteenth-Century France* (New Brunswick, NJ, 1983).

—— *Death and the Afterlife in Nineteenth Century France* (Princeton, NJ, 1993).

—— 'The Varieties of Religious Experience in Urban France', McLeod (ed.), *Age of Great Cities*, pp. 165–90.

—— 'Religion and French Identity: the Origins of the Union Sacrée', in Hutchison and Lehmann (eds), *Many are Chosen*, pp. 57–79.

Kudlick, Catherine J., *Cholera in Post-Revolutionary Paris: A Cultural History* (Berkeley, CA, 1996).

Kuhlemann, Frank-Michael, 'Zwischen Tradition und Modernität: Volksschule und Volksschullehrer im wilhelmischen Ostwestfalen', in Meynert, Mooser and Rodekamp (eds), *Pickelhaube und Zylinder*, pp. 327–46.

Lagrée, Michel, *Mentalités, religion et histoire en Haute-Bretagne au XIXe siècle* (Paris, 1977).

—— 'Exilés dans leur patrie (1880–1920)', in Lebrun (ed.), *Catholiques*, pp. 369–411.

—— *Religions et cultures en Bretagne, 1850–1950* (Paris, 1992).

—— 'Sport et sociabilité catholique en France au début du XXe siècle', in P. Arnaud and J. Camy (eds), *La naissance du Mouvement Sportif Associatif en France* (Lyon, 1986), pp. 327–35.

Lalouette, Jacqueline, *La Libre pensée en France, 1848–1940* (Paris, 1997).

Lambert, Yves, *Dieu change en Bretagne: La religion à Limerzel de 1900 à nos jours* (Paris, 1985).

—— 'Vers une ère post-chrétienne?', *Futuribles*, 200 (1995), pp. 85–111.

Lamberti, Marjorie, *State, Society and the Elementary School in Imperial Germany* (New York, 1989).

Langlois, Claude, 'Permanence, renouveau et affrontements', in Lebrun, *Catholiques*, pp. 291–368.

—— *Le catholicisme au féminin* (Paris, 1984).

—— 'La déchirure', in Timothy Tackett, *La Révolution, l'Église, la France: Le serment de 1791* (Paris, 1986), pp. 319–37.

—— 'Catholiques et laïcs', in Nora (ed.), *Lieux de mémoire*, vol. II, pp. 2327–58.

Laqueur, Thomas Walter, *Religion and Respectability: Sunday Schools and Working Class Culture, 1780–1850* (New Haven, CT, 1976).

Larkin, Maurice, *Church and State after the Dreyfus Affair* (London, 1974).

—— *Religion, Politics and Preferment in France since the 1890s: La Belle Époque and its Legacy* (Cambridge, 1995).

Lawrence, D. H., *Selected Poems* (Harmondsworth, 1972).

Lawrence, Jon, *Speaking for the People: Party, Language and Popular Politics in England, 1867–1914* (Cambridge, 1998).

Lawson, Joseph, *Letters to the Young on Progress in Pudsey during the last Sixty Years* (Stanningley, 1887).

Lebrun, François (ed.), *Histoire des catholiques en France* (Toulouse, 1980).

Lecky, W. E. H., *History of the Rise and Influence of the Spirit of Rationalism in Europe*, 2 vols (London, 1893).

Lehmann, Hartmut, '"God Our Old Ally": The Chosen People Theme in Late Nineteenth- and Early Twentieth-Century German Nationalism', in Hutchison and Lehmann (eds), *Many are Chosen*, pp. 85–107.

—— (ed.), *Säkularisierung, Dechristianisierung, Rechristianisierung im neuzeitlichen Europa* (Göttingen, 1997).

Lentin, Antony, 'Anglicanism, Parliament and the Courts', in Parsons, Moore and Wolffe (eds), *Religion in Victorian Britain*, vol. II, pp. 88–106.

Lepovitz, Helena Waddy, 'The Industrialization of Popular Art in Bavaria', *Past & Present*, 99 (1983), pp. 88–122.

Lewis, Donald M., *Lighten their Darkness: The Evangelical Mission to Working Class London, 1828–1860* (London, 1986).

Liberles, Robert, 'The So-Called Quiet Years of German Jewry, 1849–1869: a Reconsideration', *Yearbook of the Leo Baeck Institute*, 41 (1996), pp. 65–74.

Lidtke, Vernon L., 'August Bebel and German Social Democracy's Relation to the Christian Churches', *Journal of the History of Ideas*, 27 (1966), pp. 245–64.

—— 'Social Class and Secularization in Imperial Germany: The Working Classes', *Yearbook of the Leo Baeck Institute*, 25 (1980), pp. 21–40.

—— *The Alternative Culture* (New York, 1985).

Liedhegener, Antonius, *Christentum und Urbanisierung: Katholiken und Protestanten in Münster und Bochum, 1830–1933* (Paderborn, 1997).

Lightman, Bernard, 'Robert Elsmere and the Agnostic Crisis of Faith', in Helmstadter and Lightman (eds), *Victorian Faith*, pp. 283–311.

Lill Rudolf, 'Kirche und Revolution', *Archiv für Sozialgeschichte*, 18 (1978), pp. 565–75.

Linden, F., *Sozialismus und Religion* (Leipzig, 1932).

Lisco, F., *Zur Kirchengeschichte Berlins* (Berlin, 1857).

Loreck, Jochen, *Wie man früher Sozialdemokrat wurde* (Bonn, 1977).

Lorenz, Walter, 'Personal Social Services', in Jochen Clasen and Richard Freeman (eds), *Social Policy in Germany* (Hemel Hempstead, 1994), pp. 148–69.

Lorimer, Douglas A., 'Race, Science and Culture: Historical Continuities and Discontinuities, 1850–1914', in Shearer West (ed.), *Victorians and Race* (Aldershot, 1996), pp. 12–33.

Lowerson, John, *Sport and the English Middle Classes* (Manchester, 1993).

Loyer, François, 'Le Sacré-Cœur de Montmartre', in Nora (ed.), *Lieux de mémoire*, vol. III, pp. 4253–69.

Luckmann, Thomas, *The Invisible Religion* (English translation, London, 1967).

Machin, G. I. T., *Politics and the Churches in Great Britain, 1832 to 1868* (Oxford, 1977).

——*Politics and the Churches in Great Britain, 1869–1921* (Oxford, 1987).

——'British Churches and the Cinema in the 1930s', in Diana Wood (ed.), *The Church and the Arts*, Studies in Church History 28 (Oxford, 1992), pp. 477–88.

McHugh, Paul, *Prostitution and Victorian Social Reform* (London, 1980).

McIlhiney, D. B., 'A Gentleman in Every Slum: Church of England Missions in the East End of London, 1837–1914' (Princeton University PhD thesis, 1977).

McIntire, C. T., 'Changing Religious Establishments and Religious Liberty in France, 1787–1908', in Helmstadter (ed.), *Freedom and Religion*, pp. 233–301.

Macintyre, Stuart, *Little Moscows* (London, 1980).

MacKenzie, John M., 'Heroic Myths of Empire', in idem. (ed.), *Popular Imperialism and the Military, 1850–1950* (Manchester, 1992), pp. 109–38.

McLaren, A. A., *Religion and Social Class: The Disruption Years in Aberdeen* (London, 1974).

McLeod, Hugh, 'Class, Community and Region: the Religious Geography of Nineteenth-century England', in Michael Hill (ed.), *Sociological Yearbook of Religion in Britain*, 6 (1973), pp. 29–72.

——*Class and Religion in the Late Victorian City* (London, 1974).

——'White-collar Values and the Role of Religion', in Geoffrey Crossick (ed.), *The Lower Middle Class in Britain, 1870–1914* (London, 1977), pp. 61–88.

——'Protestantism and the Working Class in Imperial Germany', *European Studies Review*, 12 (1982), pp. 323–45.

—— 'New Perspectives on Victorian Working Class Religion: the Oral Evidence', *Oral History Journal*, 14 (1986), pp. 31–49.

—— 'Religion in the British and German Labour Movements: a Comparison', *Bulletin of the Society for the Study of Labour History*, 50 (1986), pp. 25–36.

—— 'Building the "Catholic Ghetto": Catholic Organisations, 1870–1914', in W. J. Sheils and Diana Wood (eds), *Voluntary Religion*, Studies in Church History 23 (Oxford, 1986), pp. 411–44.

—— (ed.), *European Religion in the Age of Great Cities* (London, 1995).

—— *Piety and Poverty: Working Class Religion in Berlin, London and New York, 1870–1914* (New York, 1996).

—— *Religion and Society in England, 1850–1914* (Basingstoke, 1996).

—— *Religion and the People of Western Europe, 1789–1989* (Oxford, 1997).

—— 'Dechristianization and Rechristianization: the Case of Great Britain', *Kirchliche Zeitgeschichte*, 11 (1998), pp. 21–32.

—— 'Protestantism and British National Identity, 1815–1945', in Peter van der Veer and Hartmut Lehmann (eds), *Nation and Religion: Perspectives on Europe and Asia* (Princeton, NJ, 1999), pp. 44–70.

McManners, John, *Church and State in France, 1870–1914* (London, 1972).

McMillan, James F., 'Women in Social Catholicism in Late Nineteenth- and Early Twentieth Century France', in W. J. Sheils and Diana Wood (eds), *Women in the Church*, Studies in Church History 27 (Oxford, 1990), pp. 467–80.

—— 'Reclaiming a Martyr: French Catholics and the Cult of Joan of Arc, 1890–1920', in Diana Wood (ed.), *Martyrs and Martyrologies*, Studies in Church History 30 (Oxford, 1993), pp. 359–70.

Magraw, Roger, 'The Conflict in the Villages: Popular Anti-Clericalism in the Isère', in Zeldin (ed.), *Conflicts*, pp. 169–227.

—— 'Popular Anti-clericalism in Nineteenth-century Rural France', in Obelkevich, Roper and Samuel (eds), *Disciplines of Faith*, pp. 351–70.

Mallmann, Klaus Michael, ' "Aus des Tages Last machen sie ein Kreuz des Herrn . . ."? Bergarbeiter, Religion und sozialer Protest im Saarrevier des 19. Jahrhunderts', in Schieder (ed.), *Volksreligiosität*, pp. 152–84.

Malmgreen, Gail (ed.), *Religion in the Lives of English Women, 1760–1930* (Beckenham, 1986).

Mangan, J. A., *Athleticism and the Victorian and Edwardian Public School: The Emergence and Consolidation of an Educational Ideology* (Cambridge, 1981).

—— *The Games Ethic and Imperialism* (Harmondsworth, 1986).

—— 'Social Darwinism and Upper-Class Education in Late Victorian and Edwardian England', in J. A. Mangan and James Walvin (eds), *Manliness and Morality: Middle Class Masculinity in Britain and America, 1800–1940* (Manchester, 1987), pp. 135–59.

Marbach, Rainer, *Säkularisierung und sozialer Wandel im 19. Jahrhundert* (Göttingen, 1978).

Marcilhacy, Christiane, *Le diocese d'Orléans sous l'épiscopat de Mgr Dupanloup* (Paris, 1962).

——*Le diocèse d'Orléans au milieu du XIXe siècle* (Paris, 1964).

Margandant, Ted, 'Primary Schools and Youth Groups in Pre-war Paris: Les "Petites A's"', *Journal of Contemporary History*, 13 (1978), pp. 323–36.

Marrus, Michael R., *The Politics of Assimilation: A Study of the French Jewish Community at the Time of the Dreyfus Affair* (Oxford, 1971).

Marsh, Peter T., *The Victorian Church in Decline* (London, 1969).

——*Joseph Chamberlain: Entrepreneur in Politics* (New Haven, CT, 1994).

Martin, David, *A General Theory of Secularization* (Oxford, 1978).

——*Tongues of Fire: The Explosion of Protestantism in Latin America* (Oxford, 1990).

Martin, Philippe, 'Christianisation? Déchristianisation? Rechristianisation? La question de la sacralisation de l'espace dans la France catholique (XIXe–XXe siècles)', *Kirchliche Zeitgeschichte*, 11 (1998), pp. 51–68.

Martin Du Gard, Roger, *Jean Barois* (Paris, 1921) [first published 1913].

Marx, Karl, and Engels, Friedrich, *On Religion* (Moscow, 1957).

Mason, Tony (ed.), *Sport in Britain: A Social History* (Cambridge, 1989).

Mass Observation, *Puzzled People* (London, 1947).

Masterman, C. F. G., *The Condition of England* (London, 1909).

Masterman, Lucy, *C. F. G. Masterman: A Biography* (London, 1939).

Mather, Judson, 'The Assumptionist Response to Secularization, 1870–1900', in Robert Bezucha (ed.), *Modern European Social History* (Lexington, MA, 1971), pp. 59–89.

Meiwes, Reilinde, 'Religiosität und Arbeit als Lebensform für katholische Frauenkongregationen im 19. Jahrhundert', in Götz von Olenhusen et al., *Frauen*, pp. 69–88.

Meller, Helen, *Leisure and the Changing City, 1870–1914* (London, 1976).

Mergel, Thomas, *Zwischen Klasse und Konfession: Katholisches Bürgertum im Rheinland, 1794–1914* (Göttingen 1994).

——'Die subtile Macht der Liebe: Geschlecht, Erziehung und Frömmigkeit in katholischen rheinischen Bürgerfamilien', in Götz von Olenhusen et al., *Frauen*, pp. 22–47.

——'Ultramontanism, Liberalism, Moderation: Political Mentalities and Political Behavior of the German Catholic *Bürgertum*, 1848–1914', *Central European History*, 29 (1996), pp. 151–74.

Mews, Stuart Paul, 'Religion and English Society in the First World War' (University of Cambridge PhD thesis, 1973).

Meyer, Michael A., *Jewish Identity in the Modern World* (Seattle, 1990).

——*Response to Modernity: A History of the Reform Movement in Judaism* (Detroit, MI, 1995).

——(ed.), *German–Jewish History in Modern Times*, vol. 2: *Emancipation and Acculturation, 1780–1871* (New York, 1997).

Meynert, Joachim, Mooser, Josef and Rodekamp, Volker (eds), *Unter Pick-elhaube und Zylinder: Das östliche Westfalen im Zeitalter des Wilhelmismus, 1888–1914* (Bielefeld, 1991).

Michelet, Jules, *Du Prêtre, De la Famille, De l'Église* (Paris, 1845).

Moody, Joseph N., *The Church as Enemy: Anticlericalism in Nineteenth-Century French Literature* (Washington, DC, 1968).

Moore, James R., 'Freethought, Secularism, Darwinism: The Case of Charles Darwin', in Parsons, Moore and Wolffe (eds), *Religion in Victorian Britain*, vol. I, pp. 274–319.

——'The Crisis of Faith: Reformation Versus Revolution', in Parsons, Moore and Wolffe (eds), *Religion in Victorian Britain*, vol. II, pp. 220–37.

Moore, Robert, *Pit-men, Preachers and Politics* (London, 1974).

Moore, R. Laurence, *Selling God: American Religion in the Marketplace of Culture* (New York, 1994).

Mooser, Josef, 'Arbeiter, Bürger und Priester in den konfessionellen Arbeitervereinen im deutschen Kaiserreich, 1880–1914', in Jürgen Kocka (ed.), *Arbeiter und Bürger im 19. Jahrhundert* (Munich, 1986), pp. 79–105.

——'Katholische Volksreligion, Klerus und Bürgertum in der zweiten Hälfte des 19. Jahrhunderts. Thesen', Schieder (ed.), *Religion*, pp. 144–56.

——'Das katholische Milieu in der bürgerlichen Gesellschaft: Zum Vereinswesen des Katholizismus im späten Kaiserreich', in Blaschke and Kuhlemann (eds), *Religion im Kaiserreich*, pp. 59–92.

Morgan, Kenneth O., *Rebirth of a Nation: Wales, 1880–1980* (Oxford, 1981).

Morris, J. N., *Religion and Urban Change: Croydon, 1890–1914* (Woodbridge, 1992).

Morris, R. J., *Cholera 1832* (London, 1976).

Motzkin, Gabriel, 'Säkularisierung, Bürgertum und Intellektuelle in Frankreich und Deutschland', in Kocka (ed.), *Bürgertum*, vol. III, pp. 141–71.

Müller, Karl Julius, *Aberglaube und Occultismus in Berlin und der Provinz Brandenburg* (Berlin, 1899).

Munson, J. E. B., 'The London School Board Election of 1894: a Study in Victorian Religious Controversy', *British Journal of Educational Studies*, 23 (1975), pp. 7–23.

——*The Nonconformists* (London, 1991).

Newman, Aubrey, 'The Office of Chief Rabbi: a Very English Institution', in Nigel Aston (ed.), *Religious Change in Europe, 1650–1914* (Oxford, 1997), pp. 289–308.

Nietzsche, Friedrich, *Jenseits von Gut und Böse* (1886).

Nipperdey, Thomas, *Deutsche Geschichte, 1800–1866* (Munich, 1983).

——*Religion im Umbruch* (Munich, 1987).

Nolan, Mary, *Social Democracy and Society: Working-Class Radicalism in Düsseldorf, 1890–1920* (Cambridge, 1987).

Nora, Pierre (ed.), *Les lieux de mémoire*, 3 vols (2nd edn, Paris, 1997).

Nord, Philip, *The Republican Moment: Struggles for Democracy in Nineteenth-Century France* (Cambridge, MA, 1995).

Norman, Edward, 'Church and State since 1800', in Gilley and Sheils (eds), *Religion in Britain*, pp. 279–90.

Obelkevich, James, *Religion and Rural Society: South Lindsey, 1825–1875* (Oxford, 1976).

—— 'The Religion of Music', in Obelkevich, Roper and Samuel (eds), *Disciplines of Faith*, pp. 550–65.

Obelkevich, James, Roper, Lyndal and Samuel, Raphael (eds), *Disciplines of Faith* (London, 1987).

Ormières, Jean-Louis, 'Les rouges et les blancs', in Nora (ed.), *Lieux de mémoire*, vol. II, pp. 2395–2432.

Ozouf, Jacques, *Nous les maîtres d'école* (Paris, 1973).

Ozouf, Jacques and Mona, *La république des instituteurs* (Paris, 1992).

Ozouf, Mona, *L'école, L'Église et la République* (Paris, 1963).

Paletschek, Sylvia, *Frauen und Dissens* (Göttingen, 1990).

—— 'Frauen und Säkularisierung Mitte des 19. Jahrhunderts', in Schieder (ed.), *Religion*, pp. 300–17.

Parry, J. P., *Democracy and Religion: Gladstone and the Liberal Party, 1867–75* (Cambridge, 1986).

Parsons, Gerald, Moore, James R. and Wolffe, John (eds), *Religion in Victorian Britain*, 5 vols (Manchester, 1988–96).

Paz, D. G., *Popular Anti-Catholicism in Mid-Victorian England* (Stanford, CA, 1992).

Pelling, Henry, *Social Geography of British Elections, 1885–1910* (London, 1967).

Pérouas, Louis, *Refus d'une religion, religion d'un refus en Limousin rural, 1880–1940* (Paris, 1985).

—— *Les Limousins, leurs saints, leurs prêtres, du XVe au XXe siècle* (Paris, 1988).

Petuchowski, Jakob, 'Frankfurt Jewry: a Model of Transition to Modernity', *Yearbook of the Leo Baeck Institute*, 29 (1984), pp. 405–18.

Phayer, J. M., *Sexual Liberation and Religion in Nineteenth-Century Europe* (London, 1977).

Pickering, W. S. F., *Durkheim's Sociology of Religion* (London, 1984).

Pieper, P., *Kirchenstatistik Deutschlands* (Freiburg im Breisgau, 1899).

Pin, Émile, *Pratique religieuse et classes sociales* (Paris, 1956).

Pohl, Karl-Heinrich, 'Katholische Sozialdemokraten oder sozialdemokratische Katholiken in München: Ein Identitätskonflikt', in Blaschke and Kuhlemann (eds), *Religion im Kaiserreich*, pp. 233–53.

Pollmann, K. E., *Lansdesherrliches Kirchenregiment und soziale Frage* (Berlin, 1973).

Prelinger, Catherine, *Charity, Challenge and Change: Religious Dimensions of the Mid-Nineteenth-Century Women's Movement in Germany* (New York, 1987).

Prochaska, F. K., 'Body and Soul: Bible Nurses and the Poor in Victorian London', *Historical Research*, 60 (1987), pp. 336–48.

Rae, John, *Conscience and Politics* (London, 1970).

Reeken, Dietmar von, 'Protestantische Milieu und "liberale" Landeskirche?' in Blaschke and Kuhlemann, *Religion im Kaiserreich*, pp. 290–315.

Reid, Ivan, *Social Class Differences in Britain* (London, 1977).

Reif, Hans, *Westfälischer Adel* (Göttingen, 1979).

'Religious Worship (England and Wales)', *Parliamentary Papers* (1852–3) vol. 89.

Rémond, René, *L'anti-cléricalisme en France: De 1815 à nos jours* (2nd edn, Paris, 1992).

—— 'La fille ainée de l'église', in Nora (ed.), *Lieux de mémoire*, vol. III, pp. 4321–51.

Rendall, Jane, *The Origins of Modern Feminism* (London, 1985).

Ribbe, Wolfgang, 'Zur Entwicklung und Funktion der Pfarrgemeinden in der evangelischen Kirche Berlins bis zum Ende der Monarchie', in Elm and Loock (eds), *Seelsorge und Diakonie*, pp. 233–63.

—— (ed.), *Geschichte Berlins*, 2 vols (Munich, 1987).

Richards, N. J., 'Religious Controversy and the School Boards 1870–1902', *British Journal of Educational Studies*, 18 (1970), pp. 180–96.

Richarz, Monika, *Jüdisches Leben in Deutschland*, 3 vols (Stuttgart, 1979).

Roberts, Elizabeth, *A Woman's Place: An Oral History of Working-Class Women, 1890–1940* (Oxford, 1984).

Robson, Geoffrey, 'Religion and Irreligion in Birmingham and the Black Country' (University of Birmingham PhD thesis, 1997).

—— 'The Failures of Success: Working-Class Evangelists in Early Victorian Birmingham', in Derek Baker (ed.), *Religious Motivation: Biographical and Sociological Problems for the Church Historian*, Studies in Church History, 15 (Oxford, 1978), pp. 381–91.

Rogers, Rebecca, 'The Socialization of Girls in France under the Influence of Religion and the Church', in Kraul and Luth (eds), *Erziehung*, pp. 139–58.

Rohde, Joachim, 'Streiflichter aus der Berliner Kirchengeschichte von 1900 bis 1918', in Wirth (ed.), *Beiträge*, pp. 217–42.

Rolffs, E., *Das kirchliche Leben der evangelischen Kirchen in Niedersachsen* (Tübingen, 1917).

Roof, Wade Clark, and McKinney, William, *American Mainline Religion* (New Brunswick, NJ, 1987).

Rose, Gillian, 'Locality, Politics and Culture: Poplar in the 1920s' (University of London PhD thesis, 1989).

Ross, Ellen, 'Survival Networks: Women's Neighbourhood Sharing in London before World War I', *History Workshop Journal*, 15 (1983), pp. 4–27.

—— 'Hungry Children: Housewives and London charity', in Peter Mandler (ed.), *The Uses of Charity: The Poor on Relief in the Nineteenth-Century Metropolis* (Philadelphia, PA, 1990), pp. 161–96.

Ross, Ronald J., *Beleaguered Tower: The Dilemma of Political Catholicism in Wilhelmine Germany* (Notre Dame, IN, 1976).

—— *The Failure of Bismarck's Kulturkampf: Catholics and State Power in Imperial Germany, 1871–1887* (Washington, DC, 1998).

—— 'The Kulturkampf: Restrictions and Controls on the Practice of Religion in Bismarck's Germany', in Helmstadter (ed.), *Freedom and Religion*, pp. 172–95.

Royle, Edward, *Victorian Infidels* (Manchester, 1974).

—— *Radicals, Secularists and Republicans: Popular Freethought in Britain, 1866–1915* (Manchester, 1980).

Rückleben, Hermann, 'Theologischer Rationalismus und kirchlicher Protest in Baden 1843–49', *Pietismus und Neuzeit*, 5 (1979), pp. 66–83.

Ruppin, Arthur, *Soziologie der Juden*, 2 vols (Berlin, 1930–1).

Ryan, Mary, 'A Woman's Awakening: Evangelical Religion and the Families of Utica, New York, 1800–1840', in Janet Wilson James (ed.), *Women in American Religion* (Philadelphia, PA, 1980), pp. 89–110.

Samuel, Raphael, 'The Roman Catholic Church and the Irish Poor', in Swift and Gilley (eds), *Irish in Victorian City*, pp. 267–300.

Saß, Friedrich, *Berlin in seiner neuesten Zeit und Entwicklung* (Berlin, 1983) [first published 1846].

Satlow, Bernt, 'Die Revolution von 1848. Die Kirche und die soziale Frage', in Wirth (ed.), *Beiträge*, pp. 177–96.

Scannell, Paddy, and Cardiff, David, *A Social History of British Broadcasting*, vol. 1: *1922–1939* (Oxford, 1991).

Schäfer, Gerhard, 'Die evangelische Kirche in Württemberg und die Revolution 1848/9', *Pietismus und Neuzeit*, 5 (1979), pp. 39–65.

Schauff, Johannes, *Das Wahlverhalten der deutschen Katholiken* (Mainz, 1975) [first published 1928].

Scheidgen, H.-J., *Deutsche Bischöfe im Ersten Weltkrieg* (Cologne, 1991).

Schieder, Wolfgang, 'Kirche und Revolution. Zur Sozialgeschichte der Trierer Wallfahrt von 1844', *Archiv für Sozialgeschichte*, 14 (1974), pp. 419–54.

—— 'Konfessionelle Erneuerung in den christlichen Parallelkirchen Deutschlands im 19. Jahrhundert', in Lehmann (ed.), *Säkularisierung*, pp. 223–8.

—— (ed.), *Volksreligiosität in der modernen Sozialgeschichte* (Göttingen, 1986).

—— (ed.), *Religion und Gesellschaft im 19. Jahrhundert* (Stuttgart, 1993).

Schlögl, Rudolf, *Glaube und Religion in der Säkularisierung* (Munich, 1995).

Schloßmacher, Norbert, 'Der Deutsche Verein für die Rheinprovinz', in Blaschke and Kuhlemann (eds), *Religion im Kaiserreich*, pp. 474–502.

Schmaltz, K., *Kirchengeschichte Mecklenburgs*, 3 vols (Schwerin and Berlin, 1935–52).

Schmidt, Erich, *Meine Jugend in Groß-Berlin* (Bremen, 1988).

Schmidt, Martin, 'Die Entchristlichung in der neuzeitlichen Kirchengeschichte im deutschsprachigen Gebiet', *Zeitschrift für Kirchengeschichte*, 79 (1968), pp. 342–57.

Schnabel, Franz, *Deutsche Geschichte im 19. Jahrhundert*, vol. 4: *Die religiösen Kräfte* (Freiburg im Breisgau, 1937).

Schwank, Willi, *Kirche und Sport in Deutschland von 1848 bis 1920* (Hochheim-am-Main, 1979).

Schwentker, Wolfgang, *Konservative Vereine und Revolution in Preußen 1848/49* (Düsseldorf, 1988).

Scotland, Nigel, *Methodism and the Revolt of the Field* (Gloucester, 1981).

——*Agricultural Trade Unionism in Gloucestershire, 1872–1950* (Cheltenham, 1991).

Seeley, Paul, 'O Sainte Mère: Liberalism and the Socialization of Men in Nineteenth-Century France', *Journal of Modern History*, 70 (1998), pp. 862–91.

Sewell, W., 'Social Change and the Rise of Working Class Politics in Nineteenth-Century Marseilles', *Past & Present*, 65 (1974), pp. 75–109.

Shanahan, W. O., *German Protestants Face the Social Question* (Notre Dame, IN, 1954).

Simon-Rits, Frank, 'Kulturelle Modernisierung und Krise der religiösen Bewußtseins', in Blaschke and Kuhlemann (eds), *Religion im Kaiserreich*, pp. 457–73.

Singer, Barnett, *Village Notables in Nineteenth-Century France: Priests, Mayors and Schoolmasters* (Albany, NY, 1983).

Smith, Bonnie G., *Ladies of the Leisure Class: The Bourgeoises of Northern France in the Nineteenth Century* (Princeton, NJ, 1981).

Smith, Elaine R., 'Jews and Politics in the East End of London', in David Cesarani (ed.), *The Making of Modern Anglo-Jewry* (Oxford, 1990).

Smith, Helmut Walser, *German Nationalism and Religious Conflict: Culture, Ideology, Politics, 1870–1914* (Princeton, NJ, 1995).

——'Catholics, the Nation and Nationalism in Nineteenth-century Germany', paper read at conference 'Religion and Nationalism', University of Amsterdam (1995).

Smith, Leonard, *Religion and the Rise of Labour* (Keele, 1993).

Smith, Mark, *Religion and Industrial Society: Oldham and Saddleworth, 1740–1865* (Oxford, 1995).

Sorkin, David, *The Transformation of German Jewry* (Oxford, 1987).

——'The Impact of Emancipation on German Jewry', in Frankel and Zipperstein (eds), *Assimilation and Community* (Cambridge, 1992), pp. 177–98.

Sperber, Jonathan, 'Roman Catholic Religious Identity in Rhineland-Westphalia, 1800–70', *Social History*, 7 (1982) pp. 305–18.

——— *Popular Catholicism in Nineteenth-Century Germany* (Princeton, NJ, 1984).

——— *Rhineland Radicals: The Democratic Movement and the Revolution of 1848–1849* (Princeton, NJ, 1991).

——— *The European Revolutions, 1848–1851* (Cambridge, 1994).

——— *The Kaiser's Voters* (Cambridge, 1997).

Stark, Rodney, and Bainbridge, William Sims, *The Future of Religion: Secularization, Revival and Cult Formation* (Berkeley, CA, 1985).

Stark, Rodney, and Iannacone, Laurence R., 'A Supply-Side Reinterpretation of the Secularization of Europe', *Journal for the Scientific Study of Religion*, 33 (1994), pp. 230–52.

Steinhoff, Anthony, 'Protestants in Strasbourg, 1870–1914: Religion and Society in late Nineteenth-Century Europe' (University of Chicago PhD thesis, 1996).

Strikwerda, Carl, *A House Divided: Catholics, Socialists and Flemish Nationalists in Belgium* (Lanham, MD, 1997).

Strumhinger, L., ' "A bas les prêtres! A bas les couvents!" The Church and the Workers in Nineteenth-Century Lyon,' *Journal of Social History*, 11 (1978), pp. 546–53.

Summers, D. F., 'The Labour Church and Allied Movements of the late 19th and early 20th Centuries' (University of Edinburgh PhD, 1958).

Sun, Raymond, ' "Before the Enemy is within our Walls": a Social, Cultural and Political History of Catholic Workers in Cologne, 1895–1912' (Johns Hopkins University PhD, 1991).

Swift, Roger and Gilley, Sheridan (eds), *The Irish in the Victorian City* (London, 1985).

Sykes, Richard, 'Popular Religion in Dudley and the Gornals, *c*. 1914–1965' (University of Wolverhampton PhD thesis, 1999).

Tal, Uriel, *Christians and Jews in Germany: Religion, Politics and Ideology in the Second Reich, 1870–1914* (English translation, Ithaca, NY, 1975).

Tallett, Frank, and Atkin, Nicholas (eds), *Religion, Society and Politics in France since 1789* (London, 1991).

Tallett, Frank, 'Dechristianizing France: the Year II and the Revolutionary Experience', in Tallett and Atkin (eds), *Religion in France*, pp. 1–28.

Taylor, Lawrence J., 'Stories of Power, Powerful Stories', in Badone (ed.), *Religious Orthodoxy*, pp. 163–84.

Tews, Johannes, *Berliner Lehrer* (Berlin, 1907).

Thabault, Roger, *Mon village* (Paris, 1945).

Thompson, David, 'R. W. Dale and the "Civic Gospel" ', in Alan Sell (ed.), *Protestant Nonconformity and the West Midlands of England* (Keele, 1996), pp. 99–118.

Thompson, Paul, *Socialists, Liberals and Labour: The Struggle for London, 1885–1914* (London, 1967).

Thompson, Paul, with Tony Wailey and Trevor Lummis, *Living the Fishing* (London, 1983).

Thorne, Susan, 'Protestant Ethics and the Spirit of Imperialism: British Congregationalists and the London Missionary Society, 1795–1925' (University of Michigan PhD thesis, 1990).

Townsend, Mary Lee, *Forbidden Laughter* (Ann Arbor, MI, 1992).

Tressell, Robert, *The Ragged Trousered Philanthropists* (London, 1955) [1st published 1914].

Tschannen, Olivier, *Les théories de la sécularisation* (Geneva, 1992).

Tsuzuki, Chushichi, *Edward Carpenter, 1844–1929: Prophet of Human Fellowship* (Cambridge, 1980).

Turner, Frank M., *Between Science and Religion* (New Haven, CT, 1974).

—— 'The Victorian Crisis of Faith and the Faith that was Lost', in Helmstadter and Lightman (eds), *Victorian Faith*, pp. 9–38.

——*Contesting Cultural Authority: Essays in Victorian Intellectual Life* (Cambridge, 1993).

Urdank, Albion, *Religion and Society in a Cotswold Vale: Nailsworth, Gloucestershire, 1780–1865* (Berkeley, CA, 1990).

Ustorf, Werner, *Theologie im revolutionären Bremen: Die Aktualität Rudolph Dulons* (Bonn, 1992).

Vance, Norman, *The Sinews of the Spirit* (Cambridge, 1985).

van Rooden, Peter, 'Secularization, Dechristianization and Rechristianization in The Netherlands', in Lehmann (ed.), *Säkularisierung*, pp. 131–53.

Vincent, John, *Pollbooks: How Victorians Voted* (Cambridge, 1967).

Volkov, Shulamit, 'Antisemitism as a Cultural Code: Reflections on the History and Historiography of Antisemitism in Imperial Germany', *Yearbook of the Leo Baeck Institute*, 23 (1978) pp. 25–46.

—— 'Die Verbürgerlichung der Juden in Deutschland', in Kocka (ed.), *Bürgertum*, vol. II, pp. 343–71.

Vorländer, Herwart, *Evangelische Kirche und soziale Frage in der werdenden Industriegroßstadt Elberfeld* (Düsseldorf, 1963).

Waddy, Helena, 'St Anthony's Bread: The Modernized Religious Culture of German Catholics in the Early Twentieth Century', *Journal of Social History*, 31 (1998), pp. 347–70.

Wahl, Alfred, 'Confession et comportement dans les campagnes d'Alsace et de Bade', 2 vols (University of Metz doctoral thesis, 1980).

—— *Les archives du football: Sport et société en France, 1880–1980* (Paris, 1989).

Wald, K. D., *Crosses on the Ballot* (Princeton, NJ, 1983).

Walkenhorst, Peter, 'Nationalismus als "politische Religion"?' in Blaschke and Kuhlemann (eds), *Religion im Kaiserreich*, pp. 503–29.

Walker, Pamela J., 'A Chaste and Fervid Eloquence: Catherine Booth and the Ministry of Women in the Salvation Army', in Beverly Mayne Kienzle and Pamela J. Walker (eds), *Women Preachers and Prophets through Two Millennia of Christianity* (Berkeley, CA, 1998), pp. 288–302.

Walkowitz, Judith R., *Prostitution and Victorian Society* (Cambridge, 1980).

Waller, P. J., *Democracy and Sectarianism: A Political and Social History of Liverpool, 1868–1939* (Liverpool, 1981).

Walvin, James, *Leisure and Society, 1830–1950* (London, 1978).

Ward, Mrs Humphry, *Robert Elsmere* (London, 1952) [first published 1888].

Ward, W. R., *Religion and Society in England, 1790–1850* (London, 1972).

Wassermann, Henry, 'Jews and Judaism in the Gartenlaube', *Yearbook of the Leo Baeck Institute*, 23 (1978), pp. 47–60.

Watts, Michael R., *The Dissenters*, vol. 2: *The Expansion of Evangelical Nonconformity* (Oxford, 1995).

Weber, Eugen, *Peasants into Frenchmen* (London, 1977).

Weinbren, Dan, 'Building Communities, Constructing Identities: the Rise of the Labour Party in London', *London Journal*, 23 (1998), pp. 41–60.

Weindling, Paul, 'Jews in the Medical Profession in Britain and Germany', in Brenner, Liedtke and Rechter (eds), *Two Nations*, pp. 393–405.

Wendland Walter, *Siebenhundert Jahre Kirchengeschichte Berlins* (Berlin, 1930).

Whyte, J. H., *Church and State in Ireland, 1923–1979* (2nd edn, Dublin, 1980).

Wigley, J., *The Rise and Fall of the Victorian Sunday* (Manchester, 1980).

Wilkinson, Alan, *The Church of England and the First World War* (London, 1978).

——*Dissent or Conform? War, Peace and the English Churches, 1900–1945* (London, 1986).

Willard, C., 'Notre Dame de l'Usine', in Bédarida and Maitron (eds), *Christianisme et monde ouvrier*, pp. 245–55.

Willey, Basil, *More Victorian Studies: A Group of Honest Doubters* (London, 1956).

Williams, Bill, *The Making of Manchester Jewry, 1740–1875* (Manchester, 1976).

Williams, Jack, 'Churches, Sport and Identities in the North, 1900–1939', in Jeff Hill and Jack Williams (eds), *Sport and Identity in the North of England* (Keele, 1996), pp. 113–36.

——*Cricket and England: A Cultural and Social History of the Inter-war Years* (London, 1999).

Williams, Sarah C., 'Religious Belief and Popular Culture: a Study of the South London Borough of Southwark *c.*1880–1939' (University of Oxford DPhil thesis 1993).

——*Religious Belief and Popular Culture in Southwark, c.1880–1939* (Oxford, 1999).

Williamson, Philip, 'The Doctrinal Politics of Stanley Baldwin', in Michael Bentley (ed.), *Public and Private Doctrine* (Cambridge, 1993), pp. 181–208.

Wilson, Bryan, *Religion in Secular Society* (London, 1966).

——*Contemporary Transformations of Religion* (Oxford, 1976).

Wilson, Stephen, 'Saints and their Cults in the Churches of Central Paris', in idem. (ed.), *Saints and their Cults* (Cambridge, 1983), pp. 233–60.

Winock, Michel, 'Jeanne d'Arc', in Nora (ed.), *Lieux de memoire*, vol. III, pp. 4427–73.

Winter, J. M., 'Spiritualism and the First World War', in R. W. Davis and R. J. Helmstadter (eds), *Religion and Irreligion in Victorian Society* (London, 1992), pp. 185–200.

Wirth, Günter (ed.), *Beiträge zur Berliner Kirchengeschichte* (Berlin, 1987).

Wolff, Robert Lee, *Gains and Losses: Novels of Faith and Doubt in Victorian England* (New York, 1977).

Wolffe, John, *The Protestant Crusade in Great Britain, 1829–1860* (Oxford, 1991).

——*God and Greater Britain, 1843–1945* (London, 1994).

Worthen, John, D. H. *Lawrence: The Early Years, 1885–1912* (Cambridge, 1991).

Wright, T. R., *The Religion of Humanity* (Cambridge, 1986).

Wurster, P., *Das kirchliche Leben der evangelischen Landeskirche in Württemberg* (Tübingen, 1919).

Wuthnow, Robert, *The Restructuring of American Religion* (Princeton, NJ, 1988).

Yeo, Eileen, 'Christianity in Chartist Struggle, 1838–42', *Past & Present*, 91 (1981), pp. 109–39.

Yeo, Stephen, *Religion and Voluntary Organisations in Crisis* (London, 1976).

——'The Religion of Socialism', *History Workshop Journal*, 4 (1977), pp. 5–56.

Zeldin, Theodore (ed.), *Conflicts in French Society* (London, 1970).

——*France 1848–1945*, 2 vols (Oxford, 1973–7).

Émile Zola, *L'Assommoir* (English translation, London, 1995) [first published 1877].

——*The Earth* (English translation, Harmondsworth, 1980) [first published 1887].

——*Doctor Pascal* (English translation, Stroud 1989) [1st published 1893].

——*Lourdes* (English translation, Stroud 1993) [first published 1894].

——*Paris* (English translation, Stroud 1993) [first published 1898].

Zwahr, Hartmut, *Zur Konstituierung des Proletariats als Klasse* (Berlin, 1978).

Index